ISBN 978-1-331-18443-0
PIBN 10155435

This book is a reproduction of an important historical work. Forgotten Books uses
state-of-the-art technology to digitally reconstruct the work, preserving the original format
whilst repairing imperfections present in the aged copy. In rare cases, an imperfection in
the original, such as a blemish or missing page, may be replicated in our edition. We do,
however, repair the vast majority of imperfections successfully; any imperfections that
remain are intentionally left to preserve the state of such historical works.

1 MONTH OF
FREE
READING

at

www.ForgottenBooks.com

By purchasing this book you are eligible for one month membership to ForgottenBooks.com, giving you unlimited access to our entire collection of over 1,000,000 titles via our web site and mobile apps.

To claim your free month visit:

www.forgottenbooks.com/free155435

English
Français
Deutsche
Italiano
Español
Português

www.forgottenbooks.com

Mythology Photography **Fiction**
Fishing Christianity **Art** Cooking
Essays Buddhism Freemasonry
Medicine **Biology** Music **Ancient**
Egypt Evolution Carpentry Physics
Dance Geology **Mathematics** Fitness
Shakespeare **Folklore** Yoga Marketing
Confidence Immortality Biographies
Poetry **Psychology** Witchcraft
Electronics Chemistry History **Law**
Accounting **Philosophy** Anthropology
Alchemy Drama Quantum Mechanics
Atheism Sexual Health **Ancient History**
Entrepreneurship Languages Sport
Paleontology Needlework Islam
Metaphysics Investment Archaeology
Parenting Statistics Criminology
Motivational

LECTURES ON PEDAGOGY

THEORETICAL AND PRACTICAL.

BY

GABRIEL COMPAYRÉ,

AUTHOR OF "HISTOIRE DE LA PEDAGOGIE," PROFESSOR IN THE NORMAL
SCHOOLS OF FONTENAY-AUX-ROSES AND SAINT CLOUD, AND
MEMBER OF THE CHAMBER OF DEPUTIES.

TRANSLATED, WITH AN INTRODUCTION, NOTES,
AND AN APPENDIX,

45557

BY

W. H. PAYNE, A.M.,

CHANCELLOR OF THE UNIVERSITY OF NASHVILLE AND PRESIDENT OF THE
PEABODY NORMAL COLLEGE; AUTHOR OF "CHAPTERS ON SCHOOL
SUPERVISION," "OUTLINES OF EDUCATIONAL DOCTRINE," AND
"CONTRIBUTIONS TO THE SCIENCE OF EDUCATION"
EDITOR OF "PAGE'S THEORY AND PRACTICE
OF TEACHING "; AND TRANSLATOR OF
COMPAYRÉ'S "HISTOIRE DE
LA PEDAGOGIE."

BOSTON:
D. C. HEATH & CO., PUBLISHERS.
1887.

PRESS OF HENRY H. CLARK & CO., BOSTON. .

TRANSLATOR'S PREFACE.

In recent years the literature of education has been enriched by no contributions superior to Compayré's "Histoire de la Pédagogie" and "Cours de Pédagogie, Théorique et Pratique." The qualities that are so conspicuous in the first, — wise selection of material, absolute clearness of statement, judicial fairness in the treatment of open questions, critical insight, width of intellectual perspective, elegance of diction, — also characterize the second; and these two volumes may be accepted as the best résumé yet made of the history, the theory, and the practice of education.

M. Compayré is too wise, too catholic, and too honest to be an extremist, and his familiarity with the history of education has preserved his respect for the thinkers and teachers of the past, and has saved him from the illusion that a revolution in doctrines and methods is imminent. As the reader proceeds from chapter to chapter he is affected by the words of a judge whose sole preoccupation is the truth, and not of an attorney who is addressing a jury-box. In the wide and wise economy of things, partisans and extremists doubtless have their uses; but the habit of mind that is most worthy of cultivation is temperance, candor, and judicial fairness in dealing with a question so complex and difficult as that of education. This is the prevailing spirit of every volume which has proceeded from the pen of M. Compayré.

These lectures will commend themselves to that class of teachers, now happily growing in numbers, who are looking to psychology as the rational basis of their art. They will discover, perchance to their surprise and delight, that psychology is not an occult science, but that the main laws and essential facts of the intellectual life can be expressed in intelligible terms. This subject, like every other upon which man makes a trial of his thought, finally shades off into transcendental vagueness and uncertainty; but happily the portions that have a real value for guidance lie quite within the compass of the common understanding. For the purposes of disinterested science the mind may be analyzed as though it were an inert thing, just as a dead body may be dissected, and most psychologies seem to have been written from this point of view; but for the teacher's use the mind should be studied in its cardinal movements when engaged in the process of learning. Such in the main is M. Compayré's treatment of the subject in Part First of these Lectures.

The thoughtful reader can hardly fail to experience the charm of the author's ardent patriotism. In this volume the teacher is considered as enlisted in the service of the state, working for her preservation, her prosperity, her glory; and the common school is a mould out of which shall issue the highest type of republican citizenship. The teacher who surveys his work from this vantage-ground must be made of poor stuff if he does not feel a conscious pride in his calling, and does not attain a higher success by keeping steadily and clearly in view this goal of his efforts.

In America, as in France, the state by deliberate intent as well as by a necessary evolution has become an educator. The public school is a civil institution, but on this account it is neither godless, unchristian, nor immoral. Between the church and the state there has come about a division of functions, and there is no good reason why they may not coöperate as honorable and helpful allies. This thought has never been more tersely and beautifully expressed than in these words by our author:

" We shall continue to build on our solid bases of justice, charity, and tolerance the human city, while leaving to the ministers of religion the task of building beside it what Saint Augustine called the city of God."

The teacher's happiness and professional improvement both require that he should have an educational creed as an intellectual and moral support. In education, as in politics and religion, a firm belief in certain first principles is necessary in order to give stability to character and to make continuous growth possible.

For the ends here pointed out, it is not required that educational creeds should be uniform, the essential thing being merely that each teacher hold fast to some system of probable truth; but it is necessary that each one's creed be elastic enough to accommodate new truths or modifications of old truths. We may well take alarm when we are no longer conscious of such internal modifications of our educational beliefs. The best service a book can render a teacher is to assist him in the formation of his opinions, and for this purpose it must be dispassionate in tone and must carry critical insight into all its discussions. This volume is pervaded by this spirit, so wholesome and helpful, and I experience no little happiness from the thought that by means of this translation I may help American teachers in the formation of a rational educational creed.

The catholic spirit everywhere manifested by M. Compayré justifies me in expressing mild and cautious dissent on a few manifestly open questions; and I have ventured to express my thought in a few brief articles in the Appendix.

If this volume shall meet the hearty approval that was given the "History of Pedagogy," I shall feel anew my obligations to the teaching profession.

W. H. PAYNE.

NASHVILLE, April 1, 1888.

AUTHOR'S PREFACE.

I DO not presume to offer to the public, in this volume, a complete treatise on education: my purpose is simpler and more modest. In bringing together the lectures given in the higher normal schools of Fontenay-aux-Roses and Saint Cloud, I have simply intended to compose an elementary manual of teaching. In the vast field of the principles and the practice of education, I have selected only the indispensable ideas, those of which no one who educates and instructs children can afford to be ignorant.

In the composition of this volume I have made free use of the works of my predecessors. The best praise that can be given them is to do what I have done, — quote them on almost every page. However, I have endeavored not to imitate them, in at least two respects, — their dryness and their prolixity.

Too many manuals of teaching, in fact, are but dry nomenclatures, in which the spirit of pure form reigns supreme and multiplies divisions, definitions, and distinctions of every sort, with a pedantic display which seems borrowed from the ancient logic.

On the other hand, taking advantage of the intimate relations between pedagogy and the philosophical sciences, other writers on education have given undue extension to the sphere of their art, having included in it, in fact, the whole of psychology, the whole of ethics, and the whole of philosophy.

I have sought a just medium between these extremes, and have attempted to make my treatment of the subject at once simple and of living interest.

I do not think it enough to enumerate a certain number of abstract rules and scholastic formulas: my treatment ascends to principles, but with as much discretion as possible. From the medley of modern lucubrations it lops off everything superfluous, in order to reserve for use what is really essential; it restricts itself to the clearest and the most practical conceptions.

I divide my treatise into two very distinct parts. I first study the child in himself, in his natural development, and in the formal culture of his faculties; and then, abandoning the subject of education, I examine the object of it, — that is to say, instruction and discipline, the methods of the one and the principles and rules of the other.

In the first part, I call to my aid all who have studied childhood, correcting and completing their observations by my own studies.

In the second part, I have expressly consulted those who have professional competence, who have in their own practice put to the test methods of instruction and principles of discipline. For example, in order to extract the practical suggestions that are, as it were, buried in them, I have perused the voluminous and interesting *Rapports* of the Inspectors-General upon the condition of primary instruction.[1]

Without doubt, the best system of teaching, like the best logic, is still that which we make for ourselves through study, experience, and personal reflection. Certainly, it is not required to have learned by heart and recited, as some authors of teachers' manuals still demand, a catechism of method; but in order to aid the reflection and guide the experience of each novice in instruction, the book is very far from being useless, though it do nothing more than stimulate personal reflection. It is just in this spirit, less for imposing doctrines than for suggesting reflections, that this modest volume has been written. I trust that it may receive the same welcome as my "History of Pedagogy," of which it is the sequel.

---

[1] Paris, *Imprimerie nationale,* 1879–1880, 1881–1882.

TABLE OF CONTENTS.

PART FIRST.

THEORETICAL PEDAGOGY.

THEORETICAL PEDAGOGY.

CHAPTER I.

EDUCATION IN GENERAL.

1. ORIGIN OF THE WORD EDUCATION. — "Education" is a word relatively new in the French language. Montaigne employs it only once, in a sentence often quoted : " I protest against all violence in the education of a tender soul, which is being trained for honor and liberty."[1] With this exception, he always employs the expression *institution des enfants*, from which we have the word *instituteur*. The writers of the sixteenth century were accustomed to use the word *nourriture* in the same sense, as in the well-known proverb, *Nourriture passe nature* (Nurture is more than Nature). But in the seventeenth century, "education" comes into current use to designate the art of training men.

2. EDUCATION IS THE PREROGATIVE OF MAN. — To man must be reserved the noble term education. Training suffices for animals, and cultivation for plants. Man alone is susceptible of education, because he alone is capable of governing himself, and of becoming a moral being. An animal, through its instincts, is all that it can be, or at least all that it has need of being. But man, in order to

---

[1] Montaigne, *Essais*, I., II., Chap. VIII.

perfect himself, has need of reason and reflection ; and as at birth he does not himself possess these qualities, he must be brought up by other men.

3. IS THERE A SCIENCE OF EDUCATION ? — No one doubts, to-day, the possibility of a science of education. Education is itself an art, skill embodied in practice ; and this art certainly supposes something besides the knowledge of a few rules learned from books. It requires experience, moral qualities, a certain warmth of heart, and a real inspiration of intelligence. There can be no education without an educator, any more than poetry without a poet, — that is, without some one who by his personal qualities vivifies and applies the abstract and lifeless laws of treatises on education. But, just as eloquence has its rules derived from rhetoric, and poetry its rules derived from poetics ; just as, in another order of ideas, medicine, which is an art, is based upon the theories of medical science ; so education, before being an art in the hands of the masters who practise it, who enrich it by their versatility and their devotion, who put upon it the impress of their mind and heart, — education is a science which philosophy deduces from the general laws of human nature, and which the teacher perfects by inductions from his own experience.

There is, therefore, a science of education, a practical and applied science, which now has its principles and laws, which gives proof of its vitality by a great number of publications, both in France and abroad, and which has also its peculiar designation, *Pedagogy*, although there is still hesitation in adopting it.

4. PEDAGOGY AND EDUCATION. — It is to be regretted that so many writers still confound pedagogy with education.

There is more than a shade of difference between these two terms. Pedagogy, so to speak, is the theory of education, and education the practice of pedagogy. Just as one may be a rhetorician without being an orator, so one may be a pedagogue — that is, may have a thorough knowledge of the rules of education — without being an educator, without having practical skill in the training of children.[1]

"To form a man," says Marion, eloquently, "is a fine art; a perilous undertaking. In this art do not venture the infallibility of a systematic geometry, and do not expect from it the supreme tranquillity of finely wrought demonstrations. In the prosecution of this art there will be contest, the unforeseen, brusque transitions, whims, failures, recoveries, inertia, the miracles of free and active nature. There will be all the tumultuous ebb and flow, the bursting into harmony and the degenerating into chaos, which are in man as well as in the sea."[2]

But from these difficulties in practice we must not conclude either that the rules of education do not exist, or that it is useless to know them. In medicine also how much

---

[1] M. Compayré's use of the terms pedagogy and pedagogue may be illustrated as follows: A writer who discusses educational questions from the theoretical point of view is a pedagogue, and his treatise is a work on pedagogy; while a man who directs educational affairs without actually teaching, as a superintendent of public instruction or of schools, is an educator. A history of pedagogy is an account of the rise, progress, and present state of educational theories or ideas; while a history of education is an account of the rise, progress, and present state of educational systems and establishments. In other words, education in its theoretical or scientific aspect is pedagogy; while in its practical aspect, or in its art-phase, it is education. But if distinctive terms are needed to designate these two phases, why not call education in the first sense Pedagogics, and in the second Pedagogy? We might thus escape the tautology of theoretical pedagogy and the inconsistency of practical pedagogy. (P.)

[2] Marion's Lectures on the *Science of Education*, Manuel général de l'instruction primaire, Paris, 1884, p. 13.

that is unforeseen, what freaks of nature, how many sur-
prises that baffle our fears or deceive our hopes! And
yet what we demand above all else of a physician is to
have a thorough knowledge of the principles and rules of
his art.

Let it not be said, then, that for educating men there is
required neither precision of analysis nor science. Let it
be said, rather, that all this is not enough, because living
nature, by its sudden upheavals and unexpected falls,
by its mobility and its diversity, can hold in check the
best-established calculations. But recollect, however, that
there are rules and principles, if not infallible, at least
generally efficacious. Recollect, also, that these rules are
becoming more exact day by day, and that with the progress
of science this approximation becomes greater and greater.

The further we go, the better we know childhood, and the
more deeply we fathom the laws of human nature; the more
perfect, also, educational methods become, and the more
nearly they approach the truth. It is said that experience
is everything and science nothing; but what, pray, is
science itself, if not the experience of the ancients and of
all those who have preceded us? Then let us not allow
ourselves to think, with Diesterweg, that the study of pedagogy is of no account, and that one is born an educator
just as one is born a poet.[1] Let us not fall into the prejudice of thinking that a professor or a teacher has no more
need of knowing the theoretical laws of education and
instruction than we have of learning the functions of diges-
tion from a book on physiology, in order that our food may
be properly digested. In the matter of education, that
which is worth still more than inspiration is inspiration
enlightened and regulated by science.

---

[1] *Œuvres Choisies de Diesterweg.* Hachette, 1884, p. 272.

5. PEDAGOGY, AND ITS SCIENTIFIC PRINCIPLES. — Can it be said that pedagogy has now become an organized science, and that recent progress has liberated it from those gropings and uncertainties which every science traverses in its earlier stages? We do not go so far in our assumptions. Notwithstanding the great feats already accomplished, it is still necessary to repeat to-day what Diesterweg said in 1830. The scientific coördination of the precepts and experiments of pedagogy is still rather an aspiration or a hope than an accomplished fact.

"Would to God," he wrote, "that we had made enough progress so that, I do not say all men, but merely men of culture, were agreed as to the best mode of education; that we could not only determine with certainty what is good and what is bad, and what the results are of such or such a method, but also give a reason for our conclusions."[1]

But if we still have need of seeking the solution of certain problems, we at least know where these solutions can be found, and from what sources we must draw in order to give more and more exactness to our conceptions of educa-tion. Like all the practical sciences, pedagogy rests upon certain theoretical data, or upon a scientific basis.

6. THE RELATION OF PEDAGOGY TO PSYCHOLOGY. — Just as the physician ought to know the organs and the func-tions of the body which he treats, the farmer the nature of the soil which he cultivates, and the sculptor the qualities of the marble which he chisels and of the clay which he kneads, so the teacher cannot do without the knowledge of the laws of the mental organization, — that is, the study of psychology.

In truth, the rules for teaching are but the laws of psy-

[1] Diesterweg, op. cit., p. 54.

chology applied, transformed into practical maxims, and tested by experience.

Psychology is the basis of all the practical sciences which have to do with the moral faculties of man; but the other sciences which are derived from psychology treat of but certain energies of the human soul, — logic, of thought; æsthetics, of the sentiment of the beautiful; ethics, of the will. Pedagogy alone embraces all faculties of the soul, and should put under contribution the whole of psychology.

7. Is there an Infant Psychology?—It is not, however, general psychology, the psychology of the grown man, which alone ought to inspire the teacher. Whatever may have been said about it, there is a psychology of the child, because there is a childhood of the soul. The idealists, like Malebranche, should be the only ones to assert that the human spirit has no age, that from the hour of birth it is all that it can become, and that it is already capable of comprehending the loftiest abstractions.[1] To an impartial observer it is evident that the mind is developed and formed in accordance with certain laws of growth which definitely constitute the psychology of the child. Psychology, in a word, is not an invariable geometry, establishing immutable theorems, but a history, at least for the first years of life, which relates the gradual evolution of the different faculties.

It has been truly said that if we wish to train a man, we must know the psychology of men; but we would add that if we would educate a child, we must study the psychology of the child.[2]

---

[1] See Compayré, *History of Pedagogy* (Boston: 1886), p. 193.

[2] It is safer, with Pestalozzi, to look for the man in the child, than to regard the child as being *sui generis*. The progress from childhood to manhood is an insensible transition; there is no brusque passage

8. THE RELATIONS OF PEDAGOGY WITH OTHER SCIENCES. — Of course, since pedagogy embraces the whole human being, it does not derive its inspiration from psychology alone. In order to give a competent treatment of physical education, and even of certain parts of intellectual and moral education, biology in general, and more particularly the anatomy and physiology of man, are summoned to render important services.

In the same way it would be easy to prove that pedagogy cannot dispense with the aid of ethics and logic. Education tends to lead man to his proper destination, and it is ethics which determines the real end of human actions, the essential nature of all that we call good and desirable. On the other hand, education is the culture of thought and reason, and it is logic which makes known the best methods of weighing knowledges in order to discover the truth.

Pedagogy, or the science of education, then, has its method, which consists in observing all the facts of the physical and moral life of man, or rather in making use of the general laws which inductive reflection has constructed from these facts. Let us now define with greater precision its object and the principles which ought to guide it.

9. DIFFERENT DEFINITIONS OF EDUCATION. — The educators are rare who, like Locke, have written formal treatises on education without defining it, without collecting into one single formula the elements of their system.[1] In general,

---

from one to the other, such as seems to be implied in the term " infant psychology." However, this distinction will be serviceable if it shall emphasize the need of adapting instruction to the powers and the mental needs of the child. Dr. White's discussion of this subject (Elements of Pedagogy) is valuable. (P.)

[1] See the opening paragraphs of *Thoughts on Education.*

each writer on education has his own definition, and this diversity is chiefly due to the fact that the greater number have wrongly included in their definitions the indication of the particular methods and different means which education calls to its aid.

It will not be without interest to mention in this place the principal definitions that are of note, either on account of the names of their authors or of the relative exactness of their connotations.

One of the most ancient, and also one of the best, is that of Plato : —

"The purpose of education is to give to the body and to the soul all the beauty and all the perfection of which they are capable."

The perfection of human nature, such indeed is the ideal purpose of education.

It is in the same sense that Kant, Madame Necker de Saussure, and Stuart Mill have given the following definitions : —

"Education is the development in man of all the perfection which his nature permits."

"To educate a child is to put him in a condition to fulfil as perfectly as possible the purpose of his life."

"Education includes whatever we do for ourselves and whatever is done for us by others, for the express purpose of bringing us nearer to the perfection of our nature."

Here it is the general purpose of education which is principally in view. But the term perfection is somewhat vague and requires some explanation. Herbert Spencer's definition responds in part to this need —

"Education is the preparation for complete living."

But in what does complete living itself consist? The definitions of German educators give us the reply : —

"Education is at once the art and the science of guiding the young and of putting them in a condition, by the aid of instruction, through the power of emulation and good example, to attain the triple end assigned to man by his religious, social, and national destination." (Niemeyer.)

"Education is the harmonious and equable evolution of the human faculties by a method founded upon the nature of the mind for developing all the faculties of the soul, for stirring up and nourishing all the principles of life, while shunning all one-sided culture and taking account of the sentiments on which the strength and worth of men depend." (Stein.)

"Education is the harmonious development of the physical, intellectual, and moral faculties." (Denzel.)

These definitions have the common fault of not throwing into sharper relief the essential character of education properly so called, which is the premeditated, intentional action which the will of a man exercises over the child to instruct and train him. They might be applied equally well to the natural, instinctive, and predetermined development of the human faculties. In this respect we prefer the following formulas : —

"Education is the process by which one mind forms another mind, and one heart another heart." (Jules Simon.)

"Education is the sum of the intentional actions by means of which man attempts to raise his fellows to perfection." (Marion.)

"Education is the sum of the efforts whose purpose is to give to man the complete possession and correct use of his different faculties." (Henry Joly.)

Kant rightly demanded that the purpose of education should be to train children, not with reference to their success in the present state of human society, but with reference to a better state possible in the future, in accordance with an ideal conception of humanity. We must surely assent to these high and noble aspirations, without forgetting, however, the practised aims of educational effort.   It is in this sense that James Mill· wrote : —

" The end of education is to render the individual as much as possible an instrument of happiness, first to himself, and next to other beings."

Doubtless this definition is incomplete, but it has the merit of leading us back to the practical realities and the real conditions of existence.   The word happiness is the utilitarian translation of the word perfection.   A lofty idealism should not make us forget that the human being aspires to be happy, and that happiness is also a part of his destination.   Moreover, without losing sight of the fact that education is above all else the disinterested development of the individual, of one's personality, it is well that the definition of education should remind us that we do not live solely for ourselves, for our own single and selfish perfection, but that we also live for others, and that our existence is subordinate to that of others.

What are we to conclude from this review of so many different definitions?   First, that their authors have often complicated them by the introduction of various elements foreign to the exact notion of the word education, and that it would perhaps be better to be satisfied to say, with Rousseau, for the sake of uniting simply on the sense of the word, " Education is the art of bringing up children and of forming men."   But if we are determined to include in the definition of education the determination of the subject upon which it acts and the object which it pursues, we shall find the elements of such a conception here and there in the different formulas which we have quoted.   It would suffice to bring them together and to say : —

" Education is the sum of the reflective efforts by which we aid nature in the development of the physical,[1] intellectual, and moral faculties of man, in view of his perfection, his happiness, and his social destination."

10. DIVISION OF EDUCATION. — Education comprises different divisions, which correspond to a similar division of the faculties of human nature.

Whatever theory may be held as to the nature of the soul, whether it be considered as a distinct and independent substance or as related to the body as effect to its cause, the duality of the physical and the moral is no less real on this account. Hence there is a prime distinction to be made between the education of the body and the education of the mind.

But the mind itself is subdivided into a certain number of faculties. Thus it has long been the custom to distinguish intellectual education from moral education, the first cultivating the intellectual faculties and communicating knowledges, the other developing the heart and the will, and forming the sentiments, the habits, the conscience, and the moral powers.

In truth, it were preferable, having once started in this line of thought, to follow to the end the psychological division of the faculties, and to distinguish the education

---

[1] In a definition of education we cannot omit the development of the physical faculties. Yet many educators pass them by in silence. This is easily accounted for in the case of theologians, like Dupanloup, who define education as "the art of preparing for the life eternal by exalting the present life." But it is not so easy to explain what Mr. Bain says: "Physical education, however important it may be, may be kept quite separate." (*Education as a Science*, p. 3.) So an English writer, James Sully, defines education in too narrow a sense when he says that it is "the practical science which aims at cultivating the mind on the side of Knowing, Feeling, and Willing alike." (*Outlines of Psychology*, p. 15.)

of the intelligence, the education of the sentiments, and the education of the will.

Horace Mann, the American educator, distinguished the three essential parts of education in the following eloquent extract : —

"By the word education I mean much more than the ability to read, write, and keep common accounts. I comprehend, under this noble word, such a training of the body as shall build it up with robustness and vigor, at once protecting it from disease and enabling it to act formatively upon the crude substances of nature, — to turn a wilderness into cultivated fields, forests into ships, or quarries and clay-pits into villages and cities. I mean also to include such a cultivation of the intellect as shall enable it to discover those permanent and mighty laws which pervade all parts of the created universe, whether material or spiritual. This is necessary, because, if we act in obedience to these laws, all the resistless forces of Nature become our auxiliaries and cheer us on to certain prosperity and triumph ; but if we act in contravention or defiance of these laws, then Nature resists, thwarts, baffles us, and in the end it is just as certain that she will overwhelm us with ruin, as it is that God is stronger than man. And, finally, by the term Education I mean such a culture of our moral affections and religious susceptibilities as, in the course of Nature and Providence, shall lead to a subjection or conformity of all our appetites, propensities, and sentiments to the will of Heaven." [1]

11. ANOTHER DIVISION OF EDUCATION. — The preceding division is founded on the consideration of the subject, — that is, of the faculties of man ; but if we regard the object, or the end of education, other divisions are made necessary.

In fact, a general or liberal education, which is meet for all, is one thing, and a professional or technical education, which prepares only for a given vocation, is quite another. At the normal school, for example, it is not the purpose

---

[1] *Lectures on Education.* Boston, 1855, pp. 117, 118.

merely to educate men, but to train teachers; to a general education there is added a special education, an education in pedagogy.

"These two species of education," says Dupanloup, "a general and liberal education, and a special and professional education, are equally important to man. Moreover, they are not opposed to one another. Directly to the contrary, they strengthen and perfect one another; each is accomplished through the other. To neglect one to the advantage of the other would be to weaken them, and often to ruin both at once."[1]

12. LIBERAL EDUCATION. — The true term which should be applied to the education which is general and essential is "liberal education," although this term has till now been expressly reserved for the studies which prepare for the liberal professions.

If all men are free, morally free in the determination of their actions, and politically free through their participation in the government of the society of which they form a part, is it not evident that they all have the right, whatever may be their condition, to a liberal education which enlightens and emancipates their mind and their will? Formerly the classical humanities, the dead languages, were regarded as the sole instrument of a liberal education; but to-day historical and scientific studies, even reduced to their simplest elements, appear to us to be studies truly liberalizing, and constitute what might be called the primary humanities. Even the physical exercises which give agility to the body and prepare it to become at a later period the docile instrument of professional education, constitute in one sense a part of a liberal education.

"That man has received a liberal education," says Mr. Huxley, "who has been so trained in youth that his body is the ready

---

[1] Dupanloup, *De l'Éducation*, tome I., p. 312.

servant of his will, and does with ease and pleasure all the work
that, as a mechanism, it is capable of; whose intellect is a clear,
cold, logical engine, with all its parts of equal strength and in
smooth working order, ready, like a steam-engine, to be turned to
any kind of work, and spin the gossamers as well as forge the
anchors of the mind; whose mind is stored with a knowledge of
the great and fundamental truths of Nature and of the laws of her
operations; one who, no stunted ascetic, is full of life and fire, but
whose passions are trained to come to heel by a vigorous will, the
servant of a tender conscience; who has learned to love all beauty,
whether of Nature or of art, to hate all vileness, to respect others
as himself." [1]

It is not necessary, then, in order to receive a liberal
education, to aim at a high intellectual instruction. It
suffices that the elementary instruction has been directed in
such a way as to prepare for the free development of the
reason. It may be said, in one sense, that the old education of the Jesuits was not a liberal education, since it did
not tend in a sufficient degree towards the emancipation of
the will and the mind. On the contrary, a poor workman
gives his children a liberal education if he strives to open
their intelligence and to fortify their moral energy, even
though it is within his power to teach them nothing else
than the elements of the sciences.

13. THE PRINCIPLE OF NATURE. — Especially since
Rousseau's time, educational writers are fond of repeating
that the grand principle of education is conformity to the
laws of nature. We do not intend to oppose this notion.
The nearer we come to the natural needs of the child, the
more fully we take into account his aptitudes, the more
perfectly shall we adapt the objects and the methods of
instruction to the progressive development of his faculties,

----

[1] *Lay Sermons*, pp. 34, 35.

and to the greater degree shall we make of education a useful and truly efficacious work, particularly if we take account, not only of the general nature of man, but of the particular nature of each child.

"Man," says Diesterweg, "ought to become what nature has destined him to be, and it is from his aptitudes that we are to infer his destination. You will vainly attempt to train him for things to which he is not adapted. You will never make an angel of him, for he was not born for that. He neither can be nor ought to be any other thing than a man, and each individual, in his turn, becomes what his aptitudes demand and make possible. Attempt,.then, to make a Mozart of a deaf mute or of a man who has no ears."

We are not called upon, then, as was formerly done, to contend against nature, to treat her as an enemy, and to resist her as a deadly influence. On the contrary, we must have confidence in her, without, however, going so far as to abandon ourselves entirely to her. We must treat her as we would a friend to whom we listen and whom we follow, but to whom it is sometimes necessary to refuse certain concessions.

14. WHAT ARE WE TO UNDERSTAND BY NATURE? — But if the principle of nature is excellent, we cannot conceal the fact that this term is vague and that it admits of equivocation. In reality, what is called nature is after all an ideal which each educator conceives in his own way.[1]

"What," says Diesterweg in another place, "is conformity to nature? Where shall we find her? How shall we know her? What men have remained faithful to her? Must we look for them in the virgin forests of America, or in the various tribes of the South Sea, or rather in the civilized nations of Europe? Where

---

[1] In *Contributions to the Science of Education* I have discussed the term "Nature." (P.)

are the privileged beings who have been so fortunate as never to have withdrawn from the watch-care of nature?"

To find an answer to this question, there is no other way than to observe the child with impartiality at the age when the conventionalities, the fashions, and the artifices of society have not yet spoiled his native simplicity. As Rousseau said, "Let us study the man in the child."

15. RESTRICTIONS TO THE PRINCIPLE OF NATURE. — But however good our opinion may be of human nature, we should not think of humoring it in everything. Mr. Bain admits that there are evil instincts, such as anger, hatred, antipathy, jealousy, and scorn. Educators should repress and correct them, instead of encouraging and developing them.

Moreover, we are not to forget that, when abandoned to herself, nature makes only savages. It is education alone that can rescue us from the animal state and make men of us. As Kant has said, it is education that rids us of our natural savagery.

"Man cannot become man, save through education. He is only what education makes him. He who has not been disciplined is a savage."

In other terms, it is not enough that education should be inspired by nature and draw her rules from nature. Education is no less an art on this account; that is, a body of maxims founded on the experiences of successive generations of men, a body of processes brought into conformity with the new elements which progress and civilization have gradually introduced into the primitive nature of man. It is not a question of educating man in general, but the man of the nineteenth century, the man of a certain country, a citizen, a Frenchman.[1]

It is with nature in education as with universal suffrage in politics. Doubtless we must obey the majority, the law of numbers, in our social affairs, just as we must follow nature in education. But the majority itself should be inspired by reason and justice, and so natural education ought to be but the development of the reason which is in man.[2]

16. EDUCATION THE WORK OF LIBERTY. — Education, then, is not the training of an inert and passive being, but the development of a being that is free and active, whose instruction we are to provoke, and whose spontaneity we are to excite.

Education has often been likened to sculpture, its purpose being, so to speak, to chisel human souls according to a highly wrought model. The error in this comparison is forgetting that spirit is not inert matter that can be fashioned as we will, that passively submits to whatever we impose on it, as marble or wood to the chisel of the artist.

---

[1] There has been no greater mistake in educational theory than to assume that the education of to-day must be adjusted in accordance with the needs of primitive man or of primitive society. For example, as, historically, the family came before the state, it is assumed that now, when the state has been definitely organized, family duties antedate duties to civil society. But *tempora mutantur, et nos cum illis mutamur.* Primitively, parenthood preceded citizenship; but now citizenship precedes parenthood. The child must be educated, not for the primeval world of barbarism into which the parents of the race were born, but for the world re-created by human art, into which he himself was born. (P.)

[2] Emerson somewhere uses *provocation* to denote the spiritual act of teaching. Professor Jowett makes Plato (*Meno*) use the term *elicit* to express the same fact. The term *induce* perhaps expresses still more correctly the real nature of instruction as it was conceived by Socrates. (P.)

Far different is the mind of the child, which ceaselessly reacts upon that of the educator, and mingles its own activity with his. Education is a work in which pupil and teacher co-operate. Often the young co-worker resists by his caprices, by a sort of open hostility; and oftener by his inertia he disconcerts the plans of his teacher and takes no active part in them. But in an education well administered, the pupil ought to be associated with the teacher. On his part he should strive to reach the end towards which he is being conducted. By his personal efforts he should participate in the education which he receives.

"Teacher," said Pestalozzi,[1] eloquently, "be assured of the excellence of liberty, and do not allow yourself to be induced, through vanity, to devote yourself to the production of immature fruits. Let your pupil be as free as he can be. Carefully provide everything which allows you to grant him liberty, tranquillity, and unruffled humor. Everything, absolutely everything that you can teach him through the natural consequences of things, do not teach him through language. Allow him in his own person to see, hear, find, fall, get up, and be deceived. No words when the act, the thing itself, is possible. Whatever he can do himself, let him do. Let him always be busy, always active; and let the time during which you do not disturb him in the least be the greatest part of his childhood. You will find out that nature teaches him much better than men can."

17. Education a Work of Authority. — It was a wise saying of Kant that one of the greatest problems of education is to reconcile the liberty of the child with the necessity of constraint.

It is the same thought which troubled Pestalozzi when he wrote: —

"I often find myself embarrassed for having suppressed, in

---

[1] *Histoire de Pestalozzi*, par Roger de Guimps, p. 57.

the education of my children, the tone of the master's authority. Where shall I find the line between liberty and obedience?

"There are crises in which the liberty of the child would work harm to him, and even under the most favorable circumstances it is often necessary to oppose the child's will."

Education does not abandon nature to herself, but oversees and directs her, and, if necessary, constrains her. In a general way, education is the work of authority as much as of liberty, and the authority acquired by a master who knows how to make himself loved and obeyed will permit him to employ persuasion oftener than constraint. The more authority he has, the less need he will have to use it.

One of the masters of contemporary pedagogy, M. Buisson, has deftly analyzed the conditions of this authority.

"The justification of the special authority which is delegated to the teacher in education is that it is the only means of assuring the development of the pupil. In attaining this result, it is evidently necessary, on the one hand, that the teacher really have the power to contribute to this development, and, on the other, that he have the will.

"First, he must have the power, and to this end it is above all else necessary that he know what he ought to transmit, and that he have over the pupil the advantage of experience and of a full and serene possession of the knowledge whose elements he is to communicate.

"Nor is this all. Even what he thoroughly knows he must still learn to communicate. To teach, to educate, is certainly an art which has its rules and its secrets. . . . . There are necessary mental conditions, that is, aptitudes and habits, which allow the teacher, for example, if he is giving instruction, to present his subject with system, and yet with variety; to make for himself a plan, and to follow it without falling into dogmatic exactness; to know how to make a truth luminous in the minds of children, to insist on the important, and to sacrifice or postpone the accessory. If the teacher is giving moral training, his skill should permit him to notice delicately, and to correct still more delicately, faults of mind and character; to persuade and to command, as occasion requires; to encourage, when necessary, and just enough not to develop pride; finally, to govern according to well-established principles, and yet with very fine shades of treatment, those little people, so much the more difficult to manage because they are so frail and so powerless to govern themselves. There are also necessary conditions of character, the absence of which would suffice to make the effort to instruct a failure: an even temper, the gift of patience, a bearing which is not exactly that of ordinary life, but as it were a mingling of gravity and cheerfulness in manner which at once captures the hearts of children; extreme precaution in shunning the very things which in society and in the world are the most acceptable and the most sought after. There should never be irony, never contradictions and paradoxes, never anything which exalts the teacher at the expense of the pupil, — much indulgence, and no trace of weakness; nothing exciting or brusque; an inflexible firmness and a paternal gentleness; inexhaustible simplicity in all things; finally, a constant effort, which becomes insensible in the course of time, to come down to his plane, to understand him, to sustain him, to love him.

"This last word causes us to pass to the second order of conditions. The teacher must have the will to labor for the development of the child. In fact, it is not so much a question of knowledge as of will. If his heart is really fixed on enriching the patrimony of the young soul which is confided to him, the teacher will infallibly succeed, even though his knowledge is limited. If he loves his pupils, he will resolve, as it were, intuitively, a mass of those practical problems of which his art is composed; for it cannot be too often repeated that education is an art which is administered rather through experience than through formulas. The teacher will hold a just medium between authority and liberty; he will respect the initiative of the child without demanding too much of him or abandoning him too much to himself; he will gain ascendency in proportion as he is preoccupied the less with himself and the more with his pupil; he will perfect himself in order to perfect his pupil." [1]

---

[1] *Dictionnaire de Pédagogie*, art. "Education."

18. POWER AND LIMITS OF EDUCATION. — Fontenelle was certainly wrong when he said: "A good education does not make a good character, nor does a bad education destroy character." On the contrary, we believe that education plays an important part even in the formation of the higher virtues and the superior qualities of the mind. It contributes towards making or unmaking characters. But we shall not go so far as to believe, with Locke and Helvetius, that education is omnipotent. Doubtless it may be held that the power of education is ideally infinite;[1] but as a matter of fact it is limited in its action, either through the natural aptitudes and qualities of the individuals upon whom it acts, or through the time which it has at its disposal.

We shall not say, then, with Helvetius, that "all men are born equal and with equal aptitudes, and that the differences among men are due to education alone." We must take a just account both of natural qualities and of the acquired qualities which education grafts upon the natural stock.

A contemporary writer is also mistaken when he writes that "education has no effect, save upon natures of mediocre mould."[2] It is not true that birth is the only struggle endured by great men, and we freely assert that the influence of education reaches its maximum when nature subjects to its beneficent action her richest contingent of powers and faculties. Education can do nothing if it does not come in contact with germs to develop; and education reaches its highest perfection in souls when these germs are the most numerous and the best nourished by native aliment. If one were disposed to exaggerate the power of education to the point of believing that it can transform everything,

---

[1] Marion, *Cours sur la Science de l'Éducation.*
[2] Ribot, *De l'Hérédité,* p. 486.

it would suffice to remind him of the famous example of the education of the Dauphin by Bossuet, the excellence of the teacher and the positive mediocrity of the pupil. But if, on the other hand, he were tempted to doubt the efficacy of education, we would cite in proof of it the education of the Duke of Bourgogne, which, directed by Fénelon, developed almost all the virtues in a soul where nature seemed to have sown the seeds of all the vices.[1]

To deny the power of education, it would be necessary to begin by denying the influence of the habits which play so great a part in life, and almost all of which depend on the manner in which we have been brought up. Our mind, like our character, depends in great part on the manner of our education.

"Education," says Guizot, "fortifies the weak or inert faculties of childhood. No one is ignorant of the power that exercise and habit have of making the memory more facile and the attention more sustained. Our faculties, instead of deteriorating, grow stronger by use. Examples of the successful application of the will to the perfecting of a given quality are innumerable."[2]

19. EDUCATION AND SCHOOL. — It is true that in order to justify the power which we ascribe to education, we must transcend the limits of the school and interpret education in its widest and broadest sense. In fact, there is not only the education properly so called, that which proceeds from the direct action of teachers; but there is the education of the family, and also that of the social environment in which we live. There are what have shrewdly been called the *occult coadjutors* of education, — climate, race, manners, political institutions, religious beliefs. There is also a

---

[1] See Compayré, *op. cit.*, Chap. VIII.

[2] Guizot, *Conseils d'un père sur l'éducation*, in *Méditations et Études*.

personal education, that which one gives himself, and which continues all one's life.

But the agency of the school is none the less important on this account, nor the responsibility of the teacher less fearful. Self-education is scarcely more than the continuation of the good habits learned at school. As to exterior influences, they are but auxiliaries which can accomplish nothing without the coöperation of a regular education, or enemies against whom we must react through a good training in the schools. What Leibnitz said becomes more and more true, that " the masters of education hold ,in their hands the future of the world."

20. EDUCATION IN A REPUBLIC. — Under a republican *régime*, in a great democracy education acquires a new importance, because there must then be demanded of the virtue, the wisdom, and the liberty of each citizen, the order and the peace which .despotism had before imposed on ignorance and passive obedience.

"Republican institutions," says Horace Mann, "furnish as great facilities for wicked men in all departments of wickedness, as phosphorus and lucifer matches furnish to the incendiary."[1]

But these dangers do not discourage the great American philanthropist, for, in the first place, it is impossible to take a backward step. "The sun can as easily be turned backwards in its course, as one particle of that power which·· has been conferred upon the millions can be again monopolized by the few."

But it is also in the name of human dignity and of its rights that it is meet to demand the free development of natural energies, and protest against every system which would assume to stifle them.

---

[1] Horace Mann, *op. cit.*, p. 148.

"In despotisms the divinely formed soul, created to admire through intelligence this glorious universe; to go forth through knowledge, through sympathy with all human fortunes; to know its Maker and its immortal destiny, is driven back at every door of egress, or darkened at every window where light could enter, and is chained to the vassal spot which gave it birth, where the very earth, as well as its inhabitant, is blasted by the common curse of bondage. In Oriental and African despotisms, the mind of the millions grows only as the trees of a noble forest could grow in the rocky depths of a cavern, without strength or beauty or healing balm, in impurity and darkness, fed by poisonous exhalations from stagnant pools, all upward and outward expansion introverted by solid barriers, and forced back into unsightly forms. Thus it has always fared with the faculties of the human soul when concerned in despotism. They have dwelt in intellectual, denser than subterranean, darkness. Their most tender, sweet, and hallowed emotions have been choked and blighted. The pure and sacred effusions of the heart have been converted into hatred of the good and idolatry of the base, for want of the light and the air of true freedom and instruction; the world can suffer no loss equal to that spiritual loss which is occasioned by attempting to destroy, instead of regulating the energies of the mind." [1]

21. CONCLUSION. — Education, then, ought to be at once an excitation and a restraint. Let us not fear to affranchise, to emancipate minds, if we are wise enough at the same time to discover the secret of teaching them moderation and self-government, if through sufficient culture we help them to find within themselves the restraint necessary to reform their passions and evil instincts.

This is why character building is the supreme end of education. After all, it is according to our character that we act, and it is of much more consequence that we act well than that we think well. It is true that our character depends preëminently upon our sentiments and our thoughts;

[1] Horace Mann, *op. cit.*, pp. 144, 145.

or, in other terms, that moral education depends in part upon intellectual education. But moral education is none the less the final term of our efforts.

And to attain this end it is evidently not sufficient to possess wisdom, instruction; there must be joined to these moral qualities the virtues of the heart and the will. It has been said that the effort of education is to form men. To this end let teachers begin by being men themselves.

"Whoever undertakes the education of another should begin by completing his own. Émile Souvestre has exemplified this truth as follows: A young father, in anticipation of the birth of a child, surrounds himself with books on education. But the reading of these works only increases his uncertainties. Finally, he begins to reflect, and, considering the boundless influence of the father and mother, upon the tablet which he had prepared for taking notes, below the title, *Educational Precepts*, he wrote merely these words: *to become better.*" [1]

---

[1] Chauvet, *L'Education*, Paris, 1868, p. 73.

CHAPTER II.

PHYSICAL EDUCATION.

22. A Sound Mind in a Sound Body. — "A sound mind in a sound body, — this," says Locke, "is the short but complete definition of happiness in this world." Such, therefore, ought to be the double purpose of education. Physical education should not be separated from intellectual and moral education. And this for two reasons: first, because bodily health and strength are desirable and good in themselves, because they make a part of that complete and perfect life which is the will of nature and the dream of education; and then because the development of the body is one of the conditions, one of the means, of the development of the soul, — because the higher life of the spirit is not possible, except it have for a support a robust and healthy physical life.

23. Physical Education for the Good of the Body. — There have been times when men could believe that the ideal was to despise the body, and even to humiliate it and mortify it, that this lower element of our being was entitled to no respect, to no care, and that human perfection was in proportion to the diminution and the decay of the material forces. Mysticism proposed, as the unique purpose of life, spiritual perfection; and asceticism, the practical application of the principles of mysticism, took up arms against the body, to reduce it to terms by fasting, by tortures, by privations of every description, — if possible, to annihilate it, as the source of all sin and of all evil.

We of to-day have recovered from these chimeras. We regard man as a whole which is not to be mutilated in any of its parts. Simply because they are inferior in dignity to the spiritual forces, the energies of the physical organism none the less deserve to be respected and developed.

"As remarks a suggestive writer," says Herbert Spencer, "the first requisite to success in life is 'to be a good animal'; and to be a nation of good animals is the first condition of national prosperity. Not only is it that the event of a war often turns on the strength and hardiness of soldiers; but it is that the contests of commerce are in part determined by the bodily endurance of producers." [1]

Moreover, it is not simply a question of positive and practical interest; the preservation of health is one of our duties. Every conscious infraction of the laws of hygiene is a culpable act, and, as Herbert Spencer has justly observed, every prejudice voluntarily done to health is a physical sin.

24. PHYSICAL EDUCATION FOR THE SAKE OF THE MIND. — A thing not less positive is that there is a solidarity of interest between mind and body. As the physical and the moral are, so to speak, the under and the upper textures of the same fabric, it would be folly to suppose that we could with impunity derange the under without by the same act compromising the upper.

The Greeks understood this, and they associated the body and the mind in one harmonious education, in order to make man at once "beautiful and good." It was by them that Montaigne was inspired when he wrote his admirable chapter on the "Training of Children."

---

[1] Spencer, *Education*, p. 222.

"It is not enough to toughen the mind of the child; his muscles must be toughened also. The mind is too hard driven if it is not assisted; it has too much to do to fill two offices alone. I know how much mine, so prone to be preoccupied with itself, suffers from being tied to a body so delicate and sensitive; and in my reading I often notice that in their accounts my authors adduce as examples of magnanimity and courage, what ought the rather to be attributed to thickness of skin and hardness of bone."

And further on : —

"It is not a soul, nor yet a body, which we are educating, but a man, and we must not divide him. And, as Plato says, we must not train one of them without the other, but we must drive them abreast like a span of horses harnessed to the same shaft."

The moral faculties do not freely expand, except when the body is in full health; and besides, when they have once been developed, they do not come into free exercise unless they can avail themselves of firm and agile members. A good bodily constitution "renders the operations of the mind easy and sure;" and at the same time that it contributes towards forming the mind, it is a necessary condition for the outward manifestation of spirit, and prevents the mind from falling back upon itself, lost in futile contemplations.

I well know that we sometimes meet with intelligences of the first order, and with strong and courageous wills, united to weak and sickly bodies. A man whose physical life is but a perpetual discomfort may be distinguished from all others by the energy of his mind and the elevation of his heart. The example of Pascal, the invalid and the man of genius, occurs to the mind of every one. It may really happen in certain cases, by a mysterious reaction, that bodily sufferings may refine and stimulate the moral faculties. In such cases, pain is the principal agent in this unusual progress of the intelligence. But these exceptions prove nothing as against the general law. With good health, Pascal might have lived longer, and probably would have lost nothing of his genius. According to the expression which he himself used, it will not do to despise the *bête*, for sooner or later it will have its revenge. It had its vengeance on Pascal by killing him.

"Physical perfection serves to assure moral perfection. There is nothing more tyrannical than an enfeebled organism. Nothing sooner paralyzes the free activity of the reason, the flight of the imagination, and the exercise of reflection; nothing sooner dries up all the sources of thought than a sickly body whose functions languish, and for which every effort is a cause of suffering. Then have no scruples; and if you would form a soul which is to have ample development, a man of generous and intrepid will, a workman capable of great undertakings and arduous labors, first, and above all, secure a vigorous organism, of powerful resistance and muscles of steel." [1]

25. PHYSICAL EDUCATION AS A PREPARATION FOR PROFESSIONAL EDUCATION. — Physical education, like intellectual and moral education, does not consist merely in a disinterested culture of natural powers, but tends towards a practical end; it ought to be a preparation for life, and, by reason of its very nature, a preparation for professional education, or at least for bodily skill.

It is hardly possible to introduce into the education of all men what Locke and Rousseau desired, the apprenticeship to a trade; but, nevertheless, under all circumstances it is well to know how to use one's hands and one's limbs.

"One of the highest compliments we can pay a man," says Saint-Marc Girardin, "is to say that he knows how to surmount difficulties, not through artful discourse or through ingenious conversation, but, if necessary, through manual dexterity also; to

---

[1] F. Marion, *Cours sur la Science de l'Education.*

come off conqueror, not merely in great things, but in small; not to be continually in need of using the arms of others in order to lengthen his own, and to be embarrassed neither by his own body nor by what it has to carry; but that he is versatile and active, that he is neither awkward nor effeminate, — in a word, that he can live without having a bell within reach, and a servant within sound of the bell."[1]

It is especially in the common school, by reason of the special destination of those who attend it, that physical education ought to take a practical direction, and thus prepare boys for the future occupations of the laborer and the soldier, and girls for the duties of the household and for the occupations peculiar to women.

On this point, the official programme of French instruction expresses itself as follows : —

"The purpose of physical education is not merely to fortify the body and strengthen the constitution of the child, by placing him in the most favorable hygienic conditions; but it should also give him, at an early hour, qualities of deftness and agility, that manual dexterity and that promptness and certainty of movement which, valuable for every one, are more particularly necessary for pupils in the common school, the most of whom are destined for manual occupations."[2]

26. PRINCIPLES OF PHYSICAL EDUCATION. — It is in the education of the body that the greatest credit seems to have been given the notion that nature should have her own way, that she should be intrusted exclusively with the care of developing the organs and regulating their functions. It were a grave error thus to hand over the health and life of the child to accidents and hazards of every species. Here, as everywhere, we must aid nature, and to aid her we must know her.

---

[1] Saint-Marc Girardin, J. J. ROUSSEAU, Tome II. p. 112.
[2] Programmes annexed to the official order of July 27, 1882.

To be wholly rational, physical education should be based on a profound knowledge of the different sciences which treat of the human body. Hygiene bases its practical rules upon the theories of physiology; gymnastics is founded upon the elementary principles of anatomy; and, in general, physical education applies the great laws of the science of the body, just as intellectual and moral education applies the great laws of the science to the soul.

27. PHYSIOLOGY OF THE CHILD. — Let us add that for the body, as well as for the soul, there is an infancy — that is to say, a peculiar state of growth — which precedes maturity. It is not, then, merely the general physiology and anatomy of man that the educator is bound to consult, but, in order to be really fit to fulfil his task, he should himself construct, as a rule for his procedure, a real physiology of the child.

Like the psychology of the child, his physiology is a history which accompanies little by little the evolution of the body, the successive formation of its organs, and the organization of the different parts of the nervous system. Let us not forget that the child is not a ready-made being, a finished product, but a weak and fragile creature, "whose muscles, nerves, and organs are in the milk, so to speak," and develop but gradually, owing to a slow but incessant growth.

28. IMPORTANCE OF PHYSIOLOGICAL CONCEPTIONS. — It is doubtless to parents in particular that falls the obligation to know enough of the laws of life not to abandon the education of their children to the quackery of nurses and to blind and irrational modes of treatment. In one of his eloquent pages Mr. Herbert Spencer has reminded them of their duties on this point.

"To tens of thousands who are killed, add hundreds of thousands that survive with feeble constitutions and millions that grow up with constitutions not so strong as they should be, and you will have some idea of the curse inflicted on their offspring by parents ignorant of the laws of life. Do but consider for a moment that the regimen to which children are subject is hourly telling upon them to their life-long injury or benefit, and that there are twenty ways of going wrong to one way of going right, and you will get some idea of the enormous mischief that is almost everywhere inflicted by the thoughtless, haphazard system in common use. Is it decided that a boy shall be clothed in some flimsy short dress, and be allowed to go playing about with his limbs reddened by cold? The decision will tell on his whole future existence, either in illness or in stunted growth, or in deficient energy, or in maturity less vigorous than it ought to have been, and consequent hindrances to success and happiness. Are children doomed to a monotonous dietary, or a dietary deficient in nutritiveness? Their ultimate physical power, and their efficiency as men and women, will inevitably be more or less diminished by it. Are they forbidden vociferous play, or (being too ill-clothed to bear exposure) are they left indoors in cold weather? They are certain to fall below that measure of health and strength to which they would else have attained." [1]

But though the responsibility in this matter rests chiefly upon parents, teachers also, if they have neglected to inform themselves of the laws of the physical life, if they set them at defiance by unreasonable commands or by ill-timed prohibitions, — teachers also may exercise a fatal influence upon the health and vitality of children. Then let them take a serious view of their responsibilities, and study with care anatomy and physiology as presented in the normal schools. Let them supplement these studies by their personal observations upon the children of their schools; let them take account of their physical aptitudes,

---

[1] Spencer, *Education*, pp. 56, 57.

of their differences in temperament, and of the natural weakness or strength of their constitution. Thus prepared in the lessons which they give in gymnastics, in their precautions and advice in matters of hygiene, they will not be the mere routine adherents to a programme, but will the better execute the orders whose meaning and application they comprehend. They will put a liberal interpretation upon the dead letter of the law; through their personal experience, and through their enlightened interest in the particular temperament of each child, they will make this letter a living thing. •

29. POSITIVE AND NEGATIVE EDUCATION OF THE BODY. — Granting everything that can be claimed for the natural vigor of the child's constitution and of his spontaneous development, there still remains a vast field of activity open to the previsions of the educator.

On the one hand, the life of the child must be shielded from everything which may be the cause of disturbance, dissipation, and debility, of whatever would have a tendency to impair bodily health, such as excessive brain labor. Here, properly speaking, is the domain of negative physical education, that which consists in conserving and protecting the natural forces, and which is almost all summed up in prohibitions, in the warnings pronounced by hygiene.

On the other hand, it is necessary to supplement and stimulate the work of nature, to develop and fortify the physical powers; and this deliberate intervention becomes more and more necessary, in proportion as the intensive culture of the intellect is carried to excess, and to the abuses of intemperate study and overcrowded programmes. This will be the purpose of a positive physical education, of an education which will comprise all the exercises and all the sports of childhood, all the practices recommended by hygiene, and all the movements which constitute gymnastics.

Hygiene and gymnastics, these are the two elements of physical education, and both are equally necessary. The first is, in some sort, a good method of conduct, a kind of ethics for the body; the other is to physical activity what study is to intellectual activity, a wholesome and strengthcuing exercise. Both conspire to endow the body with health and vigor; but hygiene has especial reference to health, and gymnastics to vigor.

30.. School Hygiene. — Volumes have been written upon hygiene, and we do not propose to recite even the essential things which might be said on such a subject, either from the point of view of school hygiene or of the hygiene of children and pupils. On this point we refer our readers to special treatises.[1]

Hygiene, according to Rousseau, is not so much "a science as a virtue;" that is, it consists above all in abstaining from whatever is bad, in shunning all excesses, and in being temperate in all things. Temperance is the half of hygiene. The child whose diet is plain, whose life is simple, who is spared every occasion for overtaxing his powers, who knows nothing of indigestion, of violent pleasures and excessive fatigues, — such a child has already accomplished much in the way of healthful living.

---

[1] See particularly *Leçons élémentaires d'hygiène*, by Dr. George (Paris: Delalain); *l'Hygiène et l'Education dans les internats*, by Riant; *L'Instruction* of July 28, 1882; the article *Hygiène*, of Dr. E. Pécaut, in the *Dictionnaire de pédagogie;* lastly, the *Rapports* of the Commission on School Hygiene, Paris, 1884.

The English reader is referred to the following books: Charles Kingsley, *Health and Education;* Archibald Maclaren, *A System of Physical Education;* D. F. Lincoln, *School and Industrial Hygiene.*

However, hygiene permits a certain number of positive injunctions which relate either to the general cleanliness of the body, to diet, or to clothing. The common principle of all these injunctions ought to be not to yield too much to the inclinations of nature, nor yet to interfere with her too much.

31. THE PRINCIPLE OF PHYSICAL HARDENING. — Such, however, is not the opinion of a certain number of educators who, like Locke for example, give a much greater extension to the principle of physical hardening, and who, under the pretext of not spoiling nature by an excess of mildness and complacency, end by refusing her the most legitimate gratifications. It is doubtless well to inure children to hardships, not to enervate them, but to bring them up in country fashion. However, we should always take into account the diversity of temperaments.

"If your son is very robust," said Madame de Sévigné shrewdly, "a rude education is good; but if he is delicate, I think that in your attempts to make him robust you would kill him."

And even the most robust constitutions cannot be subjected to all trials. Locke is wrong when he forbids warm clothing in winter. Herbert Spencer is wiser on this point, when, in the clothing of children, he would take account of the natural sensations of heat and cold.

"The common notion about 'hardening,'" he says, "is a grievous delusion. Children are not unfrequently 'hardened' out of the world."

It is chimerical to suppose that by forced modes of procedure and by habits early acquired, we can accomplish everything through the plasticity of the physical organs. There are things contrary to our physical constitution, to which the organism cannot become accustomed. This is what Goldsmith tried to illustrate when he related this anecdote :

"One day Peter the Great took it into his head that it would be best for all sailors to form the habit of drinking salt water. He immediately promulgated an order that all naval cadets should henceforth drink only sea-water. The boys all died, and there the experiment stopped."

Then let us be wise enough to give sufficient place to the requirements of nature, and not revert to the old ascetic tendencies which led to dangerous deprivations and hardships ; but let us be equally on our guard against paying homage to the optimism, as unwise as it is seductive, of those who, like Herbert Spencer, assert that it is necessary in everything to revere the sacred order of nature and satisfy all the desires of the child, as for example his immoderate appetite for sweetmeats.

32. CLEANLINESS. — Cleanliness is a virtue, according to Volney ; a half virtue, according to others. What admits of no doubt is that the opposite of cleanliness is a great fault, since it compromises the dignity of the human person by giving an offensive appearance to the body. " There is a closer relation than we think," said Madame Pape-Carpantier, " between physical cleanliness and moral purity."

But cleanliness is valuable in itself, as a hygienic rule, as an element of health, and as a preventive of contagions which give rise to diseases, light or severe.

Hence the importance of giving attention to cleanliness. It rests chiefly with the family to insist on its observance ; but by his advice, by his example, and also by the attention which he gives to the subject, the teacher can do much towards giving the child habits of cleanliness.

33. FOOD AND CLOTHING. — Without saying, with Feuerbach, that "man is what he eats," and without accepting the absolute assertion of Herbert Spencer, that "the well-fed races have been the energetic and dominant races," we cannot accord too much importance to alimentation, to the quality and the quantity of food.

Mr. Spencer declares that there are too many rules in the nursery, just as there are too many in the state, and that one of the greatest evils resulting from this state of things is that children are too much restricted in their diet. "The food of children," he says, "should be highly nutritive; it should be varied at each meal; and it should be abundant."[1]

The child, then, should eat till his hunger is satisfied. Eating to excess is the vice of adults rather than of children. Indigestion, with children, is almost always brought on by a reaction against privations, against a prolonged fast.

As to garments, they should be full and loose, so that the body shall feel at ease in them, and that nothing shall interfere with the functions of the organism. "Hygienists condemn the premature use of the corset for girls, and at all times the tunic for boys."[2]

Locke, with his usual austerity, required the child to play bareheaded, and never to wear warm clothing; he even favored the idea of requiring him to wear the same garments winter and summer. Mr. Spencer, on the contrary, finds that it is folly to clothe children in thin garments. The French criticise the English custom of allowing children to go bare-legged and thinly dressed; while the English blame the French for the silly things invented by the *Petit Courrier des dames*, which recommends garments that

---

[1] *Education*, p. 224.

[2] See Fonssagrives, *Éducation physique des garçons*, p. 57.

are either inconvenient or insufficient.[1] Mr. Spencer concludes that if clothing should not be so heavy as to produce
an uncomfortable warmth, it ought always to be warm
enough to prevent all feeling of cold.

34. OTHER HYGIENIC REQUIREMENTS. — We are far from
having enumerated all the precepts of hygiene ; there are
others bearing on sleep, on work, on recreations, and upon
punishments. Hygiene particularly recommends physical
activity as a means of counterbalancing cerebral toil and
intellectual fatigue. Activity is one of the conditions of
health. We are nourished, not by what we eat, but by what
we digest, as a physician has told us ; and Trousseau adds,
" We digest with our limbs as well as with our stomach."

But at this point hygiene is almost confounded with gymnastics, of which we now proceed to speak.

35. GYMNASTICS. — Generally too much neglected in
France, but holding a prominent place in Switzerland and
Germany, gymnastics begins to affect the habits of our
schools.[2] French legislation has ordained it, and official
manuals have codified its requirements.[3]

---

[1] See Spencer, *Education,* p. 250.

[2] The law of March 15, 1850, placed the teaching of gymnastics among
the optional studies of primary instruction. The decree of March 24,
1851, included it among the obligatory studies of the normal schools.
The decree of March 13, 1854, introduced it into the lycées. A decree
of 1869 (Feb. 3) organized it in the lycées and colleges, in the normal
schools, and in the primary schools. Numerous circulars published
since that period have given precise instructions and detailed precepts.
Finally, the law of January 27, 1880, makes obligatory the teaching of
gymnastics " in all the institutions of public instruction for boys ; "
and the decree of July 27, 1881, says expressly that " each day, or at
least every other day, gymnastics shall occupy a recitation hour during the course of the afternoon."

[3] See the *Manual* of Captain Vergnes.

This subject is being gradually organized, and if it does not always meet with competent instructors, it at least responds everywhere to the taste of pupils.

But let us be on our guard lest this taste become an infatuation. When the educator has made many efforts to introduce a new subject into education, and has at last been successful, his part changes; most often he has to repress excesses of zeal, and to maintain within just limits that very branch of instruction which he had the greatest difficulty in introducing. All the sciences, all the arts, whatever they may be, are in their very nature encroaching, once the doors of the school have been opened to them. They are but means, but they are disposed to make themselves accepted as ends. In the French colleges the study of Latin, which should be but one of the modes of intellectual culture through the use of a foreign language, has become the supreme end of education, and there is no longer any other thought than to make latinists.[1] Let it not be so with gymnastics, whose purpose is not to make gymnasts, prodigies of strength and agility, but simply to give power and suppleness to the muscles; to govern and facilitate the play of the bodily movements; to assure to laborers vigorous limbs, good corporeal tools; to prepare for all men

---

[1] It is worthy of note, in passing, that teachers often misconceive the destination of their pupils. In particular this mistake is made by specialists, as in the classics and the sciences, who proceed on the hypothesis that all their pupils are to become specialists, — philologists or naturalists. In such cases the presumption is set up that the sciences must be rediscovered. The story of Agassiz and the student with the fish, so often quoted to illustrate the true method of teaching science, does not represent the average pupil, who needs to learn science chiefly for the same reason that he learns history, for the sake of general information. This subject is discussed at some length in *Contributions to the Science of Education*, Chap. III. (P.)

the elements of a robust health and a long life; and, finally, to develope the physical energies, just as study developes the moral energies.

Doubtless gymnastics has need of apparatus and rigging, and for the moment this is one of the difficulties which retard its introduction into village schools; but let it be as far as possible independent of these aids, or at least let it not abuse them. Let there be no machines that are too complicated, no contrivances that are too scientific. The report of the special commission appointed in 1868 had the prudence to condemn "exercises which demand too great an expenditure of strength, and which might be the cause of accidents." So let us proscribe all the niceties, all the refinements, which would end in transforming the lesson in gymnastics into a training of jugglers or of adepts in feats of strength, — in a word, all the exercises which do not have the single purpose of giving the child a body fit for action and able to resist fatigue.

36. OTHER RESULTS OF GYMNASTICS. — But gymnastics has not physical development solely in view.

A shrewd observer of children, Mademoiselle Chalamet, has remarked that gymnastics also proposes, " (1) to discipline the child; and (2) to afford him repose from intellectual labor, and, by this very means, to make the resumption of it more easy and more profitable." [1]

Gymnastics, in fact, by regulating the movements of the body, by imposing regular and rhythmical evolutions, by requiring exact movements, executed with precision and promptness, — gymnastics communicates habits of order and decision, whose effect survives the exercises which have produced them, and which, by a sort of inner contagion, are even transmitted to the soul. This result would cer-

---

[1] Mademoiselle Chalamet, *L'École maternelle*, p. 275.

tainly be attained if the evolutions of pupils were to be accompanied by songs, as recommended by Amorås, who introduced gymnastics into France.[1]

On the other hand, gymnastics does not labor merely for the future by enlarging and strengthening the chest, by giving suppleness to the limbs, and by contributing to the health of the child. It also acts immediately upon the state of the body, whose forces it renews, and upon the nervous system, which it tempers; it has a happy effect upon studies, because it re-establishes the equilibrium in the organism, and at the same time gives the mind more vigor and elasticity. Gymnastics, like play, takes the child weary, enervated by study and cerebral effort, and restores him to intellectual labor refreshed and active. But it will do this on one condition, that we never pass the limit beyond which fatigue would begin. An excessive exercise of the body makes the mind inert, while moderate exercise reanimates and refreshes it. Especially in our day, when an over-crowded programme subjects the child to severe intellectual efforts, when " a system of high-pressure education," as Mr. Spencer says, requires excessive application, an alternation of physical and mental exercises becomes more and more necessary in order to re-establish and renew without cessation the forces which the abuse of mental labor is not slow to exhaust.

37. MILITARY GYMNASTICS. — It is not only in our day, as one might suppose, that men have thought of exercising children in the handling of arms.

---

[1] In the *Rapport* of Dr. Javal, *Sur l'Hygiène des écoles primaires* (Paris: 1884), we find the following precept: Children must be prevented from singing during violent gymnastic exercises and while running. But evidently this prohibition does not apply to elementary exercises, to rounds, and to evolutions.

"I saw yesterday," wrote Madame de Sévigné, "a little boy whom I found to be a fine fellow. He is seven years old, and his father has taught him to handle the musket and the pike. It is the finest thing in the world. You would love that little child. This exercise limbers his body and makes him deliberate, dexterous, and resolute. To my mind, this is better than a dancing-master."

It is needless to insist on the utility of military gymnastics, which is a preparation for the duties of citizenship and an apprenticeship in the habits of a soldier, at the same time that it offers most of the advantages which can be obtained from the practice of ordinary gymnastics. It is sufficient to call to mind the place which military drill has long held in the schools of Germany.

38. GYMNASTICS FOR GIRLS. — We must not conclude from the fact that the law of 1880 is content with imposing upon boys the obligation to receive instruction in gymnastics, that such instruction is not adapted to girls.

"Women," said Monsieur Laisné, "have need of gymnastics even more than men ; for in their case the obstacles which civilized life opposes to physical development are much more numerous and even much more fatal."[1]

Herbert Spencer vigorously combats the prejudice which excludes girls from physical exercises. He conceives for them an education as boisterous and as active as that of their brothers. He even urges them to violent sports and to long walks, to whatever can produce in them a robust physical development. He would have them run like madcaps and grow up amid gambols and rude sports. There is no fear, he adds, that this will afterwards affect the delicacy and grace of their manners.

---

[1] Laisné, *Gymnastique pratique*, Preface, p. 13.

"If the sportive activity allowed to boys does not prevent them from growing up into gentlemen, why should a like sportive activity allowed to girls prevent them from growing up into ladies? Rough as may have been their accustomed playground frolics, youths who have left school do not indulge in leapfrog in the street or marbles in the drawing-room."[1]

Doubtless it is unnecessary to subject the two sexes to the same régime. Plato and some utopists of the French Revolution are the only ones who could dream, in their passion for equality, of an education absolutely the same, in which girls should be dressed like boys, and, like them, should mount horse and bear arms. No; nature requires that we take into account the difference which she has established in physical constitution as in social destination. There should be special programmes and distinct manuals of gymnastics for the two sexes. Certainly there should not be required of women the prolonged running, the violent leaps, and the feats of strength, — any of those exercises, in a word, — which are befitting only to the muscular strength of men. We must ever keep in mind with what a delicate and frail being we have to do.

But with these reservations, it is safe to say that, at least in towns, young women need to be subjected to gymnastic discipline.

"The boy always finds a means of escaping somewhat from the influence of bad lodging and an unwholesome mode of life. He is out of doors, walks the streets, idles about town, lives much in the open air. But the girl, on the contrary, is sedentary, remains within doors, escapes no restraint. The direct consequence of this is a greater debility, which can be repaired only by more energetic and more assiduous care. What physician in the poorer quarters of cities has not been painfully struck by that muscular feebleness, by that nervous debility, and by that impoverishment

---

[1] *Education*, p. 225.

of the blood which characterize the young women of the lower
classes, and make of them, at a late period, the victims of grave
nervous disorders, or at least women rarely capable of sustaining
with impunity the fatigues of maternity?" [1]

39. OFFICIAL PROGRAMMES. — It has not been thought
sufficient to recommend gymnastic exercises, or even to
impose them by law; the programme of this new instruction
has recently been prepared. Already, in 1872, in the
schools of Paris, instruction in gymnastics had been organized according to a regular plan.

"The lessons, based on the elementary principles of general
anatomy, comprise exercises in walking, simple movements, movements combined with the xylofer,[2] the handling of dumb-bells,
jumping, and, for the oldest pupils, parallel bars and the
ladder. All the movements are accompanied by an easy and
pleasing song, which helps to strengthen the muscles of the
respiratory organs." [3]

We now present the text of the official programme established in 1882 : —

INFANT CLASS. — Plays, rounds, evolutions, rhythmic movements, the little games of Madame Pape-Carpantier. Graduated
exercises.

ELEMENTARY COURSE. — Preparatory exercises, movements and
flexions of the arms and legs. Use of the dumb-bells and bar.
Cadenced running. Evolutions.

INTERMEDIATE COURSE. — Continuation of the exercises in the
flexion and extension of the arms and legs. Practice with dumb-
bells. Exercises with the bar, rings, ladder, knotted cord, sus-
pended bars, fixed horizontal beam, the pole, the trapeze. Evolutions.

---

[1] *Revue pédagogique*, Nov. 25, 1882, article by M. E. Pécaut.

[2] An instrument recommended by Dr. Tissot in 1870, constructed
by Laisné in 1873, whose purpose is to expand and develop the chests
of children.

[3] M. Gréard, *L'Enseignement primaire à Paris*, p. 113.

HIGHER COURSE. — Continuation of the same exercises. Exercises in equilibrium upon one foot. Arm movements, combined with walking. Exercises two and two with the bar. Races, jumping. Cane exercise (for boys).

40. PLAY AND GYMNASTICS. — As it has been justly said, gymnastics, understood as a science of movements, as a systematic and exact art of physical exercises, — gymnastics, when introduced into the school, is but an additional lesson there. Now it is particularly of physical activity that it is true to say that, in order to attain its purpose, it ought to be agreeable, to please the child, to conform to his tastes. If pleasure does not attend them, physical exercises will not have the salutary effect that is expected of them. From this point of view, the monotonous, artificial, and unnatural movements of gymnastics are certainly not worth the free and joyous effort that comes from activity in play.

"The truth is," says Mr. Spencer, "that happiness is the most powerful of tonics. By accelerating the circulation of the blood, it facilitates the performance of every function, and so tends alike to increase health when it exists, and to restore it when it has been lost. Hence the essential superiority of play to gymnastics." [1]

In pursuing his formal strictures against gymnastics, which " must be radically defective as not supplying these agreeable mental stimuli," the English educator remarks that it has still another fault; the prescribed movements which it imposes, necessarily less diversified than the movements which result from free exercises, develop but a part of the muscular system, exercise only particular organs, and consequently do not produce an equal distribution of activity among all parts of the body.

---

[1] *Education*, pp. 257, 258.

The legitimate preference which Mr. Spencer accords to play, to the spontaneous activity of the child, almost necessarily leads him to the extreme and false conclusion that gymnastics is a bad thing, and that it can be accepted at best only as a make-shift, — " formal exercises of the limbs are better than nothing."

We are far from sharing this opinion, and it seems to us that Laisné was more just in his appreciation when he wrote :

"Ordinary sports, with their inconveniences, disordered and unsystematic, cannot replace gymnastics; but, conversely, gymnastics, regular and systematic as it is, ought not to supersede play where all children abandon themselves to the frolics of their age."

41. NECESSITY OF PLAY. — This is not the place to discuss exhaustively the question of sports. In fact, sports do not affect physical education alone; they have intimate relations with the culture of the imagination and with æsthetic education, and we shall have occasion to return to the subject.

But it is well to state before going further how important it is, from a sanitary point of view, that the child should play, and how much it were to be regretted should the habit of playing disappear from our schools, as it tends, alas! to disappear from social life.

"Play in the open air, which invites to jump, to run without interruption, to shout at the top of the voice, which causes the blood to circulate vigorously, and gives color to the cheeks, — this is the agent of all others for physical development. The English and the Americans well know this, and with them play is a national institution."

The French, on the contrary, play less and less, and the fault is due in part to the habits contracted in the colleges, and also in part to the teachers, who, in general, have disparaged sports too much, — "those nothings which are everything in the life of a child." Froebel is almost the only one who has given that attention to the subject which it merits.

"We should not consider play," he says, "as a frivolous thing; on the contrary, it is a thing of profound signification. . . . . By means of play the child expands in joy as the flower expands when it proceeds from the bud; for joy is the soul of all the actions of that age."

42. PHYSICAL EXERCISES IN ENGLAND. — Physical education still counts so many adverse critics among the French that it is not useless to invoke the example of foreign nations. No one will deny that the Anglo-Saxon race stands in the front rank among the human races, and it owes its superiority in part to its taste for physical exercises.

On this point let us quote the testimony of an acute observer, M. Taine.[1]

"There are gentlemen in England," he says, "whose ambition and training are those of a Greek athlete. They restrict themselves to a particular diet, abstaining from every excess in food and drink. They develop their muscles and subject themselves to a rational system of training. . . . .

"Sports hold the first place, said an Eton master, and books the second. A boy stakes his reputation on being a good athlete. He spends three, four, five hours a day in boisterous and violent exercise. He will splash about for hours in ploughed fields and miry meadows, falling into the mud, losing his shoes, and pulling himself out as best he can. . . . . The university continues the school, and in it there reigns an active, popular, almost universal taste for athletic exercises. Playing at cricket, rowing, sailing,

---

[1] M. Taine, *Notes sur l'Engleterre*, Paris, 1872, Chap. IV., *L'Education.*

training dogs to hunt rats, fishing, hunting, riding on horseback, coaching, swimming, boxing, fencing, and recently amateur soldiering, — these are the most interesting occupations for the young men. . . . . Doubtless muscular training carried to such an extent entails some rudeness in manners; but, by way of compensation, this athletic and gymnastic discipline has this double advantage, that it chills the senses and pacifies the imagination. Moreover, when the moral and mental life is afterwards developed, the soul finds, to support it, a more healthy and a more substantial body."

We do not desire, any more than M. Taine does, to disguise the faults which this extreme attention to the physical life, this mania for muscularity, is likely to engender. Plato, two thousand years ago, drew the portrait, but little flattering, of the man who trains only his body, "who lives in ignorance and awkwardness, with no symmetry and no grace."[1] English education must often end in producing coarse natures, dolts; but, on the other hand, it hardens the body and tempers character.

43. Conclusion. — It is only till lately that the theory and the practice of education have given to physical exercises their proper place; and already, in presence of the progress, still uncertain, of gymnastics, some minds have taken the alarm. It is to be feared, some say, that the new generations may be "trained to passive obedience through the development of physical exercises." It is even said that education, thus conducted, lowers man towards the level of the beast.[2] This is surely misplaced zeal to hurl anathemas against a thing the most innocent and the most legitimate in the world, the development of physical power. If it were necessary to choose between mind and

---

[1] *Republic*, 411.
[2] See the Lent Sermon of the Bishop of Versailles, 1885.

gymnastics, we would freely exclaim, Long live mind! Down with gymnastics! But surely there is no need of such a choice. The mind can derive only good from a moderate exercise of the body. As to saying that the habit of passive obedience will be the result of this new taste for physical discipline, it is to forget that well-worn truth that a man is so much the more free, so much the more independent, as he has more power at his disposal. We have never observed that in the religious orders, where passive obedience is most strongly recommended, and where the maxim *perinde ac cadaver* has reigned, much attention has been given to physical development. In such cases asceticism has flourished, not gymnastics.

CHAPTER III.

INTELLECTUAL EDUCATION.—GENERAL PRINCIPLES.

44. Is there an Intellectual Education?—It is still the general usage to reserve the word education to designate the formation of morals and character. The precise object of education proper, in distinction from instruction, is the culture of the will and the heart, as opposed to that of the intelligence.[1] There is, however, an intellectual education, but it is something more than instruction, though it includes it and depends in great part upon it.

"The mind," said Locke, "is the principal part of human nature, and education ought to bear chiefly upon what is within man." It cannot be doubted, in fact, that the intelligence and the interior faculties are, still more than the physical faculties, the object of education, either by reason of the dignity of thought,—"for it is from this source that we must gain the power to rise,"—or because, nature and instinct playing a less important part in mental development, the intervention of the educator is here particularly necessary.

45. Relation of Intellectual Education to Physical and Moral Education.—Intellectual education is by no

---

[1] H. Marion, *Leçons de psychologie,* p. 49. The meaning of this term is not so restricted by English writers, who apply it in the same sense to body, mind, and character; though the essential idea in each case is that of discipline or formation, rather than of instruction or information. (P.)

52

means an isolated thing, separated from all the rest. On the contrary, it is but a fragment of the general education of man, having intimate relations with physical education, and also with moral education.

When science shall have succeeded in solving the question, still obscure, of the relations between the physical and the moral, between brain and thought, the influence of the education of the body upon the education of the mind will become perfectly apparent. But even now, it is sufficient to have observed children to be convinced that their intellectual evolution corresponds to their state of health, to the nature of their temperament, to their strength, or to their weakness of body.

And, on the other hand, notwithstanding the clamorous assertions of Herbert Spencer, with respect to the impotency of instruction and its moral sterility, it is evident that the education of the mind is a preparation for that of the heart and the character, and that there is an element of truth in the old Socratic maxim, "Knowledge and virtue are one."[1]

46. DEFINITION OF INTELLECTUAL EDUCATION. — Everything which contributes to making the mind active, to developing, strengthening, and training it, and also to enlightening and ornamenting it, forms a part of intellectual education. But there is an important distinction to be made: it is one thing to build a house, and another thing to furnish it.[2] And so, with respect to the intelligence, it is one thing to cultivate it for itself, by developing

---

[1] See Compayré, *History of Pedagogy*, p. 380.

[2] A very true statement of the case will be made, if we say that the purpose of intellectual education is to train or discipline the mind and to furnish it, and that this furnishing is to serve two purposes, use and enjoyment. (P.)

its faculties, and another thing to furnish it with the knowledges which constitute either the elements of wisdom or real
science.

Then we shall not confound instruction proper, the study
of whatever must be learned and known, with the general
culture of the intelligence, the educative effort by virtue of
which the child leaves school not only instructed, but capable of carrying forward his own instruction; teachable,
furnished with strong and pliant faculties, with an agile
and firm memory, with accurate judgment, and with the
power of exact reasoning.

"Education," says Dupanloup, "consists essentially in the development of the human faculties.

"If the care of the master and the efforts of the pupil do not
result in developing, extending, elevating, and strengthening the
faculties; if they are limited, for example, to providing the mind
with certain knowledges, and, if I dare say it, to storing them
away there without adding to its breadth, its power, and its natural activity, education will not have taken place; there will be
nothing but instruction. I would no longer recognize in this process that grand and beautiful creative work which is called education, *educare*. The child might be, strictly speaking, instructed,
but he would not be educated. Even the education of the intellect would be imperfect.

"In this there would be at most only an instruction of low
quality, and in some sort passive, such as a weak and incomplete being might receive." [1]

In other terms, education has not only to present knowledges to a mind already formed, but its very first duty is
to form that mind.

47. THE INSTRUCTION AND EDUCATION OF THE MIND. —
Intellectual education is, then, something besides instruc-

---

[1] Dupanloup, *De l'Éducation*, liv. 1er, chap. ii.

tion: it is the end and aim, — instruction is but the means of attaining it. But instruction is not only valuable in itself: it is the essential means, the most powerful instrument, of intellectual education.

Instruction, in fact, brings to the mind the aliment it needs for nourishment, for adding to its growth and stature.

On this point American educators are fond of comparing the mind with the body, and try to show that knowledge is the aliment of the spirit.

"The appetite," says Mr. Baldwin, "craves food, and in the presence of suitable food the entire digestive apparatus acts; food is converted into muscles; muscles are used; the result is physical power. The soul longs for knowledge; in the presence of suitable knowledge every faculty of the soul is roused to action; the child knows, feels, chooses, acts; the result is increased mental power." [1]

No doubt the mind, if not fed, would become impoverished and enfeebled. Even in mature age the intelligence, if it does not renew its provision of ideas by study, languishes and grows weak, just as the body becomes emaciated under the influence of privations and of prolonged fasting. For a still better reason, at the period of its early development the intellect cannot grow strong if it is not nourished; and it is instruction which is the aliment of the spirit.

I add that if the aliment is well chosen, if the knowledges are presented with order, with discernment; if the studies are systematic and well conducted; not only will the mind become strengthened by them, but it will also

---

[1] Baldwin, *The Art of School Management*, New York, 1881, p. 313. See the same principles developed in *The Principles and Practice of Teaching*, by James Johonnot, p. 15.

be trained.   The natural fruit of instruction, wisely admin·
istered, is not only wisdom but precision in the play of
the faculties, — in a word, intellectual education.

It is true, on the other hand, that instruction, if poorly
administered, might still transmit knowledge, but it would
be valueless for the general culture of the mind.   Incomplete studies leave dangerous flaws in the intelligence;
they develop only one or two faculties at the expense of
all the others.   Studies that are too hasty weary the
mind, and may enervate it for life; pushed too far, they
encumber and weigh it down; irregular and disconnected,
they becloud and deform it.

48. METHODS OF CULTURE AND METHODS OF INSTRUC-
TION. — Instruction and intellectual education, then, are
things which are inseparable.   All the faults and all the
excellences of instruction will be re-echoed in the development of the faculties, and will contribute, for good or ill,
to the culture of the mind.

There is no other means of cultivating and forming
the intellectual faculties than exercise, — exercise which is
judicious and prudent; and there is no other intellectual
exercise than instruction under its different forms.

Does it follow that the educator ought immediately to
undertake the examination of the different branches of
instruction in order to study their methods, and that he
has no other course to follow, in order to direct intellectual education and to determine its laws?

By no means.   There are two different points of departure in pedagogy, — either the thinking subject who
is to be educated, or the objects which are to be taught.
In the first case we start from the nature of man, consider the laws of the formation of the faculties, and propose general methods of culture in conformity with these

laws. In the second case we start from each one of the several branches of instruction, determine their nature and characteristics, and then determine the methods of instruction which are in conformity with these characteristics.

In other terms, there are methods of culture inferred from the laws of psychology, and methods of instruction which, while striving to accord with psychology, are based chiefly on the nature of the knowledges which are to be taught.

We shall first study the methods of culture, by examining the different faculties one after another; but before entering upon this detailed examination, it is necessary to reply to some general questions which govern the whole subject, and to recall certain principles which apply without distinction to all the parts of intellectual education. Moreover, it is not best to make too much of these considerations, which, simply because they are very general, offer no great practical interest. An American educator enumerates no less than fourteen general principles of intellectual education.[1] We shall not imitate his example, for to do this it would be necessary to enter upon the task of transcribing in this place all the results of psychological study. We shall assume that these results are known for the most part, and shall limit ourselves to a few observations on the order of development of the faculties, on their necessary harmony, on the essential characteristics of intellectual education, and on the applications to education which result from them.

49. ORDER OF THE DEVELOPMENT OF THE FACULTIES. — Is it true that all the intellectual faculties expand at once, just as at nightfall all the stars glow in the heavens? Or,

----

[1] J. P. Wickersham, *Methods of Instruction*, pp. 37-51.

on the contrary, do they develop only successively, as the flowers unfold one after another on the stalk which supports them?

Educators have resolved the question differently. If we are to believe Rousseau, the mind is formed, so to speak, of successive layers; there are stages, steps, in the evolution of the intellect. To the faculties of sense, which manifest themselves from the earliest years, there succeed very much later the faculties of abstraction and of reasoning.

Other writers, who approach nearer the truth, incline towards the contrary exaggeration, and for the principle of succession substitute that of simultaneity.

"We would bring all the faculties under the view of the educator," says E. Joly, "for the purpose of studying them in the light of a useful and practical principle. This principle we would formulate as follows: The intellect is an aggregate of faculties which are developed simultaneously, and lend one another mutual assistance." [1]

The truth is that all the mental faculties, if we consider them in their germs, appear in the child at the same time; but they acquire their full power, attain their maturity, only one after another, and in an invariable order determined by the progress in age.

Herbert Spencer, in well-known pages of his "Education," has determined the laws of intellectual evolution. He proves that the mind proceeds from the simple to the complex, from the concrete to the abstract, from the particular to the general, from the indefinite to the definite, from the empirical to the rational. [2]

From these he concludes that we should first present to

---

[1] E. Joly, *Notions de pédagogie*, p. 32.

[2] For Joly's criticism on the laws laid down by Mr. Spencer, see *Notions de pédagogie*, pp. 46 *et suiv.*

children only simple subjects for study, sensible objects, particular things, in order to lead them forward step by step to complex truths, to abstract generalities, to conceptions of the reason; and he draws the further inference from them that we can require of the infant intelligence only incomplete and vague notions, which the travail of the spirit will gradually elaborate and classify.

50. The Intellectual State of the Child. — Closely examine the child, and you will see that his faculties resemble those of the grown man more closely than is generally supposed.

"The child of five years," says Madame Necker de Saussure, "is in possession of all the intellectual faculties accorded to humanity. Some of these faculties, weak and but little used, and often called into play by the most frivolous motives, express themselves as yet only by insignificant acts; but nevertheless we see them manifest themselves." [1]

In the simple fact of drawing back his hand from the fire because he has once been burned by it, the child exhibits memory, judgment, and inductive reasoning. It is none the less true that, in general, he feels more than he reasons, and that when he reasons he does so in his own way.

"The perceptive powers," says Mr. Wickersham, "are stronger and more active in youth than the other intellectual faculties." [2]

And the American educator adds:

"A child is merely an animal until there is awakened in him the power of self-consciousness. After this I can find no time when all his faculties are not active in some degree; but his perceptive powers are the strongest and most active during the whole period of childhood and youth."

---

[1] *L'Éducation progressive*, Tome I., Préface.
[2] J. P. Wickersham, *Methods of Instruction*, pp. 40, 41.

"We nowhere find nature beginning anything," says Madame Necker de Saussure; "we never surprise her at creating; she always seems to be developing."

In other terms, if the child is already, from the intellectual point of view, a little man, if we find in him the germ and almost the equivalent of all the faculties of mature age, at least these faculties do not affect the same aspects in his case, are not all presented with the same degree of power and precision. Just as all articles of food do not agree with the stomach of the babe, which as yet digests only milk, so all reasons are not fit for the reasoning of the child. He already feels the need of finding an explanation for things, of seeking their cause and purpose; but he will accept for such explanations reasons which are trivial and puerile. The progress accomplished by man from his early years up to maturity introduces into the mind no powers which are really new; but it modifies their character, increases their vigor, and extends their compass. All the faculties are awakened at the same time in the human intelligence, just as upon a race-course all the runners start at the same instant; but they do not advance at the same pace, — some take the lead, while others fall behind, and they reach the goal only one after another.

51. Progressive Education. — Intellectual education will take account of this successive development of the faculties. It will be progressive; it will not forget that in its slow evolution the mind changes its identity from moment to moment; that there are ages for the intelligence as for the body; that little by little the primitive dispositions are renewed and transformed; and that the moral nature is insensibly created. Consequently, in the aid which it will bring the child, either for exciting or for moderating his faculties, education will adapt itself exactly to the conditions

of nature and to the changes which occur in the soul with the march of time; it will accompany the mind in all the stages of its progress, and will adapt itself to all its movements; it will be, as Mr. Spencer has said, "the objective counterpart of the subjective development of the mind."

52. EQUILIBRIUM AND HARMONY OF THE FACULTIES. — From having recognized the differences which nature has established, with respect to the degree of development, among the faculties of the child, we shall not on that account come to forget the unity of the human soul. Education should be progressive, and not successive, as Rousseau wished. The author of the *Émile*, so to speak, cut the existence of the child into distinct sections, as the period of sense-perception, the period of judgment. No! the mind of the child is already an organized and complete whole, which contains in germ all the faculties; and if it is not possible to put them all upon the same footing, to make them all march abreast, at least there is not a single instant in life when we should not try to cultivate and develop them all, though in different degrees.

The independent culture of each faculty should not make us lose sight of the final aim, which is the harmony and the equilibrium of all the faculties.

"The equilibrium of the faculties, in the human intelligence, is what the equilibrium of forces is in the physical world, — it maintains order without hindering movement. Every faculty strong enough to suspend or cripple the action of other faculties is a despot; and in order to be sound the mind needs to be free." [1]

Let us be on our guard against minds in which certain intellectual dispositions dominate exclusively and smother

---

[1] Guizot, *Conseils d'un père sur l'éducation.*

the others.   When certain faculties destroy the equilibrium, genius, it is true, sometimes appears ; but the more often that which results from this unequal education is incoherence, disorder, and impotence.

The ideal of a good intellectual education is a mind in which all the faculties occupy a place proportionate to their value and importance, just as the ideal of a physical education is a complete body in which all the organs are harmoniously ˙ developed and all the functions regularly co-operate in the maintenance of life.

"The principal rule," says Kant, "is to cultivate no faculty solely for itself, but to cultivate each in view of the others; for example, the imagination for the sake of the intelligence."

Just as in the soul, as a whole, the sensibility and the will ought to be neither sacrificed nor preferred to the intelligence, so in the intelligence itself no aptitude ought to be neglected, no one ought to be the object of a privileged culture.

53. THE FACULTIES SHOULD LEND ONE ANOTHER MUTUAL SUPPORT.—The harmony of the faculties so nicely conforms to the intent of nature, and so to the purpose of education, that these different faculties are mutually helpful, and it is almost impossible to develop one without at the same time preparing for the development of the others. Nicole had called attention to this fact.

"Instruction," he said, "gives neither memory, imagination, nor intelligence, but it cultivates all these elements by strengthening one through another.   We aid the judgment by memory, and we relieve the memory by imagination and judgment." [1]

It is only in minds badly trained that the different

---

[1] *De l'Éducation d'un prince,* p. 35.

faculties come into collision and manifest, so to speak,
anarchical tendencies. A sound mind is a real organism,
in which everything has its own place, but in which all
things work together towards the same end.

54. GENERAL CHARACTERISTICS OF INTELLECTUAL EVOLU-
TION. — From all that has preceded it follows that the
point of departure in intellectual education is the unequal
march, the progressive evolution, of the different faculties,
and that the term, the aim, is the development — I do
not say equal, but proportionate and normal — of these
same faculties. We now see where we are going and
whence we set out.

But by what routes shall we go? According to what
general principles ought the educator to govern his conduct? It is not sufficient to say that education as a
whole will conform to the order of nature. Nature, in fact,
is a grand and vague word, which educators and moralists interpret just as it pleases them, and under cover of
which they give currency to the most various and often
to the most singular conceptions.

Without entering into the details of method, which shall
be the purpose of the chapters composing the second
part of this work, it is proper to determine at this point
some of the laws of intellectual evolution and the educational results which flow from them.

55. THE MIND IS NOT A VASE TO BE FILLED, BUT A FIRE
THAT IS TO BE MADE TO GLOW. — The mind is not a *tabula
rasa*, a blank page, on which we have but to write, a
simple receptacle which it suffices to fill just as we fill a
measure with grain; but it is an aggregate of germs which
aspire to develop themselves.

How many times have teachers transgressed this psychological law! Do we not violate it every day when our chief concern is to cram the mind of the child, to accumulate a mass of knowledge, at the risk of smothering the intelligence, which we should only arouse and excite? The overcrowding of modern programmes is increasing from day to day, to the great detriment of intellectual liberty. Even supposing that the mind is at birth a vase ready made, it would still be an insoluble problem to propose to have contained in a vase of invariable dimensions ten, twenty, or a hundred times as much matter. But besides, it is not the purpose of education to produce prodigies of memory, erudites capable of discussing whatever is knowable.

"The purpose of study," says Gréard, "is above all else to create the instrument of intellectual labor, to make the judgment surer; and for this purpose it is not necessary to teach all that it is possible to know, but that of which it is not permissible to be ignorant." [1]

Then let us renounce the pretensions of those who would have the human intelligence the résumé of universal knowledge. Let us no longer admire feats of strength like those mentioned by Dupanloup.

"One pupil recited the whole of the *Telemaque*, another recited a grammatical analysis which contained more than sixty thousand Greek and French words."

Let us return to the old maxim, *Non multa, sed multum.* It is better to know a few things thoroughly than to know all things superficially.

56. RESPECT FOR THE LIBERTY AND THE VOLUNTARY EFFORT OF THE CHILD. — The teachers who still believe that

---

[1] *Mémoire sur la question des programmes dans l'enseignement secondaire,* 1884.

the mind is an inert, passive capacity, of course have no regard for the liberty of the child; there is no occasion for respecting powers whose existence is not admitted. But all those who believe that nature has planted in the intelligence vital principles, which await only a favorable occasion and a proper stimulus to awaken and expand, feel on the contrary the need of not hampering and not opposing the natural evolution of the mind.

Allow the child who is beginning to think the largest liberty possible. Do not bend his intelligence to artificial forms; do not compel him to endure by force too many didactic lessons; do not impose on him a diet which he is not capable of digesting.

"When men," says Mr. Spencer, "received their creed and its interpretations from an infallible authority deigning no explanations, it was natural that the teaching of children should be dogmatic. While 'believe and ask no questions' was the maxim of the church, it was fitly the maxim of the school. Conversely now that Protestantism [Mr. Spencer should add, 'and philosophy'] has gained for adults a right of private judgment, and established the practice of appealing to reason, there is harmony in the change that has made juvenile instruction a process of exposition addressed to the understanding."[1]

57. WE MUST KNOW HOW NOT TO BE IN HASTE. — "The most useful rule of all education," said Rousseau, "is not to gain time, but to lose it." Under the form of a paradox, this was saying that it is not wise to make haste, and that education ought to act upon the frail and delicate intelligence of the child with a slowness copied from nature.

"Let us protect ourselves," says Madame Pape-Carpantier to the same effect, "against that unthinking zeal, or that culpable vanity, which would exact from the child all that his elastic intelligence

---

[1] *Education,* p. 97.

can produce, at the risk of exhausting it, at the risk of destroying the fruit in the flower."

58. ATTRACTIVE LABOR. — It is a truth now generally admitted that there are no studies really profitable, save those which respond to the needs of the intelligence, and there provoke an agreeable excitation. Herbert Spencer earnestly recommends that the tastes of the child shall be taken into account. "Work," says Gréard, "being but the development of natural activity, the exercise of that activity ought certainly to make the child happy."

The pleasure which the child feels is in fact the sign that his mind is developing with ease, that he is assimilating the knowledge which has been presented to him. On the other hand, his repugnances, his indolence, and his inertia prove that the instruction which displeases him has been presented at too early a period, or has been presented in a bad way.[1]

---

[1] Following Mr. Spencer, M. Compayré assigns two reasons why studies may be disagreeable to a child: (1) They may be unseasonable or (2) they may be badly presented. There is still another reason: they may involve a mode of mental activity which has not yet been developed so fully as to proceed with facility, and hence with pleasure. Under the most favorable circumstances, the beginning of a new subject will often be unpleasant, because the mind has not yet become accustomed to this new mode of exercise. If we regard symmetry and harmony of development as one aim of education, a pupil's dislike of a study may indicate that he ought to pursue it.

It should be added also that a study will grow tedious when the mental activity it involves reaches the fatigue-point. In a word, the same rules may be applied to mental as to physical activity. In both cases free and spontaneous activity is agreeable; activity that is constrained, or that reaches the fatigue-point, is tedious or disagreeable. But these last conditions are often inevitable, and are even desirable, for robustness, power, and manliness can be attained in no other way. In a larger sense, there is no discipline like a noble sorrow. (P.)

Pleasure, then, is not a thing to be despised in instruction; it will give to the faculties an unusual animation. And it is not necessary, in order to make the child happy in his work, to attempt to enliven instruction by amusements which impair its character. It is sufficient to follow a proper order, one adapted to the powers of the child. Mental activity is agreeable in itself.

"Where young people are taught as they ought to be, they are quite as happy in school as at play, seldom less delighted — nay, often more — with the well-directed exercise of their mental energies, than with that of their physical powers." [1]

59. NECESSITY OF EFFORT. — But the legitimate desire to make study agreeable, to sweeten the toil of the child, ought not to make us forget the necessity of effort. Let us not yield to the temptation of saying, with Fénelon, "everything should be done with pleasure." According to the amiable author of the *Éducation des filles*, everything should be learned while playing. This is neither possible nor desirable. Let us avoid whatever is repulsive, but let us not go so far as to proscribe what is laborious.

"School is a forced culture," says Kant. "We should accustom the child to work. . . . . It is to render him a very poor service to accustom him to regard everything as play. . . . ."

"Whatever is done to make study agreeable," says Rousseau, "will prevent children from profiting by it. . . . . And so Madame de Staël says : 'The education that takes place by amusing one's self dissipates thought. Pain of every kind is one of the greatest secrets of nature, and the mind of the child ought to accustom itself to studious efforts, just as our soul should be accustomed to suffering.' "

"Asceticism is disappearing out of education, as out of life," Mr. Spencer has said, in his brilliant way. Yes ; but

---

[1] Professor Pillans, quoted by Herbert Spencer, *Education*, p. 159.

for the old-time asceticism there must not be substituted a sort of pedagogic epicureanism, distinguished by instruction which is amusing as well as by discipline which is lax.

Pain ought not to be purposely proscribed in education. It awakens new ideas in the soul; it stirs the mind to depths scarcely suspected before the suffering came. No stimulus is equal to that of pain, for liberating the human personality from the disguises which envelop it.

"Man is an apprentice; pain is his master!"

60. THE INNER DEVELOPMENT OF THE MIND. — The idea of an inner and spontaneous development of the mind is not a new thing in pedagogy.

"Properly speaking," says Nicole, "it is not the teacher nor outside instruction, which causes things to be comprehended; they do nothing more than expose them to the interior light of the mind, by which alone they are comprehended; so that when there is not the concurrence of this light, instruction is to no more purpose than as though one were to exhibit pictures in the night."

In fact, in an education properly administered, it is of less importance to assure the superficial instruction, the exterior culture and adornment of the mind, than to secure its inner and profound development. "To instruct a child," said Madame Neckèr de Saussure, pithily, "is to construct him from within."

Let us, then, reject all methods of instruction which, like those of the Jesuits, leave inactive the inner forces of the soul. To find for the mind occupations which absorb it, which lull it like a dream, without wholly awakening it; to call attention to words, to niceties of speech, to the trivial facts of history, so as to reduce by so much the opportunity for thinking; to provoke a certain degree of intellectual activity, prudently arrested at the point where reflective reason succeeds a garnished memory; — in a word, to stir the mind from without just enough to rescue it from its natural ignorance, but not enough to make it really act for itself by a manly display of all its faculties, — such was the method of the Jesuits. It is good for nothing but to make grown-up children, not men.

61. MEANS TO BE EMPLOYED. — It is not our purpose in this place to enter upon details of method; this is a subject which we shall resume further on (see Part Second). Let us merely illustrate, by a few quotations, the extent to which modern educators, particularly American educators, are preoccupied with the inner activity of the mind.

"The teacher should never do for the child what it can do for itself. It is the child's own activity that will give strength to its powers and increase the capacity of the mind. The teacher must avoid telling too much or aiding the child too frequently. A mere hint or suggestive question, to lead the mind in the proper direction, is worth much more than direct assistance, for it not only gives activity and consequently mental development, but cultivates the power of original investigation."[1]

Mr. Wickersham, another American educator, proceeds in the same vein:

"The condition of the learner should not be one of passive reception, but of earnest self-exertion. One trial of strength should induce other trials; one difficulty overcome should excite an ambition to triumph over other difficulties. The teacher should create interest in study, incite curiosity, promote inquiry, prompt investigation, inspire self-confidence, give hints, make suggestions, tempt pupils on to try their strength and test their skill."[2]

Mr. Wickersham continues by citing the example of a bird teaching her young ones to fly.

---

[1] Edward Brooks, *Normal Methods of Teaching*, pp. 21, 22.
[2] Wickersham, *op. cit.*, pp. 23, 24.

"One of my best lessons in teaching was taught me by a robin. It was in my garden, and the mother-robin was teaching her young brood to fly. A little robin sat upon the nest and seemed afraid to move. The mother-bird came and stood by its side, stroked it with her bill, and then hopped to a neighboring twig and stood awhile, as if to induce the little bird to follow. Again and again she repeated her caresses, and then hopped nimbly to the same twig. At length the little bird gained courage, and to the great joy of its mother shook its weak wings, started, and stood by her side. Another more distant twig was now selected, and further effort brought the little bird to it also. And so the process was repeated many times, until the timid fledgling, now grown quite bold, could sail away with its mother over woodlands, fields, and meadows."

Under a pleasing form the above is a paraphrase of this thought of Froebel: " Let teachers not lose sight of this truth: Always and at the same time they must give and take, precede and follow, act and let act."

62. INTELLECTUAL INEQUALITIES. — In spite of Jacotot's paradox, "All intelligences are equal," it is certain that profound differences separate minds in their native constitution, and that these intellectual inequalities do not all come from the fact that we do not all have the same tastes and the same will. The teacher should know how to take into account this diversity of faculties, and should recall the maxim of Locke, "There are perhaps no two children who can be brought up by exactly the same methods."

However, do not let us push the significance of these observations too far. Do not let us diversify intellectual education without limit. While paying regard to natural inequalities for the purpose of correcting them, and to special aptitudes for the purpose of favoring them, let us not forget that we must propose to all pupils the same aim, and that, in general, it is possible to lead them to it. As

Madame Guizot said, "Save in some special and rare cases, we are all made for everything. . . . We must not so devote our faculties to one special line of action as to become unfitted for every other."[1]

63. SPECIAL APTITUDES. — It is not best, then, to follow the current of nature with absolute compliance, and when a child gives evidence of particular dispositions, to fall in, so to speak, with his predilections, and to devote him by preference to the things for which he has a marked aptitude. On this point it seems to us that Nicole is lacking in wisdom and moderation.

"There are children," he said, "who should be busied with scarcely anything except what depends on the memory, because they have a prompt memory and a weak judgment; and there are others who should devote themselves to the things that depend on the judgment, because they have more judgment than memory."[2]

No; without asserting that education ought to cast all minds in the same mould, nor that we should try to bring all intelligences up to the same level, let us not renounce the purpose to have them pursue a common ideal. For guarding the personality of each pupil, and for assuring sufficient liberty to his particular dispositions, we have done enough when, for the old tyrannical and oppressive methods, we have substituted the new methods, which appeal to the spontaneity and the voluntary effort of the child.

64. INTELLECTUAL EDUCATION ITSELF SHOULD HAVE A PRACTICAL AIM. — Even in our day we too often forget the old Latin adage, *Vitæ, non scholæ, discitur* (It is for life,

---

[1] *Lettres de famille sur l'éducation*, p. 77.
[2] Nicole, *De l'Éducation d'un prince*, p. 35.

not for school, that instruction is given). Preparation for life, — such is the true definition of instruction, especially of common-school instruction. It is not a grammarian, it is not a logician, as Montaigne says,[1] but a man that is to be trained. Then let us not demand that intellectual education should develop the brilliant faculties whose purpose is mental adornment, the faculties which serve for display, serviceable to men of leisure, but not adapted to the humble and laborious condition of the common people. What is needed is a manly training of the useful faculties, those of which it may be said that they are arms for the battle of life. Doubtless the common school is not a technical or professional school, but it ought to be a practical school. "The end of education," justly remarks an American writer, "is not to teach pupils to know and use books, but to know and make right use of themselves."[2]

---

[1] See *Compayré's History of Pedagogy*, p. 103.
[2] Baldwin, *op. cit.*, p. 313.

CHAPTER IV.

THE EDUCATION OF THE SENSES.

65. The Beginning of Intelligence. — He who would know in its completeness the nature of the intelligence should study the child beside his cradle.

At first he is but a little, inert mass, that awakens only to cling to his mother's breast or to weep; and yet in that body still so frail there slumber the germs of a complete moral personality. Upon contact with the exterior world all these germs will expand, all that latent life will awake, all that is potential will become active. It seems as though an invisible hand were pouring, drop by drop, into that delicate and fragile vase, soul and intelligence.

In a few days a smile will come to animate the lips of the infant; movements more and more characteristic will give evidence of his vitality; they will express either his instincts or simply his general need of activity. Finally, at the end of a few months, a sort of prattling — feeble cries indefinitely repeated — shows that this feeble child already has some glimmers of intelligence, and that he wishes to communicate them.

We have often heard of the slowness with which nature proceeds in organizing the faculties of the child. I confess that it is rather the contrary that impresses me. When we think of the origin of the child, that only a few months ago he had no formal existence, how can we fail to be astonished at that prodigy which is renewed every day, and which gives

73

rise in so brief a time to a new being, nearly similar in everything, except stature, to the authors of his life? Especially how can we fail to admire the intellectual progress which, through the acquisitions of the senses, is accomplished within a few years? "The period in which the child has no teacher," says Egger, "is perhaps that in which he learns most and most rapidly. Let one compare the number of ideas acquired between birth and the age of five or six, with those which he acquires in the years following, and he will be astonished at this great precocity."[1]

66. SENSATIONS AND PERCEPTIONS. — We assume to be known whatever psychology and physiology teach of the organs and the functions of the five senses, — seeing, hearing, touching, smelling, and tasting. Let us dwell only on what it is important for the educator to know, if he would proceed successfully in the education of the senses.

The sensations peculiar to the five senses are not merely *affective* perceptions, — that is, sources of pleasure or of pain, — but they are also *representative* perceptions, that is, the sources of images, of ideas, and of knowledges.[2] While the interior sensations, those which accompany the play of the organic functions, teach us nothing of the nature of the organs where they are developed, the exterior sensations inform us of the qualities of the objects which produce them, and those objects themselves.

From the earliest years of life perception is quite readily disengaged from sensation, and the perception is already knowledge, — it consists essentially in distinguishing the difference between objects.

"Mind," says Mr. Bain, "starts from discrimination. The con-

---

[1] Egger, *Observations sur le développment de l'intelligence*, 1879.

[2] Rousseau was wrong in saying, "The first sensations of children are purely affective: they perceive only pleasure and pain."

sciousness of difference is the beginning of every intellectual exercise." [1]

And at the same time that the mind, through successive perceptions, discriminates objects from one another, it soon comes to discriminate itself from these objects. Self-consciousness, the inner sense, is inseparable from the development of the external senses.

67. IMPORTANCE OF SENSE-INTUITIONS. — The notions furnished by the senses are one of the essential elements of the human intelligence. It were an error to think that the senses do not give us ideas. "Before the age of reason," said Rousseau wrongly, "the child does not receive ideas, but images." From the fact of being sensible, the representations of sight and of hearing are none the less ideas.

Doubtless the consciousness, applied to the interior modifications of the self, is a fruitful source of knowledge; but how much richer and vaster is the domain of exterior perception!

Our abstract and general ideas themselves are but the derivatives of a mental effort which compares, separates, and unites the concrete data of the senses.

Doubtless it is no longer necessary to make of the senses the only source of intellect, as Locke, Condillac, and Comenius also taught. [2]

The mind has its own constitution and its necessary laws; natural or acquired, innate or hereditary, reason exists prior to the senses and governs their exercise; as, for example, when it obliges us to admit an external reality, the cause and basis of sensible representations.

---

[1] Alexander Bain, *Education as a Science*, p. 15.

[2] "It is certain," says Comenius, in the preface to the *Orbis Pictus*, "that there is nothing in the understanding which had not before been in the senses."

But, nevertheless, the senses are the origin of the most of our knowledge ; they enrich the mind with a multitude of notions. It suffices, to judge of their importance, to see to what a wretched condition is reduced the intelligence of the unfortunates who have been deprived of several, or even of a single one, of their senses. The mind is not, as certain philosophers have supposed, a force which is self-sufficing ; it has need of nourishing itself from without, through an incessant communication with nature ; in a word, it is, in large measure, but the conscious echo of an external world.

68. GENERAL CULTURE OF THE SENSES. — The senses are in great part organized and formed by nature. A natural evolution carries forward each of them to its point of normal perfection. There is, however, for the faculties of sense-perception, as for all the others, an education proper, a real culture, which alone can secure to the senses all the precision, all the delicacy, of which they are susceptible.

The starting-point in this education of the senses depends upon physiology and hygiene. The integrity and the health of the organs must be protected. In the education of the vision, for example, the first duty belongs to the oculist. The senses are the instruments, the material tools, which must be kept clean, strong, and in a normal condition. But nature presents, in the case of a great number of individuals, grave imperfections which ought to be corrected so far as this is possible, and corrected at first by physical means. Some are near-sighted, some have imperfect vision, some are color-blind ; some are hard of hearing, and some almost deaf. For these difficulties medicine and hygiene offer remedies, or at least palliatives.

Sometimes an infirmity of the senses is caused, not by a defect in the special construction of the organ, but by a general weakness of the constitution. By fortifying the whole body and the general health, we assure the health and vigor of the organs of sense-perception. Finally, education, from this first point of view, ought carefully to avoid all the material causes of the enfeebling of the senses, — bad conditions of lighting, for example, — which might injure the natural and normal sensibility of vision.

But all has not been done when we have provided, through hygiene, for the health of the organs of sense. It is much to have good tools at our disposal, but this is not enough; we must know how to use them. Like all the faculties, the senses are perfectible. Between what they are naturally, and what they can become by a methodic and regular culture, there is a considerable margin. Exercise is the great secret of this education of the senses. It is by practice that the painter and the musician, the artisan and the artist, learn to see and to hear with a degree of accuracy and power to which the untaught do not attain. We know what marvellous power is attained by the hearing of savages and huntsmen, the touch of the blind, and the sight of sailors. Laura Bridgman, deaf, dumb, and blind, has succeeded through touch alone in distinguishing the colors of the different balls of yarn or of silk which she employs in her sewing and embroidery.

Finally, we must recollect that the senses are mutually complementary. Touch corrects the illusions of sight and extends its sphere. Sight illumines and guides the hearing. Besides these individual and special perceptions, natural perceptions, as the psychologists say, each sense has its *acquired perceptions*, which it owes in part to the co-operation of the other senses. Hence, again, the educator has a new occasion for intervention, for the purpose of aiding the senses in mutually controlling and correcting themselves, and in becoming by their accord the admirable and infallible instrument for acquiring a knowledge of the material world.

69. OPINION OF ROUSSEAU. — Rousseau is the first who understood the importance of the education of the senses.

"A child," he says, "is not so tall as a man; he has neither his strength nor his reason, but he sees and hears as well as he, or nearly as well. . . . The first faculties which are formed and perfected in us are the senses. These are the first that should be cultivated; they are the only ones that are forgotten, or that are most neglected.

"To exercise the senses is not merely to make use of them, but it is to learn to judge correctly by them; it is to learn, so to speak, to feel, for we can neither touch, nor see, nor hear, except as we have been taught."

What pleases us particularly in Rousseau's thought is that he does not consider the senses simply as instruments for perfecting the mind; but he studies them in themselves and seeks the means of training them. It is not merely the cd-ucation of the mind through the senses which concerns him, but above all the education of the senses themselves.

70. METHODS OF PESTALOZZI AND FROEBEL. — To Rousseau belongs the merit of having recommended theoretically the education of the senses, but to Pestalozzi and to Froebel belongs the honor of having put it in practice, of having introduced it into the domain of school work.

According to Pestalozzi, the point of departure in all intellectual education is to be found in the sensations. It was through things themselves that he wished to develop the intelligence of his pupils. It was not enough for him to have the objects seen, but they must be touched also; the child turned them about in all directions, until he had perfectly caught their form and observed their qualities. Pestalozzi went still further; he obliged the child to weigh, measure, and analyze the material things which he had taken into his hands, and at the same time he drilled the pupil in naming, in designating by the proper word, the qualities, the relations, the dimensions which his sight or his hand had distinguished in the objects. "See and name," was the principle of his elementary method of instruction.

It is in the same spirit that Froebel successively developed before the eyes of the child the marvels of the six gifts ; that he first exhibited to the sight concrete objects, such as balls of colored wool and geometrical solids ; and that he taught him to distinguish their contents, form, and material, "in such a way," says Gréard, "as to accustom him *to see*, — that is, to seize the appearance, form, resemblances, differences, and relations of things."

71. THE SPECIAL EDUCATION OF EACH SENSE. — Madame Necker de Saussure is not wholly right when she requires that the child shall carry forward the training of the five senses simultaneously. In fact, some of the senses are more precocious, and others more tardy, in their development ; and, besides, the senses are of unequal importance, and, not rendering the same services, do not deserve the same attention. Finally, each of them has its own conditions and its own laws. Hence the educator needs to study them one after another and to cultivate them separately, without, however, losing sight of their mutual relations.

72. SMELL AND TASTE. — Smell is perhaps the one of all the senses that is developed latest. Rousseau is right in claiming that children remain for a long time insensible to good and bad odors. Moreover, we can scarcely understand why smell is called "the sense of the imagination," on the pretext that odors and perfumes often recall memories which have long been slumbering.

Taste, on the contrary, just because it responds to the essential need of infant life, alimentation, — taste is very

early developed. Sensations of taste would be the first,
were they not preceded by vague tactile sensations. The
infant at once recognizes the sweetish taste of milk. If
he is offered water, or milk but slightly sweetened, he
rejects it. He refers everything to the sense of taste, and
carries all objects to his mouth.

Smell and taste are both inferior senses which have
scarcely any connection with the intellectual life. They
furnish us sensations rather than perceptions. They are the
agents of the physical life and of the digestive functions.
They put us on guard against certain dangers. They instruct us concerning aliments and liquors. They are the
sources of pleasures and pains, rather than of knowledges
and ideas. By their tendency towards excesses, by their
unhealthy stimulus, they may contribute towards developing
and nourishing evil appetites, such as gluttony and drunk-
enness; but the part they play in the life of the spirit is
mediocre, if not wholly null.

They fall, then, chiefly under the cognizance of moral
education, which must undertake to restrain them, to moderate their excesses, and to repress their caprices, their
daintiness, their excessive and violent preferences.

"Let the diet of the child," says Rousseau, "be plain and simple;
let his palate be made familiar only with moderate savors, and
let him contract no exclusive taste." "The abuse of odors and
perfumes," says Bernard Pérez, "enervates the body and enfeebles
the will. I would not have a bouquet in the infant's chamber,
or perfumes in his baths, on his hair, or upon his garments.
However, I would have him very sensitive to the sweet odors of
flowers."[1]

Taste and smell may, however, render some services to
the intelligence. The chemist recognizes a body by its

---

[1] Bernard Pérez, *L'éducation des le berceau,* p. 49.

characteristic odor ; he distinguishes substances as sapid and insipid. The taster recognizes the vintage and the age of wines simply from the impression which they produce on his palate. There is, then, some interest, from the intellectual point of view, in training even the senses of smell and taste, in rendering them more clever in discerning shades of sensible impressions.

73. EDUCATION OF THE SENSE OF HEARING. — The perceptions of hearing have a wholly different importance. Hearing makes us acquainted with sound and the different qualities of sound, — acuteness, gravity, intensity, volume, timbre. In this way hearing brings us into relation with a multitude of objects. But what is especially to be noted is that hearing is particularly the social sense, since by means of it we hear the voice of our fellows and know their thoughts. Hearing is also an artistic sense, since it makes possible music, the most popular, the most insinuating of all the arts.

The hearing is often defective. " The number of children who have imperfect hearing is much greater than is commonly supposed." [1]

In many cases the only cause of this weakness is the uncleanliness of the ears, and can easily be corrected ; but in other cases there is a natural and organic infirmity, — the child confounds certain syllables and certain words with words and syllables of similar assonance. With pupils thus poorly endowed the teacher ought to be particularly indulgent. He ought to bring them as near to himself as possible in the class-room, and should oblige himself and all their companions always to speak very distinctly.

The natural education of the hearing is relatively rapid.

[1] See the *Rapport* of Jacoulet, already mentioned.

The infant hears from the first day of its life. "On the thirty-sixth day," says M. Cuignet, "the child that I am observing as yet recognizes no one with his eyes, no matter who takes him or who walks with him; but he recognizes his mother by her voice."[1] The slightest sound makes the babe tremble in its cradle.

But what is slower and more delicate is the musical education of the hearing. At first all noises please the child. He loves noise for the sake of noise. In the matter of music he is no harder to please than animals, apes, and bees. It seems that his acoustic sense finds pleasure simply in being excited, in whatever way it may be. The more he is stunned, and the more he stuns others, the happier he seems. The culture of the musical sense is then a necessity, particularly to-day when singing has become a part of education, and because inaptitude in singing is the result of a defective culture of the hearing.

In general, in the education of the hearing, we should be guided by the following rules : —

"For the hearing, as for all the other senses, moderation is indispensable if we would preserve its integrity and its sensibility. We become accustomed to noise, it is true; but its effect is none the less pernicious. On the other hand, the complete absence of noise gives to the hearing an unhealthy sensibility, like that contracted by the sight of persons who have long been deprived of light."[2]

74. EDUCATION OF THE TOUCH. — The general sensations of touch are very early developed, because the entire body is its organ. At a very early period the infant shows that it is sensible to hard and rough contacts, to slight pressures, and that it suffers from them. A sensation of contact which

---

[1] M. Cuignet, *Annales d'oculistique*, Tome LXVI., p. 117.

[2] Dr. Saffray, *Dictionnaire de pédagogie*, art *Ouïe*.

would be indifferent to an adult makes it scowl or cry, and the touch of a warm and caressing hand causes it a very lively pleasure.

But we must distinguish the primitive sensation, wholly passive, of touch in general, from the active sensation whose essential organ is the hand. The infant first feels with the lips. As to the hand, it learns rather slowly to make use of it. For many months it notices objects without making an attempt to grasp them.

"It is easy," says Madame de Saussure, "to observe the gropings of experience in the manner in which the infant learns to make use of touch. This sense is slow in obeying the orders of the will. It is obliged, in some sort, to receive the stimulus of the sense of sight, whose education it in turn perfects."

75. THE CHILD'S POWER OF SIGHT. — At the .age of three or four years the child already astonishes us by the admirable precision of his sight, by the ease and deftness of his vision. It seems that he has looked at nothing, and yet he has seen everything.

The mature man, and even the young man, preoccupied with thought or with inner emotion, often looks only with distraction upon things without; but the child, free from after-thoughts, eager and curious, in the freshness and power of his nascent faculties lets nothing escape him of all that is presented by the shifting scenes of reality; we might say that his whole soul is in his eyes. A clever observer of children, M. Legouvé, has called attention to this in a humorous vein : —

"The child is all eyes. He has an incomparable power of vision. Compared with him, we are blind. Take your son with you into a chamber, a workshop, or a palace, and on coming out interrogate him. You will be amazed at all he has seen. At a single glance he has made an inventory of the furniture, the **walls,** the objects useful and ornamental. A professional could not have done this so quickly. All children are born appraisers." [1]

76. NATURAL DEVELOPMENT OF THE SENSE OF SIGHT. — But the child does not acquire this marvellous perspicacity of vision all at once. The sense of sight does not escape the law of natural education and of progressive development which presides over the organization of all the faculties. The eye learns to see, just as the tongue learns to speak and the legs to walk.

It would doubtless be an exaggeration to say that the infant at the moment of birth is but a little blind creature ; but the truth is that if he sees enough at the first to be hurt by the light, he does not see enough to distinguish objects.

During the first days of his life the child is afraid of the light. He is attacked by a sort of natural *photophobia,* [2] which is explained by the delicacy and imperfection of his visual organs, and is analogous to the cases of morbid photophobia caused by inflammation of the eye or other diseases. Bring a candle near a new-born child, and it will close its eyes, or at least will squint badly. The eye will conceal itself, so to speak, and will shut itself up in the obscure corner of the orbit in order to escape the light. But after a little time all is changed ; the infant manifests a marked taste, a sort of appetite, for the light. It will sometimes suffice, to cure his crying, to place a candle near his cradle. Let it be noted, however, that for the babe a few weeks old the light ought not to be too intense. That it may be endurable, it should be soft and should not dazzle.

But for some time the child enjoys the light, rather than perceives it ; he does not know immediately how to determine

---

[1] *Nos Filles et nos Fils,* p. 171.
[2] That is, " fear of light."

objects. When he is finally in a state to determine them, the first stage of progress will be his ability to follow them with his sight by a movement of the ball of the eye. A second stage of progress is his ability to turn his head, and so to prolong his attention.

But when he has gone so far, the child is not yet in full possession of the faculty of sight. Adult vision has a certain sweep in breadth; that is, it embraces a certain field of vision to the right and left. Besides, it has a certain range in depth; it grasps objects placed before it at a greater or less distance. Now, it is easy to prove that if we observe little children their vision has not at once its normal width and depth. Little children quickly lose from view the objects placed before them; and, on the other hand, if we suddenly change to the right or left the object which they are observing, that object escapes their notice.

In other terms, their field of vision is still very limited, both in depth and in breadth. Nature, in this case as in all others, proceeds with perfect art, by little increments of progress, by insensible developments; she grants to the babe only limited perceptions in harmony with its condition; she does not unfold to it, all at once, the spectacle of the visible universe; she discloses this to him little by little, with caution and discretion; she does not create the senses and the faculties at a single stroke, but organizes them little by little.

77. IMPORTANCE OF THE PERCEPTIONS OF SIGHT. — The perceptions of sight are still more rich, still more important, than those of hearing and touch. Sight is particularly the scientific sense; it is this which reveals to us the color, form, and size of objects. What more admirable than this "touch at a distance," which permits us to grasp the contour of the things in the midst of which we live, and which

makes it possible for us to penetrate even the immensity of
the starry heavens? While we may discuss at great length
the comparative misfortunes of blindness and deafness, it
seems undeniable that the blind man is still more unfortunate
than the one who is deaf, for he is deprived of the sight of
the innumerable beauties of the universe; though the deaf
man is the more sad, because less isolated than the blind
man, he is the more conscious of his misfortune, feels more
keenly what he has lost.

Let us not forget that sight, like hearing, is an æsthetic
sense, without which we would enjoy neither painting, sculpture, nor architecture. There are beautiful colors and beautiful forms, as there are beautiful sounds; but there are
neither beautiful odors nor beautiful flavors. In a word,
beauty seems to be connected only with the senses of sight
and hearing.

78. EDUCATION OF THE SIGHT. — A complete pedagogical
study of the sense of sight would comprise a considerable
number of precepts, some relating to what might be called
the education of the sight, and others more directly connected with its instruction.

The education of the sight consists in whatever gives
deftness and power to the faculty of seeing. To this end
the first thing to be done is to treat it carefully.

"For the first months," says M. Pérez, "the chief care should
be to protect the sight of the child, to surround with safeguards
that weak and delicate sense, to shield the eye from impressions
that are too intense, from glaring light and colors, and to surround the child and bring him into relations with objects which,
so far as possible, have a color that is soothing. . . . Neither
upon the child nor about him should there be anything that is
gaudy."

And it is no less necessary to protect the sight from all

the circumstances and all the habits which might injure it, in order to preserve that power of *adaptation* and of accommodation which permits the eye to see distinctly objects placed at very different distances. On this point heed should be paid to all the hygienic recommendations relative to the faults in the lighting of school-rooms, to the vicious arrangement of seats and desks, to methods of writing incompatible with the proper position of the one who writes, to the premature teaching of writing, and to the use of books too finely printed. "The sight is wantonly abused," says M. Fonssagrives.[1] M. Hermann Kohn shows that myopia is five times more frequent with the children in towns than with those in the country, because the sight of the first, restricted to small rooms, cannot acquire the habit of extending itself to a distance.

The Commission on School Hygiene, appointed by decree of January 24, 1882, whose reports were published in 1884, concludes that myopia in children should be regarded as the consequence of a bad posture.[2] "How many cases of acquired myopia there are," says Madame Pape-Carpantier, "and of so-called color-blindness, which are merely the result of a confirmed habit of improper seeing in the early years of life, and of the absence of all examination with respect to colors! For one real organic defect, there are perhaps ten that might have been avoided by the normal use of the sense that is to-day perverted."

79. INSTRUCTION OF THE SIGHT. — What we call instruction of the sight has reference to everything which it can be habituated to discern in order to fulfil its office, — first

---

[1] *L'éducation physique des garçons*, p. 183. We shall return to these questions of the hygiene of vision in our remarks on the teaching of reading and writing.

[2] See the *Rapports* just referred to.

colors, then forms, and finally distances. Contemporary
educators attach a great importance, perhaps an exaggerated
importance, to school discipline in the distinction of colors ;
but what is certainly useful is the rapid and accurate perception of the form and the position of objects ; that is,
accuracy of sight.

In order to acquire this endowment, the child ought **to be**
habituated to notice a great number of objects, and to notice
them in different situations. A graduated series of little
plays, of little experiments, of excursions directed by the
teacher, where the pupil's attention shall be called to distant
objects which are to be reached by gradual approaches ; an
incessant correction of the sense of sight by the sense of
touch ; the objects which were first presented to the sight
being finally placed within the hands of the child, so that he
may feel and measure them and compare appearances with
reality, the illusions of sight with the realities of touch, —
these are some of the precautions recommended by expe-
ricuce.

80. THE REFLECTIVE EXERCISE OF THE SENSES. — The
essential psychological condition for the normal development
of perception is attention. It is one thing to see, to hear,
to touch, and another to observe, to listen, to feel.

Care will then be taken that the child does not use his
senses in a heedless manner. For this purpose it is best not
to present to him too many objects at one time, or at least
not to bring before his vision too rapidly too great a succession and variety of objects. His mind must be fixed on a
small number of things, and he must be made to examine
them under all their aspects ; in a word, his faculty of
observation must be called into play.

81. PEDAGOGICAL INSTRUMENTS. — No one has better

enforced the worth of the education of the senses than Madame Pape-Carpantier:[1] —

"It is," she says, "the most valuable and the most attractive of all the teacher's duties, and some day it will have a place in the official programmes."

And in her enthusiasm she goes so far as to dream of the invention of artificial instruments which would be for the education of the senses what books are for the culture of the mind. For setting an example she proposes certain pieces of apparatus designed to aid pupils in their sensible perceptions, as the movable color-bearer or spectral top, the polyphone, etc.

For ourselves, we have little confidence in the utility of these instruments and machines. On the pretext of serving nature we must not supplant her and substitute ourselves for her. The real instrument for the development of the senses is attentive exercise, observation.

82. PERCEPTION AND OBSERVATION. — Observation might be defined as methodical perception, that prolonged perception which the attention directs towards a determined object. Seeing (*voir*) is instinctive and natural vision; marking with the sight (*regarder*) is attentive and reflective vision; observing is regulated and consecutive vision.

"A useful book was written with the title, 'How to Observe.' These three words might serve as a motto to guide us in the most important part of our early education, — a part, unfortunately, only too much neglected. All the natural sciences are particularly valuable, not only as supplying the mind with the most rich, various, and beautiful furniture, but as teaching people that most useful of all arts, how to use their eyes. It is astonishing how much we all go about with our eyes open, and yet seeing nothing. This is because the organ of vision, like

---

[1] *Notice sur l'éducation des sens.* Paris, 1878.

other organs, requires training; and by lack of training and the
slavish dependence on books becomes dull and slow, and ulti-
mately incapable of exercising its natural function. Let those
studies, therefore, both in school and college, be regarded as
primary, that teach young persons to know what they are seeing, and to see what they would otherwise fail to see. Among
the most useful are Botany, Zoölogy, Mineralogy, Geology, Chemistry, Architecture, Drawing, and the Fine Arts. How many a
Highland excursion and Continental tour have been rendered
comparatively useless to young persons well drilled in their
books, merely from want of a little elementary knowledge in
these sciences of observation!"[1]

Doubtless the sciences of observation, as their name indicates, are the best discipline for teaching the art of observation ; but long before the child can be initiated into any
science whatsoever, it is already possible, with respect to
everything that presents itself to his notice, to habituate
him to observe, and to cultivate his natural curiosity.

"The child is born with the desire to observe and to know.
The interior life being not yet awakened in him, he belongs
entirely to the phenomena of the exterior world. All his senses
are on the alert; all the objects that his sight or his hand en-
counters attract him, interest him, delight him."[2]

83. OBSERVATION IN THE CHILD. — Before being voluntary,
the observation of the child is, so to speak, unconscious.
I mean that he observes without willing it, without reflection, stimulated by an instinctive curiosity.

"It is not through caprice that the child is ever reaching his
hands out towards the objects which are beyond his grasp, and
weeps when his desires for them are refused. At the age when
he needs to amass a fund of knowledge, the eyes as yet scarcely
suffice to inform him of the angles or the contours of these ob-

---

[1] John Stuart Blackie, *On Self-Culture*, pp. 2, 3.
[2] M. Gréard, *op. cit.*, p. 77.

jects; he must feel them. . . . The breaking of toys is due to the same system of observation. The child has a thirst to know by means of what mysterious springs the eyelids of a doll close the eyes, how the sheep bleats, how the horse moves. This is why, from the dawn of humanity, the child has always broken his toys." [1]

But this natural curiosity, which is exercised upon everything, may be deliberately managed by a skilful teacher, and directed to objects which he deems the most useful to be known; so that, while exercising his powers of perception and observation, the child acquires a stock of necessary knowledge.

84. MR. SPENCER'S PARADOX. — With the habitual temerity which he carries into his assertions, Mr. Herbert Spencer declares that success in everything depends upon the power of observation; and he invokes the testimony of the naturalist, the physician, the engineer, and the scientist. Let this be granted; but in pursuing his line of argument he does not stop till he falls into ambiguities. "The philosopher," he says, "*observes* the relations of things." It is only through the effort of reflection and reason that the philosopher can seize the relations of objects and the laws of nature; and to confound these acts with observation is to play upon words.

Observation is doubtless the starting-point in a great number of scientific discoveries, but on the condition that it is made fruitful through reflection. It is from within, not less than from without, that the formation of mind must take place.

85. DANGERS FROM AN ABUSE OF SENSE-TRAINING. — The

---

[1] Champfleury, *Les Enfants*, p. 227.

importance of the education of the senses must not make us
blind to the dangers which the mind would incur from an
exclusive culture of sense-perception.

"The sight of scientific phenomena," says M. Gréard, "amuses
children. They would willingly sacrifice everything else to it, —
arithmetic, history, grammar. This is a clear proof of the valuable aid which can be derived from these demonstrations in
giving expansion to their opening faculties. Perhaps we may
also see in this a warning. If it is undoubtedly useful that
children should find pleasure in examining the forms and exterior arrangements of objects, in following the decomposition
and the recomposition of a body, and in observing in its natural
manifestation in its pictorial representation the play of some
great law; it must be confessed that, after a little time, when
their senses have been corrected, sharpened, amused, and trained,
this kind of study is for them less a labor than a distraction;
it occupies them rather than gives them exercise. We have
banished ennui[1] from our primary schools. Let us consider
whether we have not gone a little too far in dismissing effort
from them."

Let us not forget that the mind ought to be something
else than the fruitful mirror of exterior reality.

86. CONSEQUENCES OF A PROPER EDUCATION OF THE
SENSES. — It must not be inferred that in devoting itself to
the education of the senses education has in view only the
formation of an animal of penetrating sight and acute
hearing, simply capable, like Émile at the age of twelve,
of judging of distances, of handling objects, — in a word, of
recognizing himself in the midst of the obstacles of the
material world. No; the education of the senses is the
necessary preface to the education of the mind. Confusion
too often glides into the intelligence under cover of incom-

---

[1] "Ennui, the disease of unfurnished minds."— BENTHAM.

plete and defective perceptions. On the contrary, clear and distinct perceptions are solid supports for the higher faculties of the intelligence ; and the clearness of sense-intuitions, which are the elements and the materials of all the ultimate constructions of the intelligence, illuminates the mind as a whole. Without an exact and precise knowledge of the visible and tangible properties of objects, our conceptions would run the risk of being false, our deductions defective, our whole mental effort sterile. The culture of the senses is not, then, as Madame Pape-Carpantier has justly observed, "a useless pastime, a sort of• interlude in serious lessons ;" but it is a serious lesson in itself, the success of which interests all the faculties of the mind.

CHAPTER V.

CULTURE OF THE ATTENTION.

87. INNER SENSE OR CONSCIOUSNESS. — We call inner sense or consciousness the knowledge which the mind takes of itself and of whatever takes place within itself. Consciousness, like an inward light, illumines and accompanies all psychological states, all mental acts. It is thus less a distinct faculty than a quality common to all the faculties of the mind, whose characteristic is inability to act without knowing that it acts. In the last analysis it is nothing else than the intelligence knowing itself and knowing all that takes place in the exercise of the different mental faculties.

88. DIFFERENT DEGREES OF CONSCIOUSNESS. — In the child the intelligence or consciousness does not attain its full clearness at a single stroke. It passes through different stages. Obscure and confused in the mere infant, it informs him vaguely of whatever takes place within him. Little by little it becomes more clear and more distinct; it connects with the *me* the phenomena that take place within. Finally, it acquires its full power when, governed by the will, it manifests itself under its reflective form.

It then takes the name of *reflection* when it applies itself to the mind itself, and the name *attention* when it is directed to what is outside of us. "The term reflection," says M.

94

Janet, "expresses the return of the mind upon itself and upon its thought; it is inward attention."[1] And so atten-tion is outward reflection.

89. EDUCATION OF THE CONSCIOUSNESS. — The education of the consciousness is involved in the education of all the faculties. The more we develop the different powers of the soul, the more we assure the clearness and the strength of the perceptions of consciousness.[2] Under its first form, consciousness almost wholly escapes the action of education. It is of itself and through the natural increment of its powers that the soul clarifies itself, so to speak, and comes to render to itself an account of its acts. The educator need not interfere to hasten this natural progress, which is due to growth and to age.

And, once developed, the consciousness does not even then permit a special culture. Its power is always measured by the degree of force which the different faculties attain.

However, in that which concerns that part of the consciousness whose immediate object is the *me*, and which is the basis of the feeling of personality, education has a part to play in fortifying psychological reflection and in assuring to the human personality the complete possession of itself. But, considered in general, consciousness, as we have said, is confounded with the intelligence, and the first care of the teacher should be to assure the progress of the intel-

---

[1] M. Janet, *Cours de Morale.* Paris, 1881, p. 65.

[2] In the early development of the spirit we know the part played by what contemporary philosophers call unconscious impressions, or what Leibnitz has called unobserved perceptions. Care should then be taken that the child's surroundings be wholesome and pure, and that nothing evil glide unnoticed, so to speak, into his soul. Even before the awakening of consciousness, there is a negative education which consists in shielding the child from all unwholesome influences.

ligence by subjecting it to the direction of the will, or, in other terms, by rendering it attentive.

90. ATTENTION AND EDUCATION. — "The important point," said Condillac, "is to make the child comprehend what attention is." No; the important point is to teach him to be attentive, and the way to succeed in this is, not to explain to him the theoretical conditions of attention, but it is to know them himself, so as actually to place the pupil in those conditions by presenting him objects which are within the compass of his ability, and which will excite his interest.

Nothing can be expected of those languid or too mobile spirits whom no study interests, no lesson captivates. On the contrary, everything is to be hoped for from an attentive intelligence, which can fix itself upon the subjects which it studies. The teacher is sure of success, and instruction really begins only on that day when he has held the attention of his pupils for a certain number of minutes. If he has to do only with inattentive auditors, he renews the toil of Sisyphus and pours his knowledge into a barrel without a bottom.

91. DEFINITION OF ATTENTION. — Perfect attention, in its final form, is the characteristic of an intelligence that is self-possessed, self-governed, and that applies itself to whatever it will. In a word, it is the liberty of the spirit. The attentive intelligence is not at all at the mercy of external impressions or of the capricious and involuntary suggestions of the memory and the imagination. It voluntarily devotes itself to the objects which it has chosen; it is its own master.

Attention is not a special faculty; it is a general mode of all our intellectual operations. It associates itself with all of them; with exterior perception, with consciousness, with imagination, with reasoning, and assures to them their maximum of power. Everybody knows the difference between seeing and noticing, hearing and understanding, touching and feeling. Attentive consciousness is reflection, which penetrates with a profounder gaze into the recesses of the inner world of sentiments and thoughts. Progressive degrees of memory are directly related to progressive degrees of the attention ; and the reason is not really firm and strong, except when it is reflective, that is to say, attentive.

92. GENERAL IMPORTANCE OF ATTENTION. —It is sufficient to have defined attention, in order to judge of its influence and its effects. The history of brilliant scientific discoveries and of the great works of human art is for the most part but the recital of the efforts of the attention. Newton said that he had discovered the laws of universal attraction, "by always thinking on the subject." Buffon. defined genius as "a long patience." In more modest degrees, all the results of the toil of thinking are direct proofs of the importance of attention.

But there is in some sort a counter-proof ; the infirmities of the mind are connected with weakness of the attention. The idiot and the imbecile are incapable of fixing their mind upon any given object. The monomaniac is the slave of a fixed idea, which wholly absorbs him. The maniac, on the contrary, in a single instant pursues a thousand different thoughts, powerless to fix his attention upon any one of them. In all its degrees, madness is especially an incapacity of being attentive, of controlling one's mind ; the intelligence is no longer its own master,—as we say, it is alienated.

Attention, then, is the characteristic of a normal state of the intelligence, and, so to speak, the health of the spirit. So we need not be astonished that certain philosophers—

Laromiguière, for example — have considered attention as the basis of all the intellectual faculties.

93. ATTENTION IN THE CHILD. — If this is so, if attention is the perfect form of the intelligence, the conscious act *par excellence*, that which implicates the participation of the will and the entire personality, it is evident that it cannot manifest itself all of a sudden in the child, at the age when the faculties are in a state of development.

The child is naturally distracted, and distraction is the very opposite of attention. At first the child is the sport of the sensations, which come in succession and draw him hither and thither. A little further advanced in age, he is at every moment turned aside by his imagination, by his recollections, by the incoherent ideas which spring . forth, we do not know how, from his consciousness. His intelligence is almost as mobile as his body. It is dominated by other forces ; it is, so to speak, in tow of the involuntary impressions which are ever coming to throw themselves across his toil and his studies. To call it back and fix it is a serious business.

So do not let us expect or demand of the child real, absolute attention. We might as well command immobility on a bird ; and yet it is necessary as soon as possible to make the child attentive, for even the most elementary instruction requires this. We must at any cost secure from him that effort of attention which is so painful to him, which seems so contrary to his nature, that *concentration*, as the English psychologists say, so little consonant with the natural scattering of his ideas and with the volatile mobility of his imagination.

At first the problem seems insoluble, and if it is not so it is because there are certain intermediate degrees which nature has provided for, between the state of ordinary inattention, which is the point of departure, and the habit of attention, which is the final term of the series.

94. INTERMEDIATE STATES. — The powers of the mind are not on the start what they will one day be. Sometimes even they are totally different in their early stages from what they will become later on, and present characteristics almost opposite to those which they will manifest in their mature and final form. This is the case with attention, which may be defined as the voluntary mode of the intelligence, but which at first is involuntary and irreflective.

Let one read the chapter which M. Pérez, an ingenious observer of children, has devoted to the early developments of the attention, and he will be convinced that the attention of the child is but the shadow and the phantom of real attention.[1] In the examples which M. Pérez has collected, attention is now confounded with an imperious need, like that of the babe who fixes its gaze upon the breast of its nurse; now with a vivid sensation, like that of the infant a month old, who is able to follow for three or four minutes the reflected light thrown on a table placed near the window; and even with mobility of impressions, as in the case of that little girl of three months who is represented to us as " attentive to everything that was going on about her, to all sorts of sounds, to the noise of footsteps in the room." In these different circumstances in which the infant gives proof of attention, " the observing subject," M. Pérez admits, " seems less to belong to himself than to belong to the object observed." Now this is exactly the opposite of attention. Far from being exclusively a sensation, or a condescendence of the mind to the multiplied impressions of the senses, atten-

---

[1] M. Pérez, *Les trois premières années de l'enfant.*

tion consists especially in dominating the sensations, in order to follow voluntarily a thought preferred to all others. It is not the rebound or the result of an excitation from without, but it proceeds from an inward effort. As to "that habit of attention, prompt, capriciously distributed, that is, indifferently accorded to everything," it is indeed the very characteristic of infancy, but it is the very negation of attention proper.

95. The Beginning of Attention. —And yet it is in this way, and in this way alone, that attention makes a start. There is no other means of cultivating it, in early years, than to habituate the child to those vivid, dominating impressions which hold and captivate his mind, and which are the shadows or images of attention.

When he has several times fixed his sight on bright colors and brilliant forms which fascinate him, when he has turned his ear to the loud voice that controls him and the harmonious sounds that charm him, he may be gently induced to turn his thoughts of his own accord to these ordinary objects of his contemplation. To the usual excitation from without there will gradually respond a voluntary movement from within. To involuntary attention there will succeed attention resulting from his free will. There is no other secret for calling the mind to liberty than at first to imprison it in continuous and peremptory sensations. It is curious to see how, by a natural evolution, by the mind's native power, the interior energy will manifest itself; how the will by degrees will insinuate itself into the habit of imposed labor and of thought held by constraint upon the same point.

96. Imposed Attention. —There is, then, no other advice to give the educator, for this early culture of the

attention, than to impose on the child the prolonged examination of a given object. From that state which simulates attention there will insensibly issue real attention. The best plan will be to place the child in such conditions that nothing will excite distractions.[1] Put a child who is learning to read in a garden with his primer, and there amid the sensations which eddy about him it will be almost impossible to fix his mind. He will be continually interrupting his spelling with all sorts of exclamations: "There goes a butterfly! There flies a bird!" On the other hand, place the same child in a room scantily furnished and somewhat gloomy, where the solicitations of sense are rare, proceed in such a way that he sees only his book, and you will find that he will repeat his lesson with but little resistance. Without doubt you have not to do, in this case, with a mind truly attentive, making a voluntary effort to follow a given direction; but you have before you only a passive being, whom you hold by artificial means, subject to a single sensation, that of the syllable which you are causing him to spell, and who will escape from you on the first occasion, to become the slave of a new sensation. But in that species of subjection in which he is held by a single impression to the exclusion of all others, the mind is gradually strengthened. He will lose the habit of dissipation and mobility; he will devote himself more and more, and with an ever-growing alacrity, to the objects of study which you propose to him. After having allowed himself to be constrained, he will finally consent to it; he will give his attention until at last he will of his own accord attach himself to the objects of study towards which his own

---

[1] "Cause a calm to reign around the infant, so that the impressions he receives through the senses may be distinct." (Madame Necker de Saussure, T. II., p. 125.)

choice draws him. And even in the attention of the mature man there will always remain something of the involuntary and the enforced, the irresistible attraction of a favorite thought, of a study of predilection, of a dominant taste.

97. OTHER CHARACTERISTICS OF THE CHILD'S ATTENTION. — When the child has grown and has reached the school age, we may demand of him some degree of voluntary attention and count on some effort on his part; but how many expedients we must still employ, not to weary his nascent attention, but to stimulate it and hold it! Here again we must consult the nature of the child and take into account the special characteristics of his mind. To each one of these characteristics there will correspond a series of pedagogical precepts.

At first the limit of the child's attention is short; it is soon exhausted. Moreover, he voluntarily applies it only to sensible objects. Its power is still limited, and to fixedness of mind there does not always correspond immobility of body. Finally, in a general way, the attention is weak, and there must be a resort to all sorts of stimulants in order to arouse it and keep it at its work.

98. SHORT DURATION OF ATTENTION. — We say nothing new in remarking that children are not capable of a long intensity of thought.

"Horace Grant has shown that, beyond from five to ten minutes for young children, and from thirty to forty-five for older pupils, the attention is wearied and intellectual effort comes to an end." [1]

Generally the child displays his whole power at the be-

---

[1] M. Fonssagrives, *L'Éducation physique des garçons.* Paris, 1870.

ginning of his task; but he is soon at the limit of his strength, and needs to be occupied with something else, or even to have no task on hand, but to refresh himself with play or with absolute repose. Be careful, then, to proceed gradually. Let the lessons be short at first; they will grow longer in proportion as the pupil's power of attention is developed. Also introduce variety into the exercises. Change is a rest. As much as possible alternate school work with recreation, which, as the etymology of the term indicates, truly remakes or creates anew (re-creates) the exhausted forces.

99. EXERCISE OF THE ATTENTION THROUGH THE SENSES. — The inability of the child to follow abstract ideas is another platitude. A sure means of making him inattentive, of weakening perhaps for life his power of attention, is to teach him too early general truths, rules, formulæ, — anything which repels him because he does not comprehend it easily. General ideas have no value for children. In their view the only realities are facts.

M. Egger cites a striking instance of this inability of the child to comprehend the abstract:

"At the age of three and a half years, Émile, who was being taught to read the figure 3, the number of a house, refused to do it 'because there was only one figure there.' He could not understand how a single symbol could indicate plurality."

It cannot be too often repeated that at first the child can assimilate only knowledge coming through the senses. Appeal, then, to the senses, and so far as possible save beginners from abstractions. One of the reasons which best justify the use of object lessons is that they are based directly on this fundamental principle, that it is best to exercise the attention on concrete and sensible objects before applying it to abstractions.

100. EXTERIOR SIGNS OF ATTENTION. — Another characteristic of the child's attention is that it is rarely accompanied by the exterior signs which announce it in the mature man. The thinker who reflects remains motionless, with fixed eyes and bowed head. But observe the child who is repeating his lesson. It is impossible for him to stand still; his eyes wander to the ceiling, to the right, to the left; his legs, his arms, his whole body, is in motion. I knew a little girl who could not learn to read, save on the condition of sewing at the same time; and it was a pleasure to see her mechanically drawing her needle with her little fingers, while she was at the same time spelling out the words of her primer placed on the knees of her mother. In a word, the child has need of movement, even when he is studying. Intellectual activity does not suspend his physical activity. The attention of which he is capable does not wholly absorb him.

101. NEED OF MOVEMENT. — This being true, it will be best to make provision for this need of movement, and not to require of the child an absolute immobility. Let us not demand of him what is impossible at his age, that during the time he spends in school he shall be a thinking statue. Let us not require of him the exterior signs of attention, provided he be really attentive.

Let us the rather seek for methods which, while furnishing occasion for gratifying his need of physical movement, at the same time aid the effort of thinking. The child learns to write more easily than to read, because the task of writing calls his hand into use, and consequently gives him greater pleasure.

Whatever may be thought of them, the phonomimic processes have the advantage of introducing gestures and movements into the study of the alphabet, and so of breaking up the immobility which is so unendurable to children. One of the merits of Froebel's system is that it calls into exercise at the same time the senses and the instinct to movement.

It would be dangerous, however, to yield too much to the physical petulance of the child. The order of the school could not easily accommodate pupils ever on the move, whose notion would be to learn to read while skipping about the room. Moreover, if the child were not guarded in this respect, he would be allowed to. contract uncomely habits, disagreeable tricks. And Miss Edgeworth, who seems, however, to have overestimated the extent of this danger, writes not without reason, —

"If a boy could not read without swinging his head like a pendulum, we should rather prohibit him from reading for some time, than suffer him to grow up with this ridiculous habit."[1]

102. STIMULANTS OF ATTENTION. — "The interest inspired by the subject itself," an educator has said, "is a unique talisman for developing the attention." How to create interest, — such, consequently, ought to be the principal anxiety of the teacher.

Real attention, like affection, does not permit constraint. It bestows itself on those who know how to gain it. Hence nothing is more important than the choice of the subjects to be taught, and particularly the manner of teaching them.

Without doubt we must guard against the dangers of an education that is too compliant, too easy, which makes an abuse of what is diverting, and which excludes effort. We should not forget, however, that pleasure is the most powerful stimulant to effort. So far as possible, let us remove the obstacles that are upon the route of this attention still

---

[1] *Practical Education,* Vol. I., p. 106.

wavering, which will not keep its track unless it finds what is agreeable there.

Nothing is indifferent to what can contribute towards making instruction attractive. The talent of teachers will always be the surest pledge of the pupil's attention. But in default of talent, simplicity, clearness, cleanness of exposition, will have a happy effect on the dispositions of those who hear. Even the tone of voice and the attitude of a teacher who, as has been said, knows his business, who gives proof of the interest which he takes in those whom he instructs, — these things will contribute towards exciting the interest of those who learn and listen.

It is not required to make everything agreeable and attractive; but it is to be recollected that only that which affects the sensibility, that which is agreeable or painful, can with certainty arouse the attention, and that only that which is agreeable can hold it.

103. CURIOSITY. — In this search for the attractive and the interesting the educator is aided by the very nature of the child. In fact, the mind of the child is far from being repugnant to attention.

Curiosity, that grand mobile of the intelligence, which Fénelon has admirably defined to be a propensity of nature which goes in advance of instruction, — curiosity, if skilfully excited and duly satisfied, — will be the natural source of attention.

A bishop of the nineteenth century, less liberal than Fénelon — Dupanloup — has only harsh words for the curiosity of the child.

"The soul, trivial, dissipated, curious, open on all sides, lets everything slip away and keeps nothing. No serious work is possible with it or in it." [1]

---

[1] Dupanloup, *De l'Éducation*, Tom. III., p. 465.

Curiosity, which is in fact the characteristic of a mind open on all sides, impatient to know, ardent for research, is, on the contrary, whatever Dupanloup says of it, a precious inclination, a happy aptitude, which it is only needful to know how to employ with skill and discretion. It is a sort of intellectual appetite, which should be furnished only with wholesome aliment.

Happy the teachers who have to do with intelligences naturally curious! But especially happy are those who know how to excite curiosity and to keep it active. For this purpose we must skilfully appeal to the tastes of the child and favor them, yet without overtaxing them. "Eagerness to derive advantage from a taste," says Madame Necker de Saussure, "is often the cause of our killing it."

"The manner in which the child is instructed," says M. Lacombe in the same vein, "necessarily has the disadvantage of preceding curiosity, of preventing its rise, or at least of suddenly arresting its movements. In fact, what do we do? We take a child, set him on a bench, and teach him off-hand a multitude of things of which he has never observed the existence, which he did not anticipate, and which consequently he could not desire to know. We extinguish his curiosity before it had a chance to be aroused. As to the things of which he has been able to catch some glimpse, and which perhaps have puzzled him, we bring them before him all at once, thoroughly, and with greater detail than he desires. We overwhelm his curiosity almost before it is born. We teach him so many things by compulsion which he no longer has the least desire to know."

Then let us manage the curiosity of the child. Let us not smother it by satiating it too soon. Let us reply to his questions, as Locke recommends; but let us also allow him the privilege of seeking for himself, by personal observation, the satisfaction which he desires. Curiosity cannot

truly become the germ of attention, unless it is in part
handed over to itself, unless it is not too quickly satisfied,
unless we give it time to put forth an effort after the truth.

104. Effects of Novelty upon Attention. — One of
the best means of exciting the curiosity, and hence the
attention, is to present to the child objects which are new.
Contrast wakes up the mind, but on one condition, — that
it be not too violent, and that the new study do not introduce the child into a world absolutely strange to his
previous experiences. In subjects entirely new, says Miss
Edgeworth, we make superabundant efforts of attention,
and so weary ourselves without profit.

Who does not know by experience that the beginning
of a science, notwithstanding the attraction of novelty,
is particularly painful? In order to reach the truth we
must reconcile and unite into one the two proverbs,
"Wholly new, wholly beautiful!" and, "It is only the
first step which costs!"

105. Effects of Variety. — It is less the novelty than
the variety which is of importance in the education of the
attention.

An alternation of occupations and exercises animates a
class. It is necessary to know how to pass from exposition to interrogation, from one kind of labor to another.
The reason of this is that these different exercises are
addressed to faculties somewhat different. When one faculty is wearied it is necessary to grant it some respite
and to make an appeal to a neighboring faculty. The
mind of the child, moreover, is eager for change. Often
a simple change in tone, a different intonation in the
voice of the teacher, suffices to revive the attention which
was beginning to drowse. Nothing is so difficult to follow,

to listen to with attention, as a monotonous discourse delivered without inflections.

106. FEW THINGS AT ONCE. — Our anxiety to vary, to diversify instruction, need not cause us to fall into confusion. A multiplicity of subjects disconcerts the attention, rather than aids it.

"He would be a foolish teacher," says Mr. Sully, "who gave a child a number of disconnected things to do at a time, or who insisted on keeping his mind bent on the same subject for an indefinite period." [1]

We do not hold the attention, or at least we weary and overdrive it in a way to make its efforts useless, when we present to it too many subjects at once. We distrust verbose teachers whose thought overflows its limits and whose words succeed one another with an extreme volubility. No durable effect nor profound impression is to be expected from their lectures. The pupil, like the teacher, reaches the end of such an oratorical race, out of breath. The state of mind into which the erudition and precipitate delivery of the teacher plunge the pupil recalls the consternation of those Esquimaux whose history is given by Miss Edgeworth.

Newly arrived in London, they had visited in one day all the monuments of the capital, under the conduct of a guide who was in too much of a hurry. On their return, when they were asked what they had seen, they did not know what to say. It was with difficulty that one of them, repeatedly urged to speak, and finally rousing himself from his torpor, could say while shaking his head, "Too much smoke, — too much noise, — too much houses, — too much men, — too much everything!" [2]

---

[1] *Elements of Psychology,* p. 104.
[2] *Practical Education,* Vol. I., pp. 98, 99.

107. EXTERNAL CONDITIONS OF ATTENTION. — It is dangerous, says Miss Edgeworth, to employ stimulants foreign to the subject studied. So far as possible, the interest should certainly be made to come from the study itself, and set in motion the inner springs of the attention. This, however, is not a reason for disdaining the aid which can come from without, nor for disregarding the importance of the material conditions in which the child may be placed.

The following, according to M. Bréal, are some of these conditions :

"So far as possible the teacher should keep his position, holding the class under his eyes and requiring that all eyes should be turned towards him. The instruction is not to begin till all the children have taken an erect and composed attitude. A rap on the table or a word agreed upon is the signal that the recitation is to begin. The questions should be addressed to the class as a whole; and so the teacher will always first ask the question, and then will allow the pause necessary for finding the reply; and only then will he name the pupil who is to reply. If the pupil begins by trying to find the reply after he has been called on,. it is a proof of inattention. If the response made by a pupil is correct, it may be demanded again of a fellow-pupil. If it is faulty, it should be corrected by him. The important parts of the lesson are repeated in concert by the whole class. As soon as inattention appears, the teacher stops. A means of reanimating the class, but a means which should not be abused, is to call up the class and reseat it at a word of command. The pupils should always respond in a very loud voice; but the teacher may speak in a moderate tone. The pupil's ear soon becomes accustomed to explosions of voice, and then they are good for nothing." [1]

To these precautions there must be added others which experience suggests. Attention varies with the hours of the day, with the days of the week, and with the inter-

---

[1] *Dictionnaire de pédagogie,* art. "Attention."

val which separates work and the taking of food. Attention is stronger in the morning class than in the afternoon class, and stronger during the first hours of the session than during the last. A wise teacher will take account of all these differences, in order to regulate the order of studies. He will begin with the exercises that are the most difficult, and will postpone to the end of the session those which require the least effort.

108. DISTRACTIONS NOT TO BE TOLERATED. — The play of an intellectual faculty can be truly assured only by repressing the faults which are opposed to it. We must then make war against distraction at all hazards; and after having done everything to correct it by mild means, we must resort even to punishments in order to suppress it.

"Distractions," says Kant, "ought never to be tolerated, at least in school, for they end by degenerating into habits.
"The finest talents are lost in a man who is subject to distractions. . . . . Inattentive children only half hear, reply wholly at random, and do not know what they read."

109. CASES WHERE ATTENTION IS IN REVOLT. — Defective attention comes either accidentally from passing circumstances, which it is relatively easy to modify, or from the general indifference of a mind at all times incapable of becoming fixed.

In the first case the remedies to be employed will be but the application of the recommendations already given, which consist in placing the mind in the conditions most favorable for the development of the attention.

These rules, moreover, ought to be applied with care, while taking into account the exceptions to which they are subject. Thus, it is a general law that the pupil's attention is particularly strong at the beginning of the lesson, when it has not yet been wearied. And yet who has not noticed that the child has some difficulty in making a start? Generally, when a child begins his lesson, he is embarrassed, and it requires several minutes to recover himself, to rearrange the dispersed forces of his mind. At first he is restive, like a horse which must be whipped to a start.

The situation is more serious when we have to do with natures wholly sterile, and when inattention is the sign of a general indifference of the mind. Locke says this indifference of disposition is the worst fault that can manifest itself in a child, and the most difficult to correct, because it has its source in the constitution.

But in truth this incurable inattention is very rare. The more often the child, even the most inattentive in class, because the lessons which he receives there have no attraction for him, recovers all his ardor and all his energy, either in his play or in a favorite occupation. It is necessary, then, to observe his character with care. If he is indifferent in all his actions, there is little hope in the case; but if there are things, whatever they may be, which attract his preference, and which he does with pleasure, take care to cultivate this particular taste; make use of it to exercise his activity and to secure his attention. Once fixed and developed on one point, the attention will radiate upon others, and gradually extend itself to the studies which had at first repelled him.

110. Moral Consequences of Defective Attention.— It is not only in study, in intellectual labor, that attention is profitable. The conduct of life and the virtues of character have no less need of it than excellences of the intelligence have. Defective attention in practical life is the synonym of thoughtlessness and heedlessness. To be habitually attentive is not only the best means of learning and progressing

in the sciences, and the most effective prayer which we can address to the truth in order that it may bestow itself upon us; but it is also one of the most precious means of moral perfection, the surest means of shunning mistakes and faults, and one of the most necessary elements of virtue.

CHAPTER VI.

CULTURE OF THE MEMORY.

111. IMPORTANCE OF THE MEMORY. — There is no occasion to speak at length on the utility of memory. Because an abuse was once made of it, because the other faculties of the mind were wrongly sacrificed to it in systems of education in which the instruction was exclusively confided to it, educators have presumed to decry it, to hold it in suspicion, and to treat it almost as an enemy. Have they thought what education would become without memory? Have they reflected that there is not a moment, so to speak, when instruction can do without its aid? It envelops and accompanies the other faculties, and supplies them all with aliment.

"Memory," said Pascal, "is necessary to all the operations of spirit."

"Without memory," wrote Guizot, "the noblest faculties remain useless." The moral life itself, as well as the intellectual life, reposes upon memory, and, as Chateaubriand says, "the most affectionate heart would lose its tenderness if it no longer recollected."

Surely to-day no one any longer allows the memory to exercise over the mind a domination that belongs only to the judgment and to personal reflection. For the memory, as for the other powers of the soul, an exclusive culture is dangerous; but it would be as absurd to abjure memory, because an abuse has been made of memoriter recitations, as

114

to exclude reasoning because an unwarranted use has been made of the syllogism. Infinitely useful for all the purposes of practical life, memory is at the same time the most valuable of pedagogical instruments. There is not a faculty whose services the educator has more frequent occasion to call to his aid ; not one which he ought more earnestly to seek to develop and train, in view of a preparation for life. It is the direct source of much of our knowledge, and the guardian of it all. Mr. Bain does not hesitate to say that it is "the faculty that most of all concerns us in education."[1]

112. MEMORY IN THE CHILD. — It is precisely at the age when everything is to be learned, that the memory is the most naturally strong. Educators grant with one accord that childhood is the privileged period of memory. Mr. Bain estimates that the period in which the "plasticity of the brain" and the power of mental acquisition are at their maximum, extends from the sixth to the tenth year. In general, the child is so happily endowed in respect of memory that he retains words and phrases which have no meaning for him, or even which have no meaning whatever.

Memory is dependent in great part on the vital forces and the nervous system. In the child, whose brain is increasing in size from day to day, whose nerves vibrate with an energy which belongs only to forces still young and plastic, whose sensibility has lost nothing of its freshness and primitive vivacity, the memory ought necessarily to develop with a marvelous facility. Later, in the adult, in the mature man, the reflective powers of the mind will come to aid the memory ; but they will never succeed in equaling that spontaneous memory of early years, open to all impressions, the natural and easy product of the young and still unemployed organs.

---

[1] *Education as a Science*, p. 20.

Moreover, the power of the child's memory derives advantage from the weakness and inactivity of the other faculties. The mind is still unoccupied ; consequently it fills itself without effort. Later preoccupations, cares, and personal reflections will more or less obstruct the road to impressions from without. New memories will have difficulty in finding a place in the intelligence already encumbered with old memories. They will be jumbled and confounded in the mind, like new characters which we would engrave on paper already covered with writing. The memory of the child is a white page on which everything is easily impressed, a clean mirror in which everything is reflected.

113. OPINIONS OF ROUSSEAU AND MADAME CAMPAN.— What shall we think, then, of the opinion of certain educators, according to whom the child, at least the young child, has no real memory?

"Although memory and reason are two different faculties," wrote Rousseau, "the one is never really developed without the other. . . . Children, incapable of judging, really have no memory." [1]

And on her part Madame Campan declares that "the memory is not developed till the age of three years." [2]

It suffices to study the opinion of Rousseau closely, to be convinced that the disaccord with him is simply apparent, that it comes from a misunderstanding of terms. The memory which Rousseau denies to the child is that of abstract ideas ; he is the first to accord to the child a memory of sounds, forms, and, in general, of all the sensible notions.

As to the assertion of Madame Campan, it has reference to this fact of general observation, that the mature man

---

[1] *Émile* (Boston, 1885), pp. 78, 79.
[2] *De l'Éducation*, I., III., Ch. I.

does not recall the events of the first two or three years of his life. These first years are to us as though they had not been; a black night covers them over in our consciousness, and the darkness is unbroken save by a few gleams, as by the remembrance of some grave accident or of some catastrophe. Leibnitz cites the case of a child who became blind at the age of two or three, and after that recalled none of his visual perceptions.[1]

Does this mean that even during those years at the beginning of life when the consciousness is still obscure, the child's memory does not act, does not acquire? It would suffice, to refute Madame Campan, to recall the fact that at the age of three years the child generally knows how to speak, and that the knowledge of words and the mother tongue supposes a considerable display of memory. Only, the first acquisitions of the memory are weak and fragile; they need to be fixed and fortified by a renewal of the same impressions, like delicate sketches over which the brush should pass several times, in order to hold the fugitive colors, always ready to be effaced.

114. CHARACTERISTICS OF INFANT MEMORY. —The child's memory has its own good qualities, and also some defects.

The first of the good qualities, in children well endowed, is a rare power of acquisition. While the tired memory of the old man takes delight in languidly calling up the images of past times, that of the child is always in movement, always in quest of new knowledge, just as easily acquired as eagerly sought, for the child sees everything, hears everything. Nothing escapes his young and active senses. He distinguishes objects and persons. He has a marvelous aptitude for retaining words and learning lan-

---

[1] Leibnitz, *Nouveaux Essais sur l'entendement*, Liv. I., Ch. III.

guages. In certain conditions he will learn two or **three**
at once. What the adult and the mature man will accomplish only at the cost of painful labor, at the time
when the jaded memory has come to rebel against the
registration of new ideas, the child will do with ease,
and without giving a thought to the work.

Another characteristic of the child's memory is the literal precision, the vigorous exactness of his recollection.
M. Legouvé justly compares the child to an appraiser who
notes everything, who omits no detail. With a punctil-
iousness worthy of being quoted as a model for an historian, the child recalls the least particularities of things.
When we relate to him a fable or a story which he knows,
do not imagine that you can change a single particular, a
single word, without hearing his cries and protestations:
"That is not it!"

On the other hand, the memory of the child has weaknesses which only progress in age can correct. It fails
especially in this, that it is but little qualified to give an
exact location in time of the recollections which he has
acquired. The complete memory supposes an appreciation
of duration of which the child is incapable, because this
appreciation requires the co-ordination of recollections.
Who has not heard children of two or three years of age
relate as an event of yesterday a transaction which they
witnessed several months before ? Too often recollections
float in the mind of the child like disconnected pictures or
pictures detached from their frame.

115. CULTURE OF THE MEMORY. — Montaigne made the
just remark that we are most often engaged in furnishing
the memory, but that we forget to form it. The essential thing, in fact, is not merely that the child should
leave school with his mind well garnished with **recollec-**

tions and facts; it is also important that he have at his
disposal a flexible and strong memory, in a condition to
be still more enriched, to appropriate to itself new ideas,
and to adapt itself to the requirements of life.

There are, then, two distinct aims in the culture of the
memory. First, it must be made to acquire the most
knowledge possible, which is the object of the whole
course of instruction. In the second place, it must be
strengthened and developed in so far as it is a faculty
of the mind. This no doubt results in part from the
instruction itself, but it also requires some special precautions, the sum of which constitutes what may be
called the education proper of the memory.

116. Is this Necessary?—But is this special culture
of the memory necessary? And, if it is proved that it is
necessary, is it possible?

We do not hesitate to reply in the affirmative, notwithstanding the contrary opinion of Locke.

Locke's special argument for calling in question the utility of training the memory in school, is the constant use
which we make of it in the world and in life. He says
that memory is so necessary in all the transactions of
life, there are so few things in which we can do without
it, that there would be no occasion for fearing that it
will become enfeebled and blunted for lack of exercise,
if exercise were really the condition of its power.

Without doubt life will be a good training for the
memory, but on one condition, which is, that the memory has already been made pliant and broken to labor
by the studies of youth, and that the man receive it
from the hands of the scholar as an instrument already
fashioned. There is no teacher who is not authorized
to contradict the opinion of Locke, for all know by ex-

perience that the best memories have need of long efforts in order to attain their maximum of power; that mediocre memories would soon grow rusty if they were not constantly exercised; and that finally the memories naturally poor would always remain sterile, if they were not early cultivated.

117. Is such a Culture possible?—But Locke goes still further. His ultimate thought is, not that the culture of the memory is useless, but that it is impossible. Exercising the memory on such or such an object "no more fits the memory for the retention of anything else, than the graving of one sentence in lead makes it the more capable of retaining firmly any other characters."[1] Here again the English educator is in contradiction with facts.

Whatever notion we form theoretically of the nature of the memory; whether we connect it entirely with organic conditions, as Luys and Ribot do, or whether we consider it an independent power of the soul, with all spiritualist philosophers, it is practically certain that memory makes progress through skilful attention and intelligent exercise, and that it is not true to say that it depends entirely on a "happy constitution."

Another paradox would be to hold, with Jacotot, by a contrary exaggeration, that education can do everything; that at birth memories are equal in all children, and that inequalities come exclusively from negligence, from lack of care, from inattention, and from lack of culture. Without speaking of extraordinary and exceptional memories, which make light of all difficulties, like that of a Villemain, repeating a discourse after having heard it, of a

<hr/>

[1] See Compayré's *History of Pedagogy*, pp. 207, 208.

Mozart writing the "Miserere" of the Sistine Chapel after hearing it twice, of a Horace Vernet, or of a Gustave Doré, painting portraits from memory,—without invoking the testimony of these prodigious memories, which attest by their brilliancy the potency of nature, there is no humble school where upon the pupils' benches the teacher does not distinguish notable differences in natural aptitudes for learning and remembering.

The inequality of different minds, says Mr. Bain, with respect to the assimilation of knowledge, in circumstances absolutely the same, is a well-known fact; and this is one of the obstacles presented by simultaneous instruction given to a certain number of pupils arranged in the same class.

118. EXERCISE OF THE MEMORY.—We shall assume, then, as settled, that it is necessary and possible to cultivate the memory. Now, there is no other means of cultivating it than to exercise it. But to exercise it profitably, and to reach conclusions that are really practical, it is not sufficient to study the memory in general or as a whole, but we must make an analysis of its elements.

119. DIFFERENT QUALITIES OF THE MEMORY. — "A good memory," says Rollin, "should have two qualities, two virtues, — first, that of receiving promptly and without difficulty what is intrusted to it, and then that of guarding it faithfully." To these qualities a third should be added, that of easily *restoring* what has been quickly learned and exactly retained. My memory is poor, if it does not allow me to dispose of all I know with facility and promptness; if, as Montaigne says, "It serves me when *it* pleases, rather than when *I* please."

These different qualities of memory are not always found

united.[1] It happens that one who learns quickly also forgets quickly. The memories that are the quickest are often the most treacherous. Their acquisitions resemble fortunes too rapidly made; they lack solidity. Often that which comes easily also goes easily.

But these qualities, however, do not exclude one another; there is usually a solidarity among them. The ideal is to have them all at once, and the education of the memory ought to have in view the perfecting of each of them, by particular attention and by a special culture.

120. PROMPTNESS IN APPREHENDING. — It is particularly in this quality that the memory is dependent on nature, upon innate tendencies. Art is powerless to establish equality between those docile, malleable intelligences, of vivid impressions, which impregnate themselves, so to speak, with everything that they perceive, and those slow, indolent, unyielding spirits, which learn only with great difficulty the little that they do learn. Let us not conclude from this, however, that we must despair of correcting, at least in part, these natural defects.

"We must not be easily discouraged," Rollin very justly says, "nor yield to that first resistance of the memory which we have often seen conquered and broken by patience and perseverance. At first, only a few lines should be given such a child to learn, but he should be required to learn them with exactness. We may try to mollify the disagreeableness of this work by presenting to him only things which are agreeable, such, for example, as the fables of La Fontaine and thrilling stories. An industrious and earnest teacher may work with his pupil, sometimes allowing him to beat and get the start, and thus making him feel that by his own power he can do much more than he

---

[1] It appears to me wholly exaggerated to say, with M. Marion, "The three qualities of memory are almost never united."

thought he could.[1] In proportion as we see progress making we may gradually and insensibly increase the daily task."

In other terms, carefully manage the weak memories by requiring of them only moderate and graduated exercises; do not discourage them on the start, but rather stimulate them by skilfully preparing little successes for them and by inspiring them with some confidence in themselves; such is the spirit of the practical counsels of Rollin.

Let us add that weakness of memory not being an ultimate fact of mental life, since it proceeds from and depends upon the absence of certain conditions, such as the lack of vivid impressions and unsteadiness of attention, we shall have done much towards limbering up dull memories if we have known how to awaken the sensibility and give stability to the mind of the child.

In particular, whatever will fortify the attention will aid the memory. Now, there is no better way to make a pupil attentive than to explain to him clearly and make him perfectly comprehend whatever is taught him. The *Conduite des Écoles chrétiennes* (edition of 1860) declares that "pupils learn only with great difficulty what they do not comprehend."[2] Pascal said of himself that he never forgot what he had once comprehended. Whatever may be said to the contrary, there is no disaccord between the memory and the judgment. In making all his instruction exact, in multiplying his explanations, the teacher is not working alone for the judgment, but also for the memory.

---

[1] "We have often had learned before us, — with us, rather, — in ten minutes, by a whole class and perfectly, a half page of text, a short fable of La Fontaine. Try this plan of teaching to all your pupils some given lesson, which you explain and cause to be comprehended, and you will see produced astonishing results of infant memory." — E. Rendu, *Manuel*, p. 202.

[2] *Conduite à l'usage des Écoles chrétiennes*, p. 16.

That which will also contribute to promptness in learning is order, the logical connection of the facts which are presented to the child; in a word, it is the association of ideas.

"It is indubitable," says the Port Royal logic, "that one learns with a facility incomparably greater, and that he retains much better, what is taught in the true order; because the ideas which have a natural sequence arrange themselves much better in our memory and revive one another much more easily." [1]

121. TENACITY OF RECOLLECTIONS. — Recollections methodically acquired, the possession of which is pledged by the attention that has fixed them in the mind, and by the intelligence that has comprehended their meaning, generally speaking defy forgetfulness. In other terms, all the efforts which are made to facilitate the acquisition of recollections also assure their conservation.

There are, however, some particular rules to be observed relative to the second quality of memory. The first of these is repetition, which is one of the necessary means of training the power of recollection.

It is an old pedagogical maxim that repetition is the soul of instruction: *Repetitio mater studiorum.* We must often recur to the same things, and not fear the tedium of a frequent return to the same ideas. "We retain," said Jacotot, "only what we repeat." He concludes from this, in accordance with the adage, *Multum, non multa,* that it is sufficient to learn one thing, and to know that well. The continued repetition of one single book would be the ideal of instruction. Strange exaggeration, which, on the pretext of strengthening the memory, would result in impoverishing it! Extent of knowledge is not less desirable than solidity. But it remains none the less true that, freed from the narrow bounds in which Jacotot inclosed it, and employed under all

---

[1] *Logic de Port-Royal,* 4e partie, Ch. X.

its forms (recall, pure and simple, of what has been said, summaries, general review), repetition is one of the essential conditions for the development of the memory.

"It is not often," says Mr. Bain, "that one single occurrence leaves a permanent and recoverable idea; usually, we need several repetitions for the purpose. The process of fixing the impression occupies a certain length of time; either we must prolong the first shock, or renew it in several successive occasions. This is the first law of memory." [1]

Another important condition of the fidelity of recollection is the rigorous and exact precision of the ideas which are intrusted to the mind. We must not be satisfied with half-way work, and this is why in certain cases a literal repetition, and in all cases a detailed and minute knowledge of what has been learned, should be required of the child. In the interesting chapter in which she takes those to task who have proposed to replace the study of words by the study of things, Madame Necker de Saussure rightly observes that these two studies are inseparably connected.

"The pupil is told to give his effort only to the sense of the words employed in his lessons, without giving his attention to the words, and that when he recites his lesson, if it is seen that he comprehends the sense of it, we should be satisfied, whatever expressions he may use to render an account of it. Nevertheless these expressions are almost always very vague, very inexact, for children are not very skillful *redacteurs*. This boasted comprehension remains confused and soon disappears, because it has not been fastened to fixed and positive words." [2]

122. PROMPTNESS IN RECALLING. — The precious and rare quality called presence of mind depends in great part on this third form of the memory. The best means of de-

---

[1] *Education as a Science*, p. 20.
[2] *L'Éducation progressive*, Tom. II., p. 286.

veloping it will be, in the first place, frequent interrogations. By unexpected questions the child must be made to exert himself, and, so to speak, to jog his memory. He must be accustomed to recover himself promptly, and from among so many others to seize the recollection demanded of him. In this way we shall awaken slumbering memories which have treasures, but do not know how to make use of them.

Another important recommendation is to oppose routine, and whatever there is of the mechanical in the use of the memory. The child who is quick to learn is too often inclined to repeat mechanically what is taught him, in the order and form in which he has been taught. He will repeat without perturbation a chronological series of the kings of France, and will recite without the change of a word a theorem of geometry; but if he is slightly disturbed in this purely mechanical process, he comes to a standstill. There is no other means of correcting this fault, or of preventing it, than frequently to take the child at unawares by questions in which the natural order is inverted, and then to compel him to repeat under another form, or with some change of expression, what he has committed to memory.

123. MEMORY AND JUDGMENT. — One dominant thought ought to govern all the efforts of the educator in this careful search for the means of cultivating the memory; and this is not to develop it to the injury of the judgment.[1]

A prejudice somewhat widely current is to the effect that "the memory is the almost irreconcilable enemy of the judgment." (Fontenelle.) Through cultivating their memory certain people come to leave their judgment fallow. We then have to do with insupportable pedants who do not

---

[1] The following is the epitaph of the Père Hardouin, a Jesuit of the seventeenth century, the author of learned works: " Hic jacet vir bonæ memoriæ expectans judicium."

think for themselves, or who risk their own thought only under cover of a quotation; who know only what others have thought and said. Said Kant, "What is a man who has a great memory, but no judgment? He is but a living lexicon."

Surely we must be on our guard, even at school, against an excess of memory work. To this faculty is applicable in particular the rule proposed by Kant: "Cultivate separately no faculty for itself; cultivate each in view of the others." Unduly cultivated, the memory annuls, so to speak, the other faculties, and, according to the saying of Vauvenargues, "we must have memory only in proportion to our intelligence."

But there is nothing to fear of the memory, provided we hold it to its place and consider it only as an auxiliary faculty, "as a marvelous instrument," to use Montaigne's phrase, "without which the judgment can hardly perform its office." When intrusted to a living, active mind, which preserves the liberty of its judgments, things committed to the memory, however numerous they may be, animate and vivify the intelligence, far from benumbing and stifling it; they furnish it without encumbering it. Moreover, they are here the starting-point of a whole harvest of new ideas. As Mlle. Marchef-Girard has said, with some exaggeration, "the memory is not a tomb, but a cradle in which ideas grow."[1]

124. MEMORY AND VERBAL REPETITION. —The discredit into which memory has sometimes fallen, is chiefly due to the confusion made between memory proper and repetition, that is, a particular form of the use of the memory. Even were we to proscribe verbal repetition, and renounce

---

[1] *Des Facultés humaines*, p. 275.

learning by heart, it would be none the less necessary to develop the memory.

But verbal repetition itself is far from deserving all the criticism which it has received.

125. Opinion of Herbert Spencer. — Herbert Spencer is one of those who have the most vigorously condemned the method of memoriter recitations.

"The once universal practice of learning by rote is daily falling more into discredit. All modern authorities condemn the old mechanical way of learning the alphabet. The multiplication-table is now frequently taught experimentally.

"In the acquirement of languages, the Grammar-school plan is being superseded by plans based on the spontaneous process followed by the child in gaining its mother tongue. . . . . The rote-system, like other systems of its age, made more of the forms and symbols than of the thing symbolized. To repeat the words correctly was everything; to understand their meaning, nothing: and thus the spirit was sacrificed to the letter. It is at length perceived that, in this case as in others, such a result is not accidental but necessary, — that in proportion as there is attention to the signs, there must be inattention to the thing signified." [1]

In this quotation we again observe Mr. Spencer's habitual faults, his lofty, absolute assertions, devoid of measure and so of justness. That abuse was once made, and is still made, of memory lessons, no one denies; we still recall what painful and dreary hours of study we spent at college in repeating in a low voice long texts of Greek, Latin, and French. But because too much was formerly learned by heart, at college and even at school, is it any reason why nothing at all should now be learned by heart?

126. Arguments pro and con. — The adversaries of

---

[1] *Education*, pp. 103, 104.

verbal repetition defend their position on various grounds. American educators are distinguished for the ardor of their attacks. Thus James Johonnot asserts that the system of instruction which consists in making pupils learn by heart has no longer any justification in modern societies, where it is of less consequence to maintain blind traditions and inconsiderate respect for the past, than to fortify the reason and to promote personal reflection.[1]

Evidently the argument is valid only against a system of memorizing carried to an extreme in which is required a literal repetition, word for word, in all branches of instruction, even in those where it is least appropriate, as in the sciences and in ethics.

Other educators allege that the result of memoriter tasks is not worth the trouble that is taken to attain it. What does it profit a pupil to repeat ready-made phrases and to acquire a knowledge that is purely verbal? "To know by heart is not to know," Montaigne has said. Moreover, literal repetition requires an intense effort and a great sacrifice of time. The mind is wearied and exhausted in this effort; and while the pupil is tormented and burdened by his lessons, the time passes, precious time, which might be better employed.

We reply that, at least in certain cases, the idea cannot be separated from the only words which adequately express it, and that it is necessary, consequently, to retain them exactly. We are not really masters of our own thoughts until we have found the words which are fit to express them. In quite a large number of cases, to know by heart is the only means of knowing.

From another point of view, effort is necessary in education. It is not well to treat the child too tenderly,

---

[1] *Principles and Practice of Teaching*, New York, 1881, p. 171.

and to absolve him from all labor in verbal memorizing, on the ground that he will have understood and vaguely retained the meaning of what is taught him. The objections which we have just examined bear against the abuse of verbal repetition employed indiscreetly and to excess, rather than against the discreet and moderate use of literal repetition, in subjects where it is indispensable.

127. Where Literal Repetition is necessary. — An English educator, Mr. Fitch, has concisely stated the rule that determines the cases in which literal repetition is necessary:

"When the object is to have thoughts, facts, reasonings reproduced, seek to have them reproduced in the pupil's own words. Do not set the faculty of mere verbal memory to work. But when the words themselves in which a fact is embodied have some special fitness or beauty of their own, when they represent some scientific datum or central truth, which could not otherwise be so well expressed, then see that the form as well as the substance of the expression is learned by heart."[1]

According to this, it is easy to fix the limit which verbal repetition should not pass. In grammar, the principal rules; in arithmetic, the definitions; in geometry, the theorems; in the sciences in general, the formulæ; in history, a few summaries; in geography, the explanation of certain technical terms; in ethics, a few maxims; these are things which the child ought to know word for word, *verbatim*, on the condition, of course, that he perfectly understands the meaning of what he recites, and that his attention is called to the thought not less than to the form of expression. Nothing should be intrusted to memory except that which the intelli-

[1] Fitch, *op. cit.*, p. 135.

gence has perfectly comprehended. Everything else must be referred to the liberal memory of thoughts, not to the strict memory of words; and it is as mischievous as it is useless, and as dangerous as it is difficult, to require long pages of history, of grammar, and of physics, to be learned by heart.

128. EXERCISES IN MEMORIZING. — There is, however, another important use of verbal repetition, — the literal study of choice extracts, selections in prose and verse suitable for enriching and adorning the memory of children. "Exercises in exact memorizing are not sufficiently employed in our schools."[1] There is no better means of forming the taste of pupils, of teaching them to feel and enjoy eloquence and poetry, the power of beautiful thoughts and the charm of fine language. Even a careful reading does not always suffice; it must be accompanied from time to time by verbal recitation. By this means you constrain the memory to an effort of marked intensity, to a real concentration of the attention. You also oblige the child to speak. Finally, by this means the child penetrates more deeply into the processes and the art of the great writers; he appropriates their style and forms within himself a treasury of beautiful models which the mind of the pupil unconsciously recalls when he himself comes to write.

The recitation of authors is not only an exercise in memory, but also in language and pronunciation; and finally, it is an excellent preparation for writing, for original composition. But we do not forget the difficulty there is in choosing selections for recitations. In fact, in the pages which are to be learned by heart there must be

---

[1] E. Rendu, *Manuel de l'enseignement primaire*, p. 201.

found united the talent of the writer and the simplicity of a thought which is just, pure, in a sense popular, and within the range of the young hearers whom we are instructing.

129. Abuse of Verbal Memorizing. — We should be careful, however, not to go to extremes. On this point we recall the saying of Dr. Johnson. One day, as he was visiting a school where the custom of learning fables was in fashion, a lad stepped forward to declaim a selection for the Doctor, while at his side his younger brother was preparing to recite another selection for him. "My little fellows," said Johnson, interrupting the one who was speaking, "could you not recite for me your verses both at once?" But it is not merely because they are insupportable to others that we condemn those who are too much given to recitation, but because they render no sort of service to themselves and waste their own time. We have not the least admiration for those wonderful feats of memory which consist, for example, as Rabelais has said, in making sport of them, in reciting a book from beginning to end, backwards and forwards.

"I would prefer," said Madame de Maintenon, in speaking of her pupils of Saint Cyr, "that they retain only ten lines which they perfectly understand, rather than learn a whole volume without knowing what they are repeating."

130. Choice of Exercises. — Little and well, — such, then, will be the rule in the matter of memorizing. In making selections, preference will be given to extracts which are interesting and varied, now in verse and now in prose, and especially in verse for little children. Care will be taken to read them aloud to the class before causing them to be learned, so that the exercise in recitation shall at first be a reading lesson. Then these exercises will be carefully explained. We are not of those who think that the memory should ever anticipate the intelligence,[1] and that it is well to begin with a sort of mechanical culture of the memory by requiring things to be learned which are not understood. The child, doubtless, with his marvelous facility at memorizing, will submit to this mechanical labor; but in doing so he will contract a dangerous habit from which he will suffer all his life, — that of repeating like a parrot phrases of which he can give no account.

131. SUMMARY OF THE CONDITIONS FOR THE DEVELOPMENT OF THE MEMORY. — An English educator, Mr. Blackie, has happily summed up the principal conditions to be fulfilled for assuring strength of memory, or for re-enforcing its weakness.[2] These conditions are the following:

1. The clearness, vivacity, and intensity of the original impression.

2. The order and classification of the facts.

3. Repetition. "If the nail does not go in at one stroke, let it have another and another."

4. The power of logical sequence. "The man who is slow to remember without a reason, searches after the causal connection of the facts, and, when he has found it, binds together by the bonds of rational sequences what the constitution of his mind disinclined him to receive as an arbitrary and unexplained succession."

5. The artificial relations established between the things remembered.

6. The use of written notes. "The lack of a memory naturally good," said Montaigne, "caused me to make one of paper."

---

[1] See Appendix A.

[2] Blackie, *op. cit.*, p. 19 *et seq.*

To these conditions, which are all of the psychological order, there must be added, for the sake of completeness, the physical conditions.

"The first general circumstance favoring retentiveness," says Mr. Bain, "is the physical condition of the individual. . . . . . It includes general health, vigor, and freshness at the moment, together with the further indispensable proviso that the nutrition, instead of being drafted off to strengthen the mere physical functions, is allowed to run in good measure to the brain." [1]

Everybody knows by experience that the power of the memory is greater after a meal than before it, after sleep than before it.

132. MNEMONIC DEVICES. — Educational writers have often recommended the use of artificial methods, which, by establishing an artificial bond between recollections, insure their durability and facilitate their recall.

But, in the first place, mnemonic devices have the disadvantage of accustoming the mind to arbitrary and superficial associations of ideas. Had they, with respect to the development of the memory, all the efficacy which is ascribed to them, it would still be necessary to condemn them, by reason of the mischievous influence which they might exert upon the judgment and the reason.

---

[1] *Education as a Science*, p. 22. However much disposed we may be to take into account the physical conditions, we believe that in pedagogy we must be cautious of considerations of this nature. We do not see what education can gain from observations like these: "The words which we make use of in our thoughts do not appear in consciousness, except through the activity of the special cells which are situated, *in general*, in the third frontal convolution of the left hemisphere." (From an article on the *Récitation classique*, by M. Douliot, in the *Revue de l'enseignement secondaire*, mai, 1885.)

But still further, what must we think of these devices as they affect the memory itself?

"Artificial bonds of association," says Mr. Blackie, "may also sometimes be found useful, as when a school-boy remembers that Abydos is on the Asiatic coast of the Hellespont, because both Asia and Abydos commence with the letter A; but such tricks suit rather the necessities of an ill-trained governess than the uses of a manly mind. I have no faith in the systematic use of what are called artificial mnemonic systems; they fill the fancy with a set of arbitrary and ridiculous symbols, which interfere with the natural play of the faculties. Dates in history, to which this sort of machinery has been generally applied, are better recollected by the casual dependence, and even the accidental contiguity, of great names." [1]

The true mnemonics is that which is founded on the real relations, the natural association of ideas, and upon the method and logical order which should be introduced into instruction. On the contrary, the mnemonics which is based on artificial resemblances and conventional relations may be useful for preserving a particular remembrance; but it is injurious to the general culture of the memory. Everything that aids the memory does not, in fact, strengthen it; and it contracts bad habits by being furnished with exterior supports and artificial aids, which disqualify it for relying upon itself and upon the nature of things.

133. THE ASSOCIATION OF IDEAS. — The association of ideas is one of the essential laws of the development of the memory, in the sense that our recollections are connected with one another, that their connection fixes them in the mind, and that, once associated by any bond whatever, the appearance of one suffices to evoke the other. This is why

---

[1] Blackie, *op. cit.*, pp. 20, 21.

new studies, which by the attraction of their very novelty excite the attention, fatigue and disconcert the memory, because the ideas which they suggest to the mind do not find these points of support, that is, other analogous ideas to which they can be attached.

In the culture of the memory the teacher will then take advantage of the association of ideas and of its different principles, — some of them accidental and exterior, like contiguity in time and space ; others intrinsical and logical, like the relation of cause to effect.   The more relations that are established among the items of knowledge, the greater will be the association of ideas, and the more active and tenacious the memory. Saint François de Sales said, in a pointed way : " A good way to learn is to study ; a better is to listen ; the very best is to teach ! "

If the best way to learn is really to teach, it is precisely because the teacher is obliged to classify and co-ordinate the knowledges which he teaches, and to subject them to a rigorous and methodical order.

134. Different Forms of the Memory. — " We speak of the memory," says M. Legouvé ; " we should say memories."   In truth, there is a memory of facts, a memory of words, a memory of ideas, a memory of dates, of places, and still others ; and these different memories, while not excluding one another, are rarely found united in the same person.   One who retains imperturbably a series of figures and computations will be incapable of recalling the forms of objects and the appearance of persons. It is habit, it is frequent and repeated exercise, which contributes more than nature to the development of these different dispositions. Each profession, each trade, tends to favor the one or the other. At school, the duty of the teacher should be to oppose these specializations of the memory and not permit

it to be devoted exclusively to the acquisition of a single kind of knowledge.

In a word, the memory ought to be developed in all directions, in behalf of abstract ideas as in behalf of sensible images and notions. It should be a flexible and general power of acquisition, which lends itself to all the labors of thought and to all the occupations of life. If it is but the guardian of a privileged class of recollections, it will still render important services, but services which are restricted and particular; it will no longer be the universal faculty which it should be, the servant of the intelligence, a servant, moreover, with which we cannot dispense.

CHAPTER VII.

CULTURE OF THE IMAGINATION.

135. OFFICE OF THE IMAGINATION.—The imagination is not one of those essential faculties which, like the memory, take part in all the mental operations, or, like the judgment, are constantly making manifest the activity of the spirit. It is impossible to imagine an intelligence which cannot recollect, which cannot judge; but it is possible for us to conceive of a man without imagination.

The judgment is the normal act of the intellectual life; the memory is one of its necessary conditions. The imagination is but an auxiliary, accessory faculty; it merely intervenes on occasion to aid, and sometimes to impede in their development, the other powers of the soul.

136. BENEFITS OF THE IMAGINATION.—We by no means deny the great and real services which the imagination is called to render, either in practical life, in literature and the arts, or even in science. We do not forget that it embellishes existence by the golden dreams with which it lulls us, that it nourishes our hopes, and that it fills by its sweet contemplations the chasms and intervals of active, reflective life. Nor do we forget that it is the inspirer of poetry and the handmaid of art, and that without it literature would be but a cold and insipid photograph of reality. The scientist himself has need of imagination, for it suggests to him fruitful hypotheses and bold inventions, which often put him

138

on the route toward the truth ; and a philosopher has said that a chapter on logic might be written with this title: *Errors committed through default of imagination.*[1]

137. DANGERS OF THE IMAGINATION. — But if it is easy to extol the imagination and its benefits, it is none the less so to decry it and point out its dangers. Of how many errors and illusions is it not the source ! Pascal harshly characterized it as "the enemy of reason," "the mistress of error and falsehood." Malebranche called it "the madcap of the house," to express the error and the disorder which it can excite in the soul.

The education of the imagination will not, then, be merely a work of excitation and development.

Like the sensibility, like all the disturbed and disturbing faculties, susceptible of good and of evil, the imagination must be supervised, restrained, and directed.

"Other faculties," says Madame de Saussure, "furnish no occasion for constraint. Every innocent exercise which tends to strengthen the attention, the reason, and the memory forms a part of our plan, and we can employ it without hesitation in the work of development; but the moment the imagination becomes the subject of our attention, all becomes more delicate and dangerous. To restrain, to regulate, to moderate, is often more necessary than to develop; and yet who would extinguish the imagination?"

138. ITS POWER IN CHILDHOOD. — All the philosophers save Rousseau, who, continuing to isolate himself in his paradoxes, denies imagination to the child, after having denied him memory, — all the observers of childhood are in accord in recognizing in this period of life the precocious development of the imagination. Madame de Saussure, who has

---

[1] Paul Janet, *Philosophie du bonheur,* p. 61.

written upon this subject one of the finest chapters of her excellent book, declares that at the beginning of life the imagination is " all-powerful." [1]

It is Kant's opinion that the infant imagination is extremely vivid, and that it needs to be governed, not to be enlarged.

139. ITS DIFFERENT FORMS. — But before going further, in order to introduce greater clearness into a question of such delicacy, it is important at this point to distinguish the two principal forms of the imagination, — one which is ordinarily called the representative imagination, which is hardly more than vivid memory, the faculty of recalling with the eyes closed what we have seen with the eyes open ; the other, which is in truth the imagination proper, that which invents and combines under new forms the images borrowed from the memory. The representative imagination, moreover, is the starting-point of the other, the humble cradle of a faculty summoned to the most brilliant destinies.

"The imagination," says Madame Pape-Carpantier, "that precious endowment, has been given to the child in order to permit him, when he has imitated what he has seen, to construct for himself, in his turn, things that are new. Thus this faculty is endowed with an incessant activity, which is ever urging the child to action. It is only rarely, then, that we have to stimulate the imagination ; but we have to offer it wholesome aliment and open to it straight and becoming paths." [2]

140. THE REPRESENTATIVE IMAGINATION. — We might be tempted to think that the representative imagination, manifestly useful to the artist and the painter, who need

---

[1] *Éducation progressive*, Tom. II., p. 297, Ch. VIII.
[2] Madame Pape-Carpantier, *Cours complet d'éducation*, 1874.

to form vivid representations of objects, renders no service to the child and plays no part in the earliest education; but a little reflection suffices to prove the contrary.

A vivid representation of the letters of the alphabet
will be of great service in teaching to read and write
quickly and well. Further on, in the tracing of maps,
in the study of geometry, and still more in the exercises in drawing, children well endowed with respect to
the imagination, and accustomed to conceive with clearness the material forms of objects, will have no difficulty
in surpassing their comrades.

Even in the study of orthography, the representative
imagination has its importance. How shall we explain
the fact that one child, as intelligent as another, who
has even read much more, is nevertheless much slower
in learning to spell? The cause of this is probably in
the weakness of the representative imagination. Certain
children, who read readily, in some way do not follow
the text except by the thought; their eyes are not sufficiently fixed upon the words themselves and upon the
elements which compose them. So that, when asked to
write from memory a word which they have read for the
tenth time, they bungle and disfigure it, they do not reproduce all its letters; like unskillful draftsmen, who
through defective imagination cannot represent with exactness the object which they have seen and which they
wish to draw from memory.

141. CULTURE OF THE REPRESENTATIVE IMAGINATION. —
Though the representative imagination, like the memory,
is instinctively very powerful, it may nevertheless be
the object of a special culture. Exercises in intuition,
like those employed by Pestalozzi, are especially adapted
to this education. Mr. Bain states that almost the only

means of strengthening this faculty is by making additions to our knowledge ; but on this condition, however, that we have due regard to the precision of the knowledge communicated, and to the clearness and vividness of the perceptions we acquire. A multitude of ideas, confusedly and vaguely conceived, would tend only to befog and obscure the imagination. In order to imagine well, we must begin by seeing well.

Accustomed to conceive clearly and distinctly whatever the senses perceive, the imagination will become a good instrument of intuition, invaluable not only for recalling objects that we have seen, but also for representing objects that we have not seen. In fact, the imaginative faculty, in its higher manifestations, is something more than the mere photographic reproduction of what has been really perceived ; it allows us to conceive with clearness any object whatever from a simple verbal description of it. It is a great help in the study of history and geography, because it places the child in a position to see, with the eyes of the mind, the places, the events, and the men that are the subjects of the lesson. It animates instruction, gives vividness to ideas and coloring to events, and so inspires an interest in the subject in hand.

Care must be taken, however, that the child does not make a misuse of the conceptive faculty. Very much disposed to think by images, he has not at his disposition, in the early years of his life, that algebra of thought called language. Back of each word that he pronounces, he sees with its details of form and color, the object designated by that word. If pushed too far, this is a dangerous habit, because it obstructs the clearness and the celerity of thought, and causes the pupil to loiter amid useless imaginings. The image should **not** stifle the idea and obstruct the work of abstract thought, by mingling with them a train of sensible representations.

Let us add that the representative imagination should not be considered merely an instrument which is to be made deft and strong. It is a direct source of acquisitions; it peoples our consciousness and heart with a world of images and recollections.

Hence the need of careful oversight and of choice in the first impressions of the imagination. The child must be shielded from whatever is ugly, repulsive, and immoral. Madame de Sévigné was fond of repeating the saying, "To the pure all things are pure." In other terms, in a soul healthy and pure unwholesome impressions leave no trace of evil. Perhaps this is true of consciences already formed and of characters already established, whose inclinations are strong enough, whose habits are sufficiently fixed to reject every impure alloy, and which can encounter the most pernicious impressions with impunity; but this saying is not applicable to the child whose mind, in the process of formation, is impregnated with everything that touches it and opposes resistance to no impression.[1]

That which is best adapted to the early culture of the imagination is the spectacle presented by nature. Before he is capable of becoming interested in the works of man, the child is already disposed to admire " the grand poem which the finger of God has written on the surface of the earth."

"Often take children," says Gauthey, "to the bosom of nature, that they may there revel at will in colors, forms, and perfumes."[2]

---

[1] "New vases preserve the taste of the first liquor that is put into them; and wool, once colored, never regains its primitive whiteness." — QUINTILIAN.

[2] Gauthey, *De l'Éducation*, Paris, 1854, Tom. I., p. 464.

142. PICTURES PROPERLY SO CALLED. — It is no longer necessary to call the attention to the importance of pictures and to the part which they may play in instruction. On every hand the art of picture-making is being developed, and the representations of real objects are scattered everywhere, — upon the walls of our schoolrooms, in works of standard literature, upon the covers of pupils' note-books.

" Could we show objects to children and have them touched and handled, it would doubtless be best; but if objects are out of reach, or are of such a nature as to make direct presentation impossible, the teacher who can draw calls to his aid books of engravings, maps, or pictures.[1]

The picture, then, has gained for itself a place; and since the day of Comenius, who in his *Orbis Pictus* was the first to employ it as a means of instruction, it has become popularized and at the same time perfected. Children love them; there is no doubt on that point. Some teachers assert that girls are even more fond of them than boys are. At any rate, pictures are the first poesy of childhood, and are to be commended in the first place because they furnish amusement and recreation. But they are also a means of developing the representative imagination. of fixing the attention, and of making study attractive. Finally, they are a school of positive instruction, and at the same time a preparation for an education in art.

143. THE CREATIVE IMAGINATION. — The expression *creative imagination* has the sanction of usage, but it is certainly inexact. The imagination acts, invents, arranges according

---

[1] Du Mesnil, *Lettre à M. Jules Ferry*, 1880, p. 21.

to its fancy, magnifies, contracts, modifies in a thousand ways the elements it borrows from reality, and groups the images furnished by the observation and the memory in accordance with an ideal which it conceives; but in no true sense does it create.

144. DOES IT EXIST IN THE CHILD? — Whatever name we give it,[1] — and we prefer to call it the active or inventive imagination, — it is developed at a quite early period. There comes a moment in the life of the child when the spirit is no longer merely a faithful memory and a passive reproduction of what the senses have perceived; when from the shock of multiplied representations and from the clash of various images, there burst forth, under the stimulus of the sentiments, a certain number of new and original conceptions which attest the native fecundity of the spirit. Of course all infant intelligences are not alike in this respect. Perhaps to a greater degree than any other, the inventive faculty supposes a strength of intelligence and a power of sensibility which are very unevenly distributed by nature; but it may be affirmed that, with equal intelligence, the child will have the most imagination who has read most, traveled most, observed most things, witnessed most spectacles, — who, in a word, has at his disposal most material which can be utilized in new combinations and constructions.

Nothing is more varied, however, than the play of the childish imagination in the thousand pastures where it strays in pursuit of artless fictions and innocent falsehoods.

145. MYTHOLOGICAL TENDENCY. — At first, the child has a marked tendency to personify all the objects which sur-

---

[1] English psychologists call it the *constructive* imagination, in distinction from the imagination that is simply reproductive.

round him, to represent them to himself after his own image, to enter into conversation with animals, and even with inanimate things.   His mental state is very like that of primitive people, who attribute life and feeling to material objects, and invest all things with human or divine qualities.   "The sun has risen," a child was told.   "Who then is its maid?" he asked.   The Greeks believed that Apollo drove the chariot of the sun through the heavens.   The little child imagines that the sun should be taken out for a walk by an attendant, just as he is himself.

There is no great good to be expected from a tendency which renews for each child the ridiculous crudities and dangerous superstitions of the infancy of the race.   However, we may take advantage of this tendency in creating an interest in the reading of fables.[1]   The child, in order to enjoy La Fontaine, needs really to believe that the animals and plants speak, and that they are really the authors of the acts which the poet attributes to them.[2]

Notwithstanding Rousseau, who would have us show children only what is true, let us allow the little learner to wander off into fairy-land.   The full day of reason will come soon enough to dissipate the shadows and phantoms of the imagination.

146. POETICAL TENDENCY. — The difference between the mythologist and the poet is that the former has an artless belief in the fictions of his imagination, while the later enjoys them without believing in them.   The poet yields to a

---

[1] See the judicious article of M. Antoine (*Fables*) in the *Dictionnaire de Pédagogie.*

[2] Gauthey gives an account of a little girl who, visiting a museum of natural history, asked to see some crickets, and two were shown her. "Which of these two crickets," she said, "is the one that had that talk with the ant?"

semi-illusion like that which we experience at the theatre. Without being wholly the dupes of the events which take place in the drama played before our eyes, we are partially deceived. We become interested in the characters of the play just as though they were real, and yet we know that they are not.

"Children are born poets," says an observer of infancy; "and this is why we must entertain them with poetical ideas."

The childish imagination easily invents for itself fictions which charm it, and dramas where it assigns parts to imaginary characters. The son of Tiedemann imagined conversations between cabbage-stalks. "Children," says M. Egger, "contrive for themselves the instruments needed in their little dramas."

"We give them playthings for the purpose, but there are not enough of these for all the scenes which they imagine, and the same toy will often answer for several parts, and sometimes for very different ones."[1]

Madame Necker de Saussure mentions a great number of instances which exhibit this poetical tendency of the child to represent to himself something besides what he has seen; and she concludes thus

"The entire existence of little children is dramatic. Their life is a pleasing dream, purposely prolonged and sustained. Always inventing scenes, scene-painters, and actors, their days glide away in fictions, and in their childish fancies they are almost poets."[2]

Far from discouraging this poetic instinct of the child, our only thought should be to give it free play. Thus, when he is weary of inventing fictions for himself, let us

---

[1] M. Egger, *op. cit.*, p. 13.
[2] Madame de Saussure, I., III., Chap. V.

purposely furnish him with them. Let us tell him those fabulous stories for which he is so hungry. Let us control his taste for imaginary things so as to direct it in our own way, and in this way let us superadd to the spontaneous development of the childish imagination the new excitation which comes from the imagination of another.

147. TALES. — The austere Kant excludes tales from education. It is impossible to assent to his opinion. Tales bring joy to the spirit of the child, and joy forms a part of intellectual hygiene. Moreover, they arouse the intelligence, and, as Mr. Sully observes, the child who at home takes most delight in listening to stories will, other things being equal, do the best at school. Have no fear, then, of tales, real tales, even of those which have no moral pretension and conceal no serious lesson under their pleasing fictions.

"When stories are told children," says Mlle. Chalamet, "why not do it simply for the purpose of amusing them? Why not be satisfied with telling a story for the story's *sake*, to satisfy the craving of the imagination for food?"[1]

It is not claiming enough, however, to recommend tales simply as amusements. If they are carefully chosen and are simple, delicate, and chaste, if there is nothing in them that is gross or in bad taste, stories will have a higher effect; they will be for the teacher a sure means of fixing the attention by interesting it; they will be an allurement to future studies, and also a preparation for the understanding of real poetry, to which it is important that no man should be a stranger.[2]

---

[1] *L'École maternelle*, p. 234.

[2] "What is the origin of the singular taste that men have for fairy stories? Is it because falsehood is pleasanter than truth? No; fairy stories are not falsehoods, and the child who is amused or frightened by them is not deceived by them for an instant.

148. NARRATIVES. — But it would be an error to think that the childish imagination can be exercised only by nourishing it on fictions, by alluring it into fairy-land. The imagination may be as well applied, and even with greater profit, to what is actually real.

"By far the most useful exercise of this faculty is when it buckles itself to realities; and this I advise the student chiefly to cultivate. There is no need of going to romances for pictures of human character and fortune calculated to please the fancy and elevate the imagination. The life of Alexander the Great, of Martin Luther, of Gustavus Adolphus, or any of those notable characters on the great stage of the world who incarnate the history which they create, is for this purpose of more educational value than the best novel that ever was written, or even the best poetry."[1]

In truth, history would be unintelligible without imagination. In order that it may instruct the child, it must be like a series of pictures passing before his eyes, and his mind must dwell upon them as in a museum, where the attention is fixed now upon the portraits of great men and now upon the countries where the historical events have occurred.

As soon as possible, therefore, we should pass from purely fictitious stories to narratives which are truthfully exact; but in these narratives let us speak to the child in the language of the imagination, — that language in which, as it is said, *the words have color*. Let us expect no good result from instruction that is always dry and abstract, where the brilliant picture and vivid painting never come to animate and embellish facts.

Stories are the ideal, something truer than the actual truth, the triumph of the good, the beautiful, and the true." (Laboulaye, Introduction to the *Contes bleus*.)

[1] Blackie, *op. cit.*, p. 13.

149. NECESSITY OF POETRY. — Rousseau, as we have said, would have us present to the child only the naked truth. This would be to exclude him forever from the enjoyment of poetry, which is made of fictions, and where the truth is always veiled. Certain positive spirits of our day might perhaps put up with this impoverishment of the imagination, but for ourselves we could not submit to such a sacrifice. There never will be enough poetry in the world, I do not say simply to embellish and cheer existence, but to elevate and ennoble it. Popular education cannot dispense with it, and it is especially in the common schools that we must open wide the doors to the poets.

"It is in common school instruction more than in any other that fiction is beneficent, indispensable, and should have a large place. There, where the culture is perforce limited to what is strictly necessary, aims only at the useful, the practical, and ends early to give place to the positive needs of life, — it is there especially that it is important to throw a pure ray of poesy that may glitter, if possible, forever. For the child of the higher classes life, with its natural revelations, books, travel, the theatre, works of art, intellectual associations, will perhaps end in repairing the errors or supplying the deficiencies of early education; but for the pupil of the common school life the most often holds in reserve only a long lesson of hard experience, of dreary economy, and of prosy calculation. If light is to cheer such an one, it must come from you. This is why it must be given him, and it must be as brilliant as possible. Verily the human soul is so constituted that it cannot dispense with fiction, or, even if you prefer it, with an ideal world. Save it from the stupid and dangerous marvels of superstition, — nothing is wiser; but do your very best to supply its place. If you do not, one of two things will happen. You will either succeed in shriveling the soul and in drying up the source of inner poesy, or, what happens much more frequently, you will snatch it from one dream only to plunge it into another, but perchance a still more dangerous one. Whoever has reflected on the prodigious credulity of the socialistic utopist will easily comprehend our thought." [1]

150. ROMANCES. — Romances are the fairy tales of mature age, and grown persons find as much delight in them as a child does in the story of Cinderella or of the ass's hide. But without withholding them entirely from children, the reading of them must be carefully guarded. In every case, those that are put into the hands of children must be selected with scrupulous care. Moral stories, like most English romances; scientific stories, like those of Jules Verne; and even romances of pure imagination, may be read without danger, and even with profit.

151. PERSONAL CREATIONS OF THE CHILDISH IMAGINATION. — The imagination of the child is not merely a contemplative faculty which is delighted with the pretty stories and inventions of others; but it is also an active faculty which needs to create on its own account, which manifests itself by real productions, by personal constructions, at first in play and later in exercises in literary composition and in drawing.

Before Froebel, Comenius had noticed that " children love to build houses out of clay, chips, or stones."

The Père Girard writes:

"The creative imagination, under the form of a mania for constructing or for destroying, is already apparent in tender years; for if the little child wishes to give proof of his power to destroy, he loves also to produce, in his way, what is new and beautiful. Notice how he arranges his little soldiers, his houses, his sheep, and how he delights in his new combinations. He calls his mother that she too may enjoy them." [2]

---

[1] Article *Fiction,* by Dr. Élie Pécaut, in the *Dictionnaire de Pédagogie.*

[2] The Père Girard, *De l'Enseignement régulier de la langue maternelle,* I., III., p. 88.

152. The Imagination in Play. — It is in play that the child first gives proof of his nascent imagination. There he invents, combines at leisure, and freely abandons himself to the caprices of his fancy.

It is to be noted that the playthings which most captivate the child are not those elaborate toys which, by their very perfection, leave his talent for invention nothing to do, but rather those which the best lend themselves to the development of his personal activity.

"The child is ever intent on creating. A hole in the ground is a creation. Out of that dirt which comes from the hole, and which he heaps with his hands, the child raises mountains that appear to him of an incalculable height. A heap of dust represents the architecture of fairies.

"The penny doll which the child fancies to be so beautiful produces the same mirage.

"The other, the rich doll arrayed in silk, needs nothing, and the child, conscious of this, disdains it. But that little creature whose only dower is its blue eyes, its placid face, its red cheeks, and the eternal smile on its cherry lips, what a power of imagination is required to dress it in a rag of calico which shall be its robe, and a bit of tulle which shall be its neckerchief!

"The penny doll develops the imagination of the child, just as of yore the poet developed that of the people." [1]

To the same effect Madame de Saussure calls attention to the fact that " the playthings which the child invents are those which please him the most;" and M. Egger says : " It is very true that instead of the toy so elaborate in form, the child often prefers something rude which his imagination can transform according to his fancy." [2]

Let us be slow to check the child in the free and frank expansion of his imagination. After having been called

[1] M. Champfleury, *Les Enfants,* p. 154.
[2] M. Egger, *op. cit.,* p. 42.

into play by the amusements of early life, it will be found ready for serious service in work and in study.

153. EXERCISES IN LITERARY COMPOSITION. — The work of literary composition no doubt calls into play all the faculties of the mind, memory, judgment, etc. ; but the imagination also plays an important part, especially if a narrative or a description is to be written. At first it will be best to make an appeal simply to the representative imagination. The little story-teller, with reference to such or such an incident of his life, will tell what he has seen, and will have simply to show that he has made a good use of his eyes. But gradually he will be accustomed to do more than this, — to invent, of his own accord to combine imaginary events. Provided we adapt the subjects to the age of the child, draw them from his own experience, and put him in a condition to find in his own recollections the materials of his composition, he will joyfully devote himself to this personal labor.

154. DRAWING AND THE ARTS. — Let us also mention, among the most natural exercises of the imagination, drawing, singing, and the fine arts in general.

"With Pestalozzi," says Gauthey, " drawing was particularly an art of the imagination. Provided with a few data, his pupils invented all sorts of figures and combinations of figures, and they often reached very remarkable results in respect of originality and elegance.

"Such an exercise forms the taste and the inventive spirit of children destined for very diverse occupations. The gardener, the locksmith, the cabinet-maker, the upholsterer, the mason, — all have need of the inventive faculty as well as of taste. To develop their powers in these directions is to prepare them for the greatest success in their several employments."[1]

---

[1] Gauthey, op: cit., I., p. 47.

155. DISCIPLINE OF THE IMAGINATION. — From what has preceded it follows that there is a true scholastic culture of the imagination.[1] We have shown in particular how we may develop this faculty; how by following nature we may succeed in exciting it. Let us not forget that the imagination must also be disciplined, tempered, and controlled.

"Nothing is more dangerous," said David Hume, "than the ardor of the imagination. Man of a powerful imagination may be compared to those angels whom the Scripture represents as covering their eyes with their wings."

In fact, the ardent conceptions of the imagination obscure the mind and conceal from us the truth. They exalt the emotions and precipitate us into the madness of the passions. They benumb activity and throw us into an enervating revery. As a tempered imagination is useful and necessary for equipoise of spirit, by just so much is an excess of imagination fatal to good sense, to energy of character, and to rectitude of conduct.

What means, then, may education employ for keeping the imagination within proper limits? The best is to invoke the aid of counter forces. To repress it directly, to make a straightforward attack upon it, is a difficult thing. It is wiser and surer to find a counterpoise for it in the development of the reason and of the faculties that depend upon the reason. If you have to do with a child of exalted and inflamed imagination, call into its highest activity his power of observation and give ceaseless extension to his positive knowledge. You will never temper that ardent imagination, always prone to escape into the land of chimeras, save on

---

[1] M. Rousselot is wrong in saying that "such is the nature of the imagination that it is not, to the same degree as the other intellectual faculties, susceptible of a special education, I mean of a scholastic training." (*Pédagogie*, p. 125.)

the condition of putting it in charge of a vigorous reason and a judicious reflection, and of giving it, so to speak, good and reliable neighbors, by surrounding it with strong and disciplined faculties which guard it, which leave their impress upon it, and which, while developing themselves, constrain it to become one of them.

Another means of governing the imagination and keeping it within bounds is to give it occupation, to furnish it with wholesome and nourishing aliment, so that it may not go in search of questionable food.

"To exercise the imagination," says Madame Necker, "is as necessary as to hold it in check; and perhaps we hold it in check only when we exercise it."

Whatever we may do, we cannot destroy the imagination; it is not possible to have it die of inanition. It would, moreover, be a great evil to dry up in man the fruitful source of so many beautiful and noble things. But, however we may regard it, the imagination is certainly an indestructible force of the soul. It is better, then, to have it for us than against us; better to trace for it its channel than to run the risk, in abandoning it to itself, of seeing it pass its bounds in reckless disorder.

"Madame de Saussure has shown that the imagination, that irresistible power, even when we think we have brought it under subjection, takes the most diverse forms; that it dissembles its real proportions, and with a secret fire animates the most wretched passions. If you refuse it air and liberty, it slinks off into the depths of selfishness, and, under coarse features, it becomes avarice, pusillanimity, or vanity.

"We also need to see with what benign earnestness Madame Necker spies its first movements in the soul of the child; with what intelligent care she seeks to make of it, from the very moment of its birth, the companion of the truth; how she surrounds it with whatever can establish it within the circle of the good. The studies which extend our intellectual horizon, the spectacle of nature with its numberless marvels, the emotions of the fine arts,— nothing seems to her either superfluous or dangerous for directing the imagination in the good way. She fears to see it escape, through lack of pleasures sufficiently enticing, into other routes." [1]

156. SOME SPECIAL DANGERS TO SHUN. —Besides the great dangers to which a giddy or impetuous imagination subjects the mind and the heart, there are, even in the ordinary development of a mediocre imagination, certain rocks to shun.

Thus it is important to prevent the child from confounding fiction with reality. It sometimes happens to us, when in our sleep we have been fiercely haunted by an impassioned dream, that we are obliged on awakening to make an effort to chase away the phantoms that beset our mind and to convince ourselves of our mistake. The child who as yet has no exact notions on the real and the possible, who is almost absolutely ignorant of the laws of nature, may easily be the victim of an analogous dupery of his imagination. Take care that he, does not introduce pure fictions into the woof of his thoughts as so many notions that are true. Let us warn him, when we are relating a fable to him, not to give credence to our account. As M. Egger says, "Much time is necessary for the notion of the *probable* to be formed and fixed in his mind." Let us not allow ourselves to think that the very strangeness of our inventions is a sufficient guaranty, and that it foils the credulity of the child.

The excessive credulity of the child is a sufficient reason why we should proscribe all terrifying stories, such as those of the black man, which unskilful and unwise teachers use in order to govern the child.

"One of the things we most often forget is the effect of en-

---

[1] Preface to the 8th edition of the *Éducation progressive.*

tire ignorance. We call natural what we have already seen, and we do not perceive that for the child who has seen nothing, everything is equally natural. For him the possible is without limits." [1]

157. REVERY.—Another vicious tendency of the imagination is to lose itself in vague contemplations, and to resign itself to indolent and listless reveries. How often are we turned aside from serious attention, and from definite and determined action, by the uncertain phantoms which are floating in our mind?

Revery may become a disease of the intelligence. Of course it is not to be supposed that there can be completely eliminated, even from the most studious and thoughtful consciousness, those parasitic conceptions of the imagination, any more than we can entirely extirpate noxious weeds from the best cultivated field. But for all that we must prevent revery from degenerating into a habit, and for this purpose we must as much as possible occupy the mind with the labor of consecutive and sustained reflection ; we must furnish the imagination with substantial aliment, such as beautiful verses which have been learned by heart, and grand deeds which occur to the memory the instant the mind has a moment's leisure. It is especially the unoccupied imagination that is disposed to revery. Give the imagination and the other faculties work to do, and you will cure the child of revery, that indolence of the thought.

158. IMPORTANCE OF THE IMAGINATION.—One will perhaps be astonished at the importance which we have ascribed to the culture of the imagination. No doubt this faculty cannot be compared, for the services it renders, to the memory or the judgment. It is not to the same degree a ped-

---

[1] Madame de Saussure, *op. cit.*, I., III., Chap. **V.**

agogic faculty; but we shall never concede to positive and exclusively scientific thinkers that there can be a possibility of sacrificing it. In all ages an important place has justly been given to it in instruction. In fact, the literary compositions in use in colleges are in part but exercises of the imagination. Let these be restricted in order to extend by so much the domain of real and exact knowledge, of facts and practical instruction. We are quite willing that this should be done, but pray do not presume to suppress them.

"I much fear," says Mr. Blackie, "neither teachers nor scholars are sufficiently impressed with the importance of a proper training of the imagination. . . It is the enemy of science only when it acts without reason, — that is, arbitrarily and whimsically; with reason it is often the best and the most indispensable of allies." [1]

With certain children whose minds are languid and inactive, who are "born old," it is not enough to exercise the imagination. It must be stimulated, not merely to awaken them to the poetic life, but also in the more modest interest of their success in practical affairs. In all cases the imagination is one of the stimulants of activity, the inspirer of happy inventions, or at least the cause of useful expedients.

---

[1] Blackie, *op. cit.*, pp. 12, 13.

CHAPTER VIII.

THE FACULTIES OF REFLECTION, JUDGMENT, ABSTRACTION, REASONING.

159. JUDGMENT AND REASONING. — To judge and to reason are distinct operations of the mind, irreducible to any other. In the activity of the intelligence there are three degrees, three essential moments : conceiving or having ideas, judging or associating conceptions, reasoning or combining judgments. Just as judgment is the coupling of two ideas united by an act of affirmation expressed by the verb *to be*, so reasoning is a sequence or a series of judgments united one with another in such a way that the last seems to be the legitimate conclusion and necessary consequence of those that precede.

160. DEFINITION OF JUDGMENT. — Judgment, in its psychological acceptation, is the essential act of thought, the life, so to speak, of the mind. It is in the judgment that ideas are united and made alive ; it is in the proposition, the verbal expression of the judgment, that words, the signs of ideas, are brought together and take bodily form.

The judgment, moreover, dominates and embraces the other operations of the mind. In fact, judgments are the source of our ideas, and they also serve as conclusions to our reasonings.

The perceptions of the senses and of the consciousness supply us with ready-made judgments, — primitive judgments, so to speak, — from which the mind detaches, either immediately particular ideas, or, by a slow process of abstraction, general ideas.

But there are also reflective judgments, which suppose an attentive comparison of ideas previously acquired, and in which there is always mingled a beginning of reasoning, if not a complete and formal reasoning.

161. DIFFERENT SENSES OF THE WORD JUDGMENT. — It is, then, in seizing the relations of ideas that consists the essential function of what Rousseau called the "judicial faculty." But in ordinary usage the word judgment is often diverted from its psychological meaning.

Thus Madame Necker de Saussure uses the term judgment to signify nothing more than practical sense, good sense applied to the affairs of real life.

"What it is very essential to develop," she says, "is that particular branch of the faculty of reasoning which is applicable to the conduct of life, — that which we are accustomed to call judgment."[1]

This is to forget that the judgment is also employed in the sciences and in speculative research, and that the observer, the scientist, and the philosopher judge no less than the man of action.

Another more common use of the word judgment consists in construing it in a still more restricted sense, as the synonym of good judgment. Language is easily optimistic, and often gives to words their most favorable meaning. To say of some one that he has good judgment is to affirm that he has an accurate mind ; that he is deceived less often than others ; that he has, as it were, a natural affinity for the truths ; that he weighs things surely and well. And

---

[1] *De l'Éducation progressive*, I., VI., Ch. VI.

this, of course, when it is a question of judgments that demand penetration and discernment. We do not say that a man has judgment because he is capable of affirming that snow is white or that fire burns.

162. IMPORTANCE OF THE JUDGMENT. —It is in this sense that the Port Royal logic commends the judgment as the master quality of the mind.

"There is nothing more estimable than good sense and accuracy of mind in the discernment of the true and the false. All the other qualities of the mind have limited applications, but exactness of reason is universally useful in all stations and in all the employments of life. . . . So the principal endeavor should be to form one's judgment and make it as accurate as it can be; and to this end should tend the greatest part of our studies. We use the reason as an instrument for acquiring the sciences, and, *vice versa*, we should make use of the sciences as instruments for perfecting the reason, accuracy of mind being infinitely more valuable than all the speculative knowledge to which we can attain by means of the most accurate and well-established sciences."

Port Royal certainly puts too low an estimate on the sciences and their positive results, the knowledge which they transmit; but nevertheless there is no exaggeration in declaring that the purpose of all study is the formation of the judgment, and that all the other faculties should be held subordinate to the judgment. Though having a great memory, we may be incapable of getting on in life, and having a vivid imagination, there is ever danger of going astray; but endowed with great judgment we move squarely forward, and there is no difficulty we cannot surmount.

163. CULTURE OF THE JUDGMENT. — So, since the days of Montaigne and Port Royal, the culture of the judgment has become, so to speak, the watchword of French pedagogy.

Even the most refractory have come to comprehend the importance of the judgment. In the preface to the new edition of the *Conduite des Écoles chrétiennes* (1860), the Frère Phillip expresses himself thus:

" Of late years elementary instruction has assumed a particular feature which we must take into account. Proposing as its chief end the formation of the pupil's judgment, it gives less importance than heretofore to the culture of the memory; it makes especial use of methods which call into play the intelligence and lead the child to reflect, to take account of facts, and to release him from the domain of words in order to introduce him into that of ideas."

164. JUDGMENT IN THE CHILD. — Judgment being inseparable from thought, the infant judges at a very early period of its life. Its first perceptions are already judgments, the affirmation of what it sees and what it hears. It is not yet capable of reflective judgments, but it is of those spontaneous judgments which are but the immediate adhesion of the mind to a perceived truth. Long before it is able to speak, perception determines for it little beliefs manifested by its gestures, its smiles, its movements. It judges that the candle burns when it has once been burned, and it draws back to avoid it. It judges that an object is within its reach, when it reaches out its hand to seize it. Doubtless it is often deceived in this appreciation of distance, but this error is also a judgment.

" We may see by the various methods which young children employ to reach what is above them, to drag, to hurt, to lift different bodies; that they reason, — that is to say, that they adapt means to an end, before they can explain their own designs in words." [1]

We know, however, that the child, in his first attempts at

---

[1] Miss Edgeworth, *Practical Education* (London: 1811), II., p. 332.

speaking, does not at once succeed in giving an exact and complete expression to his judgments. Do not demand of him propositions in regular form. He usually suppresses the verb *to be*, that logical copula of ideas in a sentence. The verb *to be* is, in some sort, an abstract verb. The child prefers attributive verbs, which are concrete. In default of an actual verb, he invents one, as by transforming an adjective into a verb. He will say, *Paul buds*, instead of *Paul is bad*. The most often his judgment, when expressed, will be but a simple juxtaposition of subject and attribute, as *Paul wise*, *Paul bad*. His repugnance at employing the verb *to be* is equaled only by his awkwardness in making use of it; and the same defect has been observed in the case of deaf-mutes, who when learning to write usually employ expressions like these: *I am eat bread*, for, *1 eat bread*. But it must not be inferred from this insufficiency of language that judgment is incomplete in the child. It is only the verbal expression that is at fault. The child mentioned by M. Taine, who instead of saying, *Le soleil se couche*, said, *ça brûle, coucou* (*ça brûle*, something brilliant, like fire; *coucou*, the act of setting) might have employed strange expressions, but he nevertheless formulated a very definite judgment.

165. REFLECTIVE JUDGMENTS. — It is more difficult to say at what period in the life of the child the faculty of reflective judgment is developed. In order to attain this end it is necessary that the mind shall have ceased to be at the mercy of sensible perceptions, that it shall have gained possession of itself, that it shall have become capable of attention, and finally, that it shall have at its disposal not merely a large number of particular observations which are the materials of its reflections, but also of general ideas which supply it with terms of comparison.

The child is very prompt to seize resemblances, and his
first personal judgments are founded on analogies, and most
often these are superficial.   M. Egger cites some interesting
examples of these.

"The son of a learned grammarian, of the age of five
and a half years, said to his father, 'Are there feminine verbs?
Why so?   *Pondre* is a feminine verb, for we always say *elle* (she)
pond, never *il* (he) *pond*.'"

"At the age of four years and two months Émile sees that
the window of a smoking-room is closed. He asks how the
smoke will escape, and replies by pointing out the cracks left
even when the window is closed. . .   'For,' says he, 'the smoke
is *very small*; it is like water; when I put water in my hands
it goes through there'; and he points out the interstices between
his fingers."

166. EARLIEST EDUCATION. — There is hardly any opportunity for the intervention of the teacher in the elementary
development of the child's judgment.   That negative education which Rousseau preached, but which he was wrong in
prolonging too far, — that which consists in letting nature
have her way, and in simply preventing any evil influence
from altering the normal course, — negative education is
admirably adapted to the first years of childhood.   The important thing at this age is not so much to act upon the
judgment by a special training, as to protect it from the
gross errors and prejudices which, under cover of the ignorance and credulity of the child, install themselves too easily
in the mind, and there gain an indestructible hold.

In what concerns primitive judgments, there is no other
advice to give than that which relates to the education of the
senses, whose purpose is to assure the clearness, exactness,
and strength of the perceptions.   As to the judgments of
comparison, which indicate that real mental activity has
already begun, it is best to show them indulgence, and not

to be incensed because they are simple and even ridiculous, but rather to encourage them, because, however childish they may appear, they are the prelude of an infinitely precious quality, the liberty of the spirit.

167. SCHOOL TRAINING OF THE JUDGMENT. — It might be said, not without reason, that the influence of the family is greater than that of the school upon the formation of the judgment. In fact, in the relative freedom of domestic life, the child, left a little more to himself, finds some occasions to observe and to exercise his mind. But it is none the less true that the child's studies, if wisely conducted, are excellent exercises in personal reflection, and that in them there is a school training of the judgment.

168. GENERAL METHOD. — In many German schools it is thought well to devote certain hours each week to the training of the judgment. We do not quite understand what those *classes in judgment* can be, which remind us of the *classes in virtue* imagined by the Abbé de Saint Pierre. Can we conceive of a teacher saying to his pupils, "Now, boys, we are going to exercise ourselves in judging?"

No, the education of the judgment ought not to be sought in special lessons; it will result from all the exercises of the school. In fact, there is no instruction which cannot be employed, in the hands of a good teacher, in provoking the initiative of the pupil, in calling into play his reflection, and in exciting the powers of the mind. If you resolutely avoid the processes of a mechanical instruction and of a passive education; if you know how to appeal to the natural activity of the child; if you encourage him by your questions to think for himself; if you "let trot" the young spirit before you; the judgment of your pupil will be developed naturally, spontaneously, just as all the powers are developed when they are relieved from the bonds which hamper them, and they are left to pursue an unobstructed course. The more of liberty and life you introduce into studies, the more the pupil will exercise his judgment, and the more, consequently, he will develop his faculty of judging.

169. SPECIAL METHODS. — There are, however, some special precautions to be observed in forming the judgment, especially in the case of the youngest children, and by reason also of the diversity of natures.

The judgment of the child is often timid, and it must be fortified. It is sometimes rash, and it must be checked and taught discretion. It is easy for it to be inaccurate, and it must be disciplined.

170. LIBERTY OF JUDGMENT. — At first the child seems more disposed to accept with docility all that is taught him, than to manifest judgments of his own. Just as he has learned to speak by accurately repeating the words which he has gathered from the lips of his mother, he at first learns to think by repeating the thoughts of others. To remedy this inactivity of the mind, much dependence must be placed on nature and on progress in age. When he has passively acquired a certain amount of knowledge, the child will of himself come to compare his ideas and to grasp new relations between them. The duty of the teacher will consist chiefly in promoting in the child this natural tendency, in aiding him by presenting subjects for reflection adapted to his tastes, and in suggesting to him easy thoughts, through the comparison of similar objects or through the contrast of different objects.

But if it is desirable that the teacher know how to stimulate minds, it is above all necessary that he shun whatever may oppose and restrain their natural expansion. We are but too often responsible for the servility of mind which we condemn in our children. Hardly have they ventured an inaccurate judgment when we protest, grow angry, and humiliate them by remonstrances too harsh and too strong; in a word, we discourage them, and for not having been indulgent enough to their first attempts, we disqualify them for thinking, or at least rob them of the desire to express their thoughts. Coldly greeted when they have attempted to make themselves understood, they will no longer dare to open their mouths; ever after they will remain shy; they will be inert and passive, like children who no longer venture to walk, if scolded too severely when they make their first false step.

It is necessary, then, to fortify by constant stimulation the child's liberty of judgment, and to be careful not to discourage it when it goes astray, by ridicule or reprimands.

171. DISCRETION IN JUDGMENT. — But no sooner have we succeeded in training the personal judgment of the child than we must be on our guard against striking another rock, — the misuse of judgment, or rashness in judgment. It is always thus in education; the most precious qualities are no sooner developed than they are liable, if not watched, to engender grave faults. When a child has once been taught with great difficulty to speak, a new anxiety is imposed on the instructor, — that of teaching him to keep silent. And so, when we have attained the important end of sharpening the intelligence of the child, we must be on our guard lest it take too many liberties, lest it venture upon rash judgments, lest it become quizzing and loquacious. And then there must be a change in method; we must pursue a course almost the reverse of the one we have just recommended, and mildly check the free movement which we had provoked. The educating art, like military tactics, consists of marches

and countermarches, vigorous forward movements followed by prudent retreats.

"A perplexing problem in the training of children," says Mr. Sully, "is to draw the line between excessive individual independence and undue deference to authority."[1]

The difficult thing is not to cut short the rashness of the child's judgment; we can without difficulty make him blush at his presumption. The difficulty is in convincing him of his error, without throwing him into a confusion which would paralyze his courage.

Even when he deceives himself the most grossly, let him develop his little thought, and try to comprehend it. And then do not be content with barely telling him that he is mistaken, but show him by apt and clear explanations in what respect and in what way he has been deceived; lay before him the causes of his error; make him understand that there are things which transcend his judgment, and that even in those of which he can judge he ought not to do so until after having carefully reflected. Finally, while leading him back to the truth upon the particular point of his mistake, guard him against falling into similar errors upon other points, through the fact of his thoughtlessness and lack of reflection.

172. ACCURACY OF JUDGMENT. — In putting the child on his guard against his disposition to form judgments on matters of which he is ignorant, or of forming hasty judgments on things which he knows, much has already been done to assure the accuracy of his judgment. In fact, the cause of inaccurate judgments is most often either ignorance, or thoughtlessness and precipitation. Hold the judgment of the child upon the things he knows well, and he will

---

[1] Sully, *op. cit.*, p. 443.

hardly ever be deceived. Be sure that he is attentive, and you will thus diminish the chances of error.

"The true rule for forming correct judgments," said Bossuet, "is to judge only when we see clearly; and the means of doing this is to judge with great attention."

Another way of forming the personal judgment of the child is to begin by giving him a good comprehension of the judgments of others; but only good models should be set before him.

But here, as everywhere, we must rely upon the power of example. Present to the pupil only judgments which are trustworthy, and which have been rigorously tested. The terms in which they are expressed should be clearly explained to him; he should be obliged to consider the meaning of whatever he studies; and in this way he will come insensibly to give exactness to his own personal judgments.

173. JUDGMENT AND ABSTRACTION. — A judgment is a mental construction, and, like every construction, it presupposes materials. The materials of judgments are ideas, either particular ideas which simple perception accumulates, or abstract and general ideas which the mind elaborates. Just as the perfection of a construction depends in part on the quality of the materials which are employed in it, so the accuracy of a judgment is determined by the clearness and precision of the ideas which serve to form it.

Let us, then, examine by what means the educator may assure the normal and rapid development of the faculties of abstraction and generalization.

174. ABSTRACTION AND GENERALIZATION. — We do not separate abstraction and generalization. An abstract idea is in fact at the same time a general idea, — the idea of a quality common to several individuals, or the idea of a

group of individuals which resemble one another by one or several common qualities, — for example, the idea of *reason*, or the idea of *man*. We do not generalize save as we abstract, and *vice versa*. The child considers apart a quality which in reality is united to other qualities. This abstraction results either from an unconscious analysis or from an attentive and reflective analysis. He then finds this same quality in other objects ; and hence he is led to grasp in one simple and same mental glance, either that general quality in itself, or the persons or the things which possess it. But this is an incomplete description of the mental operations of the child ; it is necessary to give a nearer and more precise view of what takes place.

175. FORMATION OF GENERAL AND ABSTRACT IDEAS. — Language certainly plays an important part in the formation of general ideas. This is not saying that it is necessary to coincide entirely with the absolute opinion of philosophers who assert that without the aid of words the child would be unable to grasp the relations of things ; but to say the least, words are necessary for fixing and defining abstract ideas, and for permitting the facile and rapid use of them.

The child first learns a word which has been pronounced in his hearing and which designates an individual and determinate object, — the word *papa*, for example. Thereafter he will apply this term to his father, and also to other persons.

Let a gentleman of about the same height, with a strong voice and with similar clothes, present himself to him, and he will also address him by the name *papa*. The word was individual, but he makes it general ; he employs it not to designate a person, but to express a class.[1] There is, then,

---

[1] M. Janet justly remarks that the child generalizes the word *papa* more readily than the word *mamma*.

in the child an instinctive tendency to generalize, to seize the resemblances of things.

Of course, if the child generalizes the individual words that we suggest to him, he also generalizes, and for a better reason, general terms. If he hears the term white applied to the paper which he sees, he will perhaps individualize this abstract term for a while, and in his mind whiteness will be applied at first only to paper, — it will be exclusively the whiteness of paper; but the child will soon come to employ the same word to express the whiteness of all other white objects.

176. GENERAL IDEAS BEFORE LANGUAGE. — Words are thus the essential agents in the work of generalization, which takes place very early in the mind of the child; but careful observation proves that the child is capable of generalizing even before he has learned to speak.

It could not be otherwise, since animals themselves have the rudiments of general ideas. Dogs, for example, clearly distinguish beggars, at whom they must bark, from all those who are not beggars, and who must be allowed to enter. So the infant exhibits a preference for young and pretty faces, and thus outlines a process of generalization. M. Pérez mentions the case of a child eight months old, that had for a favorite toy a tin box provided with an opening into which he stuffed whatever would enter it. The moment any object whatever was given this child, he would turn it over in all directions to find an opening in it; "he thus had the general idea of that property of opening and capacity which he had perceived in several objects, and which he sought for in all." [1]

177. THE CHILD'S TENDENCY TO GENERALIZE. — How-

---

[1] M. Pérez, *Psychologie de l'enfant*, 2d ed., p. 234.

ever, it is when the child has learned to speak that his instinct
to generalize becomes particularly manifest. As we have said,
he has a marked tendency, by reason of the vivacity of his
memory, to seize resemblances, and even, by the aid of his
imagination, to invent them. He generalizes in defiance of
every rule, of every established classification. He constructs new classifications, sometimes very original, based on
superficial analogies and far-fetched, vague resemblances.

On this point the observers of children cite a great number
of examples. An English child who had learned the meaning of the word *quack* (duck), employed the word indifferently
to designate water, all sorts of birds, insects, and liquids,
and even coins, because on a French piece of money he had
noticed an eagle. These indiscriminating and misleading
generalizations are no doubt due, in the first place, to the
poverty of the child's vocabulary. The child is like a man
who, not having many dishes, eats all parts of his repast
from the same plate; likewise he forces several meanings
into one single word. It is thus that the Romans called
elephants *oxen* of Lucania. But they are not merely reasons
of economy that govern the child. If he transfers words
from one meaning to another, it is because he has a marvelous aptitude for discovering among things resemblances
which escape even the perspicacity of the mature man.

"A little girl two and a half years old had on her neck a
consecrated medal. She had been told, 'It is the good God.' One
day, seated on her uncle's knee, she took his eye-glass and said, 'It
is my uncle's good God.' A little boy a year old had traveled
several times on a railroad. The engine with its whistling
and smoke had struck his attention. The first word he had
pronounced was *fafer* (chemin de fer); and after that a
steamboat, a coffee-pot, — all objects that hiss, make a racket,
throw out smoke, — were for him *fafers*."[1]

[1] M. Taine, *De l'Intelligence*, Tom. II.

**178. WHAT ARE WE TO THINK OF THE CHILD'S REPUG-
NANCE FOR ABSTRACTION?** — The first pedagogical conclusion
that can properly be drawn from these facts is that the repugnance of the child for generalization and abstraction is only
apparent. What he does not like is abstractions which he
cannot resolve, which are presented to him too early or
imposed on him without preparation, — abstractions which
he does not comprehend, because he has not conceived them
himself by a spontaneous effort of his own mind. Put him
in the presence of things, bring together before him objects
of the same kind, and his instinct to generalize will readily
find free scope. In order to teach him general terms, wait
till he has collected experiences enough, and has had under
his eyes concrete examples enough to comprehend with
exactness their meaning. Particularly do not require him
all at once to make abstractions and generalizations in the
domain of moral ideas. Direct this reflection towards sensible things, the only ones which are as yet accessible to
his intelligence.

179. ABUSE OF ABSTRACTION IN TEACHING. — For a long
time there has been an abuse of abstraction in teaching;
for example, in grammar, when definitions and rules have
been made to precede examples, and when in general the
child was harassed by a multitude of general terms which he
does not comprehend, or which he only partially comprehends. The following is a logical order, perhaps; but it
was going counter to the order of nature. This vicious
method is now discountenanced. Mr. Bain remarks that it
is now a rule universally recognized, that in order to reach
a general or abstract idea, the essential preparation is a
knowledge of the particular facts.

180. IMPORTANCE OF GENERAL OR ABSTRACT IDEAS. — In

order to react against the abuse of abstraction, it is not
necessary to banish it from the school, or even to postpone
it.   If abstract ideas are the most difficult of all to acquire,
they are at the same time the most important.   Particular
intuitions have no value save on one condition, that they
gradually lead the mind up to the general ideas which govern
and include them.   Do not let us tarry too long in the education of the senses, which should really be but an introduction to abstract thought.   It would amount to nothing to
make a multitude of particular objects pass before the eyes
of the child, if at the same time he were not made to form
the habit of generalization.

181.   DIFFICULTIES OF ABSTRACTION. — That which makes
the process of abstraction complicated and difficult for the
child is that generalization admits of different degrees.   If
it were a question merely of the first general notions, — those
which issue spontaneously, so to speak, from the comparison
of objects which are sensible and familiar to the child, — his
instinct, as we have said, would suffice of itself to lead him
there.   But these generalizations, compared one with another, give rise to new generalizations, higher and more
abstract.   As a rule, we are not careful enough to make the
mind ascend these different steps one after another; we
neglect the intermediate steps, and plunge the child too
quickly into the highest abstractions.

The difficulty is aggravated by reason of the impossibility,
in respect of a great number of abstract ideas, of presenting
to the eyes of the child the particular objects whose relations
they express.   How many general ideas there are which can
be communicated to the child only through words!   And he
has great difficulty in understanding these words, because
they surpass the range of his imagination.   Now, there is no
lesson, however elementary it may be, either in grammar,

in geography, in history, or in arithmetic, that does not require the use of a great number of those abstract terms, for which the child has made no corresponding intuitive preparation.

In a word, if the first steps in the field of generalization and abstraction are easy; if the child takes pleasure in classifying and grouping in the domain of material objects; progress is difficult, and there is required a real intellectual effort to rise to higher conceptions, to succeed in handling abstractions themselves, and to detach them from every association with particular objects and sensible realities.

182. PEDAGOGICAL RULES. — 1. The first rule, as we have said, is that abstraction should always be preceded by corresponding intuitions. It is necessary to follow the methods which English teachers recommend under the title of methods of *juxtaposition* and of the *accumulation of examples*, — methods which consist in collecting objects; in placing them in symmetrical juxtaposition, in order the better to bring out the resemblances; in multiplying examples, and in choosing them in such a way that the interest is not directed to their particular characteristics and that the attention is made to bear upon their relations.

Mr. Bain dwells on the choice of examples in these terms:

"The number and the character of objects," he says, "must also be taken into account. They may be too few, or they may be too many; they may even have the effect of obstructing the growth of the general idea.

"The selection must be such as to show all the extreme varieties. Identical instances are not to be accumulated; they merely burden the mind. Varying instances are necessary to show the quality under every combination. To bring home the abstract property of soundness, or the circle, we must present concrete examples in varying size, color, material, situation, and circumstances. To explain a building we must cite instances of buildings for all kinds of uses." [1]

Mr. Bain is wrong in giving the first place to extreme varieties. It is better to present to the child, for each class of objects, average specimens in which the characteristics common to the whole class appear in some relief, and are not obscured by particulars that are too striking. In other words, it is necessary to aid the child's effort at generalization, by assisting his mind in making an easy transition from one object to another. Extreme varieties, separated by too wide an interval, would certainly hinder the perception of resemblances; they should be the last presentations made.

As to the number of examples, it varies in different cases. Mr. Bain remarks that for certain notions, as that of a simple quality, — weight, for example, — one or two examples are sufficient, while it is necessary to collect a large number to give an exact idea of large classes of objects, such as houses, plants, etc.

2. A second rule consists in graduating the generalizations.[2] It is necessary that the child, when presented with an abstract idea of the first grade, should be able to indicate the individuals which compose it; but it is also necessary, when he rises to a generalization of a higher degree, that he should be able to decompose it by giving an account of the simpler, more elementary ideas which serve to support it. An aggregate of abstract ideas is like a vast machine whose parts work into each other. In order that the machine work, it is of the first importance that no part be wanting, and that all the intermediate parts be in their place.

3. Finally, it is necessary to guard the use of words, to

---

[1] *Education as a Science*, p. 193.

[2] See the article *Abstraction*, by M. Buisson, in the *Dictionnaire de Pédagogie*.

define with exactness all the terms which we employ in the instruction of the child. The pupil is only too much inclined to be content with a vague and confused notion of general terms. This natural indolence should be corrected; the pupil should be enlightened by exact definitions; and he should be required to give proof of his understanding, either by employing synonymous expressions or by giving particular examples included under the abstraction which has been defined.

183. REASONING. — The process of abstraction, of generalization proper, which has to do with ideas and conceptions, is one thing; and reasoning, which associates and combines judgments, is quite another. It is not required to recall in this place what the psychologists teach us of the nature of this operation and of its two different forms, induction and deduction.[1] Nor have we to dwell on the rules which logic prescribes for reasoning. Our object is simply to show how education develops and cultivates the child's power of reasoning.

184. IMPORTANCE OF REASONING. — It is easy to comprehend the importance of this intellectual operation. Without reasoning, knowledge would be restricted to the narrow circle of the immediate intuitions of the reason and of the direct perceptions of experience; the human intelligence would be prohibited from passing beyond the limited horizon of the senses and of consciousness, and of conceiving the general laws which constitute science, and by means of which the mind embraces the entire universe.

On the other hand, we must not forget that reasoning may be abused; that too much logic misleads and deceives

---

[1] See our article *Raisonnement* in the *Dictionnaire de Pédagogie.*

us; and finally, that what Molière said of the house of
the *Femmes Savantes* may as truly be said of the mind:

"How reasoning banishes reason from it!"

185. REASONING IN THE CHILD. — Locke is of the opinion
that the child is capable of reasoning, and that he listens to
reason as soon as he can speak.

Condillac, a disciple of Locke in philosophy, is inspired by
the same pedagogical doctrine.

"It has been proved," he says, "that the faculty of reasoning begins as soon as our senses begin to develop, and that we
have an early use of our senses only because we have an early
use of our reason. . . . The faculties of the understanding are
the same in a child as in a grown man. . . . We see that
children begin early to grasp the analogies of language. If they
are sometimes deceived in this, it is none the less true that
they have reasoned."

And Condillac goes so far as to compare this instinctive
initiation of the child into his native language with the
reasoning of Newton, discovering by a series of inductions
and deductions the system of the world!

Our reply to Condillac and Locke is that they have both
failed to recognize the general and abstract element in
reasoning, and that they confound the highest forms of the
highest intellectual operation with its lower forms, with
the thoughtless inferences which may be observed even in
animals.

Doubtless there is a sense in which the child reasons; but
he does this almost without knowing it, almost unconsciously. Moreover, his reasoning bears only on the particular and sensible objects which he perceives every day.
Do not require him to reason on abstract ideas. When he
grasps the analogies of language he obeys an instinctive
logic. The child of three or four years will persist in say-

ing *à le cheval, à le jardin*, because he has heard people say *à la vache, à la promenade;* he will reduce the number of conjugations and say *batter* instead of *battre,* because he has learned that most verbs are conjugated like *aimer.*

Gradually, however, the child becomes capable of real reasoning, that which implies attention, mental effort, and the conscious concatenation of judgment and ideas ; and this process of reasoning appears rather early in children well endowed.

186. EDUCATION OF THE REASON. — For the reason, as for the judgment, there is not, properly speaking, any special training ; but in whatever he teaches the child, — grammar, history, the sciences, etc., — the teacher may habituate the child to reason, and ought to do so.

"There is no subject of study which may not in the hands of an intelligent and efficient teacher be made helpful to this result. Thus the study of physical geography should be made the occasion for exercising the child in reasoning as to the causes of natural phenomena. History, again, when well taught may be made to bring out the learner's powers of tracing analogies, finding reasons for events (*e. g.,* motives for actions), and balancing considerations so as to decide what is probable, wise, or just in given circumstances." [1]

However, the teaching of the sciences remains the grand instrument for the education of the reason. In fact, the sciences are but aggregates of general knowledges, rigorously based on exact deductions and orderly inductions, presented in a methodical and logical order, and expressed with precision. There could not be a better school for the faculties of reflection. In studying the physical sciences the student accustoms himself to generalize and to make inductions with caution, and in striving to comprehend the

---

[1] Sully, *op. cit.,* p. 445.

demonstrations of the mathematical sciences he learns to make rigorous deductions.

187. PARTICULAR TENDENCY TOWARDS INDUCTION. — The child is more inclined to induction than to deduction ; just as, when he alters the meaning· of words, he generalizes them in their signification, rather than specializes them. It is easy to understand, in fact, that the mind at the first prefers to rise from the particular to the general, rather than to descend from the general to the particular. The thoughts of the child are almost all individual ; he has at his command only a small stock of general knowledge. Now all deduction supposes general principles, universal truths. From this fact there follows this pedagogical conclusion, that the inductive sciences are best adapted to the first years of instruction. Educators are in error who, like Diderot, would begin with mathematics.

188. MODERATION RECOMMENDED. — "Reasoning with children," says Rousseau, "was the great maxim of Locke, and it is the one chiefly in vogue to-day. . . . . For myself, I see nothing more silly than those children with whom one has reasoned so much." Rousseau would have a child remain a child.

No doubt we should distrust precocious reasoners ; but this should not make us fall into the opposite error, which Rousseau was wrong in recommending, through his desire to retard beyond measure the development of the reasoning faculties. Locke was wiser when he wrote :

" I think I may say there is not so much pleasure to have a Child prattle agreeably as to reason well. Encourage, therefore, his inquisitiveness all you can, by satisfying his demands and informing his judgment, as far as it is capable. When his reasons are anyway tolerable, let him find the credit and commendation of it. And when they are quite out of the way, let him, without being laughed at for his mistake, be gently put into the right; and if he shows a forwardness to be reasoning about things that come his way, take care, as much as can, that nobody check this inclination in him, or mislead it by captious or fallacious ways of talking with him. For when all is done, this, as the highest and most important faculty of our minds, deserves the greatest care and attention in cultivating it. The right improvement and exercise of our reason being the highest perfection that a man can attain to in this life." [1]

189. SPECIAL EXERCISES IN REASONING : DEDUCTION AND THE SYLLOGISM. — Though the training of the reason is for the most part the natural result of the studies pursued and of the manner in which they are taught, it is not without use to propose to the child some special exercises in reasoning.

In ordinary discourse the reasonings are rarely expressed under the perfect form of a syllogistic argument. Consequently it is very useful to drill pupils in discovering, in carefully chosen examples, the different elements of the syllogism, as the conclusion, when only the premises are stated, or that one of the premises which, in the rapidity of the argument, has been left understood. By this means the pupil will acquire the habit of disentangling the error in the reasonings, often uncertain and ambiguous, of which the discourses of men are composed. Without needing to resort to the learned rules for deduction, but simply from having reconstructed the syllogism in its three propositions, an attentive mind will easily discover whatever of the false or the equivocal has slipped into the reasoning.

First, here are examples of arguments in which the pupil will have to supply one of the fundamental propositions which are necessary to assure their validity.

---

[1] Locke, *op. cit.*, § 122.

190. To Find the Premise which is Lacking in the Following Reasonings: — There is anger that is not blameworthy. What other premise do you need to infer that certain passions are not blameworthy?

Suppose a man says, " I detest foreigners." Find another premise, which joined with this assertion authorizes the conclusion, " No foreigner deserves to be loved."

Solon ought to be considered a wise legislator, because he adapted his laws to the character of the Athenians.

A slave is a man : he ought not, then, to be a slave.

Rousseau was a man too ardent not to commit many errors.

The eruptions of volcanos and earthquakes cannot be considered as warnings sent by God to the wicked, since these scourges overtake both the innocent and the guilty.

191. To Find the Conclusion Involved in the Following Assertions : — I know that A, B, and C are blockheads, and at the same time educated men : have I the right to draw any conclusion from this?

No science can be absolutely perfect, and yet all the sciences deserve to be cultivated.

Prejudices indicate a weak mind, and we sometimes meet with prejudices in men who are very well educated.

192. To Reduce the Following Arguments to the Syllogistic Form: — Poetry is not a science. The essential characteristics of a science are truth and generality ; and poetry has neither.

No war is for a long time popular, because war always brings an increase of taxes, and whatever is prejudicial to our interests enjoys but a passing popularity.

Of two evils we must chose the least : so a temporary revolution being a smaller evil than a permanent despotism, should be preferred to it.

In the examples which we have just proposed, the effort of the pupil should be directed to three points : 1. To set forth the conclusion with clearness, — that is, the thing to be proved, in such a way as to distinguish in a proposition the *major term* from the *minor term;* 2. To discover the *middle term* of the argument, of which there should be only one in every conclusive syllogism ; 3. To determine with exactness the two premises, one of which connects the major term with the middle term, and the other the minor term with the middle term.

The syllogism once reconstructed, natural good sense usually suffices to determine the value and legitimacy of the argument. If there remains any doubt, it would become necessary to apply the rules of logic to the suspected syllogism ; and if it violates none of these rules, it is legitimate and conclusive.

193. INDUCTIVE REASONING. — In order to make pupils clearly understand the mechanism of inductive reasoning, their attention must be called to the three essential points in every induction : 1. The *conclusion*, which ought to be a *proposition*, an affirmation proving that two facts agree or do not agree ; 2. The character of *generality* in this proposition, which should be applicable to all the cases of a given order ; 3. The *method* employed in order to arrive at this general proposition, a method which is an appeal to observation and to facts.

An exact idea of the general propositions which are the result of every legitimate induction will be gained by taking examples in the different sciences.

The magnet attracts iron (physics).

Bodies fall in a vacuum (physics).

Bodies expand under the influence of heat (physics).

The simplest substances are those which manifest the strongest affinities (chemistry).

Compounds are more fusible than elements (chemistry).

The temperature of boiling water destroys animal life (physiology).

The red corpuscles of the blood are charged with carrying oxygen to the tissues (physiology).

Feeling is always united to the will and to the intelligence (psychology).

Fear enfeebles the faculties (psychology).

The more vivid the consciousness, the more tenacious the memory (psychology).

The development of the brain corresponds to the development of the muscles, and in general of all the organs (zoölogy).

CHAPTER IX.

CULTURE OF THE FEELINGS.

194. MORAL EDUCATION. — Intellectual education is surely the best of preparations for moral education. Whatever is done for developing the intelligence is far from being lost, so far as the culture of the sentiments, of the moral consciousness, and of the will is concerned. In a well-organized intelligence, all whose faculties have received the education appropriate to their destination, the moral qualities of the character germinate spontaneously. The man merely instructed is sometimes a bad man; but we doubt whether the same thing is true of a man well educated intellectually. A tempered imagination, a powerful attention, and a sound judgment, are reliable barriers which vouch for the ardor of the passions and prevent the errors of conduct.

It is none the less true that intellectual education is not sufficient, but that the other faculties also demand a special culture. The man of feeling has no less value than the man of intellect. We are not destined merely to know and comprehend, but are also made to feel and love. Moral education is, then, to be distinguished from intellectual education, and its first purpose ought to be the culture of the feelings.

195. COMPLEX NATURE OF THE FEELINGS. — Nothing so various, nothing so complex, as the psychological facts

which philosophers connect with the feelings. It is specially here, in the presence of these phenomena so diverse, which are the elements of all the virtues and all the vices of humanity, — in the presence of the manifestations of what is humblest, grossest, and also most elevated and ideal in the human soul, — it is here that it is meet to summon before us, in order to reconcile them, the extreme opinions of those who say with Rousseau that everything is good in man, and with Hegel that everything is bad.

The feelings are the common source whence the most degrading passions and the most elevated sentiments borrow their aliment. It is to them that are beholden at the same time, the sensualist who forgets himself in bodily pleasures, the selfish man who is absorbed in the pursuit of personal good, the bad man who sacrifices everything to his vindictive spirit, the man devoted and good, who has no pleasure but in making others happy, the friend, the patriot, the philanthropist, who deny themselves in order to serve the objects of their pious affection.

From this very diversity of the phenomena of the feelings, it follows that the function of education is twofold. On the one hand it must temper or even repress dangerous inclinations and bad passions, and on the other stimulate and develop the beautiful and noble elements in our emotional nature.

196. DIVISION OF THE INCLINATIONS. — The most of psychologists agree in distributing the inclinations or emotions into three classes :

1. The personal or individual inclinations, which have for their object the *me* and whatever is directly connected with it : such are the pleasures of self-love and of ambition. They are all included under one term, — selfishness.

2. The sympathetic or benevolent inclinations which

attach us to others, and for which the positivist school has invented the barbarous term *altruism:* such are the affections in general, as patriotism and love of humanity.

3. The higher inclinations, whose object is abstract ideas, as the love of the true, the beautiful, and the good.

Among these different manifestations of the feelings, the last form a class wholly distinct, — they pertain to what is highest in human nature, to ethics, to science, to art. We shall study them by themselves. At present we shall examine in their natural development and pedagogical treatment only the selfish and the benevolent inclinations. And at the first we shall throw into strong relief the inclinations which properly constitute the benevolent feelings, — love for others, in one word, the heart, through which, as the Père Girard has said, "man is all that he is."

197. THE EDUCATION OF THE HEART TOO OFTEN NEGLECTED. — For a long time the psychologists have given the feelings their proper rank in the list of the human faculties; but it seems that they have found it difficult to make themselves understood by teachers. In fact, open most of the works on pedagogy, and you will find that the chapter on the heart is generally omitted. And on this point the practice conforms only too closely to the theory. How many schools there are in which no effort is made to cultivate the emotions, the sympathetic sentiments, — all which makes men good, sociable, loving, and devoted!

Even more, it has occurred to certain writers to mention this omission as a merit in educators who should deem such a compliment a reproach. This quotation from M. Guizot is an example:

"The almost absolute silence which Montaigne has maintained on that part of education which pertains to forming the heart of the pupil, seems to me a new proof of his good judgment." [1]

198. Necessity of this Education. — We cannot assent to such an assertion; and it seems to us that the heart has as good a right as the mind to a special training.

And first, do we need to prove that the heart is worth at least as much as the mind, and that the feelings deserve the care of the educator? Is it not evident that duty itself ought the most often to be placed under the keeping of emotion? There is no virtue really secure, save that which is founded on the love of virtue. "He alone is virtuous," said Aristotle, "who finds pleasure in being so." No doubt we should distrust men who, like Rousseau, look only in their hearts for the principles of their conduct. The heart should be governed by reason, and an ardent sensibility may be allied with the strangest freaks of judgment and conduct. But let us also distrust characters that are unfeeling, too rational, which are moved only by cold reflection. They will make more mistakes than we think, unless sentiment comes to their relief.

Moreover, there are several of our affections which form an integral part of our duties. To love one's family, one's friends, one's country, is not only the source of the most delicate pleasures and the sweetest joys of life, but is also the first duty of a virtuous man.

199. Particular Difficulties in the Education of the Sentiments. — One of the reasons why educators are generally silent upon the nature of the heart, is probably the particular difficulty of this part of education.

---

[1] *Méditations et Études morales*, p. 404.

We cannot give lessons in sensibility as we give lessons in reading or arithmetic. " Affection," says Miss Edgeworth, " is not learned by heart." The teacher holds in his hands the means of exciting the intellectual powers of the child; he places objects before his eyes, communicates knowledge to him through language, and in a manner acts directly upon the faculties of the soul; but he has not the same power over the sentiments. We cannot command a child to be moved, as we require him to be attentive.

Besides, the great diversity which nature puts into human feelings complicates the problem still more. The heart, much more than the mind, is a natural endowment. Common opinion, and it is not wholly false, declares that we are born tender or unfeeling, affectionate or cold. Education seems powerless to warm up certain souls, to endow them with the life of the affections.

Notwithstanding these difficulties, there is an art of cultivating the feelings; and this art consists chiefly in placing the soul of the child in circumstances that are the most favorable for the complete development of his natural disposition.

200. DEVELOPMENT OF SYMPATHY IN THE CHILD. — Originally, the child is but a bundle of selfishness; and it is from this selfishness that there is gradually disengaged sympathy, the faculty of loving.

Very early the child evinces sympathy or antipathy, not only in respect of persons and animals, but also of inanimate things.

His toys, his wooden horses, his rubber cats, inspire him with the tenderest affection; and, on the other hand, he sincerely hates whatever hurts him or wearies him. " The switch and the wash-rag," says M. Pérez, " are to him personal enemies."

It is easy to prove that the earliest sympathies of the child are bestowed only on the persons who have given him a personal pleasure. A babe of six months will as yet bestow a smile only on its nurse and its attendant, — on its nurse, because she recalls to it the pleasing impressions of nourishment; and on its attendant, because she soothes and caresses it.

Habit and familiarity also play an important part in the development of the nascent affections, in the education of a sensibility that takes fright at whatever is new and unknown.

Later, when to the pleasures of taste and touch there are added those of sight and hearing, the sympathy provoked by these new sensations, agreeable or disagreeable, is extended to sonorous or colored objects, to animals, for example, which, by the grace of their movements or the vivacity of their cries, give to the sight or the hearing of the child the occasion of agreeable excitement.

In a word, sympathy follows step by step the successive manifestations of the pleasures of sense.

201. GENERAL CHARACTERISTICS OF INFANT SENSIBILITY. — The sensibility of the child has the same limits as his intelligence. The child bestows his thought only on actual things; his memory goes back hardly beyond the moment that has just passed; he cannot extend his inductions into the future. And so his pleasures and his pains are restricted, so to speak, to the present hour.

Hence at once the vivacity and the fugitive brevity of the child's emotions. His sensuous life is made up of momentary passions, sudden tears and smiles, violent pains, unexpected caresses, — in a word, of emotions that are as ardent as they are transient. We can see, in fact, that, being determined solely by the presence of objects, the feelings of the child are quickly excited, but, on the other hand, they extend no deep roots, they remain on the surface, and are not fixed in the soul. The child is in ecstasies over a trifle; with the spring of his young and supple powers he gives himself up to his joys and his sorrows. He bursts out in laughter, or he sheds floods of tears. He stamps with impatience and anger. But all this fire is quenched as soon as lighted. The moment the object is withdrawn or disappears, there is hardly a trace of the feeling left in him. As yet there is not enough power of thought in the mind of the child to retain and perpetuate the emotion. "As soon as new objects and new impressions present themselves to him," says Mr. Sully, "the current of passion subsides."

202. ABUSE OF THE FEELINGS IN EDUCATION. — There are educators whose favorite maxim is, "Always reason with children;" but there are others who are not less deceived when they say, "Always appeal to their feelings."

Education does not admit of any exclusive mobile,[1] and the emotions less than any other.

---

[1] The distinction between *motives* and *mobiles*, first made by Jouffroy, is worth preserving. The state of mind that precedes an act always contains two elements, an *intellectual* and an *emotional*; and usually these elements are inversely proportional. Now when the stimulus to action is mainly intellectual, it is called by Jouffroy a *motive*; but when it is mainly emotional, he calls it a *mobile*. In the conduct of men of the highest type, motives predominate; but brutes are governed wholly, and savages mainly, by mobiles. "Motives are the intellectual reasons which cause us to act in such or such a manner, such as thoughts and considerations of the mind. Mobiles, on the contrary, are the movements of the heart, the affections, the passions. For example, maternal love is a mobile, but the calculations of interest and the considerations of dignity are motives." — MARION, *Leçons de Psychologie*, p. 127. (P.)

Were sensibility perfectly developed in the child, there would be danger in confiding in it exclusively. But the child's sensibility is small and limited, and when we count on its inspiration to govern his conduct, we often place our reliance upon a nothing.

203. FALSE APPEARANCES OF INFANT SENSIBILITY. — In reality, the child is less sensitive than he seems. Deceived by appearances, we often attribute to him emotions which he does not feel.

" The actions of children continually deceive us by their exterior resemblance to ours, and we as often go astray in trying to find in them, in order to govern them, mobiles similar to those of which we ourselves are conscious. Louise, in some passing transport, leaves her play, throws her arms about my neck, and cannot leave off embracing me; it seems that all my mother's heart could not suffice to respond to the warmth of her caresses; but she leaves me, and with the same playful movement goes to kiss her doll or the arm of the chair that she meets on her way." [1]

There is an evident disproportion between the exterior manifestations of the child, his gestures, his motions, which attest the superabundance of life in his young body, and the real measure of the emotions which he experiences. Because the child is prone to cry, do not let us proceed, on false appearances, to ascribe to him a strength of emotion similar to our own. It is ridiculous to correct a child by saying to him, as Rousseau would after a fault has been committed, " My child, you have done me a wrong !" Either the child will not comprehend you, and your admonition will leave him indifferent, or he will appear affected, but will be so only upon the

---

[1] Madame Guizot, *Lettres de famille sur l'éducation,* I., p. 6.

surface; and in trying to excite a premature emotion you will have obtained only an affectation, a pretence of affection.

"When the Duchess of Orleans was ill," says Miss Edgeworth, "the children were instructed to write 'charming notes' from day to day, from hour to hour, to inquire how she did. Once, when a servant was going from Saint Leu to Paris, Madame de Silleri asked her pupils if they had any commissions. The little Duc de Chartres said, 'Yes'; and he gave a message about a bird-cage, but he did not recollect to write to his mother, till somebody whispered to him that he had forgotten it." [1]

Then let us take children for what they are, selfish little creatures, in whom the affectionate emotions grow but slowly, and without ever effacing the inclinations of personal interest.

204. GENERAL RULES FOR THE EDUCATION OF THE FEELINGS. — The attentive study of the slow and continuous progress of the feelings, rising little by little from the grossest pleasures of the senses to the most delicate emotions of the heart, is the best refutation that can be made of the error of educators who, like Rousseau, would wait till the fifteenth year for developing the moral sentiments. We cannot too early cultivate the sensibility of the child and call into exercise, in children's friendships, in the affections of the family, a sensibility destined later to become enamored of still greater objects. On this point it is necessary to conform to nature, to instinct, and from an early age to give free course to the first emotions, to the first aspirations of the heart. The education of the feelings will at first be

---

[1] Miss Edgeworth, *op. cit.*, I., p. 368.

negative; it will be content with avoiding whatever might wound or repress the nascent feelings. But little by little it will become positive; that is to say, it will seek every occasion to excite, and at the same time to regulate, the sentiments, and to associate the child's pleasures with things that are good and beautiful.

205. RELATIONS OF EMOTION TO IDEA. — The simplest psychological analysis suffices to prove that the emotions have direct relations with ideas. The feelings are exercised only upon the objects made known by the intelligence. It is an error to suppose that the heart is impoverished in proportion as the mind is enriched. Would you have a child love his country? First teach him what his country is; relate to him the history of his ancestors; describe to him the extent of his native land. When the idea has once taken form in his mind, the emotion will follow and will spontaneously attach itself to the known object. It is not enough, however, to enlighten the intelligence; we must interest the imagination. An English philosopher has remarked that coldness of heart is frequently caused by a defective imagination.

"The story of the same accident, of the same tragical event, if told in a heartless and uninteresting manner, will leave us unmoved; but related in a manner which speaks to our imagination, it will move us to the very depths of the soul. This also explains how an accident which has happened in a city that we know, in our quarter, in our neighborhood, moves us infinitely more than if it had happened at a distance, in a foreign city, or in an unknown country."[1]

The development of the feelings is thus intimately connected with the progress of the intelligence. We have no

---

[1] M. Marion, *Leçons de Psychologie*, p. 182.

direct hold on the emotions ; we cannot evoke them at
the word of command ; but by indirect means, by appealing to reflection, by presenting to the child, either in
narratives or in real examples, situations adapted to move
him, we shall be able, by enlightening his mind, to find
the road to his heart.

The author of the *École maternelle* relates an excellent
lesson in filial affection. A little child in a *salle d'asile*
had lost his mother. On coming back from the cemetery
he had returned to school, where with the thoughtlessness of his age he talked and laughed with his companions. When the time for opening school had come,
the mistress spoke as follows :

"My children, we will not sing to-day, for to sing we must be
happy and content. Now we cannot be content because here is
a little child who is not happy. He has had the greatest misfortune that can befall a child; he has lost his mother, who loved him
so much. To-night when he goes home he will not find his dear
mother there to kiss him. You, my children, who find your mother
at home, think while kissing her how happy you are in not having lost her. Love your mother ; and to show that you love her,
never cause her any sorrow." And the mistress added, "Be
very good to Charles, who no longer has a mother to love him."[1]

206. COMMUNICATION OF FEELING. — If feeling cannot
be taught directly, there is a compensation in the fact
that it can be communicated. Sensibility is contagious.
Surround the child with affection and love, and he will
respond to this appeal. His heart will be moved if
he feels the beating of other hearts. All the faculties of
the soul have a tendency to radiate, to expand ; but this
is especially true of the emotions. If you discover coldness and insensibility in a mature man, do not condemn

---

[1] Mademoiselle Chalamet, *L'École maternelle*, p. 87.

him hastily; for the fault is probably due to his parents, his first teachers, or to his surroundings, rather than to himself. Madame de Maintenon was reason itself, but her *Solidité*, as Louis XIV. called her, was somewhat lacking in sensibility and benignity. This fault was certainly due in part to her education; her mother had kissed her but twice in her whole life, and then after a long absence.

The best means of making a child affectionate is to treat him with affection. Love is born of love. The soul opens and yields itself to the affection which is bestowed upon it. Surrounded by persons of gentle passions and benevolent dispositions, habituated to be an object of indulgence and affection, the child will naturally become gentle and affectionate. He will learn to feel the goodness whose effects he has experienced.

"Let the teacher love his pupils, and their hearts will respond to his own. Love is naturally communicative; it invites a gracious and sympathetic return. The child very well knows when he is loved; he sees it in the glances, in the words of his teacher, and when he recognizes in his teacher a patience full of affection, his heart grows tender and inevitably becomes attached to one who consecrates himself to him with such devotion. Then he runs to him with joy; in his teacher he has found a friend and a father. "It is here that I take my stand," said Pestalozzi; "I would have my children able at each moment, from morning till evening, to read on my face and to divine upon my lips that my heart is devoted to them; that their happiness and their joys are my happiness and my joys." [1]

207. RELATIONS OF EMOTION TO ACTION. — An ex-

---

[1] Gauthey, *De l'Éducation*, II., p. 8. It is not useless to note, with Madame Pape-Carpantier, that this affection of the teacher for his pupils ought to be particular, individual. "That children may love, love them. Love them, not from the heights of a lofty philan-

cellent means of cultivating the feelings is to provide occasions and procure the means for calling them into exercise. The Abbé de Saint Pierre required as school exercises acts of benevolence and justice. At least we may require of children, in their own family, acts of tenderness towards their brothers, respect for their parents, and at school, acts of good-will towards their schoolmates. By the very fact that he has been accustomed to practice a virtue, the child will acquire the feeling which ordinarily accompanies and inspires that virtue. By giving alms he will learn to love the poor; by doing others a service he will come to love humanity. But on one condition, however, — that the acts suggested to the child are suited to his nature, that they already accord with his tastes, and that they are not constrained and forced. Only then will the child find in the act accomplished a new source of pleasure, and this pleasure, once tasted, will stimulate him to repeat the act. It is a truth which deserves recognition, that we love only because we find pleasure in loving.

But care must be taken not to be satisfied with appearances. In sentiment, as in religion, it is the reality which is important, not the exterior formalities. The rich child, for example, gives money freely to the poor, when he has it; but he who lives in abundance does not know the value of money, he feels no privation from what he has done. Then accustom the child only to acts adapted to his age, whose significance he can comprehend.

In this exercise of the child's sensibility, care should be taken to have him understand the effects which his acts

---

thropy, — you will then be too far away from them; love all the children on the globe, if your soul is large enough; but love above everything else, and in particular, each one of those who are intrusted to your care. No abstract affection, but much affection in the concrete."

produce on the feelings of others. Defective sympathy often comes from the inattention of the child, who does not take into account the feelings of others. He would be more affectionate, more loving, if he knew just how much his disobedience and his faults grieved those who love him. Then make him reflect, either on the pain he caused his parents by his bad conduct or on the pleasure he has given them by his good conduct. The day the child has formed a just idea of the consequences of his conduct he will really experience the delights of sympathy and affection ; he will seek his pleasure in the pleasure of others ; he will have passed the narrow circle of selfishness.

208. THE GENERATION OF FEELINGS ONE BY ANOTHER. —If it is true that feelings are communicated from one heart to another, it is not less true that by a sort of interior generation a feeling once excited in the soul gives birth to other feelings. The different affections form as it were a chain. If the child seizes one end of it, he will easily go from one link to another, and the entire chain will pass through his hands. At first let us appeal to the simplest feelings, those which are most familiar ; let us kindle some flame in the child's heart ; we shall see this flame gradually gaining ground ; and little by little it will extend to the whole soul.

"Children who see their father and mother love each other will also love one another. In a home where affection reigns, they are bathed in it and perspire it at every pore. Before they have learned to speak, children read affection in the eyes of father and mother ; and this affection children transmit to everything that surrounds them." [1]

---

[1] Champfleury, *Les Enfants*, p. 138.

If he has begun by loving his family, be assured that the child will also love, when the time comes, his friends, his fellow-citizens, and the whole human race.

The affectionate son, the kind companion, will also be by a sort of happy fatality an ardent citizen, a patriot, a good and generous man. It is not filial affection, but family selfishness, that sometimes turns aside the citizen from loving his own country as he ought.

209. THE FEELING OF PLEASURE AND PAIN.— Pleasure is the basis of all sensibility. It is by the vivacity of the pleasure which the child is capable of feeling that his degree of sensibility will be measured. We think we love others for their own sake; but in reality we love them for the pleasure we find in loving them. When personal, selfish interests are concerned, it is still more true that the pleasure we experience is the basis and the purpose of the feeling.

In one sense, it might be asserted that the education of the feelings wholly consists either in developing or in regulating the child's feeling of pleasure.

But there is pleasure and pleasure. By the side of the gross enjoyments of the senses there are the pure emotions of the heart. Through the development of the intelligence, education will at last succeed in making the higher pleasures more and more predominate over the attractions of material enjoyment. To put the book in place of the wine-cup, *to replace sensation by idea*, — such, according to Condorcet, is the fundamental problem of popular education; or if not by *idea*, at least by sentiment. Between the life of sensation and the intellectual life there is an intermediary more accessible to the multitude; this is the life of the sentiments, of the emotions of the heart, of family and social affections, of the sacred joys of patriotism.

It is, however, a question whether education should have

a tendency to increase the child's aptitude to feel pleasure and pain vividly, of whatever nature they may be.

According to Kant, the culture of the feelings of pleasure or of pain should be purely negative. The case of a child who takes pleasure in nothing is wholly exceptional. The feeling of pleasure is too much in conformity with nature to make it necessary to excite it. There should be only precautions to be taken against a tendency naturally so powerful.

"There is no need," says the German philosopher, "to mollify the feelings. The propensity for pleasure is more vexatious to men than all the evils of life." [1]

Surely there is nothing good to be expected from soft and effeminate natures which can act only under the impulse of pleasure. We do not believe, with Fénelon, that everything is to be done in education with an eye to pleasure-giving, and that the teacher's ideal is to have "a cheerful face" and to provide "cheerful conversation." Without believing that pain is inseparable from effort, — for there are efforts that are joyous, in which the display of activity redoubles pleasure, — we grant that effort is sometimes painful, afflictive. Now effort is the condition of progress, the instrument of education.

"Let us fight against soft impressibleness in children; but let us not forget, on the other hand, that insensibility is the worst of all faults. What can be expected of those dullish children whom nothing moves, who can neither laugh, nor even smile, whom pleasure does not excite? On the contrary, everything is to be expected of children who are inclined to joyousness, and whom pleasure inspires, but on the condition that we know how to direct, little by little, towards the good, towards the objects worthy of being loved, this need of enjoyment and this ardor for pleasure."

---

[1] Kant, *op. cit.*, p. 225.

210. EXCITATION OF PERSONAL FEELINGS. — "Sentiment will develop itself unaided," says Gauthey, "when it is concerned with self-love." In fact, it seems at first sight that the selfish feelings need only a negative, repressive discipline which merely tempers their exaggeration ; and yet all who have had the management of children know that in certain cases education should assume, even with the personal feelings, its normal function, which consists in spurring, in stimulating. In fact, there are natures so languid and sleepy that education should intervene to animate them, to excite them to self-love and to ambition.

"The egoistic impulses," says Mr. Sully, "may even be deficient and require positive stimulation. There are listless and lethargic children whom it is well to try and arouse to self-assertion. In their case it may be desirable to seek to quicken the feelings of pride, ambition, and (in extreme cases) even the distinctly anti-social feeling of antagonism and delight in beating others.... Even when there is no natural deficiency in these feelings, the education has not so much to repress them as to direct them to higher objects or aspects of objects. He seeks to transform them by refining them. Thus he aims at leading the child up from the fear of physical evil to the fear of moral evil; from the enjoyments of bodily conquest to that of mental competition ; from pride in the possession of material objects to pride in the possession of intellectual qualities."[1]

211. THE PASSIONS. — To tell the truth, the study of the passions is not a pedagogical subject. In fact, the passions, which are exalted, exclusive inclinations, and which have been defined as "habits of the sensibility," imperious and violent habits, are developed only in the progress of life. His young age and his very inexperience shelter the child from those profound disturbances, those diseases of the

---

[1] Sully, *op. cit.*, p. 506.

soul. It is in ethics, not in pedagogy, that we must look for the means to cure them; just as it pertains to logic to correct the sophisms that are rooted in conventional thought.

However, if education is not directly concerned with the passions, since in general they do not exist at the school age, it ought to anticipate their appearance. From childhood, care should be taken lest the soul become a soil already prepared for the unfolding of the passions by a preference accorded to certain emotions and by the exclusive development of certain tastes. The best guaranty, for this purpose, is to develop the sensibility in all directions. It is hardly to be feared that passion will ever gain the ascendency over a soul open to all noble sentiments, which has learned to share its faculty of loving among the different objects worthy of its love.

However, there are other precautions to be taken, which M. Marion has happily summed up in these terms:

"Vigilance is better than repression and advice. The little child must be carefully guarded, and everything done that he may grow up in perfect moral health. This dispenses with untimely recriminations and useless reproaches. Sparing children the occasions for falling, watching over their conduct without allowing them to suspect our oversight, keeping from their sight bad books and bad sights, choosing the companions with whom they associate, allowing them to hear only decorous conversation, giving them only good examples, inspiring them as much as possible with a feeling of their responsibility, — in a word, fashioning and directing their moral growth in such a way that they will be healthy and strong when the hour of the passions comes, — this is the work of a well-conducted education."[1]

---

[1] M. Marion, *op. cit.*, p. 249.

CHAPTER X.

MORAL EDUCATION.

212. Moral Education Proper. — We shall not follow the example of those educators who, with respect to moral education, include in their treatises the whole theory of duty, the whole of ethics, just as they have introduced the whole of psychology into their treatment of intellectual education. Our subject is limited; it is concerned simply with the inquiry how nature of herself develops the moral faculties, and how education intervenes in its turn to train them, to hasten their unfolding, and to perfect their development. It is not the purpose here to set forth the different applications of moral power, but we have simply to inquire by what-means this power is called into being and gradually created.

213. The Moral Faculties. — The moral faculties are distinguished from the intellectual faculties in that they tend to action, and not to knowledge. These are active, not speculative faculties. The moral faculties form the character; the intellectual faculties form the mind. The former lead us to virtue; the latter to knowledge.

Moreover, there are to be distinguished in that aggregate of moral faculties commonly called the *conscience* three different series of facts :

1. The facts of the *sensibility*, not of that general sensibility of which we have already spoken, which is diffused in the

affections of every sort, but of that which attaches us to the good, which makes us love duty, which affects us in the presence of what is good.

2. The facts of the *intelligence*, the practical reason, which suggests to us the ideas of good and evil, of merit and demerit, — in a word, moral ideas.

3. The fact of the *will*, the energy which determines us to the action which we know to be good, the good-will which inclines us to virtue.

In other terms, we must at the same time love, know, and will the good. It is not enough that our enlightened intelligence permits us to distinguish what is good from what is bad. Beyond this, and above all, it is necessary that a strong will give us the means of executing the decisions of our moral judgment; and it is also necessary, in order that the moral effort may be less painful, that feeling 'come to our aid, that the imperious orders of the reason become, as often as possible, the gracious solicitations of the heart.

214. MORAL EDUCATION AND THE TEACHING OF MORALS. — Moral education is one thing, and the teaching of morals quite another.[1] A course in morals, a body of precepts, is certainly of great service in training a man to be good. We do not think the ancient philosophy was wholly wrong when it affirmed that virtue can be taught. It can not be useless to call the attention of the child, in a didactic way, to the grand truths of conscience, to the distribution of duties, the diverse obligations of life; but nevertheless the teaching of morals is but a small part of moral education.

This education is really going on at every stage and moment of life. It begins at birth, through the examples which

---

[1] See Part Second of this work.

parents transmit to their children; it is continued at school, through the habits that are formed there, through the sentiments which are there developed, and especially through the discipline that is in vogue there; finally, it is prolonged during the whole of life, through the effort of the will and of personal education.

This education, moreover, is a complex work, in which there co-operate even more than in intellectual education, not only the child's own nature, his native dispositions and particular tastes, but the different characters of all the persons who surround him, his parents, his friends, his teachers, and in general the influences, perhaps as profound, though more unnoticed, of the social environment in which he lives.

It cannot, then, be seriously proposed to confine moral education to the narrow circle of a school course, of a series of lessons, whatever science may be introduced into them.

"The purpose of moral education is not to add to a pupil's knowledge, but to affect his will; it moves more than it demonstrates; before acting on the emotional nature, it proceeds rather from the heart than from the reason; it does not undertake to analyze all the reasons of the moral act, but tries above all else to produce it, to have it repeated, to make of it a habit which shall govern the life. Especially in the primary school, it is not a science, but an art, — the art of inclining the free will towards the good." [1]

215. IMPORTANCE OF MORAL EDUCATION. — Is there need at this time of insisting on the especial importance of moral education? Necessary at all times, it is still more so in a society like ours, where morality ought to be developed in proportion to the development of liberty itself.

"The establishment of the republican régime," says the author

---

[1] See the Act establishing common schools.

of a recent book, "by reducing the part of arbitrary authority which is made imperative, demands in return a proportional increase of that moral authority which is accepted in its stead.

"Being less governed by an external will, it is necessary that men know better how to govern themselves; what they once did through force and through fear, they must learn to do by free will and through duty."[1]

216. SUPERIORITY OF MORAL GRANDEUR.—We have said in another place that instruction or intellectual power plays an important part in the development of moral power. It sometimes happens, however, that morality does not accompany learning, nor even genius.

"As a moral man," says Mr. Blackie, "the first Napoleon lived and died very poor and very small. . . . It was an easy thing for Lord Byron to be a great poet; it was merely indulging his nature; he was an eagle, and must fly; but to have curbed his wilful humor, soothed his fretful discontent, and learned to behave like a reasonable being and a gentleman,—that was a difficult matter, which he does not seem ever seriously to have attempted. His life, therefore, with all his genius and fits of occasional sublimity, was on the whole a terrible failure."[2]

The same might be said of Rousseau, capable on occasion of heroic devotion, but powerless to apply himself to the ordinary duties of life; a man of incomparable genius, but scarcely an honorable man.

Then let us put morality in the first rank of our solici-tudes, because it is the first need of society. "We may even conceive a society composed of honorable men without instruction; but we cannot conceive a society formed of educated men without honor."[3]

---

[1] M. Vessiot, De l'Éducation à l'école.

[2] Blackie, op. cit., p. 57, 58.

[3] M. Vessiot, op. cit., p. 13.

217. Is the Child Good or Bad ?—The ideal is to make of the child a moral being who carries within himself his own rule of conduct, who governs himself by his own will, and who knows no other rule than the law of right, and who has no will except for the good.

But before nature and education have succeeded in completely developing the germs of the moral consciousness, before the child comes to be *virtuous*, many years elapse; and during this time all we can demand of the child is to be *innocent*. Our only thought is to prevent him from doing evil, or at most to cultivate the instinctive dispositions which urge him to praiseworthy actions. We can impose on him only an exterior morality, so to speak, while waiting for the reason and the will to become, in his mature soul, the solid principles of an interior morality, freely desired and realized.

Up to what point does the nature of the child adapt itself to this first education? Do we find in him only instinctive tendencies towards the good? Or, on the contrary, must we expect a stubborn resistance on the part of a nature deeply corrupt and vicious?

In other terms, is the child good or bad?

The general direction of education varies according to the reply given to this question. We are either constrained to look with favor on a nature assumed to be good, or our only thought is to repress a nature originally bad.

"Education," says Madame Guizot, "has long been a system of hostility against human nature. It was merely a question of correcting and punishing. It seemed that the only question was to take from children the nature which God had given them, in order to give them another fashioned by the teacher."[1]

On the other hand, especially since Rousseau and the

---

[1] Madame Guizot, *op. cit.*, Lettre XII.

paradoxes of the *Émile* upon the absolute innocence and the perfect goodness of the child, education tends to replace punishments by encouragements, and the "sycophants of infancy," according to the expression of Madame Necker de Saussure, think only of avoiding everything that restricts and constrains, in order to leave to nature her full and free expansion.

218. OPPOSING OPINIONS. — For our part, we shall avoid the absolute opinions of both the optimists and the pessimists, who in turn present to us infant nature under colors the most cheerful or the most sombre.

"Everything is good," cries Rousseau, "as it comes from the hands of the Author of nature. The first movements of nature are always right." ·

On the other hand, "we are born the children of wrath," says St. Paul. "All are born for damnation," proclaims Saint Augustine. And the Jansenists zealously echo the sentiment.

"You ought to consider your children," wrote Varet, "as all inclined and borne on toward evil. Their inclinations are all corrupt; and not being governed by reason, they will cause them to find pleasure and enjoyment only in the things which lead them to vice."

It is between these two extremes, between these two theses equally false, of the radical perversity and of the absolute goodness of man, that we must look for the truth.

219. THE CHILD IS NEITHER GOOD NOR BAD. — Correctly speaking, the child has not yet a moral character, and we might think the question settled by this observation of Kant:

"It is a question," he says, "whether man is by his nature

morally good or bad. I reply that he is neither, for naturally he is not a moral being; he becomes such only when he elevates his reason to the ideas of duty and of law. He could not become morally good save by means of virtue, — that is to say, a constraint exercised over himself, although he may be innocent as long as his passions are slumbering."

But Kant somewhat mistakes the question, which is, not whether the acts of the child are inspired by a moral intention, good or bad, — which no one would dare to assert, — but whether, without willing it, and by an unconscious inclination of his nature, the child is led to what is good or to what is bad. The truth is that he is led to both, and that in his composite nature vicious dispositions are associated with legitimate and praiseworthy instincts.

We grant, however, that the inclinations of the child are not, for the most part, evil in themselves. "What is evil in them," wrote Madame Guizot, "is not the inclination, but its inordinate manifestation." And Kant had said to the same effect: "The sole cause of evil is that nature is not subjected to rules."

220. THE ASSUMED EVIL INSTINCTS OF CHILDHOOD. — Let us now examine some of the accusations brought against the child.

He has been greatly traduced. "The child," said La Bruyère, "is haughty, disdainful, irascible, envious, inquisitive, selfish, lazy, fickle, etc." It is a pleasure to know that this litany of slanders emanates from a bachelor. Without intending to flatter the child, we may assert that his faults come, some from the bad education which he receives, others from his ignorance, and only a very few from an innate tendency to evil.

It is said, for example, that the child is cruel. "That age is without pity," said La Fontaine, who was less affectionate

to children than to animals. This saying is true, but the
most often this harshness is the result of a lack of intelligence. Children are without pity, because they do not understand the evil which they do. They torture a bird, because,
like little Cartesians, they do not know that the bird suffers.

Another instinct of the child, it is said, is theft. The
child resembles the savage, who has only a confused notion
of property. "He has not exactly the instinct of theft,"
remarks M. Legouvé, " but he has not the instinct of other's
property. In his case, the distinction between *mine* and
thine often consists in taking the *thine* in order to make of it
the *mine*. But is it to be wondered at that the child, who
has not studied the code, who has not, like Rousseau's Émile,
encountered a gardener Robert to explain to him the origin
of property, readily consents to take for his own use what
pleases him, but does not belong to him?

In other cases it is the grown man who, by his lack of
sense or by his example, inculcates on the child his own
faults.

Is it childish vanity that we hear mentioned? Must not
parents be blamed for this? This is stimulated by parents
who on improper occasions excite the self-esteem of their
children by exaggerating their merits. There is a well-known
story of a little girl who, having been praised by her mother
for a childish repartee, said in the presence of a lady visitor,
"Mamma, you have not told Madame what I said this morning!"

Children are charged with gluttony! I firmly believe that
Rousseau was right on this point, and that it is society, in
this case, which corrupts nature. In fact, does the greedy
child do more than desire his share of the dainties which load
the table of his parents? If the example of intemperance
were not set before him, he would be more temperate than
we think.

So falsehood is too often but the result of our bad management. "Now who has broken this piece of furniture?" we cry in a rage. Thoroughly frightened, the little culprit replies, "*I* did not do it!" The child who is treated mildly becomes confiding, but, terrified by our severity, he seeks a refuge in falsehood.

Moreover, it is not sufficient, in order to judge the child justly, to seek in his ignorance or in his bad education the explanation and the excuse for the most of his faults. We must go further, and show what good qualities, what sentiments of justice, liberality, pity, and goodness he sometimes exhibits. But we have said enough to justify those who, in judging the child, would avoid on the one hand extravagant praise and on the other passionate condemnation.

221. The Evil Instincts of the Child. — Let us acknowledge the fact, however, that certain instincts of childhood are real tendencies to evil. It is inaccurate to say that there are in nature germs only of the good. Envy and anger are natural, but they are essentially bad. Here the evil is in the inclination, not in the inordinate manifestation of the inclination.

Madame Necker de Saussure dwells, not without regret. she says, upon the vices inherent in the nature of the child.

"I speak of that momentary demoralization of the will which finds a pleasure, a particular savor, in the idea of violating a rule. . . . We observe in children something besides weakness, something besides inability to submit to the sacrifices required by duty; we see delight in throwing off the yoke of duty." [1]

To the same effect Mr. Bain devotes a special article to the "anti-social and malign emotions."

To those who would deny the existence of evil instincts,

---

[1] Madame Necker de Saussure, I., p. 304.

and would explain what is evil by the intemperance of inclinations, good in themselves, it suffices to observe that the
very intemperance is a principle of evil; that this tendency
to run riot is in nature, and consequently that human nature
is not wholly good.

222. REPRESSION OF VICIOUS TENDENCIES. — Moral education, then, will not be merely a work of excitation and of
culture; it will also have to oppose and to repress. At first,
the evil will be opposed by favoring the good. There is no
better way of correcting evil inclinations than by cultivating
those which are good; nor of fighting indolence than by
exciting to labor; nor of preventing malevolence than by
teaching to be good. It is to the same effect that Madame
Guizot wrote:

"I have always been persuaded that education had no power
against evil, except the taste for the good.

"We do not repress an evil inclination, but we fortify a good
one; and I know of no means of extirpating a fault except to
make a virtue grow in its place." [1]

"In certain cases, however, we must resort to direct repression.
The method of substitution does not always suffice. Special
remedies are required for definitely marked diseases. It is here
that discipline intervenes, with its retinue of punishments and its
necessary means of coercion." [2]

Patient with trivial faults which would be aggravated by
calling the child's attention to them and by punishing them
prematurely, discipline will be severe in the case of grave
faults. It will prevent their return, and it will chastise them
sharply if it cannot prevent them, if an obstinate resistance
makes exhortations and reprimands useless.

223. THE CONSCIENCE OR PRACTICAL REASON. — There

---

[1] Madame Guizot, *op. cit.*, I., p. 105.
[2] See Part Second of this work.

comes a moment in the life of the child when it does not suffice to correct his evil inclinations and to awaken his beneficent instincts; but when we must excite his moral consciousness and create in him the idea of a general rule of conduct, the idea of duty.

Nature has planted the germ of this idea in the intelligence, and it is to the reason,—that is, to the highest of the intellectual faculties, — that psychology ascribes the origin of moral conceptions.

Reason is the faculty of intellectual ideas, necessary and absolute; it is the natural light which enlightens every man coming into this world.

From the first dawn of his intelligence, the child is already under the direction of the reason; but this reason is almost unconscious. The child would be incapable of formulating the rational laws of which his judgments are the application. Thus a little boy of seven or eight years looks with his father for a lost object, and not finding it, he cries, "But yet it must certainly be that something is always somewhere!"

Is not this already to express, in an artless way and without succeeding in rendering a complete account of it, the necessary existence of an infinite space in which are contained all material things? And so, when a child on whom we have tried to impress the idea of the creation of the world and the idea of the Creator, replies obstinately, "But before God what was there?" is it not evident that without knowing it his young mind obeys the principle of causality, which requires that every existence should be connected with an antecedent cause?

The examples which we have just cited are connected with what Kant called the pure reason, that is, the theoretical and speculative reason, that which guides us in scientific research.

But there are other manifestations of the reason, — those which relate to practical life and to moral conduct. In this sense the reason is nothing but the moral consciousness, the belief in an obligatory law which all ought to obey. Since Kant, philosophers usually give to this the name of practical reason. Let us see if under this form the reason also manifests itself in the actions of the child.

224. THE MORAL SENSE IN THE CHILD. — At what moment may it be said that there appears in the child the essential moral idea, — that is, the distinction between good and evil, detached from every foreign element?

Certain observers of childhood seem to us to have ascribed too much upon this point to the childish intelligence. M. Pérez believes that the objective notion of good and evil can be verified at the age of six or seven months. Darwin declares that he observed the moral sense in children at the age of thirteen months.

For ourselves, we are convinced that neither at thirteen months nor at two years, nor even much later, is the child in a condition actually to discriminate good from evil. In order to believe him capable of *morality* in the strict sense of the word, it would first be necessary to accept a loose definition of the moral consciousness, — a definition which invalidatet and attenuates its import; it would then be necessary to resort to an illusory interpretation of certain acts in child-life.

Here are the facts reported by Darwin [1] and by Pérez.[2] Doddy, aged thirteen months, seemed to notice the reproaches of his father, who called him a bad boy. At the age of two years and five months, Doddy, who had been left alone, helped himself to sugar, a thing which he knew was for-

---

[1] See in the *Revue Scientifique* the account by Darwin.

[2] M. Pérez, *op. cit.*

bidden. His father met him at the moment when he came from the dining-room, and noticed something strange in his conduct. " I think," adds Darwin, " that this appearance was to be attributed to the struggle between the pleasure of eating the sugar and the *beginning of remorse*." The examples given by Pérez are of the same character. A child of eleven months obeyed when his father said, in a loud voice, " Keep still ! " This child had not yet walked alone, but his father caused him to take a few steps toward him by offering him a half of a peach.

It requires much good will to decorate with the epithet *moral*, actions in which are manifested merely the desire to gratify some sense, the fear of suffering associated by the memory with certain actions, or at most the distinction between paternal caresses and threats. The association of ideas and the memory, concurring in a conscious feeling of pleasure and pain, abundantly suffices to explain the relative obedience yielded by the child, and we decline to believe that a baby *is in possession of the moral sense* from the moment he obeys through habit or fear.

225. DEVELOPMENT OF THE MORAL CONSCIOUSNÊSS. — Not that it is necessary to deny the importance of these early sensible and utilitarian distinctions in the future acquisition of moral distinctions. Nature proceeds by successive rough drafts. For the moral consciousness, as for the attention, we must be content at first with appearances, with a foreshadowing of the real state which will be attained only long afterwards.

At first, the good is what pleases and the bad what displeases the child. Let it be so managed that he shall be pleased with only what is good. Later on, the good is what father and mother order, and the evil what they forbid. Manage in such a way that the child loves or fears his

parents enough to yield with docility to their will. Still
later, when the intelligence is capable of reflection, the good
is what is useful, the evil what is hurtful. As far as possible make the child's duty accord with his interest. Finally,
at a still higher stage, the good is what men approve, what
the civil law requires ; the evil, what is universally condemned. Make the child sensitive to public opinion.
Teach him to blush, and to feel shame for every act which
incurs general reproach.

It is not till the final term of its evolution that the
conscience comes to grasp the idea of a moral good existing
by itself, conformed to the dignity of man, which must be
practiced for the sole reason that it is good. But before the
moral idea is detached from every foreign element, — from the
seductions of pleasure, from the fear or the love inspired by
parents, from the solicitations of interest, from the respect
inspired by public opinion, how many halting-places there
are to pass through ! What painful and slow elaboration to
attain the ideal of a conscience saluting a sovereign law,
bowing before it and voluntarily conforming to its requirements !

226. The first Manifestations of Morality. — *Morality*, in the strict sense of the word, is not the act of a being
whose conduct is simply in accord with the moral law ; but
it is the characteristic of a person who intentionally and
because he wills it, submits to that law, and knowingly
accomplishes actions which he judges good.

Must we think that the child is absolutely a stranger to
morality, thus understood? Some facts seem to prove the
contrary.

"All the niceties of the moral sentiments," says M. Egger,
"are not the product of education and the privilege of a more
advanced age. For example, the instinct of remorse and of

reparation is usually exhibited by children after little revolts of the will. The child is never in better spirits than after these storms; and it is credible that he shows the intention of having us forget the sorrow caused by his disobedience." [1]

M. Pérez cites, from the Italian philosopher L. Ferri, the case of a child five years old, who, having been praised by his mother, said to her, "Mamma, I wish I could make you still happier; I wish I could always be good; tell me, why can't I always be good?" [2]

A still more probable case is that of a child noticed also by M. Pérez, who thought he was not sufficiently punished for a fault he had committed, and by a sort of spontaneous feeling of justice demanded additional correction.

227. EDUCATION OF THE MORAL CONSCIOUSNESS. — There are, then, in nature herself, the germs of morality. It would be impossible, in fact, to suggest the idea of the good, if the reason did not contain the principle of it.

"The child carries within himself the moral law, at first unconsciously, in the latent state; then little by little it disengages itself, rises from the mysterious depths of consciousness, and makes its presence felt by mute agitations; then it finds a voice, it speaks, it commands, it signifies its will by injunctions more and more clear, more and more emphatic; and finally, when it is misunderstood, by that indefinable suffering, now dull, now sharp and piercing, which is called remorse." [8]

Surely the natural evolution of the individual tends of itself to produce moral conceptions; but the educator can aid this development. For this purpose it is necessary that he exercise the child in judging of the actions of others; that in accurate and striking narratives he show him men who have

[1] M. Egger, op. cit., p. 68.
[2] M. Pérez, La Psychologie de l'enfant, p. 343.
[8] M. Vessiot, op. cit., p. 33.

done good or evil; that he be required to express his opinion on the virtues and vices of others, and invited to give
his reasons why such an action seems to him good and
another bad. The child should also be allowed to accomplish
at his own risk and peril the actions suggested to him by
his own initiative; he should be accustomed at an early hour
to make decisions, and thus acquire the feeling of his own
responsibility; and should be furnished with frequent occasions for overcoming his inclinations and for conquering his
evil instincts.[1]

In other terms, we must appeal as early as possible to the
experience of the child. Moral conceptions cannot be transmitted from without like geometrical truths; they ought to
spring spontaneously from personal reflection and internal
emotions. Conscience will be slow to appear in children
who have not been accustomed to act for themselves or to
judge of the actions of others.

"It is within himself," continues the author whom we have
just quoted, "that the child carries his rule of conduct; it is
within himself that he must be taught to look for it; and when
the teacher commands, he should try to make it understood that
it is not in his own name that he speaks, but in the name of the
moral law which is inscribed in the heart of the child, and of
which he, the teacher, is but the echo and the interpreter. To
lead the child to behave in the absence of his teacher, and of all
those who have the authority to make him do right and punish
him for having done wrong, just as he would behave in their
presence; within himself to establish a point of support against

---

[1] This was the method followed by Pestalozzi. "Instead of giving
his children direct lessons in morals, he shrewdly took advantage of
all the events which occurred in the house. They were so numerous
that each day presented many occasions for making felt the difference
between good and evil, between what is just and what is unjust.
(Pompée, *Études sur Pestalozzi*, p. 250.)

himself; to make him see that he can succeed in governing him-self without the help of others, and to lead him insensibly to do without that exterior direction; this is the true method of education."[1]

In other terms, it is necessary that every moral virtue taught to children should be intimately connected, as Pestalozzi said, "with an intuitive and sensible experience which is their own."[2]

228. DIFFICULTIES OF THIS EDUCATION.—There is such a distance between the natural state of the child, caring simply for his pleasures and his interest, and the normal state of an enlightened conscience, that at first thought we might be tempted to despair of success and to believe impossible the evolution which leads the mind to the conception of the good.

But in this delicate work nature has provided us with powerful auxiliaries; and if it is difficult to suggest to the child the abstract idea of duty, it is very much easier to accustom him practically to fulfil certain duties.

Especially when it is a question of duties towards other men, the child will be aided by his natural feelings of sympathy and benevolence; and from the practice of these duties there will gradually be evolved the idea of duty in itself.

---

[1] M. Vessiot, *op. cit.*, p. 35.

[2] "Elementary moral education," said Pestalozzi, "comprises three distinct parts: it is first necessary to give children a moral conscious-ness by awakening in them pure feelings; it is next necessary to accustom them by practice to conquer themselves in order to devote themselves to whatever is just and good; and finally, they must be led to make, by reflection and comparison, a just idea of law and of the moral duties which are incumbent on them from their position and their surroundings." (Roger de Guimps, *Histoire de Pestalozzi*, p. 206.)

"It is from the first movements of the heart," exclaims Rousseau, "that arise the first voices of the conscience; from the feelings of love and hate are born the first notions of good and evil; justice and goodness are not mere abstract terms conceived by the understanding, but real affections of the soul enlightened by reason."

The virtues relative to personal duties will be acquired with more difficulty; but here again the natural emotions, such as self-love and the sentiment of the useful, will come in aid of moral education. We are in no wise forbidden to show the child that his interest and his duty are in accord in imposing on him moderation in his desires and resistance to his evil inclinations.

But, above all and in all periods of the moral life, example will be the great teacher. Before imposing a moral law on the obedience of the child as a rule of command, it must be proposed to his imitation as an insinuating example. A child is above all else an imitator, and the great secret of moral education is to know how to take advantage of this instinct. Let us not forget that perhaps the most beautiful book of religious ethics is entitled, "*Imitation of Jesus Christ.*"

229. POWER OF THE IMITATIVE INSTINCT IN THE CHILD.—The power of the imitative instinct in the child is due to several causes; and first of all to his ignorance. Having as yet at his disposal but a small amount of knowledge and a very slender stock of ideas, the child is at the mercy of the perceptions which incite him on all sides. His supple thought, free from prepossessions, responds to the call of exterior images, and follows without resistance the current into which it is urged by the impressions which strike it. On the other hand, the child is weak; he is lacking in personality. He needs to act, but his will does not yet exist.

Powerless to act from his own initiative, he acts in accordance with what he sees others do. His weakness is the principal cause of his imitative disposition.

Sympathy is still another source of the imitative instinct. We all have a secret tendency to put ourselves in agreement, in our sentiments and actions, with the men who surround us, and particularly with those whom we love. To love any one is to desire to resemble him. The child who feels an ardent affection for his companions is naturally inclined to imitate them. The more causes of sympathy there are, such as resemblances in condition or age, the more powerfully will the imitative instinct manifest itself.

Finally, let us add that in imitation, however slavish it may appear, there is sometimes, as it were, a first soaring of the child's liberty, of his aspiration after the ideal. The child wishes to rise superior to himself ; and this is why he will imitate by preference, after his companions, his superiors and his teachers.

"All men have a tendency towards imitation, but this is particularly noticeable in the child. Not yet having a pronounced individuality and a strong character, he does not suffice for himself. He easily yields to an impulsion from without. The persons who surround him act upon him more than he acts upon them, and he is readily moulded after the pattern which they set before him, especially if they are older, stronger, more capable, and more experienced than he is."[1]

230. HISTORICAL EXAMPLES. — If it is true that none of our actions are lost to us, that each of our deeds, good or bad, has its effect upon our future conduct, and aids in directing the current of our life towards the good or towards the bad, it is also certain that the actions of other men, of those who have preceded us on this earth,

---

[1] Gauthey, *op. cit.*, II., p. 388.

as well as of those who are living around us, exercise
upon our character, however little they may be present to
our imagination, a profound influence.   The past sheds
light upon the present. Souls that have disappeared live
again in the souls of the new generation. The examples of
the ancients mould the minds of those who have just come
upon the theatre of life, and, as some one has said, "the
dead govern the living."

Present to the child, then, all the beautiful and noble
lessons which history teaches.   By narratives and por-
traitures infuse into him the virtues which have made his
ancestors illustrious.

"Towards the achievement of a noble life," says an English
teacher, "there is nothing more important than an imagination
well decorated with heroic pictures; in other words, there is no
surer method of becoming good, and it may be great also, than an
early familiarity with the lives of great and good men. . . .   There
is no kind of sermon so effective as the example of a great man.
. . .   Let us, therefore, turn our youthful imaginations into great
picture-galleries and Walhallas of the heroic souls of all times
and of all places; and we shall be incited to follow after good
and be ashamed to commit any sort of baseness in the direct
view of such a 'cloud of witnesses.'" [1]

Of course it is not proposed to make of our pupils so
many heroes, — the occasions for heroism are rare ; but still
we must not fear to present to children a very elevated
moral ideal.   He who has been made capable of being heroic
on one solemn occasion, will be more surely virtuous at
every hour of his life. Then familiarize the mind which is
to be made moral "with the real blood and bone of human
heroism which the select pages of biography present."
From this high moral excitation something will be reflected

---

[1] Blackie, *op. cit.*, pp. 81, 82.

even on the most common and the most humble social conditions.

But history holds in reserve, in order to offer them to the imitation of those who study it, very many examples of familiar and simple virtues accessible to all. The *Lives* of Plutarch, to cite but this author, contain a treasure of beautiful models by which the whole world may profit, and which are, as has been said, "the very matter out of which every moral force will always be made."

231. LIVING EXAMPLES.— But there is something which is worth even more than the example of the dead; this is intercourse with the living. The child prefers to imitate those whom he sees, those whom he meets. The finest historical narratives are cold, compared with the real and present example of a virtuous life. A good man not only assures his own virtues, but contributes to the virtue of others by the magnetic influence which he diffuses about him wherever he goes, and by the beneficent radiance of his moral qualities. There is a contagion of good, as well as a contagion of evil and of disease.

Some of the best souls in this world have acquired their moral superiority less by an effort of their will than by a natural imitation of the good people who surround them. How many families there are in which virtue is a tradition, an inheritance, which is transmitted from parents to children as surely and as directly as a patrimony! Marcus Aurelius, the wise Roman Emperor, relates in his *Thoughts* that he was indebted to several members of his family for some of his best qualities.

"My uncle," he says, "taught me patience; from my father I inherit modesty; to my mother I owe my piety."

Happy the men who, like Marcus Aurelius, breathe from the day of their birth an atmosphere of virtue, and to acquire good morals have only to submit to the gracious and natural incitements of example.

"Of all the ways whereby Children are to be instructed and their manners formed, the plainest, easiest, and most efficacious is to set before their Eyes the *Examples* of those things you would have them do or avoid. . . . Virtues and Vices can by no Words be so plainly set before their understandings as the Actions of other men will show them, when you direct their observation, and bid them view this or that good or bad Quality in their Practice. . . . Nothing sinks so gently and so deep into Men's minds as *Example*." [1]

232. EXAMPLES AND PRECEPTS. — It must not be imagined, however, that example, which is precept in action, absolves us absolutely from abstract precept, which appeals to the mind. It is well to present to the child, in a clear and expressive form, the principal maxims of duty, and to nourish his memory with beautiful moral sentences. Always present to the imagination, these formulas will lend us support against the temptations of pleasure and the sophisms of passion; they will preserve us on many occasions of weakness.

"It is well," says an author whom we have often quoted, "to carry about with us the purifying influence of a high ideal of human conduct, fervidly and powerfully expressed. Superstitious persons carry amulets externally on their breasts; carry you a select store of holy texts within, and you will be much more effectively armed against the powers of evil than any most absolute monarch behind a bristling body-guard. Such texts you may find occurring in many places, from the Kalidasas and Sakyamunis of the East, to Pythagoras, Plato, Aristotle, and Epictetus in the West; but if you are wise, and above the seduction of showy and pretentious novelties, you will store your memory early in youth with the golden texts of the Old and New Testaments." [2]

---

[1] John Locke, *op. cit.*, p. 81.   [2] Blackie, *op. cit.*, p. 79.

We do not believe in the magic power of words; but who does not know by experience what power there is in a moment of moral crisis, in an idea suddenly evoked from a maxim or from a rule of conduct, especially if this precept is associated with the recollection of the one who has transmitted it to us, — the image of a mother, a father, a venerated teacher?

But to be efficacious the precept must deeply penetrate the soul; it must not remain merely on the lips or in the memory, but must become, so to speak, a living part of the conscience. We must not be content with a borrowed morality, founded on maxims learned out of books.

"What would be thought," said the wise Plutarch, "of a man who, going to his neighbor in search of fire, and finding the hearth all aglow, should stay there to warm himself and no longer think of returning to his own home?"

This is the picture of a man who is content to recite well-conned moral discourses; who to be sure of conducting himself properly has always to consult a book, as a sort of gospel; and who has not been able to kindle in his own heart an inner fire of noble inspirations.

233. The Love of the Good. — Exercised and instructed by his own experience, accustomed to take account of his own actions, to judge the actions of others, and to weigh the consequences of them, initiated by his acts into the joy of duty accomplished, encouraged by the examples which have been set before him, sustained by the exhortations and precepts of his teachers, the child will rise little by little to the moral life. In this complex work, of which Mr. Bain has said that "the conditions to be fulfilled are so numerous that it is hardly possible to indicate with precision the best method to be adopted," the principal part belongs, not to books, not to lessons, but to the character of parents

and teachers.   The moral law cannot be for the child
a cold, impersonal abstraction ; it must be made incarnate
in a living being.   The father, the mother, and the
teacher represent to the eyes of the child the moral law ;
and they should represent it, not as impassive, unfeeling
beings, but as living personalities who are touched at the
sight of evil, who are full of affection and tenderness.   If
religion has such a profound influence upon the development of morality, it is because it presents to the minds
of men the idea of a supreme father, the benefactor of
humanity, who by his sovereign will requires virtue of his
children.   The knowledge of what is good does not suffice ;
there must be joined to this the love of what is good.   And
it is by loving virtuous men set before him for examples, and
by loving a divine model of every virtue, that the child will
come to love the good himself.

CHAPTER XI.

WILL, LIBERTY, AND HABIT.

234. KNOWLEDGE AND WILL. — The more we enlighten the intelligence the more we develop the moral consciousness. It suffices to throw a glance over the morals of the ancients and over the morals of the moderns, to judge of the progress which men have gradually made in the knowledge of their duties. Men often do wrong through ignorance of what is right. Moreover, the knowledge of what is right implies in itself a certain power of determination towards the right. To know exactly where one's duty lies is of itself one excellent condition for doing one's duty. Let us admit, however, that knowledge does not suffice, that there must be added to it will or moral energy. How many men are capable of making marvelous dissertations on all the shades of duty, and yet are incapable of becoming virtuous men! They cannot will the good which they know. It is the reason that judges what must be done, but it is the will alone which determines us to do it. The education of the will, then, is one essential part of moral education.

235. DEFINITION OF THE WILL. — In the eighteenth century the term will was sometimes employed to designate all the powers of the soul except the intelligence, — the inclinations, the tendencies, the desires; and Condillac said of the will, "that it comprehends all the operations which are born of need." In contemporary psychology the signification of the term " will " is better defined, more fixed ; and the will, or power to do what we wish, properly designates the power which the soul has of self-determination, consciously and with reflection, spontaneously and freely, towards an act of its own choice.

236. THE WILL IN THE CHILD. — The will thus understood is, like the reason, a prerogative of man. Man alone, in the full exercise of all his faculties, is capable of willing. Doubtless the animal and the child are capable of self-determination ; they act, and by an abuse of terms the principle of these determinations and actions is called will. But this irreflective power of determination and action is but a semblance of will. The child is obstinate, but he has no will. In him, as in the animal, action, however spontaneous it may be, is not master of itself. Provoked by blind desire, by irresistible need, by disorderly caprice, it is not in possession of itself ; it is but the pale image of the real human will, which reflects, calculates, knows where it goes, and consequently masters itself and governs itself.

237. DIFFERENCE BETWEEN WILL AND DESIRE. — The will is surely something else than desire. It is not possible to admit, with certain philosophers, that the will is but an ardent and strong desire, just as the attention is but a dominant sensation. The will thus understood would not affranchise us from our inclinations and our passions ; it would be but the consummation of desire. It would be included in the category of passive, fatal dispositions ; it would not be the principle of liberty.

Desire is but the solicitation of an agreeable object which procures us pleasure, and thus invites us, and sometimes determines us, to go in search of it. The will, on the contrary, is the resolution which we take of ourselves to accomplish an act, agreeable or disagreeable, as the case may be.

There are cases where desire and will are in accord, — where we will what we desire; but even then our consciousness sharply distinguishes the attraction which the thing desired exercises on the feelings, from the power which we have of yielding to that attraction.

In other cases the will is in opposition to desire; and it is then especially that the distinction between the two facts is clear and striking. For example, indolence attracts me and pleases me; all the pleasures of the *far niente* haunt my imagination; all my bodily inclinations incline me to indolence; and yet, sustained by the idea of my interest or of my duty, I resist these impulses; I will to work, and I set myself to work. How, in this case, and in all analogous cases, can we confound desire and will, the current and the power which ascends the current?

Finally, in other cases, the desire is the only thing; by its violence it carries away the soul, which has neither the time to reflect nor the power to will; but the act is then no more voluntary than the mind is truly attentive when it is dominated and absorbed by a sensation. The fixity of thought which allows itself to be captivated and made immobile, so to speak, by a powerful impression, is no more attention than the impulse of desire is will. Just as the attention disengages and transports the thought, attaches it to the object which it has chosen, or detaches it from it when it pleases, so the will withholds, arrests, or pursues the act which it has resolved on.

238. DIFFERENCE BETWEEN WILL AND IDEA. — But some one will say, if the will is distinguished from desire and from sensibility, it is precisely because it is confounded with idea and with intelligence. In fact, motives borrowed from our prevision, from our reason, are the only ones which can counterbalance the attraction of desire and assure the tri-

umph of the will; but because the will grafts itself, so to
speak, upon an idea, it is no reason for thinking that it is
the same thing as the idea. Does it not happen to us every
moment to have a very definite idea of a thing to be 'done,
and yet not to do it, because we do not will to do it?

239. RELATION OF THE WILL TO THE SENSIBILITIES. —
But after having shown that the will is something distinct
and irreducible, after having proved that it is an independent power, we must hasten to add that this independence is not absolute; that in order to will it is not
useless to desire, and that it is necessary to think.

Let us not imagine, then, that to prepare in man for the
reign of the will, we must destroy in the child the empire
of the desires. Children of little sensibility are very likely
to become men of little energy. On the contrary, lively,
ardent inclinations will be the cradle of a strong will,
provided reflection co-operates with them.[1]

Let us excite the desires of the child, while giving them
direction; let us teach him to love more and more what
he ought to love; and, enlightened by intelligence, his
desires will be transformed into wills.

But the will, however energetic we may suppose it to be,
is almost always too weak to carry on a constant struggle
with the inclinations. In this contest, it would very soon
exhaust its forces.

Doubtless the will manifests all its power only in
effort and in contest; but, happily, the contest is not
always necessary; and if there are toiling, heroic wills
which triumph over the passions which they resist, there
are also compliant, easy-going wills, which are but the

---

[1] Mr. Sully justly remarks that the exercise of physical activity is
itself a rudimentary education of the will.

adhesion of a well-endowed soul to legitimate desires. In fact, most wills are of this sort; and in the ordinary course of a well-regulated life, that which is willed is at the same time that which is felt and loved.

The end of education ought, then, to be to associate and to unite desire and will, — to bring into accord pleasure and duty. Whatever can be done to give the inclinations wisdom, will also profit the will and will make its exercise easier.

240. Relation of the Will to the Intelligence. — The philosophers of the seventeenth century, especially Bossuet, included the will among the intellectual operations. Every act of the will certainly implies an act of thought. The will might be defined a thought in action. There is no will, a philosopher has said, where there is no reason for willing. In proportion as we are more enlightened, and especially as we are more reflective; as we conceive more clearly what we have to do, and the better understand why we ought to do it, the more are we our own masters, the more do we belong to ourselves; in a word, the more will we have.

Let us, then, train the child to reflect, not to form hasty resolutions, not to yield at the first blow to the calls of his desires, and to weigh the pros and the cons before adopting a determination; and in this way we shall increase the strength of the will, whose power varies and is modified in proportion as our intellectual energy diminishes or augments.

241. The Will and Liberty. — In showing the contrasts and the agreements, between the will on the one hand and the sensibilities and the intelligence on the other, we have defined the essential characteristics of the will, which are reflection and liberty.

There are no acts truly voluntary, save those which are deliberate, which suppose that a resolution has been taken after reflection, and the voluntary act is free, precisely because it issues, not from an inconsiderate and fatal instinct, but from a studied decision and from choice. Real liberty is nothing but the faculty of choosing with reflection and with a thorough knowledge of the matter, among several possible actions, the one which we prefer, the one which we think the best. Doubtless this liberty does not give us the power to break abruptly with our past, to loose ourselves from all solidarity with what we have already done, with our inclinations and our habits of mind; it does not create acts absolutely indeterminate, independent of all condition, — in a word, it does not perform miracles. But it does enfranchise us so far as this is possible; it rescues us from the impulse of the moment, from the absolute empire of habit, from the yoke of passion, from the tyranny of fashion and of example; it permits us to govern ourselves by ourselves and by our reason, and it is in this that we are free.

242. CULTURE OF THE WILL. — The culture of the will is one of the most delicate problems of education. To develop and strengthen the will, it is first necessary to respect the spontaneity of the child, which is the germ of his independence and liberty. Parents who are too anxious to " break the wills of their children " are preparing weak and flabby characters that will be incapable of self-control.

Says Kant: "We must not break the wills of children, but only direct them in such a way that they will know how to yield to natural obstacles."[1]

---

[1] Kant, *Pedagogie*, p. 226.

The same thought inspired Rousseau, when, in the first twelve years of Émile's education, he subjected the conduct of the child to the sole rule of necessity.

" Let the child early feel upon his proud head the hard yoke which nature imposes on man, — the heavy yoke of necessity, under which every finite being must bend; let him see that this necessity lies in things, not in the caprice of men." [1]

It is going too far, however, to suppress in early education the commands of parents and teachers. It is well, on the contrary, that the will of the child feel other wills in contact with his own; but on one condition, — that these wills shall themselves be well adjusted, and that the orders through which they manifest themselves shall not be followed by counter-orders, — that they shall be clear and inflexible. The caprices of a wavering authority which contradicts itself, can have only disastrous effects. Pulled in different directions, the will of the child will itself become capricious and mobile.

The child should be neither a slave nor a despot. He should neither be constrained blindly to obey unreasonable orders, nor crossed in all his inclinations. On the other hand, he should not be gratified in all that he wishes.

" Parents," says Kant, " often make a mistake in refusing their children everything they demand. It is absurd to refuse without reason what they naturally expect from the goodness of their parents.

" On the other hand, children are spoiled by gratifying all their wishes. Doubtless they are prevented by this means from showing their bad humor, but they become all the more headstrong."

[1] *Émile*, I., II.

We must at the same time know how to yield and to resist, and especially to resist. By always gratifying the caprices of the child, by flattering his instincts, we doubtless emancipate his will, but we also make it disorderly, and in a sense weaken it. In fact, will supposes effort, domination over one's self. By resisting the child, we teach him to resist himself. It is only through the acquired habit of obeying others, that he will later become capable of obeying his own reason.

243. PRACTICAL FEELING OF LIBERTY. — There is a great practical interest in often pausing to reflect as follows, with reference to a proposed course of action: "Such a fault might have been avoided. Such a quality might have been acquired more quickly. Finally, something different and better might have been done." This is a certain means of increasing our faith in the efficacy of our acts, of fortifying in our souls the most precious thing in this world, — I mean the actual feeling of our liberty, by ridding ourselves of that harassing notion of necessity, of which Stuart Mill said, "The idea of necessity weighed upon my existence like an evil genius."

Consequently, let us accustom the child to make frequent returns upon himself, to practice in a certain measure those *examinations of conscience* recommended by the philosophers of antiquity. The *moral calendar* of Franklin, who each day recorded the infractions which he had committed on the different precepts of duty, is an ingenious application of the same thought.[1]

---

[1] In other terms, we must do for the mind what Colonel Amorôs did for the body: he gave each pupil what he called a physiological chart, in which were noted the condition of each organ at the beginning of the course in gymnastics and the progress made after each month of exercise.

244. EDUCATION IN LIBERTY. — Man is really man only when he unites a firm and ever-ready will to vivid and elevated emotions, and to an enlightened intelligence. But this quality is rarer than we think. Doubtless if we consider only that inferior will which, while saying "I will," does nothing in reality but follow inclination or habit, — in this sense we use our will each moment of our life; but if we must restrict the term will to a deliberate act, determined on with reflection, who does not see that the human conscience rarely rises to this effort? The most often we act, I do not say without motive, which is impossible, but without reflective motive, and our actions are not really willed. There are men who are almost absolutely lacking in will, who in some sort do not belong to themselves, but who live a passive, mechanical life, the slaves of their own passions and the toys of exterior influences. Even those who reflect the most do not reflect as much as they might. There are within us treasures of energy which we do not know how to take advantage of, and we certainly have more reserve power than we have will.

245. NO ACT IS INDIFFERENT. — For real training in liberty, and for assuring to it all its power, it must be borne in mind that no one of our acts is indifferent. If we yield for a single time to an evil inclination, while promising ourselves to resist it to-morrow, we are guilty of a grave imprudence; for to-morrow we will not have the same power of resistance. Every act performed is a beginning of habit, and habit fetters the will. For the very reason that we have even once acted in a certain way, we shall be a little more inclined to act again in the same way.

Then let us keep watch over all the acts of the child. Let us not excuse him from any fault on the pretext that this will be the only instance of it, and that it will be time to correct it when it occurs again. In every desire, however feeble, there is a will in germ, in every action there is the beginning of habit.

246. THE WILL AND HABITS. — The activity of the man and of the child manifests itself, as we know, under three forms : instinct, will, and habit. So far as possible, we must substitute will for instinct, — that is, reflective resolutions for blind impulses ; but must we oppose habits, as we oppose instincts? No ; for it depends on us to make habit an easy way of doing without effort what we had previously done with reflection, with will ; habit consolidates the work of liberty.

It has been said, not without truth, that " two obstacles, almost invincible, prevent us from. being the masters of our wills, — inclination and habit." It would, however, be a grave and dangerous error to attribute to these two enemies of the will a power that cannot be over- come. Inclination can always be controlled, confronted with our interests and duty, and repressed by an ener- getic act of the will. As to habit, particularly at first, it is entirely dependent on the will, since it depends on us to prevent the repetition of the act which engenders habit. Even when it has become inveterate, we may succeed in conquering it, — if not at once and by a simple effort of the will, at least by a prolonged resistance and by skillful tactics.

247. NECESSITY OF HABITS. — To a great extent, educa- tion is but the art of forming good habits. So we do not comprehend what Rousseau has said with more wit than sense : "Émile must be allowed to learn no habit, save that of having none at all."

Even Kant condemns habits, for the reason that " the

more habits a man has, the less free and independent is he."

The ideal of Kant and Rousseau would be a liberty always active, which nothing would thwart; a liberty always alert, always in movement, which would determine itself anew in every circumstance of life. But habit is an "obedience," since it enchains us to the past.[1] But the ideal of Rousseau and Kant cannot be realized. It is impossible to demand, at each moment of existence, that display of energy which is involved in each new exercise of liberty. Happily, human weakness may repose on good habits, which exempt it from efforts ceaselessly renewed, and which render the accomplishment of duty natural, easy, almost instinctive. The body cannot always be awake and erect; it must sleep and recline; and in the same way activity should not remain incessantly on the alert, — it must seek repose and must sleep, so to speak, in the easy and pleasant paths of habit. When the will has once purged the inclinations and regulated the habits, it can discharge itself in part upon the emotions and upon the routine government of the soul; like a general who, having pacified a country, sheathes his sword, but does not completely disarm, because unforeseen circumstances and changes in life may at any moment require new efforts of the will.

Does some one object that habit diminishes effort, and consequently merit? We reply, with M. Marion, "Merit and effort are not the whole of morality. I am surer that a man will do right, when the right will cost him no trouble."[2]

---

[1] See Vinet, *L'Éducation la Famille et la Société*.

[2] M. Marion, in *La Science de l'Éducation*, contained in the *Reforme universitaire*, April 1, 1885.

Then let us not demand of the will a continuous series of feats of strength. Moreover, the habits, however numerous they may be, never suppress liberty, especially if we make of liberty itself, — that is, of reflective deliberation, — a higher habit, which dominates all the others.

248. How the Habits are Formed. — There is great need, then, that education should form good habits, — habits of mind, habits of feeling, habits of action. How shall it form them? How shall it succeed in creating that second nature which will constitute the final character of the man?

In truth, the habits are formed of themselves by the repetition of the same act. Some are derived from the inclinations and instincts; others from reflective acts in which the will has co-operated. The part of the educator is, then, to keep watch, both over the instincts and the first manifestations of the will. On the start he will cut short evil tendencies, and nip in the bud vicious inclinations. Evil must be cut away to the very root.

"Habit," says Montaigne, "begins in a mild and humble fashion; it establishes in us little by little, and as it were by stealth, the foot of its authority; but it soon reveals to us a furious and tyrannical face, and we shall hardly be able to rescue ourselves again from its hold."

The teacher will prevent the rise of bad habits by opposing bad acts by all the means in his power, — by punishments if need be. To promote the formation of good habits, he will have only to encourage the child in acting, and with the aid of time the habit will be formed. It is hardly possible to impose, in a trice, new habits which will be in contradiction with the nature of the child. If the act which you command is repugnant to him, that act, performed contrary to his will, will not leave behind it a certain tendency to reproduce itself, which is the essential condition of the formation of habits. If, then, it is a question of habits that are somewhat difficult, to which the child does not tend of himself, try to manage the transitions; try to find the favorable moment when the action which we wish to transform into a habit will cost the child the least trouble. Let us be content, at first, if he performs the act with indifference; he will next repeat it with pleasure, and the habit will be formed. In a word, let us insinuate habits, not impose them. "A new idea," said Fontenelle, "is like a wedge, — it must not be driven in by the blunt end."

249. How Bad Habits are to be Corrected. — But whatever may be the supervision of the teacher, it is not claimed that under the influence of external circumstances a bad habit will not make its appearance in the child. Moreover, when he enters school the child has already contracted certain dispositions, certain bents of mind and of heart. Is it possible to correct the vicious element which custom has once introduced into the activity of the child?

Certainly this is not an easy thing; and we might almost always despair of success, if we had no other means for attaining this end than to make a direct attack on the evil inclination which has become a habit, especially if we wish to succeed in this all at once. Time has presided over the formation of habit, and time is also necessary to assure its disappearance. Let us be patient, therefore; let us be satisfied if we succeed at first in delaying the reappearance of the evil act. Little by little the empire of the will will be established, and the child will gradually rid himself of his propensity, especially if we have had skill enough to establish different habits, which draw him in another direction.

250. THE WILL AND EDUCATION, PUBLIC OR PRIVATE. — At first sight one would be tempted to believe that private education is more favorable than public education, for the culture of the will. At school, of course, everything is regulated in advance; everything is uniform; there is no initiative; there is a common level; the child is never abandoned to himself; the shortest periods of the day have their definite occupation. At home, on the contrary, the child belongs more to himself; he is not subjected to a rule so inflexible; he has the disposition of his own time and occupation; he has more initiative.

And yet, looking at things more closely, we come to be convinced that the school is worth more than the home for an apprenticeship in effort. Left with his parents, the child grows effeminate; under their direction, often uncertain and variable, his acts lack continuity; he wavers at random between their contradictory orders and his own caprices; he does not learn to obey a fixed and immutable law. Real will is obedience freely given to the moral law; and to train the child to this obedience, obedience to an exact rule is the best of preparations. "Obedience to law," says an unknown author quoted by Madame Necker de Saussure, "subjugates the will without enfeebling it, while obedience to men injures and enervates it."

Madame Necker does not hesitate to acknowledge that "public education has the decided advantage, so far as the strengthening of character and the development of manly virtues and energy are concerned."

"In the family the child escapes slackness with difficulty. In a quiet household there is no energy to display. All the weak are protected; no one needs to defend himself or to defend others. This is a happy condition, doubtless, but power of soul is not acquired in this way. At college things do not go in this way. The young man learns to know his own rights, as well as those of others. He becomes accustomed to resist solicitations as he does threats, when he believes that equity is on his side. He learns the secret of good conduct, the art of putting himself on good terms with his equals, of knowing how far he may impose on them by his firmness, or of making himself loved by his condescension." [1]

There are still other reasons that might be given. In the family the child does not easily have opinions of his own. He lives with persons who are his superiors in experience, whom he ought to respect, and whom for the most part he loves too much to annoy by differing with them in opinion. At school and college he lives with equals, and he has the right of free speech. In the family the instruction is generally too easy; the lesson, so to speak, is all *chewed;* the child has not efforts enough to make to assimilate it. At college he needs to work more for himself, and to seek in personal reflection the means of comprehending a lesson uniformly given to all.

251. SELF-EDUCATION. — It is not, however, at school that the education of the will is completed. It is only in society, in contact with the difficulties of life, that the human personality is really formed. And this is doubtless why Comenius reserved to the university, — that is, to the free life of the student, — the task of developing the will. Experience is the true school of the will.

"At college we smooth the path for the steps of the child; but difficulty is precisely the education of the will. We teach, but one really knows only what he discovers. We are guides — of whom? Of those who ought to guide themselves."

---

[1] See *Considérations sur l'éducation publique et l'éducation privée.*

This opposition which exists between the development of the personal will and school life, even the mildest and freest, disappears the day when the child is handed over to himself. It is especially then that his voluntary activity will find occasion for exercise and growth; but it is then also that his will will incur the greatest dangers. We will have taught him in vain to will in the narrow circle of childish activity; he will be likely to unlearn this in the vast field of manly activity.

"With the will," as it has been justly remarked, "the work of education is never finished. The child who has learned to read has not to go back to it; it is finished. With the will it is never finished; we are always going back to it."[1]

252. DIFFICULTY OF THE EDUCATION OF THE WILL. — With the aid of the will already formed, the success of intellectual education, as of moral education, is assured. But for the education of the will itself, where is the fulcrum, the lever upon which we shall press?

Must there not already be a little will, in order that more of it may be acquired? What shall be done with the weak natures, which have no spring in them? Is it possible to give them will, if they have none? "It is the will which we have to right," says Gauthey, "and we would have it right itself. Let weakness produce strength, and evil engender the good."[2]

La Rochefoucauld said to the same effect, "Weakness is the only defect which cannot be corrected." Happily, nature does not often propose to us this insoluble problem. It is rare, if ever, that a child is absolutely deprived of the germs of will. If he has not enough will to oppose his defects, he will always have enough of it

---

[1] Rousselot, *Pédagogie*, p. 263.
[2] Gauthey, *De l'Éducation*, II., p. 266.

to acquire certain virtues; for, according to the remark
of Bourdaloue, "it costs less to enrich one's self with
a thousand virtues, than to cure one's self of a single
fault."

253. GOOD-WILL. — It would be of no account to train
the will if there is not given it as a companion a love
for what is good. In itself, in fact, the will may be an
instrument of vice as well as an instrument of virtue.
In their way, great criminals give proof of will-power.
We may will the evil as earnestly as the good.

It is, then, good-will that it is especially important to
train and strengthen, — that good-will of which Kant said
in a page which cannot be too often quoted :

"Of all that it is possible to conceive in this world, and even
beyond this world, there is but one thing that can be regarded as
good without restriction, and this is a good-will. Intelligence, penetration, judgment, and all the qualities of mind; courage, resolution, and perseverance, or qualities of temperament, are doubtless
good and desirable qualities in many respects ; but these gifts of
nature may be extremely bad and pernicious, when the will which
makes use of them and which constitutes essentially what is called
character, is not itself good.

"A good-will does not derive its goodness from its effects, from
its results, nor from its aptitude to attain such or such a proposed
end; but simply from willing, — that is, from itself ; and, considered in itself, it should be esteemed incomparably superior to
everything that can be done by it to the advantage of a few
inclinations, or even of all the inclinations combined. Were
adverse fate or the avarice of a hard-hearted nature to deprive
this good-will of all the means for executing its designs; were
its greatest efforts to end in nothing, and were it to remain
nothing besides good-will, it would still shine with its own lus-
tre like a precious stone, for it derives from itself all its own
worth."

254. IMPORTANCE OF THE WILL IN LIFE. — Good-will, energy in well-doing, is the only thing which gives to life its value and its dignity.

"If you imagine," says Mr. Blackie, "that you are to be much helped by books and reasons, speculations and learned disputations, in this matter you are altogether mistaken. Books and discourses may indeed awaken and arouse you, and perhaps hold up the sign of a wise finger-post, to prevent you from going astray at the first start,. but they cannot move you a single step on the road. It is your own legs only that can perform the journey; it is altogether a matter of doing. . . . . You must have a compass of sure direction in your own soul."[1]

In other terms, man must find in himself his own rule of conduct and the powers necessary to bring him into conformity with it. The will is the essential agent of virtue. Moreover, it is not important merely for morality of life; it is necessary for happiness and success. Without it we would not succeed in the world, triumph over difficulties, and turn circumstances to our advantage. In affairs great or small, we have always need of the will. It is even an element in genius, which Buffon defined as "a long patience." The inventors and benefactors of humanity have accomplished their work only at the price of noble efforts and sturdy perseverance. Finally, at all steps of the social ladder, the will is the basis of the essential quality of man, — character. Character, in fact, is less the sum of our habits and tastes than the possession of a will that is strong, enlightened, just, and good, — capable of coping with events; and a character thus constituted is the ideal of moral education.

---

[1] Blackie, *op. cit.*, p. 78.

CHAPTER XII.

THE HIGHER SENTIMENTS; ÆSTHETIC EDUCATION; RELIGIOUS EDUCATION.

255. THE HIGHER SENTIMENTS. — Moral education would not be complete if it contemplated only the culture of the affectionate and benevolent emotions, the development of the conscience, and the progress of the will and the moral energy. It should also keep in view the culture of the higher emotions which depend equally on the intelligence and the sensibilities, and in which are mingled both the highest conceptions of the reason and the noblest emotions of the heart. These emotions are the love of the true, a taste for the beautiful, the love of the good, of which we have already spoken, and the religious sentiment.

256. THE LOVE OF THE TRUE. — VERACITY. — Under its humblest form, the love of the true is the horror of falsehood; under its highest form, it is the search for the truth, the scientific instinct.

Educators have often studied the means of promoting in the child the tendency to veracity, which Mr. Bain includes, with justice and benevolence, among the three fundamental virtues.

The first and the best thing to do is to give the example of the most scrupulous veracity.

Miss Edgeworth justly condemns the ingenious falsehoods which Rousseau recommends to the teachers of children. "Sooner or later," she says, "children discover that they are deceived, and then their distrust becomes incurable. 'Honesty is the best policy,' must be the maxim in education as well as in all the other affairs of life."[1]

But example is not sufficient; other precautions should be added. Rousseau has justly said that we should never tempt the veracity of the child, and question him on what he has an interest in concealing or misrepresenting. "It is better," says Miss Edgeworth, "to suffer the loss of a broken glass than to put the child's sincerity to a test." If through misplaced severity we provoke a child to dissemble his little faults, we may fear that, once having entered upon this course, he will persevere in it, and contract the habit of falsehood.

On the other hand, when the child has freely acknowledged his remissness and blundering, let us show him that we are satisfied with his sincerity, rather than provoked by his faults. "The pleasure of being esteemed and of deserving compliments," says Miss Edgeworth, "is delicious to children."

If, on the contrary, the child is disposed to lie, show him, without scolding him too much, that the result of his dissimulation is the loss of our confidence.

"A good means of correction," says M. Marion, "is to make it appear that we have less faith in the words of a child who has been caught in a falsehood, and to corroborate what he alleges by the testimony of his companions. He should be told, in a tone of severity and sadness, that we feel under the painful necessity of not believing what he says, and on the contrary should impose implicit confidence in those of his companions who have never told a falsehood.

---

[1] *Practical Education*, Chap. VIII.

"The habit of falsehood must be very inveterate, if it resist a treatment of this sort judiciously employed."[1]

In other terms, education in veracity will employ as instruments the other emotions of the child: first, his vivid desire to be loved and esteemed by his parents and teachers, and to possess their confidence; later, the feeling of personal dignity which lying abases.

257. THE SEARCH FOR TRUTH. — But this speaking the truth which we know is not all; it is also necessary to search for truth which we do not know. Education has no more serious mission than to inculcate love of truth and to wage war on credulity and error. It will be assisted in this task by the child's natural curiosity, which, once excited, aspires to know everything and to comprehend everything. It is certainly not proposed to satisfy this curiosity in all respects, especially in the primary school; but if the child cannot know all that is true, at least he should be taught nothing which is false.

Education ought more and more to indoctrinate children with the scientific spirit, and should offer to their belief, not illusions which please them, but truths which instruct them. Then let us habituate the children to accept only opinions which lie within the compass of his thought, and which he can verify for himself. Without wishing to exercise his critical spirit prematurely, let us require him to express an opinion only in earnest and after reflection. Doubtless it is not proposed to make of him a little Cartesian, who believes nothing which he cannot prove; but so far as possible let us appeal to his reason. The pleasure which naturally accompanies the attainment of truth will gradually turn him aside from blind and irra-

---

[1] M. Marion, *Leçons de psychologie*, p. 196.

tional opinions. He will come to love the truth for truth's sake ; will acquire a taste for knowledge ; will feel the need of personal research, and will taste the pleasure of discovery.

258. LOVE OF THE BEAUTIFUL. — We need not stop here to give an exact and rigorous definition of the beautiful. We leave this task to the teachers of æsthetics. For our present purpose beauty is defined chiefly by the feelings which it excites in the mind, by the charm thrown about us by the productions of nature and the works of art, by the admiration with which they fill us.

That the little child is sensible of the beautiful is a fact which cannot be disputed. Certain animals even seem to have some vague feeling of beauty. M. Pérez proves by numerous examples that even before the third year the musical instinct and the instinct of visual beauty are developed and manifested. In his affection for animals, in his preferences for certain persons, and in his taste for pictures, the child already proves that he distinguishes confusedly between what is beautiful and what is ugly. A pretty toy, an agreeable face, a brilliant flower, attract him and please him.

259. ÆSTHETIC EDUCATION. — A complete education cannot leave these natural dispositions uncultivated. It should develop them for their own sake, simply because they form a part of our nature, which would be mutilated if they were allowed to perish ; and it should develop and cultivate them for the further reason that, if well-directed, they may have a happy influence upon moral education.

A place must then be made for what might be called *æsthetic education*. In its widest extent this education would comprise an appreciation of all the beauties of nature and art, literary taste, the enjoyment of music, a knowledge of the plastic arts, and also the various talents which permit us not only to feel the beauty there is in the works of others, but to realize it in works of our own. We are not concerned here with that special culture which makes critics, artists, and poets ; but, considered simply as an element in general education, in view of assuring the happiness and relative perfection of the human being, æsthetic education is still important ; and it is to be regretted that in modern society it has not yet obtained the credit which it enjoyed among the ancients.

260. ÆSTHETIC EDUCATION AMONG THE ANCIENTS. — For making men moral, the ancients, particularly the Greeks, counted upon art even more than religion. At Athens, moral education was above all an æsthetic education. Plato thought that the soul ascends to the good through the beautiful. "Beautiful and good" are two words constantly associated by the Greeks.

"We ought," says Plato, "to seek artists who by the power of genius can trace out the nature of the fair and the graceful, that our young men, dwelling as it were in a healthful region, may drink in good from every quarter, whence any emanation from noble works may strike upon their eye or ear, like a gale wafting health from salubrious lands, and win them imperceptibly from their earliest years into resemblance, love, and harmony with the true beauty of reason.

"Is it not, then, on these accounts that we attach such supreme importance to a musical education, because rhythm and harmony sink most deeply into the recesses of the soul, bringing gracefulness in their train, and making a man graceful if he be rightly nurtured, — but if not, the reverse, — and also because he that has been duly nurtured therein will have the keenest eye for defects, whether in the failures of art or in the misgrowths of nature, and, feeling a most just disdain for them, will commend beautiful objects, gladly receive them into his soul, feed upon them, and grow to be noble and good; whereas he will rightly censure and hate all repulsive objects, even in his childhood, before he is able to be reasoned with; and when reason comes, he will welcome her most cordially who can recognize her by instinct of relationship and because he has been thus nurtured?"[1]

What Plato designates *music* would be called to-day art in general; and in his view art is, so to speak, a ladder of virtue, a preparation for the life of the reason.

The ancients were always inclined not to isolate morality, but to confound it, now with the search for the true, and now with the love of the good. While Socrates affirmed that the good and the true are the same thing, the Stoics proclaimed the identity of beauty and virtue.

261. THE ARTS AND MORALS. — In fact, there are intimate relations between the arts and morals.

"Art should be taught a child," says M. Marion, "because it has an incomparable educating power. The *beautiful* is essentially *order and harmony.* From the imagination and the mind, that order and harmony pass into the heart and soon manifest themselves outwardly by elegance and grace; a just proportion is observed in the movements, and finally it reappears in the acts. Good taste easily takes the form of self-respect. Is it not a commonplace to say that art softens public and private manners? There are faults and moral tendencies, the idea of which a mind accustomed to live in companionship with the beautiful can neither conceive nor abide."[2]

Evil, in fact, is an ugly thing; and the delicacy of a soul sensitive to beauty is offended at it and spurns it. And if we make a minute study of the different beauties

---

[1] *Republic*, pp. 401, 402.

[2] M. Marion, *Leçons de psychologie*, p. 200.

which art and nature have contrived for charming and ennobling life, the moral influence of the beautiful appears still more striking. The spectacles of nature allay the passions and envelop us in their purity and innocence. The plastic arts at the very least reveal and communicate to us the grace and elegance of the bodily movements. Music, the most impressive of the arts, to which the ancients attributed a preponderant part in moral education, transmits to the soul a certain contagion of order and harmony. Finally, poetry exalts and enchants us by its more formal inspirations; it moves us with admiration for all the beautiful deeds which it celebrates, and which it proposes as models to the enthusiasm that it excites within us.

262. THE ARTS AS A SOURCE OF PLEASURE. — The arts are not merely an element of moral culture, but deserve to be recommended also as the source of some of the sweetest, keenest, and also the most elevated emotions which human nature can enjoy. It is not possible to cut off man from pleasure; so let us try to have him seek it and find it in the pure enjoyments of art.

"We should recognize in the art emotions," says Mr. Bain, "a means of pleasure as such, a pure hedonic factor; in which capacity they are a final end. Their function in intellectual education is the function of all pleasure when not too great; namely, to cheer, refresh, and encourage us in our work."[1]

The artistic pleasures, in fact, have no disturbing or corrupting effect; they calm and pacify the soul. Far from turning it aside from serious studies, they incline it towards them; they compromise neither the delicacy of the emotions nor the strength of the reason. They oc-

---

[1] *Education as a Science*, pp. 96, 97.

cupy, better than any other diversion can, our hours of
leisure, the intervals of active life; and when we leave
them, we resume without effort and without disturbance
the labors and obligations of our profession or trade. To
those who might be tempted to deny the moral influence
of art, and who might not comprehend what power it has
to purify and ennoble the soul, we would reply further
that the æsthetic sentiments are good in themselves; that
they bring us exquisite, salutary, and wholesome joys;
and that they are also good because they replace other
emotions, and are substitutes for inferior pleasures of a
purely material order, where morals are destroyed and
the heart abased. "If we regard education as a means
of making men happy," says Mr. Bain, "it ought certainly to comprise a knowledge of the arts."

263. TESTIMONY OF STUART MILL. — In general, the
most scientific minds, those most enamored of the truth,
do not remain insensible to the charm of the arts. Thus,
in his *Memoirs*, Stuart Mill relates that his early education, under the direction of an austere father, had been
entirely devoted to abstract reflection, to logic, and to
science. At three years of age he knew Greek; at
twelve, he was a logician; at thirteen, he learned the integral calculus. What resulted from this exclusively intellectual education, from this inordinate instruction? During
his years of adolescence he was seized with a profound
sadness, a real disgust for life. At the age of twenty
he was beset each day for a winter by a wish to drown
himself. But a book of poems fell into his hands; he
formed a taste for music; and he was saved, consoled by
emotion. He then comprehended the importance of the
first emotions and sentiments which attach us to life, by
embellishing it with their charms.

264. The Arts in the Common School. — As yet the arts have had too little influence upon popular education. The child has so little time to devote to his instruction; he must in five or six years learn so many things for immediate use, must acquire so much practical knowledge, that we hesitate to impose on him this new burden which comes from even an elementary study of the arts.

And yet it is very desirable that popular education should not be exclusively subordinate to the pursuit of material interests, and that there should be reserved a place, the widest possible, for the disinterested culture of taste and the sentiment of the beautiful.

"Would not the laboring man," says M. Ravaisson eloquently, "upon whom hard necessity imposes so heavy a weight, find the best alleviation for his hard condition, if his eyes were opened to what Leonardo da Vinci calls *la bellezza del mondo;* if he also were thus called to enjoy the sight of those graces which we see scattered over this vast world, and which, made sensible to the heart, according to Pascal's expression, soothe more than anything else his sadness, and more than anything else give him the presentiment and the foretaste of a better destiny?"

265. Love for the Beautiful, how Cultivated. — From the child's earliest years he should be accustomed to inhale, so to speak, the beauties which surround him. Even in the country, where works of art are lacking, the pretty, beautiful, or sublime things presented by the spectacle of nature will suffice for this primary education in æsthetics. Later, the field-laborer will feel sustained in his rude toil by the love with which he has been inspired for rural beauty.

"Very early the child should be made sensible to the beauties of trees, flowers, birds, insects, and all those marvels which he might perhaps pass by without seeing; he must be led to

the pure source of the disinterested enjoyments of admiration." [1]

"For the language of the imagination," said Madame Necker
de Saussure to the same effect, "the first vocabulary is to be found
in nature."

Says Herder also, "It is a proof of the profound barbarism in
which we bring up our children, that we neglect to give them,
from their earliest years, a profound impression of the beauty,
harmony, and variety which our earth presents." [2]

266. INDIRECT MEANS. — At school even the decoration
of the class-room, the simple ornaments with which it is
embellished, the pictures which adorn its walls, and the
illustrations in the text-books, will be so many indirect
means for preparing the child to enjoy whatever is beautiful. It is not possible to expect that the child in our
school shall live, like the little Athenian, among the
masterpieces of art, and, so to speak, in the midst of a
world of statues. At least, so far as possible, he should
be surrounded by objects which do not shock his taste;
and even in his toys everything that is ugly or repulsive,
everything that is of a nature to produce bad habits of
hearing and seeing, should be avoided. [3] The treasures of
art should also be opened to him by visits to museums
and libraries.

---

[1] Mlle. Chalamet, *l'École maternelle*, p. 150.

[2] Herder, *Idées*, II., Chap. IV.

[3] An elegant and judicious writer, M. Rigault, strongly insists
on the disadvantages presented by the first playthings if they chance
to be ugly.

"Why is it that almost always there is made of the rattle, of
that old man in metal which is the first plaything of the child, a
deformed creature, hump-backed, with inordinate mouth and a hooked
nose reaching to the chin? The first imitation of nature which
strikes the eyes of the child is the figure of a monster. He is intro-

267. Special Exercises. — But to these indirect means there must be added special exercises. These studies, however, should remain very elementary.

"The school," says M. Rendu, "ought to make neither mechanists, agriculturists, surveyors, nor gymnasts; and no more should it make musicians. The school *initiates* the child into the sciences he will need when he becomes a man; it makes a rough draft, but does not complete the picture." [1]

M. Ravaisson, in the remarkable article to which we have already referred, gives his preference to drawing, and to the drawing of the human figure. But perhaps for the pupils of the common school, for the workmen of the future, ornamental and geometrical drawing may be more useful, and may prepare them better for the vocations which will occupy their lives.

268. Culture of the Taste. — An elementary education in æsthetics ought to develop the taste, rather than talent for execution; not that refined and purely critical taste, which simply spies out defects in works of art, and which is of advantage only to specialists; but that catholic and beneficent taste which borders on enthusiasm, which is interested in all forms of beauty, which is displayed not merely in the appreciation of literary qualities, but in the enjoyment of all the arts.

---

duced to art through the medium of the ugly. But this is not all; the body of this knock-kneed, hump-backed fellow is provided with a shrill whistle, the sound of which tortures the nascent hearing of the child. This is intended, it is said, to divert him. Here is the first idea given to him of music, — his entrance on life is greeted by a false note. I am persuaded that each year in our country the education of the child by this wretched toy destroys in germ a host of painters and musicians." (*Œuvres complètes*, IV. p. 276.)

[1] *Manuel de l'enseignement primaire.*

"Only a few are artists," says Mr. Bain, "and the rest enjoy the works produced by these. . . . . Without being able to perform, one may acquire a taste for music by listening to performances. . . . . The group of arts addressed to the eye, — painting, design, sculpture, architecture, — are the enjoyment of many; but their production is confined to a few. . . . Every literary teacher contributes to the poetic taste, both as enjoyment and as discrimination." [1]

Without doubt it is literary and poetic taste that it is easiest to develop, because, first, the masterpieces in this line are more numerous than in any other, and then for the reason that models of literary art are within the reach of all, and it is not necessary, in order to enjoy them, to force the doors of a museum.

269. ART AS A MORALIZER. — We cannot repeat too often that æsthetic culture concerns us less as a disinterested education of the artistic faculties than as an ally in moral education. It is this function of art which a contemporary moralist has placed in sharp relief in the following extract:

"We know the system of those fathers, mothers, and teachers who imagine that in education scoldings alone are efficacious, and that we form and mould the soul only by the use of maxims. In this sort of instruction, or rather régime, if the maxims are of a nature not to be easily swallowed, it is thought best to resort to a wholesome deception; the remedy is diluted in a fable, so that the patient may take it without suspecting what it is, in imitation of that physician of antiquity, who, not able to make his patient take a bitter herb, bethought himself to have a goat fed on it, so that the milk, thus impregnated with the medicinal virtue, might restore the deceived invalid to health. In this way a thousand sly and insidious ways are taken to infuse the precepts

---

[1] *Education as a Science*, Chap. XIII.

of morality. Is not this to say in effect that honesty is a frightful and disagreeable thing, which must be persistently sweetened and adulterated in order to make it palatable? Even supposing this education to be good, is it the only one? Is it not likely that children will be more profited by living with an honorable man who lives nobly, who expresses only noble sentiments, who by his discourse and his example spreads around him a beneficent influence, without ever resorting to the language of the *moralities?* It may be said that in society art resembles a noble man. If it is what it ought to be, if it is grand and pure and delicate, it instructs and purifies by its very delicacy, it teaches by its very presence." [1]

270. EXCESSES TO BE AVOIDED. — But whatever may be said of the educative virtue of art, we must nevertheless be ou our guard against exaggeration, and oppose those who say that beauty is the secret of education, just as beauty is the secret of the universe. No; unfortunately, the real education of man cannot be content with the gracious and vague inspirations of art; the child cannot thrive on hymns and sonnets, *in hymnis et canticis;* we might just as well say that he ought to be brought up in games and a perpetual recreation. Æsthetic pleasures may indeed be pure and elevated pleasures, but after all they are but pleasures; they share the nature of emotions, and the emotions cannot be the rule of life.

The abuse of the æsthetic emotions enervates and enfeebles the soul, and makes minds so extremely delicate as to be unable to confront with courage the unpleasant things of real life. "The delicate are unhappy," said La Fontaine; and he meant by this that the delicate have not force enough to resist the trials of life, to surmount its difficulties and obstacles. Let us plant in the heart a

---

[1] M. Martha, in the *Revue des Deux Mondes,* April 15, 1870.

noble aspiration after the ideal; but let us not forget
that life is made up of realities, that existence does not at
all resemble a pleasing poem, interspersed with songs, in
which we have but to follow the seducing lead of the
pleasures of taste.   There are efforts to make, struggles
to sustain, miseries to fight; and to prepare man for the
combats of life there must be a virile apprenticeship; we
must develop the reason still more than the imagination,
and must cultivate science more than art and poetry.

271. THE RELIGIOUS SENTIMENT. — Whatever may be
the importance of the religious sentiment in life, we shall
make but brief mention of it here, since this sentiment is
especially connected with doctrines and confessional beliefs, with which the philosophy of education cannot
concern itself.

While in England and elsewhere, " the schoolmaster of
the primary school is expected to be an instructor in religion, both in its own proper character and as a support
of the highest morality," we have in France preferred to
separate the school from the church, and to leave to the
ministers of the different sects the duty of catechizing
children.

Is this saying that everything relating to religious education ought to be discarded from instruction proper?
Certainly not.   Apart from forms and rites and particular dogmas, there is a natural aspiration of man towards
religion, — that is, according to the definition which M.
Marion gives of it, " towards a body of beliefs which
surpass positive knowledge, and which relate to man's
place in nature, as well as to his destiny." [1]

In our opinion the part of the educator will be mainly

---

[1] *La Réform universitaire*, 10ᵉ leçon.

negative in such cases; I mean that he ought scrupulously to respect all the beliefs of the child, and to say nothing and do nothing which may wound the religious feelings which have been inculcated in him by his parents or his ecclesiastical teachers. But must anything beyond this be done? Must the instructor depart from this attitude of deference and respect, to intervene directly and actively in the culture of the religious sentiment? Many great and good men do not hesitate to reply in the affirmative.

272. RELIGIOUS EDUCATION IN THE COMMON SCHOOLS. — M. Paul Janet has clearly defined the proper sphere of religious education in moral instruction. He speaks as follows:

"The natural coronation of moral instruction in the common school will be the knowledge of God. Children will be taught that life has a serious purpose, that men are not the product of chance, that a wise thought watches over the universe, and that a vigilant eye penetrates all. hearts.

It will pertain to the particular sects to teach and prescribe regular exercises in traditional form. Special effort will be made to awaken in souls the religious sentiment; they will be made to comprehend that the feeling and thought of God may be associated with all the acts of life, and that every action may be at the same time moral and religious, so far as it is the accomplishment of the will of Providence. *Qui travaille prie*, says the proverb. A life which strives to preserve itself pure and virtuous is a continual prayer. As to stated prayer in a particular form, it is within the domain of positive religion. It seems to us that this way of interpreting one's duties towards God can offend no one, for the state does not undertake to assert that a purely subjective piety is sufficient, and it leaves the different sects to show that it is not. Those who think in this way will feel only the more authorized to require parents to complete the religious education of their children by the instruction of the church." [1]

---

[1] *Rapport*, à la section permanent du Conseil Supérieur, 20 juin, 1882.

273. Morals and Religion. — In speaking thus, M. Janet is inspired by some of the greatest masters of modern pedagogy, especially by Rousseau and Kant.

For Kant, morals and religion are inseparable; and between them are intimate relations. But the German philosopher understands these relations as follows: "In his view, morals is the base and source of religion; it is religion which is the consequence of morals. It is because one first believes in duty imperiously revealed by conscience, that he afterwards rises to the conception of God and to the hope of an immortal destiny." [1]

"Religion," he says, "is the law which resides within us, so far as it derives its authority from a supreme legislator and judge; it is morals applied to the knowledge of God. When religion is not united to morality, it is no more than a manner of soliciting the favor of heaven. Songs, prayer, attendance at church, ought to serve only to give man new strength and new courage to work for his amelioration; they should be but the expression of a heart animated by the idea of duty. They are but preparations for good works, but not themselves good works, and one cannot please God except by becoming better. . . . The beginning must not be made in theology. Religion which is founded solely on theology has no moral element. It will embody no feelings save the fear of punishment on the one hand and on the other the hope of reward, that which will produce only a superstitious creed. Morality must then precede and theology follow; and this is what is called religion."

In other terms, God ought to appear in the consciousness only behind duty. From the idea of law we rise to the idea of the lawgiver. The reproaches of the conscience are as the ambassadors of God in our soul.

However difficult the course we have just indicated may be for the intelligence of the child, we are convinced that

---

[1] Kant, *Pédagogie*, p. 243.

it is the only one which is admissible in lay teaching, in universal instruction. Let us not introduce the child into religious controversies; let us be temperate on all those questions which divide men, and in which absolute clearness has not been attained. Religion is nothing if it is but a series of formulas learned by heart and imposed by force. Let us respect the liberty of the child, let us in no respect restrain his soaring towards the ideal, towards the infinite; but let us not constrain him by obliging him to believe what he does not comprehend. Let us aim chiefly at morals; let us build moral principles on such solid foundations that in a crisis which might carry away religious beliefs, the belief in duty would not disappear with them.

PART SECOND

PRACTICAL PEDAGOGY.

CHAPTER I.

METHODS IN GENERAL.

274. PRACTICAL PEDAGOGY. — Practical pedagogy is but
the application of the general rules established in theoretical pedagogy. After having studied the different faculties by themselves, both in their natural development and in
their school training, it is proposed to examine by the light
of these established principles the different parts of the
course of study and the principal questions of discipline.
In other terms, from the *subject* of education, the child,
we now pass to the *object* of education; that is, to the
methods of teaching and to the rules of school adminis-
tration.

275. METHOD IN GENERAL. — Method in general is the
order which we voluntarily introduce into our thoughts,
our acts, and our undertakings.[1] To act methodically
is the contrary of acting thoughtlessly, inconsiderately,
without continuity and without plan. Port Royal justly
defined method as " the art of rightly arranging a series
of several thoughts. "

Understood in this liberal sense, method is applicable to

---

[1] M. Rousselot defines method as the straightest and surest route
for the discovery of truth, or for the communication of it when it
has been discovered. This definition is not satisfactory, because
it omits the element which is absolutely essential to the meaning
of the word. Method implies calculation, reflection, will.

all the parts of education as to all the undertakings of
man. The first duty of a teacher is, not to proceed at
random, not to count upon the inspiration of the moment
and upon the good fortune of improvised effort, but
always to be guided by principles deliberately chosen, according to fixed rules and in a premeditated order. The
lack of method is the ruin of education. There is nothing to be expected from a discipline which is hesitating
and groping; from instruction which remains incoherent
and disorderly, which fluctuates at the mercy of circumstances and occasions, and which, being wholly unpre-
meditated, allows itself to be taken at unawares.

276. METHODS OF INSTRUCTION. — In a more precise
and particular sense, *method* designates a whole body of
rational processes, of rules, of means which are practiced
and followed in the accomplishment of any undertaking.
Just as for the discovery of truth there are methods
which logic prescribes, there will also be, for the communication and teaching of truth, other methods, the study
of which constitutes practical pedagogy.

Methods will vary with the nature of the subjects to be
taught. Geography will be taught differently from grammar, and mathematics differently from physics. They
will also vary with the age of the child. It is not possible to present history to the pupils of a primary school
in the same form as to the pupils of a high school. Consequently methods will vary with the different grades of
instruction. They will be one thing in a primary school
and another in a normal school; one thing in general
primary instruction, and another thing in secondary instruction.

In other terms, methods of instruction should always
conform to these three general principles: 1, the special

characteristics of the branches of knowledge communicated to the child; 2, the laws of mental evolution at
different periods of life; 3, the particular purpose and the
scope of each grade of instruction.

277. METHODOLOGY, SO CALLED. — The study of methods of instruction constitutes one of the most important
divisions of educational science. To give it a name,
foreign educators have borrowed from philosophy the
stately term *methodology*. Others have called it *didactics*,
or the art of teaching. M. Daguet ventures the designation *methodics*.[1]

Special works have been devoted to methodology, which
itself is subdivided, and comprises several parts. In
Belgium and in Switzerland the professors of pedagogy
distinguish general methodology, which treats of the
principles common to all method, from special methodology, which examines in succession the different branches
of instruction, and searches for the best means to be employed in each science and in each study. It is a distinction analogous to that which is found in treatises on
Logic, where we study general method, applicable to all
the sciences, before devoting special chapters to the
method peculiar to each science.

278. UTILITY OF METHODS. — Educators are very far
from having come to an understanding as to the utility
of methods and the necessity of studying them. Some
are disposed to accord everything to methods, and others
nothing or almost nothing.

Methods, according to Talleyrand, are the masters'
masters. "The true instruments of the sciences, they

---

[1] M. Daguet, *Manuel de Pédagogie*, Neuchatel, 1881, p. 126.

are to teachers themselves what teachers are to their pupils." [1]

Pestalozzi, who however lacked method, and assures us that "he proceeded in his instruction without knowing what he did, guided only by very obscure but very vivid feeling," — Pestalozzi put a very high estimate on those systematic rules which he had not sufficient reflective power to impose upon himself. At certain moments he pushes to fanaticism, even to superstition, his enthusiasm for methods, precisely because he was most lacking in them. He disowned himself, his own qualities of inspiration and feeling, and his ever-active and ever-vivifying personality when he pronounced these strange words :

"I believe that we must not think of making, in general, the least progress in the instruction of the people, as long as we have not found modes of teaching which make of the instructor, at least so far as the elementary studies are concerned, the simple mechanical instrument of a method which owes its results to the nature of its processes, and not to the skill of him who employs it, I affirm that a school-book has no value, except so far as it can be employed by a teacher without instruction, as well as by one who is instructed." [2]

It is not proposed to make of the instructor an automaton, and of method a mechanism which is a substitute for the intelligence and the personal qualities of the teacher. If we recommend the study of methods, it is

---

[1] "The purpose of methods is to conduct teachers in the true paths, to simplify and abridge for them the difficult road of instruction. They are not necessary alone to common minds; the most creative genius itself receives incalculable aid from them." (*Rapport à l'Assemblée constituante.*)

[2] *How Gertrude teaches her Children.*

for the especial purpose of driving from instruction
routine and questionable tradition, and not of introducing
into it, under another form, a sort of learned mechanism.
Methods are instruments; but instruments, however perfect they may be, owe their whole value to the skill of
the hand that employs them. To the paradox of Pestalozzi we oppose the wisdom of the ages, and the proverb
which says, "As is the master so is the method." Let
us also bear in mind that methods are not unchangeable
regulations, despotic and irrevocable laws; it rests with
the initiative of the teacher to modify them according to
the results of his own experience and the suggestions of
his own mind. "Methods," as Madame Necker de Saussure
says, "ought to be in a state of perpetual improvement."

Thus understood, not as laws slavishly accepted with
a superstitious respect, but as instruments which are to
be handled with freedom, methods, no one will deny,
may render important services.

"Method," says M. Marion, "is a necessary condition of success,
and, with respect to efficiency of service, it puts, as it were, an
abyss between men of equal good intent. Descartes went so far
as to say that, apparently equal as to intellectual endowments,
men differ not so much by the power they have in searching for
truth, as in the method which they employ. The truth is that in
every kind of practical work, other things being equal, he who
proceeds rationally has at least three great advantages over him
who lives on expedients, from hand to mouth. Starting with a
fixed purpose, he runs less risk of losing sight of it and of missing
his way. Having reflected on the means at his command, he has
more chances of omitting none of them and of always choosing
the best. Finally, sure both of the end in view and of the means
of attaining it, it depends only on himself to reach it as soon as
possible. 'A lame man on a straight road,' said Bacon, 'reaches
his destination sooner than a courier who misses his way.'"[1]

---

[1] M. Marion, article *Méthode,* in *the Dictionnaire de Pédagogie.*

279. Abuse of the Study of Methods. — But, convinced as we are of the utility of methods, we do not think. that it is necessary to pause to study the abstract generalities which dominate them. If this point is not guarded, the educators of our day will proceed to construct a sort of new scholastic, all bristling with learned formulas, subtile divisions, and pedantic terms. They will succeed in making of a very simple study, one wholly practical, a logic of a new kind and of a truly frightful aspect, in which fine words succeed fine words, and in which the real things are forgotten. Let us distrust the formalism which is always ready to set up its claims, because it is easier to inscribe words on paper than to awaken emotions in the heart or to enrich the mind with positive notions.

Open one of those manuals of pedagogy which are so very popular in Belgium and Germany. You will there find interminable pages devoted to the distinction between *principles*, *modes*, *forms*, *processes*, and *methods* of instruction.[1] You will there see crowded tables which contain no less than eight forms of instruction: the *acromatic* form, or that of uninterrupted exposition, the *erotematic*, or that of interrupted exposition, which contains no less than seven other distinct forms, as the *catechetic*, *socratic*, *heuristic*, *repetitive*, *examinative*, *analytic and synthetic*, and the *paralogic*. As if this were not enough, there follows a subdivision of processes, as the *intuitive*, *comparative*, *by opposition*, *etymological*, *by reasoning*, *descriptive*, *by internal observation*, *repetitive*, *synoptic*, *by reproduction*, and eleven processes besides!

---

[1] To note but one, see the *Cours de pédagogie et de méthodologi*, by M. H. Braun, inspector of the normal schools of Belgium, Brussels, 1885, p. 954.

What good can come from this tedious analysis, from this complicated enumeration, from this purely verbal science, in which hundreds of words are employed, and yet teach nothing of the things themselves? Teaching would become a very laborious art, were it necessary, in order to be a good instructor, to have lodged in the memory all these definitions of pure form, all these insipid abstractions. It is said that modern education tends to approach nature. Alas! we are far from nature with these distillers of pedagogic quintessence, who split hairs, who distinguish and analyze the simplest things, and invent several barbarous terms to designate identical operations. For a long time it was thought that it was impossible to reason well without knowing the categories and the rules of the syllogism. Let us not imagine, by a similar illusion, that in order to teach well one's memory must be stuffed with this pedagogic nonsense, with these nomenclatures as vain as pretentious.

It is not only their inutility that alarms us. We also fear that they may divert the mind from more serious interests, and that this unsubstantial food may destroy the taste for more solid and substantial aliment. We fear that that which gives instruction its real power, — life, inner emotion, free and original inspiration, — may succumb under this maze of abstractions which fetter the mind and make it bend under the weight of these dangerous puerilities.

Hence let us shun all those sterile discussions which consist in knowing, for example, which are the general principles, the special principles, the positive principles, the negative principles of teaching;[1] or, still further, " whether analysis is a *method* or a *form*."[2] Let us be satisfied with a few definite notions, and as summary as possible.

---

[1] M. Braun, *op. cit.*, p. 200.
[2] Ibid., p. 235.

280. METHODS, MODES, AND PROCESSES OF INSTRUC-
TION. — Without wishing to multiply distinctions, it is nevertheless impossible to confound with methods, properly
so-called, what it has been agreed to call modes of
teaching.

Modes of teaching depend neither on the order which
is followed nor upon the means which are employed for
instructing children; they have reference simply to the
different groups of pupils and to different ways in which
the instruction is distributed.

There is the *individual* mode, as when the teacher addresses himself to a single pupil; or the simultaneous
mode, as when he addresses himself to several pupils, as
to a whole class; or the *mutual* mode, when the teacher
stands aside and requires the children to instruct one
another.

The individual mode is really appropriate only in private
education, where a preceptor is face to face with a
single pupil. At school there is no propriety in proceeding in this way, and it is difficult to imagine a class
where the teacher repeats forty times to forty pupils what
it suffices to say once to all.

It was this system, however, or something very like it,
that was formerly employed in the early history of the
school. In the seventeenth century, for example, the
École paroissiale, a school manual of the times, says in
literal terms: "Those who go to the master to read
shall present themselves but two at once. . . . . The
teacher shall call the writers to his desk, two by two, to
correct their exercises."[1]

All that remains, all that can remain of individual instruction, in a class regularly organized, is the interroga-

---

[1] *L'École paroissiale*, 1654, 3e partie, Chap. IV.

tion which the teacher addresses to a single pupil. Such interrogations should be made with a loud voice, in order that all the pupils may participate in the exercise.

As to the mutual mode, it was but an expedient suggested by necessity at the time when teachers were scarce and resources were limited, and it was necessary at slight expense to instruct well or ill a very large number of pupils.[1] Almost universally abandoned to-day, and virtually condemned, the mutual system never had a claim in theory to be regarded as a rational mode of school organization.

There remains the simultaneous mode,[2] which is the only one possible in classes more or less numerous, if it is desired that without loss of time the sound instruction of an experienced teacher, not that of a monitor without authority, should be directly transmitted to all the pupils.

It is true that the simultaneous mode, though it is the general rule and the prevailing form of instruction, ought not to proscribe absolutely the incidental and exceptional use of other systems. So far as possible, the teacher ought, while addressing himself to all, to speak to each; he ought to take account of the vivacity of some and the slowness of others; he should vary his language, so as to accommodate himself to the different aptitudes of his pupils; finally, he should not forget that, though his instruction is simultaneous, his attention and his efforts ought to remain individual.

On the other hand, in very large schools and in those where a single teacher has three divisions to manage, the

---

[1] Swiss teachers distinguish a mode of instruction as the *magistral,* "that which is entirely given by the master, without co-operation on the part of pupils."

[2] See Compayré's *History of Pedagogy,* pp. 513, 519; also Gill's *Systems of Education,* Chap. IV.

master sometimes needs to appeal to the good-will of his best pupils, aud thus to employ something like mutual instruction. This is what is called the mixed mode.[1]

281. METHODS AND PROCESSES. — There might also be retained, although it is of less importance, the classical distinction between methods and *processes*, methods being the sum of the principles which preside over instruction, assign to it its end, regulate its order, and determine its course; while processes signify the particular means which are employed in the application of methods. Thus to demonstrate geometrical truths is a method; to exhibit them on a board, and then cause them to be repeated by the pupils, is a process. To give a didactic exposition of historical facts is a method; to require restatements from pupils is a process.

282. GENERAL METHOD. — The further pedagogy enters into the detail of methods and into the minute examination of processes, the nearer it will approach its end, which is not to construct beautiful theories, but to render practical services. However, before entering upon the different varieties of studies, before searching for the rules which are especially adapted to each of them, it is not without use to throw a glance over the general methods of instruction and the rules applicable to all the parts of the programme. Besides being interesting in itself to reduce apparent diversities to unity, and to look for essential principles in the multitude of particular applications, educators have so extended the list of methods, they

---

[1] By addressing himself to each of his pupils individually, the master learns to know his pupils better, to treat them according to their particular characters, and can better follow the development of their minds. (Wilm, *Essai sur l'éducation du peuple.*)

offer us so great a luxuriance and so stately a display
of pedagogical instruments, that it is necessary to sim-
·plify their classifications and to try to introduce some
clearness into a subject which it seems so easy to make
obscure.

283. CLASSIFICATION OF METHODS. — It is no longer
two or three methods which the classical treatises on
pedagogy distinguish; but if we are to trust these authorities, there are more than a dozen different methods. In
the presence of this endless catalogue we may well imagine that the teacher experiences a sort of dismay. Are
there, in fact, so many ways of correct procedure? Does
good instruction admit of so many refinements and complications? No; and it needs only a little attention to be
convinced that these classifications and tabular statements can be easily reduced without any detriment to
facts, and simply by pruning away a vain display of
words.

We shall then place no reliance on the *synoptical table*
of M. Daguet, who distinguishes methods as the *educative*,
the *rational*, the *practical*, the *progressive*, the *synthetic*,
the *analytic*, the *intensive*, the *inventive*, and the *intuitive*,
to which must be added, according to other authorities, the
experimental, the *socratic*, the *inductive*, the *deductive*, the
demonstrative, and the *expositive*, without counting the composite methods which result from the coupling of two simple
methods, such as the *analytic-synthetic*, the *demonstrative-
expositive*, the *demonstrative-interrogative*, etc., etc.[1] We
shall attempt to show that at bottom, behind this verbiage,
there are concealed at most two or three real distinctions;
that methods might be reduced to two, if we regard merely

---

[1] We may still distinguish as methods the systems followed by
different educators, as the methods of Jacotot, Pestalozzi, Froebel, etc.

the order which is followed in the distribution and in the connection of the truths or facts taught; and that at most there are four, if we take into account, not merely the interior nexus which connects the different propositions of which a given study is composed, but also the *form* which the teacher gives to his instruction.

284. INTERIOR ORDER OF TRUTHS WHICH ARE TO BE EXPOUNDED; INDUCTION AND DEDUCTION. — Let us begin by considering the first element, the first factor of method, — the logical order which presides over the sequence of propositions.

From this point of view, the teacher who communicates truth, like the scholar who discovers it, has at his command only two methods, induction and deduction. He either takes facts for his point of departure, and having made his pupils observe and test them, he classifies them according to their resemblances, and leads the pupil to the law which includes them; and this is the pedagogical application of the inductive method. Or he starts with general truths and definitions which he explains and causes to be comprehended, and by deduction he passes from these principles and rules to the applications and to the particular cases which naturally flow from them; and then the method is deductive.

Let us take examples. If in the teaching of grammar we first present the rule and then seek to find its applications, we proceed by deduction; but if, on the contrary, we begin by presenting to the child examples or particular cases, in order that we may then suggest the idea of the rule, the process is inductive. The teacher of geometry who at the outset lays down axioms and definitions, and then proves that such or such a theorem is the necessary consequence of them, gives a demonstration,

or, what amounts to the same thing, a series of deductions. The professor of physics who appeals to the observation of his pupils, who performs experiments before
them, who shows them the bodies which are the subjects
of study and makes an analysis of their elements, employs in succesion the different processes of induction.
In history also we proceed by deduction or induction,
according as we set out with a definition, as of the feudal
system, for example, or with the different' facts which
constitute the feudal system.

285. EXTERIOR FORM OF INSTRUCTION; CONSECUTIVE
EXPOSITION OR INTERROGATION. — But instruction does
not differ merely by the inductive or the deductive course
which is impressed on the series of propositions; there
must also be taken into account the exterior form which
is given to instruction while transmitting it to pupils. In
fact, we can proceed in two ways: we may state the
object of the lesson, and, speaking authoritatively, may
teach by uninterrupted discourse; or, by interrogating
pupils and making suggestions to them, we may make
them discover for themselves what we wish them to
learn.[1] Hence a new distinction and two different methods: the method of exposition and the method of interrogation, or socratic method.

---

[1] Suppose we have to give a lesson on the distinctive characters of
the three kingdoms of nature. I will either start with the division
of the three categories of bodies, and then pass to the distinctive characters of minerals, vegetables, and animals, and end with examples; or,
following the same course, will proceed by interrogations, such as
"What is meant by natural history? What is its triple object? Of
what does geology treat? Botany? Zoölogy? What are the essential
differences between minerals, vegetables, and animals? Give examples,
etc." (M. Horner, *Guide pratique de l'instituteur*, Paris, 1882, p. 9.)

286. Examination of the Four Essential Methods. — But let us hasten to remark that the two elements of method, *order* and *form*, are not separated in fact: on the contrary, they are united. In other terms, whether we proceed by induction or by deduction, we must either expound or interrogate. Consequently there are four general methods, to which all the others are to be referred:

1. The method of induction, in the form of exposition.
2. The method of induction, in the form of interrogation.
3. The method of deduction or demonstration, in the form of exposition.
4. The method of deduction, in the form of interrogation.

Each of these methods has its characteristics and its peculiar advantages. In a general way it may be said that the choice between deduction and induction is determined mainly by the nature of the science which is to be taught. The mathematics hardly allow the use of any method but the deductive, while the physical sciences are to be treated inductively. On the other hand, whether preference shall be given to continuous exposition or to the system of interrogation depends in great part on the age and the intelligence of the children to whom we address ourselves. When Fénelon said, though with some exaggeration, "Employ formal lessons as little as possible," he was thinking particularly of little children, to whose weakness a long, uninterrupted discourse is badly adapted. Continuous exposition is, however, necessary in a great number of cases, were it only to obviate the slowness of the instruction. On the other hand, the interrogative method has the advantage of more directly calling into play the activity of the pupil; it is the method of all others for promoting the discovery of the truth, for suggesting it without imposing it.

287. Reduction of the Different Methods to these Four Types. — With this explanation, it is easy to prove that the most of the methods wrongly distinguished by educators may be reduced to the four types which we have just established and are blended with them.[1]

For example, what is the method called the *inventive* except the method of induction and interrogation, — that which, avoiding didactic lessons, demands of the pupil a personal effort, and makes him discover for himself what we wish to teach him?

It is useless to speak of the *heuristic* method, which differs in no respect from the *inventive*, save that *inventive* comes from a Latin word, and *heuristic* from a Greek word. Diversity of expressions should not make us think that there is a real diversity in methods.

The *demonstrative* method is simply synonymous with *deductive* method, a demonstration being but a body of deductions.

The *catechetic*[2] method, which consists in stating questions and demanding replies, does not differ essentially from the *interrogative* method, nor from the Socratic method, which requires the teacher, in imitation of the celebrated Greek philosopher, to stimulate the good sense and reason of his pupils by his interrogations.

---

[1] We cannot subscribe to the opinion of M. Buisson, who, doubtless through a reaction against the abuse of multiplying methods, falls into the opposite extreme and declares that, properly speaking, there is but one method of pedagogy, a universal method which embraces the whole of education. This is the intuitive method. — See his *Rapport sur l'instruction primaire à l'Exposition universelle de Vienne en* 1875, Chap. IV.

[2] This word is very fashionable in Belgium, where it is the root of a whole family of words. M. Braun defines *catechesis*, which is the lesson given in the form of questions and answers; *catechist*, every man who teaches in this way ; and *catechumen*, the pupil instructed by this method.

It is by an abuse of words that M. Daguet decorates with the name of methods what he calls the *educative, rational, practical,* and *progressive* methods. These are the general characteristics of instruction, the essential tendencies of modern pedagogy ; they are expressions for the ends to be pursued ; truly speaking, they are not methods, — that is, co-ordinated systems of means and processes.[1]

There remain the so-called analytic, synthetic, intuitive, and experimental methods, upon which much fuller explanations are necessary.[2]

288. ANALYSIS AND SYNTHESIS. — I know of no terms more badly defined, or whose meaning has been more obscured by the misuse made of them, than the words *analysis* and *synthesis.* So it would cost me no regret to see them disappear from the vocabulary of pedagogy, where, with their pretentious and pompous airs, they bring nothing but great confusion and obscurity, without any positive advantage.

Analysis and synthesis have in reality no precise meaning, save in chemistry, where they designate two inverse operations which consist either in decomposing or in recomposing bodies, in separating or in uniting the elements which compose them. Everywhere else, in grammar, in mathematics, the words analysis and synthesis are employed only by analogy to express operations which have vague resemblances to the analysis and synthesis of chemistry.

---

[1] It has been justly observed that it is wholly improper to employ the word method to designate such or such a school process, as method of reading, of writing, of arithmetic, or of drawing. " It would seem," says M. Buisson, " that there are as many methods as branches of study or school manuals."

[2] We are far from having enumerated all the methods which it has pleased educators to distinguish and christen. There are still to be noted the *natural, moral, historical,* and *universal* methods.

289. Confused Use of these Words. — The clearest and most accurate thinkers fail in their efforts to define the signification of analysis and synthesis. For example, Littré tells us:

" The analytic method, or method of decomposition, starts from actual facts and attempts to liberate their elements. It is also called the *method of discovery.* The synthetic method, on the contrary, is that which, after having recognized a great number of truths, reunites them all under a general principle, and thus forms a synthesis of them. It is also called the *method of doctrine*, because *when we teach a science we ordinarily start from general principles in order to deduce from them their consequences.*" [1]

With due deference to Littré, the last part of this definition is contradictory. To deduce consequences from a general principle is not at all the same thing as to include a great number of truths under a general principle. In the first case the process is one of real deduction; in the second, it is rather inductive.

290. The So-called Analytic and Synthetic Methods. — A sufficient proof that it has been wrong to introduce the words analysis and synthesis into pedagogy, is the fact that different authors have not come to an understanding as to the use of these expressions. What some call synthesis others call analysis, and *vice versa.*

Thus, for the greater number of educators, analysis is the equivalent of induction, of invention, of experimental research; synthesis, on the contrary, is almost the same thing as deduction, demonstration, didactic exposition.

But this sense, which is the true one, is not universally admitted. Swiss educators, for example, go contrary to the general usage.

[1] *Dictionnaire de la langue française,* au mot *Analyse.*

"The form which is best adapted to an elementary book," says
M. Daguet, "is the *synthetic* or *progressive* form, — that is, that
which proceeds from the particular to the general. The *analytic*
form, which proceeds from the general to the particular and begins with the definition, may be followed in works which are used
in the higher course."[1]

So also M. Horner asserts that "the synonym of demonstration is deduction and analysis; that the *inventive*
process is often confounded with induction, synthesis, and
heuristic."[2] This is exactly opposed to the opinion of
M. Charbonneau, according to which "the demonstrative
method is also named *synthetic*, while the *inventive* is called
analytic."[3]

We believe that the most general usage conforms to this
last opinion. But from all these hesitations and contradictions it seems to us to follow that it is best to leave analysis
and synthesis to the language of scientists, and to eliminate
them from the vocabulary of pedagogy, where they serve
only to obscure a subject which of itself is quite simple.
In all cases it is easy to recollect from what we have said,
that the analytic method is but another term to designate
the inductive method, and the synthetic method but a synonym for the method of deduction and demonstration.[4]

291. IS THERE AN INTUITIVE METHOD? — There could be
no doubt of it, if we listen to the enthusiastic cries which
from all directions salute the advent of this royal method,
destined it seems to replace all others and to regenerate
instruction. And yet, if we consider things attentively, we
shall be convinced that the so-called intuitive method is

[1] Daguet, *op. cit.*, p. 148.
[2] Horner, *op. cit.*, p. 12.
[3] Charbonneau, *Cours de pédagogie*, p. 261.
[4] See Appendix B.

either but a special process which can and should be connected with the essential methods which we have distinguished, or, if we understand it in its most extended sense,
that it is confounded with the general spirit which ought to
animate and vivify all the parts of instruction.

292. DIFFERENT SENSES OF THE WORD INTUITION. —
Usage and fashion sometimes subject words to strange
adventures.

Here is the word *intuition*, which in the seventeenth
century signified, in theological language, 'the immediate
and mystical vision of God, and which, in philosophical
language, signified the evidence of immaterial truths and
of the knowledge of the principles of the reason; and
to-day, by some sort of confusion, this same word, de-
scended from the heights of metaphysics, is employed by
educators as the synonym of sensible and material perception.

In Switzerland, Belgium, and Germany, the *intuitive
method* is almost always confounded with instruction *through
the senses*, and especially with instruction through the sense
of sight.

" The intuitive method consists in submitting things to the
direct examination of the organs of sense, and especially of sight

" Intuitive instruction is that which is addressed to the mind and
heart through the medium of the senses, and particularly of the
sight." [1]

293. SENSIBLE INTUITION AND INTELLECTUAL INTUITION. —
But in France the meaning of the word "intuition" has
been generalized, and the intuitive method, from what our
authorities in pedagogy say, comprehends something very

---

[1] *Traité théorique et pratique de méthodologie,* par Achille V. A.
Namur, 1880, p. 153.

different from lessons addressed to the senses and teaching through the eye. There is intellectual intuition, and even moral intuition.

Intellectual intuition, according to M. Buisson, is the clear and definite consciousness of all the operations of our mind.

" I am conscious of my existence, of my desires, of my feelings, of my volitious ; I see them and feel them within myself, so to speak, more clearly and more distinctly than the eye sees colors or the ear hears sounds." [1]

The same thing would be true of the reason also, and thus intuition returns to its primitive signification, — the immediate adhesion of the mind to the great speculative truths.

As to moral intuition, M. Buisson defines it as follows :

" It is taking possession at once, by the mind, the heart, and the conscience, of those axioms of the moral order and of those in-demonstrable and indubitable truths which are the regulating principle of our conduct. There is an intuition of the good and the beautiful, as there is an intuition of the true ; only it is still more delicate, more irreducible to demonstrative processes, resists analysis to a greater degree, is more fugitive and more inexpli-cable, because it is complicated with elements foreign to the intelligence proper, and because it is commingled with the emo-tions, the feelings, the influences of the imagination, and the movements of the heart."

294. INTUITION IN ITS MOST RESTRICTED SENSE. — From these explanations it follows, first, that intuition, and con-sequently the intuitive method, designate things that are really very different.

In its most restricted sense, and taken as the synonym of

---

[1] *See Dictionnaire de pédagogie,* article *Intuition.*

sense-perception, intuition has given rise to *object lessons*, or the substitution of concrete realities for abstractions and words, as the first exercise of the intelligence.[1] We willingly accept the principle laid down by Pestalozzi, that " intuition is the source of all our knowledge ; " on condition, however, that by the word *source* we understand only the initial origin of our ideas which, borrowed first from perception and observation, have then need of being elaborated by our faculties of reflection. But it is very evident that in this sense, intuition, if it is the point of departure of a method, of the inductive method, does not constitute a method by itself.

Let us multiply intuitions for the child to our heart's content, — that is, clear and vivid perceptions ; let us even admit that intuition has something peculiar and characteristic, and that it cannot be confounded with simple perception ; let us grant that it does not suffice to present an object to the sight of the child in order that there may be a real intuition, but that in order to produce this particular state of mind special conditions are required, because the eye does not always see when it looks, because the senses grow tired, and that to excite a vivid and exact impression in the mind there is a moment to be seized which is not lasting. But for all this, it remains no less true that intuition, from this point of view, is at most but a more penetrating observation, a more intense perception of sensible realities ; and that, consequently, it may properly be an important element of the method whose object is to give us an exact knowledge of things, but not this entire method, which cannot dispense with reflection, comparison, and reason.

So also with respect to intellectual intuition, to that

---

[1] See chapter third, Part Second.

which seizes axioms at a glance, the intuitive method is still but the point of departure, the rational foundation of the deductive method, which ought doubtless to be based on well-understood principles, on evident propositions, but which constructs on these principles, by means of reasoning, a whole superstructure of science.

295. INTUITION IN ITS WIDEST SENSE. — But, understood in its wide sense, is intuition even then the principle of a distinct method of instruction? — In what does it consist, outside of its application to object lessons ? M. Buisson replies :

"It consists in a certain march of the instruction which reserves to the child the pleasure and the profit, if not of discovery and surprise, which would perhaps be promising too much, at least of initiative and intellectual activity." [1]

The intuitive method, then, would be that which, according to the saying of Fénelon, "moves the springs of the child's soul." The purpose would be to make him judge by intuition, after having taught him to perceive by intuition. "To make the child think," says M. Buisson again, "would be the essence of the intuitive method." But is not this to force the sense of the word, still to call "intuition" the personal thought, the clear and exact intelligence, which results from the efforts of attention, the active participation of the pupil in the instruction he receives? Moreover, if this is the true meaning, the real pedagogical application of intuition, is it not evident that there is here no method, properly speaking, a method always supposing a series of processes and of means, while intuition thus understood is but the general character which pertains to all instruction?

---

[1] *Dictionnaire de pédagogie*, article already cited.

Intuition ought to accompany all parts of a course of
study, just as consciousness envelops all the phenomena of
the external world. It is, so to speak, the soul of every
method and inspires all teaching which would not merely
drily transmit the commonplaces of the soul, as the light
illumines all births, but provokes the light and warmth of
the spirit, and through instruction assures education; but
when all has been said, it is not a method. To say with M.
Buisson that it consists not in the application of such or
such a process, but in the intention and general habit of
making and permitting the child's mind to act in conformity
with his intellectual instincts, is precisely to acknowledge
that it is to pedagogy what the search for truth is to science,
and the pursuit of the beautiful to poetry, — an ideal, a
supreme end, but in no wise a body of practical means, organized into a method.

296. EXPERIMENTAL METHOD. — We know what services
have been rendered science by the substitution of the experimental method for the method of pure reasoning and
abstract hypothesis. The natural sciences did not really
exist till the day when the experimental logic of Bacon
broke with the old traditions of the syllogism, and perpet-
uated a revolution which the scholars of the sixteenth
century had already provided for; till the day when thinkers
had decided to observe, to experiment, and from observed
facts to make a patient induction of the laws which governed them.

Henceforth sovereign in the domain of the concrete
sciences, when the discovery of truth is at stake, cannot
the experimental method be transported into pedagogy and
applied to the teaching of the truths which it has served to
discover? In other terms, in order to form and to instruct
the intelligence of the child, ought not the art of education

to employ the processes of observation and experiment analogous to those which science has utilized for organizing itself?

The reply cannot be doubtful, and it is easy to show that the methods brought into prominence by the educators of the last century are but different forms of the experimental method.

What, for example, is the so-called intuitive method, but a constant appeal to experiment and observation? So the method which, under different names, is called in succession the intuitive, the heuristic, the analytic, or the inductive method, and which always consists in making the pupil discover the truth which we would teach him, is but a detached fragment of the great experimental method.

In a word, the experimental method is after all but another and more pretentious name for designating the whole or a part of the inductive method.

297. General Spirit of a Good Method. — All the considerations which precede have no other practical utility than that of obliging the teacher to reflect upon the principles of instruction themselves, and upon the necessity of taking into account both the nature of the children to whom he addresses himself, and the nature of the knowledge which he communicates.

Let no one imagine that it is sufficient, in order to teach well, to know the abstract distinctions of pedagogy. The first condition for being a good teacher is always to possess a thorough knowledge of the subject which he has to teach. An English educator, M. Laurie, justly observes, "A teacher himself possessed of a disciplined intelligence and of a will fortified by religion, reason, and experience, may be working wisely towards the production in others of that which is in himself, and be *unconsciously* adapting his processes to a sound method." [1] But however well endowed he may be in respect of instruction or intelligence, he will always be inferior to a teacher who to the same personal qualities adds that which gives power, assurance, and decision, — the reflective knowledge of the natural laws for the development of the intelligence, the characteristics of each school study, and consequently the methods which most easily find the route to the mind and are best adapted to each topic of instruction.

---

[1] S. S. Laurie, *Primary Instruction in Relation to Education*, 1883, pp. 15, 16.

CHAPTER II.

READING AND WRITING.

298. SUBORDINATION OF THE DIFFERENT STUDIES. — While causing the different branches of the programme to be pursued one after another, and each by itself, the teacher will not lose sight of this general principle, that if each part ought to be studied in itself, it ought to be studied also in view of the whole; that is. it should contribute to the general education of the mind, awaken the intelligence, and furnish it with good habits of order, application, and consecutive thinking. This remark is applicable to reading and writing, which constitute the elementary basis of all instruction.

299. READING AND WRITING. — For a long time reading and writing, along with number, constituted the entire programme of the primary schools. To-day these elementary branches are no more than the conditions of more complete studies, which respond more fully to the social necessities and needs of human nature. According to a very just expression, these are instrumental knowledges ; that is to say, necessary instruments for acquiring other knowledge. But reading and writing, while they are but the preliminary means of instruction, have for this very reason a special importance.

300. THEIR PLACE IN THE COURSES OF STUDY. — " Reading and writing are necessarily the foundation of the

290

instruction given in the elementary courses," says M. Gréard. "First of all, it is necessary to make this primary basis secure." But reading and writing remain till the end of the primary course one of the principal objects of the teacher's efforts.

Even at the beginning and in the elementary course, reading and writing ought not of themselves to occupy the attention of the child to the exclusion of every other study. Different exercises in language, simple and familiar object-lessons, the elements of drawing, and notions of arithmetic and geography, may and should accompany them.

"If it is possible," says M. Gréard, "to begin the study of numbers almost at the same time, it is because spelling and numeration, and the tracing of letters and figures, are exercises of the same grade and almost of the same nature."

Dreary schools are those where the pupil has no choice except between his primer and his copy-book! Were it only for introducing variety into this monotonous work, the teacher ought to furnish the child with other occupations.

Especially should we recollect that he is not merely to make of his pupils reading and writing machines, but that his ever-present thought should be to open and stimulate the mind by positive knowledge and by moral lessons.

301. DIFFERENT GRADES OF READING. — Reading, which has been defined as " the translation of written language into spoken language," seems a very simple thing to those who know how to read ; but for the child who is learning to read, nothing is more complicated or more difficult.[1] "The extent and complicacy of this accom-

---

[1] Mr. Bain defines it as " the art of pronouncing words at sight of their visible characters."

plishment," says Mr. Bain, "make it the work of years, even when not commenced very early." When the child knows his letters, over-confident parents often shout victory and think that the whole is done. The real difficulty, however, the reading of words, begins only at that point. Months are often required for the pupil to pass from saying his letters to fluent reading.

We ought then to distinguish different grades of reading : The first grade, where the pupil learns to distinguish letters and to know their names, and where he laboriously groups them in order to pronounce syllables and words ; the second grade, where the pupil reads fluently, without hesitation, without feeling his way ; the third grade, corresponding to what is called expressive reading.

302. CAUTION AS TO THE IMPORTANCE OF PARTICULAR METHODS. — In the teaching of elementary reading, as in all parts of instruction, we must be on our guard against the superstition of method. In truth, the spirit which animates the teacher, and the intellectual and moral qualities which distinguish him, will always be worth more than the best processes. Lakanal, speaking of a commission which the Council of the Five Hundred had called for the composition of elementary books, expressed the opinion that there was not in France a single good book on the art of teaching to read and write. "Up to this time," he said, "it is the patience of teachers and pupils that has done all." But notwithstanding the progress that has been accomplished, and though we are to-day provided with a great number of good methods, it is still upon the patience and skill of the teacher that we must mainly count. The teacher ought to know how to give animation to the reading lesson, to interest the pupil in it, and if possible to make attractive an exercise which

in itself is dreary and monotonous. He will already have done much, if he has been able to inspire his pupils with the desire of learning to read.

This is what Rousseau said, though with his usual exaggeration:

"A great ado has been made," he says, "over finding the best methods of teaching to read. Cabinets and charts have been invented, and the child's room turned into a printing-office. Locke would have him learn to read with dice. Was not this a happy invention? What a pity! A surer means than all this, but one which is always forgotten, is the desire to learn. Give the child this desire, and then put aside your cabinets and your dice; every method will then succeed well with him."

To the same effect it has often been remarked that methods of reading, even the best contrived, produce results only through the manner in which they are applied.

"In this part of instruction, as in all the others, the value of the process is determined by the teacher who applies it. A given instructor has obtained in his school, through the use of means which he has devised, the most satisfactory results.

"Under his direction generations of pupils have been instructed with less effort, no doubt, than would have been required elsewhere; and he yields to the temptation, certainly very natural, to embody in a little book the method which he had invented for himself, and by this means he hopes to render to the pupils whose masters shall adopt it the same service which he has rendered his own. Unhappily the result does not always meet his expectations."[1]

303. DESCRIPTION OF THE PRINCIPAL WAYS OF TEACHING TO READ. — On first glancing at the innumerable processes which the fertile ingenuity of educators has succes-

---

[1] Mlle. Chalamet, *op. cit.*, p. 155.

sively brought into use for teaching to read, which fashion
has patronized by turns, we might be tempted to think
that it is impossible to reduce to unity this chaos of spell-
ing-books and charts of every description.[1]   After a little
more reflection, however, we become convinced that this
diversity, apparently infinite, is due rather to modifications
of detail, and to accessory and superficial combinations,
than to essential and profound differences.

The first obvious distinction is that between systems
where the teaching of reading is kept separate from everything else and administered wholly by itself, and methods
that have been very popular for a few years past, especially
in Germany, which combine the teaching of writing with
that of reading.

Let us first consider the processes in which reading is not
connected with writing.   By leaving out of account the accessory aids which introduce complications into them, these
may be reduced to two, the method by spelling and the
method by direct syllabication without spelling.

304. THE METHOD BY SPELLING (ALPHABETIC METHOD).
—The method most generally employed in France, notwithstanding the criticisms that have been made of it, is the
old way of teaching to read, which consists first in having
the letters *named* instead of having them *pronounced*, and
then in having them grouped in order to form syllables of
them.

"When we reflect on all the difficulties which this method presents, on the effort of abstraction it requires of children, on the
labor which the decomposition and the recomposition of syllables

---

[1] On the history of the different systems of reading, see the excellent article *Lecture*, by M. Guillaume, in the *Dictionnaire de pédagogie;*
also, Hall's *How to teach Reading*, Boston, 1887.

supposes, on the impossibility for the pupil to grasp the correspondence between the letters told one after another and the composite
sound which results from them; we are astonished that with
processes so defective children ever learn to read. 'Whoever
knows how to read,' says Duclos, 'knows the most difficult art, if
he has learned it by the common method.' " [1]

305. THE OLD AND THE NEW SPELLING. — Each letter
has received a name, but this name does not correspond to
the relative value which it has as a sound in the composition of words. Hence the defect, pointed out two centuries
ago by the grammarians of Port Royal, in the old method of
spelling.

"By pronouncing the consonants separately and making children
name them," says Guyot, "there is always joined to them a vowel,
namely e, which is neither a part of the syllable nor of the word,
and it thus happens that the sound of the letters as they are pronounced is entirely different from that of the letters combined.
For example, the child is made to spell the word bon, that is composed of three letters, b, o, n, which he pronounces one after the
other. Now b, pronounced alone, is be; o pronounced alone is still o,
for it is a vowel; but n pronounced alone is ene. How, then, is
the child to understand that all these sounds, which he has been
made to pronounce separately by naming these three letters one
after the other, make but the single word bon? He has been made
to pronounce three sounds, which have been distinctly impressed
on his ear, and he is then told to unite these three sounds and
make one of them, namely, bon. And Guyot proposed, in order
to remedy this difficulty, that the consonants should be called
only by their natural sounds, by merely adding the silent e, which
is necessary for pronouncing them." [2]

The new system of spelling, then, gives to the letters a

---

[1] M. Buisson, *Rapport sur l'instruction primaire à l'exposition universelle de Vienne,* 1875.

[2] *Grammaire générale de Port Royal,* Chap. VI.

sound which more nearly approaches their relative value. Besides, it decomposes the syllable into but two parts, the *sound* and the *articulation*, without taking account of the number of letters which enter into the composition of either.

The advantage of the method by spelling [alphabetic method] is that it is a good preparation for the study of orthography. But, on the other hand, as a method of reading properly so called, it is evidently longer and more difficult. But nothing prevents us from returning to spelling a little later, when it becomes indispensable for the study of orthography, and the first difficulties have been overcome. Mr. Bain has justly remarked:

"Much stress is now laid by teachers on the point of beginning to pronounce short words at sight, without spelling them, and a strong condemnation is uttered against the old spelling method. The difference between the methods is not very apparent to me; after a few preliminary steps, the two must come to the same thing." [1]

306. Phonetic Methods. — But there has become popular, particularly in Germany, in opposition to the alphabetic method, a system which consists in making the pupil grasp and reproduce the sound of each letter, without naming the written sign which represents it. From this principle has sprung a great number of different methods, all of which are connected with the idea of *statilégie*, or immediate reading without previous spelling.[2] These are also called methods by *syllabication*, because they present to the pupil, not isolated letters, but syllables.

Thus, by the old system of spelling, the word *infant* has six elements, *i-n-f-a-n-t;* by the new system of spelling it

---

[1] *Education as a Science*, p. 240.

[2] For statilégie, see the *Dictionnaire de pédagogie*, article *Lafforte*.

has three elements, *in-f-ant ;* while by the method without spelling, the word has but two elements, *in-fant.*[1]

307. SYNTHETIC AND ANALYTIC METHODS. — Educators who freely use and abuse the words analysis and synthesis, have shown no anxiety to omit these favorite expressions in the names which they have applied to the different systems of reading ; and, to tell the truth, the nature of the subject would here justify, more than anywhere else, the use of these terms.

A word, in fact, is a compound, like the bodies which chemistry analyzes. It is formed of elements, which are letters ; so that by analogy with methods in chemistry it is allowable to call analytical the method which consists in presenting at first the whole, the entire word, in order to decompose it into its elements ; and to call synthetic the reverse process, which first requires the letters to be learned, in order to form syllables of them, and afterwards to construct words.

It is in this sense that most teachers define the analytic and synthetic methods of reading.

"The analytic method," says M. Horner, "starts from the whole in order to reach the parts ; it drills pupils in first reading the word *rose* as a whole, then by syllables, *ro-se,* whence it descends to the ultimate elements of this word ; that is, to the letters.

" The synthetic method consists in starting from the ultimate elements of words, in order to reach the syllables ; from syllables the pupil passes to words, and from words to sentences." [2]

From this distinction it follows that the so-called synthetic method corresponds to the old methods. " The analytic

---

[1] Jacotot, instead of starting with the letter and the syllable, starts with the word as a whole. See *J. Jacotot et sa Méthode,* par Pérez, p. 94.

[2] Mr. Horner, *op. cit.,* p. 111, *et seq.*

method, on the contrary," says M. Horner, "almost unknown in French schools, is universally practised, or at
least recommended, in Germany and in French Switzerland."[1]

But the words analysis and synthesis are so very obscure, and so difficult to handle, that a French educational
authority, M. Brouard, asserts, to the contrary effect, that
in the analytical methods we decompose the syllable into all
its elements ; and he thus confounds them with the "old
methods."[2] According to the same author, the synthetic
method, whose essential characteristic, if we may trust the
declarations of Swiss and Belgian educators, is to start
from the simplest element, the letter, in order to rise to the
different groups which constitute syllables and words, — the
synthetic method "should not decompose, or should decompose as little as possible."

Perhaps this example of confusion and absolute contradiction in the use of the same terms will finally convince our
readers that it would be best to renounce forever, in the
language of pedagogy, those fine terms analysis and synthesis. If, however, any one feels bound to preserve them,
in order to distinguish the different procedures followed in
the study of reading, we do not hesitate to say that the only
logical signification which can be given to them is the one
from Swiss pedagogy which we have noted.

308. SIMULTANEOUS TEACHING OF READING AND WRITING.
— It must not be supposed that the system which associates
and combines the teaching of reading with that of writing,

---

[1] This is also a prevailing method in American schools of the better
class. See Appendix C. (P.)

[2] Mr. Brouard, *Inspection des écoles primaires*, p. 232. M. Guillaume
in the *Dictionnaire de pédagogie* says to the contrary and with reason,
"The most ancient method proceeded by synthesis."

and attempts to facilitate and animate each by the other, is anything entirely new. In his *Alphabet pour les enfants* (1750), Delaunay recommends parents "to put the pen in the child's hand the moment he begins to read." Montaigne relates that he was taught to read and write at the same time; and Jacotot also associated the teaching of reading with writing.

But it is chiefly within the last few years that this method has gained credit and reputation, at least in theory.

"For forty years past," says a German educator, "there has been produced but one review article in favor of the old systems by spelling; but notwithstanding this, the alphabetic method is still taught in perhaps half the schools of Germany, at least of the rural schools."[1]

M. Buisson describes this process as follows:

"In the new system of instruction, a pretty little illustrated book is given the child. This is his first book, and yet it does not begin with the alphabet, but with pictures, as of a *wheel*, a *nest*, or a *bat*. Above the object neatly drawn is the name, written in large letters; it is always a short and easy word, such as Vogel calls a *normal*[2] word. The teacher speaks to his pupils of the object which they see before them, both drawn and written; and he then shows them the characters used to write the name of that object. He next writes the entire word on the board, in order to decompose it before their eyes, and make them pronounce each vowel by itself, so as to show them how the consonants modify it; then by a sort of guess-work he sets them to hunting up a few common words in which are found the same sounds and consequently the same letters; and finally he sets them to looking in their books, here and there, for characters like those which they have just learned. This is the use that is made of the ear and the eye; that of the hand is its immediate complement, and very often the beginning is

---

[1] Quoted by M. Buisson, *Rapport*, p. 156.
[2] Buisson, Ibid., p. 154.

made with this. The teacher traces upon the blackboard a few
horizontal and vertical lines, and teaches the children a small
number of conventional terms which he will have need to use, such
as *above, below, to the right, to the left, short, long,* etc. ; and then,
when all have taken the pen in hand, he dictates to the whole
class the movements to be made, that is, the lines to be traced.
The pupils thus write in unison, and, as it were, under military
orders.   This curious exercise is much easier for them than for
us ; first, because the characters of the German running-hand are
almost exclusively rectilinear, and then because the child has generally been prepared in the *Kindergarten* by the little patterns of
Froebel, so that for him writing is but a new application of the
same exercises.   He thus learns to read and write simultaneously,
while continuing the pattern work of the *Kindergarten.*" [1]

We admire the ingenious art which presides over the
organization of such a scheme of instruction, in which the
work of the hands is associated with the exercise of hearing
and seeing ; in which the effort of the representative imagination, which reading involves, is aided by the physical activity which is required by the practice of writing ; in which
writing itself is facilitated by the preparatory exercises in
drawing, and in which, finally, there are skillfully connected
with the study of language signs little object-lessons,
which give the pupil some variety and some attraction.
One might be very glad to prefer this living and animated
method to the ordinary processes which impose on the child
" an endless repetition of sounds and unions of sounds which
signify nothing to the mind, and a pitiless repetition of
those monotonous spelling exercises which are followed by
the no less tedious exercises in writing on slate or paper."
Perhaps the day will come when this ideal method will be
generally practiced in our schools ; but we see what efforts
it requires on the part of the teacher.   As a matter of fact,

---

[1] M. Buisson, *Rapport*, p. 154.

the general characteristic of the reforms which have been suggested to the art of teaching by the modern spirit of innovation and progress is to put upon the teacher all the labor from which the pupil has been relieved. It is not then to be expected for a long time yet, that the method which we have just described can be made general in our public schools. Let it be added that whatever effort we make, whatever ingenious invention we employ, to relieve the child, we shall never succeed in suppressing in the teaching of reading all of the artificial and the mechanical that is involved in it. There can never be a method of reading perfectly natural and rational, for the excellent reason that letters are conventional signs, and that there is no natural correspondence between these signs and the ideas which they express.

309. DIFFERENT APPLICATIONS OF THIS METHOD. — But theory always anticipates practice, at least customary practice, and foreign teachers already distinguish two different ways of applying the simultaneous teaching of reading and writing, according as the analytic mode or the synthetic mode of procedure is followed. We shall not here speak of what are called the *synthetic method* and the *analytico-synthetic method of script reading*.[1] Let us simply preserve from all these tentatives the general idea which dominates them; namely, that writing being relatively easier and more attractive than reading, it is well to carry on these two exercises simultaneously. Let no one object that script letters are different from printed letters. All who have taught by this method are unanimous in declaring that the transition from script to print presents no difficulty for the child; but let us

---

[1] On this subject see interesting details in the *Rapport* of M. Buisson, already noted.

not expect that the child will learn to read by putting into
his hands the pencil or the pen.

"The fixing of the visible impressions of the alphabet is hastened if the pupil is sufficiently advanced in the power of the hand
to draw the letters with chalk or with slate pencil." [1]

310. ACCESSORY PROCESSES. — What adds to the apparent
multiplicity of methods for reading is the accessory processes which have been added to them, to fix and sustain
the child's attention.   Such are the Gervais system, where
sliding cards serve to group the letters into syllables ; the
Chéron apparatus, which replaces the tapes and cards by
standards ; the Néel charts, which simplify the use of
standards ; the Lambert method, where of two concentric
wheels one presents the articulations and the other the sound ;
the Maitre, where two tapes unroll to serve the same purpose ; the Mignon method, which employs a mural chart
with movable characters ; the Thollois method, which is a
reproduction of the typographic cabinet of Dumas ; [2] the
picture methods of Regimbeau, of Larousse, and others.
Such again is the *Phonomimic process.*

311. PHONOMIMIC PROCESS. — The principle of this process is not new.   Comenius had already placed at the
beginning of his *Orbis Pictus* a picture-alphabet, in which
to each letter there corresponded the cry of an animal, or
rather a sound familiar to the child.   This is the same idea
which inspires the phonomimic process of M. Grosselin,
applied by Madame Pape-Carpantier in her spelling-book
for the use of kindergartens.   Letters of the alphabet are
there associated with phonomimic gestures.

---

[1] Bain, *op. cit.*, p. 238.
[2] See Compayré's *History of Pedagogy*, p. 239.

312. GENERAL ADVICE. — Whatever may be the method employed, the teacher should be anxious above all else to introduce intelligence and life into the reading lesson. Let him not call into play merely the mechanical memory of the child, but let him interest his other faculties, as his judgment and his imagination. The lesson should be short,[1] interrupted if need be by questions to animate it and by diversions to make it pleasant. Let us not forget that reading is the child's first introduction to study, to school work. Let us take care that this first effort be not too difficult for him, and that he be not forever disgusted with study by his disagreeable apprenticeship to reading.

313. FLUENT AND EXPRESSIVE READING. — Fluent reading is one of the most important exercises of the primary school. By this means, in fact, the child not only becomes accustomed to overcome the difficulties of reading proper, but he is learning his native language, acquiring useful knowledge, and taking account of the meaning of words.

The choice of a good book for fluent reading is of capital importance, — it is the "walking-beam of the school." In making use of the books, let the teacher explain in advance the subject which is about to be read, and carefully illustrate all the terms employed.

"The reading lesson, with explanations," says an Inspector-General, "is one of the most encouraging signs of the progress that is being made in our primary instruction. Doubtless this explanation is often dry, confused, purely grammatical, *lexicological;* but it is a germ which will develop itself. . . . This will be the most living and vivifying part of the programme, when all teachers have comprehended the necessity of making a daily and painstaking preparation for it."[2]

---

[1] M. Rendu admits that the reading lesson may be without inconvenience from twenty to thirty minutes.

[2] Buisson, *Rapport,* page 71.

314. EXPRESSIVE READING. — "Expressive reading," says M. Rousselot, "is natural reading, whose tone is adapted to the ideas and sentiments expressed in the selection read." Without wishing to transform our schools into conservatories of declamation, there is ground for complaint that teachers generally give so little attention to the art of reading. American teachers give this subject much more attention when they require "that the child read with feeling, intelligence, and grace; that he understand what the author intended to express; that he enter into the spirit of the piece; and that he have the command of his voice."

"Every teacher should be a good reader. Not more than one in every hundred among teachers can now be called a good reader." [1]

315. CRITICAL OBSERVATIONS ON THE TEACHING OF READING. — We borrow from the *Rapports* of the Inspectors-General a certain number of critical observations gathered from actual practice, which mark with precision some of the most common faults in the teaching of reading :

"The reading exercise is not made intelligent enough; the explanations with which it ought to be accompanied are frequently lacking. The reading is heavy and monotonous. The delivery is inarticulate, dull, and confused. The teacher does not always feel himself obliged to take the lead in reading or to give a model for imitation. The reading lesson is but a mechanical exercise which leads to no useful results. The children read poorly, because they do not understand what they read. In but few schools is the reading expressive and well explained. Children seem to read as though they were running a race; they read for the sake of reading, and read too rapidly, as though the only purpose were to limber the tongue and the throat of the pupil. Many teachers imagine that the child ought to write only when he knows how to read."

---

[1] Page, *Theory and Practice of Teaching*, 1885, p. 74.

316. Proofs of Progress. — By the side of the faults just pointed out let us place the commendations given to certain schools and the proofs of the progress that has been made in many places:

"The new method of spelling is alone in use. The method in use is becoming more rational, and the process less mechanical. Writing and reading taught simultaneously. lend each other mutual aid. The teaching of reading and writing takes place at the blackboard, to the great joy of the children. Mechanical reading has been succeeded by reading that is more intelligent, better understood, explained by the teacher, and often summarized by the pupil. Teachers begin to understand that good reading should be the basis of all other work; some make a careful preparation for each lesson."

317. The Teaching of Writing. — All educators are now agreed that the child ought to be drilled in writing from the moment he enters school, and that he should not wait for this until he has learned to read fluently. More and more the truth of this pedagogical axiom will be recognized, that drawing, writing, and reading need one another and are mutually helpful.

On the other hand, it is not useless to recollect that the writing lesson itself, however mechanical it may be, may become for the teacher an occasion for calling the attention of his pupils to the meaning of the words which he copies, and to the moral significance of the sentences which he writes. From this point of view, the choice of copies presented to the child is of some importance.[1]

[1] We are disposed to think that all instruction may have a disciplinary aim, and it is for this reason that the choice of copies is not an indifferent matter. But it seems to us an exaggeration to admit, with certain teachers, that the study of writing can develop the æsthetic sense, and consequently can exercise a salutary influence on the moral nature and train the judgment.

318. DIFFERENT PROCESSES. — Properly speaking, there are no distinct methods for teaching writing; there are only different processes. The principal are the use of tracing-copies, the imitation of models, and prepared copy-books. It is astonishing that certain teachers still recommend tracing-copies and the use of black lines. This is the case with M. Rendu, who is very willing to acknowledge, however, that the practice should be at once abandoned the moment the child has become somewhat accustomed to write.

The imitation of models leaves the child to his own powers, and at first constitutes, perhaps, an exercise that is too difficult. As soon as possible, however, there must be a resort to this process, either by presenting the pupil with copies upon paper or by tracing letters and words upon the blackboard, — a practice which has this advantage, among others, of facilitating collective teaching.

Prepared copy-books, where the child at first has but to make traces, but where the guiding lines become more and more rare in proportion as the pupil advances, are the method which is best adapted to the inexperience of beginners. This system is a combination of tracing and imitation, the one which is recommended by the *Conduite des écoles chrétiennes.* This may at once be admitted, on condition that we do not prolong too far this over-agreeable exercise. "The pupil," says M. Berger, "ought as soon as possible to be drilled in freely imitating the copies and in accustoming himself somewhat to walk without leading-strings."

In the teaching of writing another difference comes from the use of slate and pencil, or of paper and pen. Pestalozzi, who made writing subordinate to drawing, strongly recommended the use of the slate, because the child handles the pencil more easily than the pen, and because upon the slate he more easily effaces his mistakes. On the other hand,

M. Brouard remarks that the slate, "the paper of the poor," is never more than an expedient, and that its use makes the hand awkward and stiffens the fingers.

319. Conditions Necessary for Learning to Write Well. — Power of representative imagination, a clear, exact, and complete conception of the forms to be traced, is one of the conditions necessary for learning to write. Another condition is that deftness of the hand which is in part natural, but which is also acquired by sufficient exercise, and precautions that may be taken to secure a correct position of the body and a proper holding of the pen.

According to the *Manuel* of M. Rendu, the elements of a correct position for writing are the following:

"The *body* straight, perpendicular, upon the bench as one sits at table;

"The *limbs* advanced, not crossed nor bent backward;

"The *left arm* oblique upon the table, supporting the body, the hand flat-wise, the fingers upon the copy-book to adjust it properly;

"The *copy-book* a little inclined to the left;

"The *right arm* free in its movements, about two-thirds upon the table, separated from the body by a hand-breadth;

"The *pen* between the first three fingers, extended without being rigid;

"The *right hand* bent neither upward nor downward, supported only by the extremities of the third and fourth fingers, bent inward in such a way that the pen points toward the shoulder;

"Finally, the *head* bent a little forward, but only enough for seeing clearly."

320. General Advice. — The teaching of writing should not be considered as a mechanical exercise for which it suffices that the pupil should have a copy-book. The teacher ought constantly to supervise this work, and the following are some of the rules to which he should conform:

The penmanship of the teacher should not only be good, but he should also have the ability to write upon the blackboard.

Preparation should be made for the writing lesson as for other lessons.

Abuse must not be made of caligraphic exercises and of mechanical copying.

All the exercises in arithmetic, composition, and especially in dictation, ought to be exercises in flowing and legible penmanship.

The teacher ought not to take part in the writing exercises while seated at his desk; after having given his lesson on the blackboard, he ought to pass from seat to seat to direct his pupils, to observe the position of body, hand, and pen, to correct faults and to re-form letters that are badly made.

"In teaching writing, teachers should not attempt to train skilful professors of caligraphy, but to prepare children for writing rapidly and legibly."

We cannot too carefully proscribe all vain caligraphic refinements, puerile masterpieces of penmanship, pen-drawings which are designed only for ornament.

321. PRACTICAL OBSERVATIONS ON THE TEACHING OF WRITING. — The following are some observations contained in the *Rapports* of the Inspectors-General, touching the teaching of writing:

" The *slate*, that simple means of giving children occupation, is rarely utilized. The teacher, instead of placing the copy upon the blackboard for the whole class, prefers to give a ready-made copy. Penmanship is rarely made a specialty. The teacher does not take the trouble to examine and correct the books. There will never be visible progress in writing while the teacher does not take upon himself the task of passing from seat to seat during the lesson, to go from pupil to pupil, to observe the position of the body and the holding of the pen, — in a word, to see how the children follow their copies, and to correct before their eyes letters which seem defective."

322. CONCLUSION. — From what has preceded, it follows that in the teaching of reading and writing, those two fundamental branches of all elementary instruction, processes that are intelligent and attractive are more and more replacing routine and mechanical processes. Writing and reading ought not to be abandoned to the hazards of a monotonous spelling or of an insipid exercise in copying; they ought to be professionally taught, as essential elements in the study of the mother-tongue.

CHAPTER III.

OBJECT-LESSONS.

323. ORIGIN OF OBJECT-LESSONS. — To-day everybody talks about object-lessons, and all teachers pretend to give them ; but thirty years ago the term was unknown, at least in France, and the repute of this mode of teaching is due to an entirely new phase of opinion.

The object-lesson is the application of the principle which Rousseau and Pestalozzi have popularized ; namely, that in instruction things must come before words, and that the senses, particularly the sense of sight, are the faculties which are first developed, and that it is to them that we must make the first appeal.

From another point of view, the introduction of object-lessons into the programme of school studies is the result of that modern tendency which more and more impels teachers to develop the educative character of instruction. In fact, the object-lesson is worth less for the knowledge which it communicates than for the manner in which it is communicated, for the effect it produces on the faculties of observation and attention, for the interest which it seeks to create by presenting to the pupil familiar notions accessible to his intelligence, and by keeping his mind on things which he already knows in part, and which we wish to have him know still better.

Let us first attempt to define with exactness the meaning which it is proper to attach to the expression *object-lessons;*

310

and we shall then inquire how that instruction ought to be administered, and on what conditions it can bear all its fruit.

324. MISUNDERSTANDINGS AS TO THE MEANING OF THE TERM. — The object-lesson has had the same fate as the so-called intuitive method; these expressions have been used at random to designate scholastic processes which have only a remote relation to them. Like all novelties, "object-lesson" has become a beautifully vague term, which each one interprets in his own way.

"A long observation of school affairs," says Mlle. Chalamet, " has convinced us that if one does not wish to be understood, he has no surer means than to speak of object-lessons. There are certainly but few questions in teaching of the practical sort, which give occasion for such strange misconceptions. Not very long ago, while speaking with one of the professors in a large school, we asked him if many object-lessons were given in his class. 'We make use of them constantly,' he replied; ' we give our pupils explanations on all subjects.' In fact, while industriously observing the work of this professor for a considerable time, we became convinced that for him object-lessons consisted in pouring forth floods of verbal explanations." [1]

It is in part to Madame Pape-Carpantier that must be attributed the responsibility for this misleading extension of the meaning of object-lessons. The models she has left us give proof of ingenious invention and exquisite tact; but they also prove that the object-lesson was for her a sort of encyclopædic process, and that she applied it to every branch of instruction as a sort of common mould into which everything was to be forced. [2]

"The object-lesson," she said, "teaches of realities themselves, and from every reality it produces useful knowledge and noble sentiment."

---

[1] Mlle. Chalamet, *op. cit.*, p. 96.

[2] Madame Pape-Carpantier, *Conférences faites à la Sorbonne en* 1867.

325. DEFINITION OF OBJECT-LESSON. — One of the best definitions which have been given of object-lessons is the one that we borrow from Mr. Bain, who has written on this subject one of the most remarkable chapters of his *Education as a Science.*

"The object-lesson is made to range over all the utilities of life and all the processes of nature. It begins upon things familiar to the pupils, and enlarges the conceptions of these by filling in unnoticed qualities. It proceeds to things that have to be learnt, even in their primary aspect, by description or diagram; and ends with the more abstruse operations of natural forces." [1]

In its last part, Mr. Bain's definition is itself a little too broad, since it tends to embrace the highest departments of the physical sciences. We are firm in the belief that the object-lesson ought to be merely a beginning instrument, and that it should not be continued to the last stage of instruction. On this point we do not share the opinion of Mr. Spencer, who would have the object-lesson so conducted in the earlier stages of instruction that it could merge insensibly into the investigation of the naturalist and the man of science. [2]

Here a few other definitions that may serve to enlighten us on the nature and purpose of object-lessons:

"The professed purpose of object-lessons," says Mr. Spencer, "is to give the child the habit of thorough observation. . . . The object-lesson is a process of instruction, one of the applications of the intuitive method." [3]

"Object-lessons may be defined as lessons designed to teach the elements of knowledge by the use of objects." [4]

---

[1] *Education as a Science*, p. 247.
[2] *Education*, p. 136.
[3] M. Platrier, *Leçons de choses* in the *Dictionnaire de pédagogie.*
[4] Wickersham, *Methods of Instruction*, p. 141.

Johonnot, an American teacher, sharply contrasts object-lessons with formal memory exercises.

" The decided superiority of the new method over the old, in arousing attention and in exciting interest, is manifest. The new instruction appeals to experience and excites the observing powers to intense activity. It feeds the mind upon real knowledge, and raises it out of the slough of inattention and listless inactivity produced by the old process of mere routine." [1]

In fact, the object-lesson is directly opposed to text-book instruction. It results from the reaction, excessive it must be admitted, which modern education has directed against instruction purely *livresque*, as Montaigne called it.

326. ABUSE OF OBJECT-LESSONS. — It may be said in a sense that object-lessons have been too successful, that people have been carried away by them, and that they have come near being brought into disrepute by the abuse which has been made of them. Besides being cried up with exces-sive enthusiasm, they have been indiscriminately applied to all branches of instruction. There have been *object-lessons* in morals and in history ; and they have been confounded with the experiments and demonstrations of science.

It is in this sense that Madame Pape-Carpantier said :

" The man of science in his amphitheatre gives an object-lesson when he performs before the very eyes of his pupils the delicate and brilliant operations with which he entertains them."

The object-lesson, as its name indicates, ought to be kept within the domain of knowledge where we have actually to deal with things which can be shown, with sensible objects which strike the eyes of the child.

But at most it is and can be but an elementary initiation

---

[1] Johonnot, *Principles and Practice of Teaching*, p. 84.

into knowledge of this sort; it ought never to take the form of a didactic lesson.

327. The New Formalism. — The object-lesson is nothing if not a living method of teaching, in which the teacher gives proof of sagacity and invention; in which he arranges, always with freedom, and if possible with originality, the common information which he wishes to communicate to his pupils; in which he intersperses his exposition with interrogations, and in which he makes a constant appeal to the child's initiative by taking advantage of circumstances, such as the replies which are made to his questions.

But the formal and scholastic spirit always asserts itself, and object-lessons, imperfectly understood, very soon become a new piece of school mechanism.

It is thus that many school-books, through a curious misconception, are entitled "Object-lessons." It has become the custom, in some primary schools, to *dictate* object-lessons; and the degeneration has gone even further than this.[1]

"To *read* an object-lesson is bad enough, but there is something worse, and we have seen one *played*. It was at a health-resort, and the watering-place had a school. One Sunday the directors invited the guests to witness the distribution of prizes. There was a programme for the occasion, and this programme promised, among other things, the *representation* of an object-lesson! In fact, two little girls appeared on the platform, one of whom was the mistress and the other her pupil; and they proceeded to recite with volubility an object-lesson in the form of a dialogue."[2]

---

[1] "No object-lesson," said Johonnot, "should be given from a book. The very name of the exercise would seem to be sufficient to render this rule unnecessary; but there have been teachers so profoundly stupid as to oblige pupils to commit to memory the model lessons given in manuals of teaching." (*Op. cit.*, pp. 91, 92.)

[2] Mlle. Chalamet, *op. cit.*

328. DIFFERENT FORMS OF OBJECT-LESSONS. — After having attempted to define the essential characteristics of every
object-lesson, we must hasten to note the fact that there are
different ways of applying this educational process.

Mr. Bain distinguishes three principal forms of the
object-lesson.

1. The object-lesson may consist in placing a concrete
object before the eyes of the pupil as a type, in order to
have him grasp an abstract idea. For example, four apples,
or four nuts, are presented to the pupil in order to develop
in him the concept of the number four.

2. The object-lesson may consist in calling into play the
five senses, as by making the pupil see, touch, and observe
the qualities of certain objects. In this form, the object-
lesson is but the education of the senses.

3. Finally, the object-lesson may be employed to increase
the number of conceptions, to make the pupil acquire a
knowledge of objects, facts, and realities, formed by nature
or by human art. It is this feature which is commonly
expressed by saying that the object-lesson cultivates or
develops the faculty of conception and imagination.

"Basing upon what the child already knows and conceives,
unknown objects may be pictured forth, and so laid hold of, as
permanent imagery for after uses. It is thus that children may
be made to conceive in a dim form the camel of the desert, the
palm-tree, the Pyramids of Egypt." [1]

329. THE PROPER DOMAIN OF OBJECT-LESSONS. — If we are
to believe American teachers, object-lessons have an unlimited
field of application, — as unlimited as nature itself. They
may be extended even to history,[2] and applied to ideal

---

[1] Bain, *op. cit.*, p. 256.
[2] Wickersham, *op. cit.*, p. 144.

things as well as to material objects. "In its enlarged sense," says Wickersham, " the term *object* means anything to which thought is or may be directed." There might, then, be object-lessons even in psychology.

Mr. Bain more wisely limits the domain of object-lessons to sensible objects alone.

" The object-lesson introduces the pupil to three great fields, — Natural History, Physical Science, and the useful arts, or common utilities of every-day life." [1]

We agree with the English educator, that the domain of object-lessons is necessarily restricted to the sciences, or rather to the familiar and ordinary subjects of knowledge, which relate directly to things that can be seen and touched. History, grammar, the abstract sciences, such as arithmetic and the moral sciences, must be strictly excluded.

330. THEIR TRUE CHARACTER. — That which finally distinguishes the object-lesson is not merely the nature of the objects to which it is applied, but the manner in which it is given. It ought not to have the didactic character of consecutive exposition, but it ought to be given always in the conversational form.

Mr. Spencer justly complains that in the manuals of object-lessons there is given a long list of the things which are to be *told* to the child. According to him, the child must be merely provoked to discover these things by his own observation. In the object-lesson it is chiefly the child that ought to speak.

" We must listen to all the child has to tell us about each object, must induce it to say everything it can think of about such object, must occasionally draw its attention to facts it has not yet

---

[1] Bain, *op. cit.*, p. 249.

observed, with the view of leading it to notice them itself whenever they recur, and must go on by and by to indicate or supply new series of things for a like exhaustive examination." [1]

The object-lesson ought to be a transition from maternal instruction to school instruction proper, an initiation into certain studies, and not a general method.

The teacher is here less a professor who sets forth what he knows, than one who stimulates the intelligence. This is why we do not think, Mr. Spencer to the contrary notwithstanding, that the object-lesson should be continued beyond the first years of school instruction. The object-lesson greatly promotes a knowledge of material things, and chiefly develops the faculty of sensible observation. Now, in the work of instruction it is necessary as soon as possible to dispense with concrete and material things in order resolutely to throw the child into the domain of abstract and general ideas. Of course, in the teaching of history and number, and in the higher instruction in the physical and natural sciences, the teacher is not forbidden to appeal to the child's imagination and to sensible representations; it is even necessary to do this on occasion. But this will be only an accident, an exception, at most a special element in the lesson. This appeal to experience will no longer constitute an object-lesson properly so-called.

331. RULES FOR OBJECT-LESSONS. — From the fact that the object-lesson is above all else a free and familiar conversation of the teacher with his pupils, it must not be inferred that it has no rules and principles.

"On the contrary," says Madame Pape-Carpantier, "it has fixed rules which are independent of the fancy of teachers. . . . Its principles and rules are the same as those which govern the operations of the human understanding."

---

[1] Spencer, *op. cit.*, pp. 133, 134.

The first of these rules is that each lesson should have **a** definite purpose, its determined scope.

" The teacher," adds Mr. Bain, "should consider what is to be the drift of the lesson. That at the outset lessons are more or less desultory, perhaps cannot be helped; but they should gradually be brought under some of the ' Unities.' "

332. THE NECESSITY OF A SYSTEMATIC PLAN. — It is not only necessary that each lesson should have its definite purpose, but also that the successive object-lessons should · be connected and, so to speak, brought into proper subordination. Object-lessons would be a chaos of sterile conversations and profitless talk, if they were disconnected and were to proceed at random in the vast field which is open to them.

" Object-lessons should be given in a systematic course, each one conveying its own teaching and bearing some palpable relation to the one that has preceded and the one that follows, thus leading the pupil to the discovery of the relations, and enabling him to associate them in memory. Desultory object-lessons are of little worth." [1]

333. PREPARATION OF OBJECT-LESSONS. — **A** thing not less necessary is that each lesson should be carefully prepared. Nothing should be left to chance in these familiar conversations, and the teacher should be all the more prepared on all the parts of his subject, as an unexpected question asked by his pupils might surprise and disconcert him.

" Object-lessons demand such a studied preparation, such· a profound knowledge of the subject, so much tact and intelligence, and finally such a judiciously arranged collection of objects, that this kind of instruction has not yet gained a foothold in the schools.

---

[1] Johonnot, *op. cit.*, p. 92.

Much has been said about them in scholastic circles, and some teachers even pride themselves that they have been successful in their use; but up to the present time they can be credited only with good intentions." [1]

334. ORDER TO BE FOLLOWED IN STUDYING THE QUALITIES OF OBJECTS. — Madame Pape-Carpantier thought it very important that in observing the qualities of objects we should restrict ourselves to an invariable order, derived, as she claimed, from the natural course which the mind follows in its perceptions. It would be necessary, on this hypothesis, to proceed always in the same manner and to call the child's attention successively to the color, the form, the use, and the matter or constituent elements of the object studied. Mr. Bain is not of his opinion.

" The most useful direction for conducting it is, first, to point out the appearance or sensible qualities of an object, and 'next to specify its uses. A better rule would be, to give the uses first (after the most obvious aspects); use is quality in act, and our interest in things is first excited by their active agency." [2]

And taking glass as an example, Mr. Bain remarks that it is useless to say to pupils that it is hard, smooth, and transparent, — things which they already very well know. That which will interest them, on the contrary, and that which will instruct them, will be to lead them to reflect on the different uses of glass, and perhaps also on the various circumstances of its discovery or on its history.

335. SCHOOL MUSEUM. — Object-lessons require the organization in the school of little school museums, where the teacher may find within his reach the objects which are to serve as a text for his lesson.

---

[1] *Rapports et inspection générale*, 1879–1880, p. 210.
[2] Bain, *Education as a Science*, p. 249.

These museums ought in great part to be constructed by the pupils themselves.

"Children are asked, for example, to bring on the morrow leaves of two trees which they have, perhaps, never thought of distinguishing, as the pear and the apple, the pine and the fir, or certain species of the poplar; or such a stone or mineral, or specimen of wood, or such a manufactured product as is found in the country, but which is lacking in the little school museum. Something ought always to be wanting in a school museum, and it would not displease me to be told that each generation of scholars is obliged to reconstruct it, so to speak, anew by its own researches. The great profit to be derived from these little museums of object-lessons does not consist in having them, but in making them."

"The school museum," says M. Cocheris, to the same effect, "is the work of time, and ought to contain samples of the local industry and specimens of the natural products which contribute to the wealth of the country."

Complaint is sometimes made, and not without reason, that in certain schools the school museums assume exaggerated proportions. It is not the purpose, in fact, to bring together a collection of curiosities, or to establish a showy museum filled with useless articles designed to strike the imagination of visitors to the school; but to collect, in order to make use of them, the objects which may really contribute to the instruction of the child. The best museum is not that where the most specimens are pressed into elegant show-cases, but that of which the most use is made.

But, generally speaking, such museums do not exist in our schools, or exist only in an embryonic state.

"School museums develop but slowly. What is easier, however, than to collect from the grocer, the apothecary, the seedsman, the druggist, from field and garden, the elements of a useful collection?

"When they exist, people do not know how to make use of them. The specimens generally disappear under a thick coating of dust."

336. PRINCIPAL MISTAKES TO BE AVOIDED. — But what is still much more important than the material conditions of the object-lesson, conditions supplied by the school museum, is the manner in which the teacher interprets this exercise.

By reason of the very liberty which characterizes this mode of teaching, the object-lesson is a delicate thing to administer ; and a great number of faults and of possible inconveniences ought to be noted and shunned.

337. SUPERFLUITY OF OBJECT-LESSONS. — Object-lessons like those which are sometimes given are certainly superfluous. They squander precious time, as Mr. Bain observes, on things children already know or which they might learn of themselves, either by their personal observation or by conversations with their parents or their companions.

We recall the tiresome exercises which Pestalozzi imposed on his pupils before the old paper-hangings of the school-room : *There is a hole in the hangings. The hole in the hangings is round*, etc. "How many object-lessons which are thus but a sterile verbiage, in which children are taught by many repetitions that snow is white, that ink is black, that glass is transparent, that a bird has two claws and one head, that a horse has two eyes, two ears, and four legs, etc. !"

338. WORDS WITHOUT THINGS. — The object-lesson, imperfectly understood, has sometimes become a purely verbal exercise. Pestalozzi, one of the first who made use of it, employed it as a means of teaching the exact meanings of words. His exercises in intuition were chiefly exercises in language. It is certainly a good and useful thing to associate with exercises in observation a drill in language. But with respect to the object which is shown the child, and under a pretext of analyzing its qualities, we must be strictly

on our guard against making use of technical and scientific terms whose meaning he is incapable of comprehending. As some one has said, one single recommendation comprehends all the others : Let the object-lesson never degenerate into a lesson of words.

339. ABUSE OF SENSE-PERCEPTION. — Mr. Wickersham, an American teacher, justly remarks that " the object-lesson system is apt to continue instruction in the *concrete* after pupils can appreciate the *abstract*."

" The elements of all kinds of knowledge must be taught in connection with objects, but an acquaintance with material things is far from being the highest end of study; and object-teaching pushed too far tends to degrade education. Back of all, there are principles, ideas, controlling things, which are the soul's most nourishing pabulum. Soon after a child has learned to count with objects, he may begin to count without them; soon after he has become acquainted with real forms, he may begin to deal with ideal ones." [1]

The object-lesson is evidently but a means for rising higher ; it is, in some sort, a passage which must be traversed in order to go farther, but where it would be unwise to tarry too long.

340. OBJECT-LESSONS NOT TO FORM A REGULAR COURSE. — The mistake of a great number of teachers has been to consider object-lessons as a special item in the programme, and consequently to carry into them the ordinary habits of instruction and the regularity of a systematic course. The object-lesson, to be in real conformity with the principles which have inspired it, ought to remain free, flexible, versatile, and animated, just like the young minds to which it is

---

[1] Wickersham, *op. cit.*, pp. 158, 159.

addressed. Too often it has degenerated into monotonous interrogations, and into dry and formal nomenclatures.

"It is not desirable," says M. Buisson, "to have the object-lesson begin and end at a fixed hour. Let it be given on the occasion of a reading or writing lesson, or in connection with the dictation exercise, with the lesson in history, geography, or grammar. If it occupies two minutes instead of twenty, it will be only the better for that. Often it will consist, not in a series of consecutive questions, but in one spirited, precise, and pointed question, which will provoke a reply of the same sort; it will often be but a sketch upon the blackboard which will be worth more than a complete description. One day the object-lesson will be a visit to an industrial establishment or to an historic monument; on another, it will be a tour of observation, or a ramble in the woods, or a hunt for insects or plants."

Like most educators, M. Buisson perhaps gives too great an extension to the meaning of the object-lesson, and wrongly confounds it with the general spirit of intelligent and attractive instruction; but with this reservation we must accept his opinion and consider the object-lesson, not as a systematic course of instruction which is to be confined within immutable limits, but as a form of instruction infinitely variable and always adapting itself to circumstances.

341. ACTUAL PROGRAMMES. — The French official programme hardly speaks of object-lessons save for the maternal schools, by connecting with them a knowledge of common objects and the first notions of natural history.

The programme of the primary schools proper is silent upon object-lessons; but yet it is evident that it recommends them implicitly, since, in the statement of reasons which precede the enumeration of the different topics of instruction, the true method is defined in these terms:

"In every branch of instruction, the teacher at the outset uses sensible objects, causes things to be seen and touched, and places children in the presence of concrete realities.

"Primary instruction is essentially intuitive; that is, counts chiefly on natural good sense, on the strength of proof, on that innate power which the human mind has to seize at first glance and without demonstration not all the truths, but the truths that are simplest and most fundamental."

342. THE METHOD OF OBJECT-LESSONS. — In one sense the method of object-lessons may be considered as synonymous with the art which ought to animate all varieties of instruction, and endeavor to make them living and practical.

With what enthusiasm did Madame Pape-Carpantier in 1868 speak of the new method!

"But what, then, constitutes the value of object-lessons? On what ground are they so popular, so highly recommended, and in fact so profitable?

" Ah! this is due to a great law terribly misunderstood, which ordains that there shall be no *patient* in education ; which requires that the pupil be an active agent in it, as active as the teacher; that he be an intelligent co-laborer in the lessons which he receives from him, and that, according to the expression of the catechism, he co-operate in the work of grace.

" That which constitutes the value of object-lessons, that which makes them agreeable and effective, is that they are in conformity with this law; that they make an appeal to the personal powers of the child; that they call into play, into movement, his physical and intellectual faculties; and that they satisfy his natural need of thinking, speaking, moving, and changing from one object to another. It is that they appeal to his mind through the medium of his senses, and that they make use of what he knows and loves, to interest him in what he does not know or does not yet love, and because, in a word, they are for him the *concrete*, and not the *abstract*." [1]

---

[1] Madame Pape-Carpantier, *Conférences*, etc., 2 partie, p. 73.

CHAPTER IV.

THE STUDY OF THE MOTHER TONGUE.

343. IMPORTANCE OF THE STUDY. — Is it really necessary to-day to insist on the capital importance of the study of the vernacular in the common school? Everybody agrees that it should be assigned the first place. "It forms," says M. Bréal, "the beginning and the center of studies, and it is for pupils the principal instrument of progress."

First, the study of the vernacular is valuable on its own account. Who can deny its immediate practical utility? One becomes truly a man only through the power to express his thought correctly and clearly. One is a citizen only on the condition of speaking the national tongue, the language of his fellow-citizen. Then, again, the knowledge of language is the key to all other knowledges. The common tongue puts us in communication with our fellows and satisfies the needs of life ; the language of literature opens to us the treasures of human thought, and technology those of formulated science.

But the study of language is valuable also through its influence on intellectual education. To know one's language is to know how to think. The extent of the vocabulary which you have at your disposal corresponds to the abundance of the ideas which you possess. The new words added to those you already know are so many conquests of your mind over the unknown. On the other hand, the propriety of the expression is equivalent to the accuracy of the thought. Finally, the grammatical correctness which you know how to put into the construction of your sentences is directly related to the logic which governs your judgments and reasonings. To acquire the mother tongue is not, then, merely to acquire verbal material, but, through the mechanism of language, to develop and train the thought, of which language is but the instrument.

344. DIFFICULTY OF THIS INSTRUCTION. — For children in easy circumstances, whose parents speak the tongue purely, the study of language offers special facilities. For them, and for them alone, the national language is the mother tongue; they have learned it without effort and by use at their mother's knee. But how many children there are who have not this good fortune! At home and in their neighborhood they hear the language spoken only incorrectly. For them the national language is truly a foreign tongue, which they must painfully study on the benches of the school.[1]

But even for children who have been brought up, so to speak, on correct speech, this instinctive apprenticeship in the mother tongue is not sufficient. There always remains for them the need at least of extending their vocabulary, necessarily restricted; of taking account of the meaning of words which they have vaguely retained, and which they understand only confusedly, of learning orthography, and finally of reflecting on the rules of grammar, without which the correctness of their style or of their language would always be poorly assured. It is nature which unties the child's tongue, and with the aid of parents teaches him to speak; but it is study alone, with the aid of teachers, which teaches him to speak well.

---

[1] What is here said of French is in a considerable degree true of English, though our speech is less corrupted by *patois*. (P.)

345. THE PURPOSE. — For a long time the study of language in our schools has been synonymous with the study of grammar. When the distinction between the parts of a discourse, conjugation, and syntax had been taught, it was thought that all had been done; to-day we have a totally different idea of the teaching of the mother tongue, of its extent and scope. This instruction comprises three essential things, and all three are of inestimable value.

It is proposed: 1. To comprehend the vernacular; 2. To know how to speak it; 3. To know how to write it.

The least that can be demanded is that the pupils in our schools comprehend their native tongue. It is certainly not proposed to teach them the twenty thousand words of which the language is composed,[1] and to make of their minds a living dictionary. What is necessary is that they know with all possible exactness the few hundreds of expressions which constitute the basis of the language. The possession of a clear and exact vocabulary is the necessary preparation for the reading of good authors. Too many children leave our schools without ever having formed a taste for personal reading, partly because they find in books too many words whose meaning they do not comprehend.

Another essential purpose of language study is to learn to speak. With many people, occasions for writing may be comparatively rare, but occasions for talking occur every day and every hour. Who, then, does not need, however humble his condition, to express himself with facility and correctness, if not with elegance? Doubtless it is not required to make praters and speechmakers, but it is necessary to put the future citizen in a condition to communicate his thoughts, to converse with his fellows, to manage his affairs, and to discuss his interests.

---

[1] The latest edition of an unabridged English (American) dictionary enumerates 118,000 words as belonging to the English speech. (P.)

Finally, written language must not be neglected, though it is of less importance than spoken language. Though comparatively new and of recent introduction into our schools, exercises in composition and dictation are not the less interesting nor the less useful. The teaching of language would be a derision if it did nothing more than cause the rules of grammar to be learned, and laboriously inculcate the science of orthography on children who would never be called on to apply these rules or to use that knowledge in compositions of their own. Grammar and orthography are excellent things, but on one condition, however, — and this is that they are used, — that they are not for children as arms in the hands of soldiers who do not know how to handle them.

346. Principles. — Thus understood, the teaching of language is an interesting and practical study, which is extending in all directions beyond the old, narrow scheme of grammatical memory-lessons and exercises in orthography. In order to attain its true purpose, this instruction must conform to the natural method, which proceeds from the example to the rule, from the experiment to the law, from common use, from the concrete instance to the general and abstract precept. Grammar must be learned through language, and not language through grammar, as Herder said; and Mr. Spencer declares that "as grammar was made after language, so it ought to be taught after it." "For a long time," as the Père Girard said, "a healthy didactics has told us, 'Few rules, many exercises.'"

The child enters the school having hardly any use of the mother tongue. Let what is lacking be supplied by graded selections from easy authors. In default of conversations which he has not heard, let the book envelop him. so to speak, in its precise terms, in its correct constructions, in an atmosphere of pure and clear speech. Let him be drilled in speaking, in constructing sentences, at first orally, and later by writing. Let the teacher give the example of exact pronunciation and of idiomatic expression. Let the blackboard present to the pupil models of simple statement; and the child, familiarized little by little with the expressions and idioms of his native tongue, will be prepared for the didactic lessons which, without this preparation, would infallibly have repelled him and wearied him without profit.

347. PROPOSED REFORMS. — From ministerial circulars we quote a few passages which clearly indicate the direction which should be given to instruction in the mother tongue.

" In the course in French, many teachers make a misuse of the grammar, and think that all has been done when they have put into the memory of their pupils a great number of rules, distinctions, and technical terms. Insist that in this study abstractions and subtleties shall be avoided; that the attention shall be given to applications and examples, especially to examples furnished by the reading and the explication of great writers. It is in this way that the language with its principal rules, its refinements, and its idioms, is learned much better than in the grammar."

" The old instruction ought to be replaced by living lessons. The grammar should be reduced to a few simple and short definitions, and to a few fundamental rules which are illustrated by examples; and in proportion as the intelligence of the children is developed, they must be supplied with the finest specimens of our literature. Here they must first be made acquainted with the signification of words, even to their nice shades of meaning, and the succession and connection of ideas; and later, the inversions and even the bold strokes of genius. In this exercise more dependence must be placed on that natural logic and grammar which children carry about with them, than upon the old mass of abstractions and formulas with which the memory is harassed with-

out profit to the intelligence.   Lhomond said a hundred years ago,
"Metaphysics is not fit for children, and the best elementary book
is the voice of the teacher who varies his lessons and the manner
of presenting them according to the needs of those to whom he
speaks."

"The teaching of grammar will henceforth be no longer limited to the purely mechanical study of rules, but these rules will
become matter for explanations by the teacher."

348. THE NECESSITY OF GRAMMAR. — It was not left
until the nineteenth century to dream of the absolute sup-
pression of the grammar in the course of instruction in language.   Nicole, in his book, the *Éducation d'un prince*,
replied in these terms to the partisans of that illusion:

"The thought of those who desire no grammar at all is but a
thought of indolent persons who wish to spare themselves the
labor of teaching it; and, very far from relieving children, this
plan infinitely burdens them, since it takes from them a light
which would facilitate the understanding of their lessons and
obliges them to learn a hundred times that which it would suffice
to learn but once." [1]

Let us pass by the question of indolence, for it would be
quite as just to say that the system which consists in putting
a grammar into the hands of pupils, and leaving them there
to clear up the subject all alone, is a thought of indolent
people; but Nicole is right in holding that grammatical
rules, preceded by explanations and illustrated by examples,
relieve the mind of the child and economize precious time.
Though the intelligence is repelled by abstract principles
prematurely imposed upon it, it is disposed of itself to
anticipate general rules which sum up its experience and
flow naturally from the examples on which it has been

---

[1] To the same effect Mr. Bain says, "The grammar abridges the
labor by generalizing everything that can be generalized."

nourished. Here it reposes with pleasure, just as a victorious army installs itself in fortresses where it makes sure of its conquest, and whence it dominates the successive advances it has made.

However elementary the study of language may be, it permits, in our opinion, the knowledge of grammatical rules, which are but the résumé of usage, the code of a language definitely fixed. Progress in teaching here consists, not in suppressing rules, but in simplifying them, and in reforming the manner in which they are taught.

349. THE TRUE GRAMMATICAL METHOD. — The true grammatical method, according to all that has just been said, consists in placing the main reliance upon the use of language, and in making the rules flow from examples which the pupil invents for himself, which he finds in books, or which the teacher suggests to him.

This was the method of the Père Gréard, who made the basis of grammatical instruction the use of the language which the child brings from home ; this use to be completed and corrected at school by the exercises which have taught him to read and write.

" Let us recollect," he said, " that a multitude of examples repeated and analyzed is the best code of language, since it introduces into rational practice the rules which by another method it would have to prescribe by arbitrary authority." [1]

It is useless to give a name to that method which is the method of reason and good sense ; we do not think that the least progress in the study of language has been made by saying, with certain educators, that it ought to be taught by the " analytico-synthetic method."

---

[1] Mr. Bain is wrong when he asserts that pupils in general cannot study grammar with profit before the age of ten.   " Grammar," he adds, " is more difficult than arithmetic."

350. THE QUESTION OF TEXT-BOOKS. — "If it is possible,
no grammar in the hands of pupils," — so says the Ministerial Circular of 1857. We do not think it is proper to go
so far, and deprive ourselves of the aid of a book in instruction as important as that of the mother tongue. A book
is necessary at least for the pupils of the intermediate and
higher courses, — a book that is well constructed, which the
teacher is to use with discretion and intelligence.

" Till lately," says M. Bréal, " the book was the principal character in the school-room, and the teacher was but the commen-
tator on the book. On the contrary, it is through the mouth of
the teacher that the children ought at first to know the rules.
The book will be consulted as a *memento*."

But however disposed we may be to magnify the office of
oral explanations, the book is necessary. This is the advice of Mr. Bain, who gives strong reasons to justify his
opinion :

" What is printed is only what is proper to be said by word of
mouth; and if the teacher can express himself more clearly than
the best existing book, his words should be written down and
take the place of the book. No matter what may be the peculiar
felicity of the teacher's method, it may be given in print to be
imitated by others, and so introduce a better class of books; the
reform that proposes to do away with books entirely, thus ending
in the preparation of another book. . . . . Again, it may be said
that the children are not of an age to imbibe the doctrines from a
printed book, but can understand them when conveyed with the
living voice. There is much truth in this, but it does not go the
length of superseding the book, which will still have value as a
means of recalling what the teacher has said, and as the basis
of preparation to answer questions thereon. If a class is to be
taught purely *viva voce*, its progress must needs be very slow." [1]

---

[1] Bain, *Education as a Science*, pp. 344, 345.

351. QUALITIES OF A GOOD GRAMMAR. — Fénelon had indicated with precision the characteristics of a good grammar.

"A professional grammarian," he said, "runs the risk of composing a grammar that is too technical, too full of observations and exceptions. It seems to me that one should limit himself to a short and simple method. At first, give only the most general rules; the exceptions will come as they are needed. The important point is to introduce a person as soon as possible into the actual application of rules by frequent use; afterwards this person will take pleasure in noting the special rules which he at first followed without paying any careful attention to them." [1]

After three hundred years, the criticisms and observations of Fénelon are still opportune, and the most competent educators of our day do no more than repeat them.

"In general," says M. Berger, "the grammars published for pupils are too full of details, and they are not yet affranchised from the plan of the Latin grammars. . . Our grammarians are too fond of classifications and distinctions which have no substantial basis. We believe that it would be possible greatly to diminish the extent of our classical grammars, without doing harm to solidity of knowledge in the matter of language. Simplicity, then, is the first quality of a good grammar; and this simplicity should manifest itself by the small number of rules. Too many grammarians still recommend simplicity in form, without conforming to it in fact; it is not necessary to distinguish propositions as subjective, completive-direct, completive-indirect, circumstantial, attributive, etc." [2]

352. HISTORICAL GRAMMAR. — We know what a complete revolution has been accomplished in grammatical studies by the introduction of the historical method.   "The

---

[1] *Lettre sur les occupations de l'Académie française*, II.
[2] See article *Grammaire, Dic. de Pédagogie*.

traditional grammar," says Michael Bréal, " formulated its prescriptions as though they were the decrees of a will as inscrutable as sovereign ; historical grammar casts a ray of good sense into the gloom." It substitutes explanations for simple affirmations ; it explains present usage by ancient usage.

" What can be more natural," says M. Brachet, "than to make the history of language contribute to the explanation of grammatical rules by going back from actual usage to the very moment when they sprang into being? Besides the advantage of being rational, the historical method has another ; the memory always retains more clearly that of which our mind has taken an account ; and the pupil will recollect the rules of grammar so much the better if they have a point of support in his intelligence. This is the method which the Germans, always solicitous to stimulate the judgment of the child, have for a long time employed in their schools for the teaching of the national language." [1]

Notwithstanding its interest, it is evident that. historical grammar can be introduced only with difficulty into the common school.

First, the historical grammar of a derivative language, like the French, goes back to the languages from which it has sprung, — to the Latin and the Greek ; and these languages really are, and ought to remain, dead languages for primary instruction. [2]

On the other hand, the purely national origin of the vernacular, the curiosities of the ancient tongue, would involve both teachers and pupils in learned researches which are beyond their sphere.

So Mr. Bain is right in saying :

" There is great interest, and some utility, in tracing the course

---

[1] Brachet, *Nouvelle Grammaire française*, preface.

[2] Notwithstanding what has recently been said about it we do not think that the introduction of Latin into the normal schools should be hoped for.

of our language from the more ancient dialects; but this subject may easily run to a disproportionate length in the first stages of English teaching. Present meanings and use are the only guidance to the employment of the language; the reference to archaic forms can sometimes account for a usage, but cannot control it." [1]

353. DICTATION EXERCISES. — The dictation exercise is the essential process, the proper use of orthography, which is learned not less by habit and memory than by the study of rules and reasoning.[2] But if dictation exercises are useful, it is on the condition that they are not abused and that they are wisely selected.

"Too many dictation exercises are required in our schools, and there is too great a disposition to seek out difficult exercises. There are schools where, on the approach of examinations, there is nothing but dictation." [3]

These exercises must not be too long [4] nor too frequent, nor should unnecessary difficulties be introduced into them.

Another important rule is, not to impose on the child dictation exercises abounding in words which he has never seen, and which he is obliged to spell at hazard. So, many educators rightly recommend teachers to spell or write on

---

[1] *Education as a Science*, pp. 349, 350.

[2] We cannot subscribe to the opinion of teachers who assert that it is useless to require exercises in orthography proper, but that it is sufficient to rely upon reading, writing, composition, and grammatical exercises to teach spelling. Especially in the primary schools, where the child is not aided in the study of orthography by a knowledge of Latin and Greek, spelling exercises are required.

[3] Article *Orthographie, Dictionnaire de Pédagogie.*

[4] In American schools consecutive texts are not generally dictated, but long lists of isolated words, as in the French collection, the *Pautex.*

the blackboard all the terms in the exercise which the pupil does not know.   Orthography is learned mainly through the sense of sight, through the memory of the eyes.[1]

Again, these exercises should correspond to the rules already learned, and should be but the application of them.

On the other hand, they should not be selected at random, without taking account of the age and the intelligence of children. They ought, like all other exercises, to contribute to the general education of the child.

Is it necessary to add that they ought always to be corrected with care, and that the faults should always be pointed out in connection with the rules which have been violated? It is not necessary to spell all the words in the exercise, but only those which are really difficult.

354. GRAMMATICAL AND LOGICAL ANALYSIS. — In the teaching of language the thought of suppressing grammatical and logical analysis should not be entertained.   An abuse has certainly been made of them, as when a teacher requires them as routine, mechanical work, devised to get rid of pupils and to avoid the need of giving attention to them.   But analysis is necessary, because for the child language is but a confused whole, whose various elements he does not distinguish and whose construction he does not clearly grasp.

Exercises in analysis may be employed in the form of oral exercises at the blackboard.   Analysis made *viva voce*,

---

[1] The plan of teaching orthography by writing words seems to be based on the assumption that when we spell a word we reproduce the mental picture of it.   On the contrary, it seems to me much more probable that for purposes of spelling our knowledge of words is nothing more than a recollection of the names and order of the letters which compose them.   That any mind really carries the mental pictures of the words in an ordinary vocabulary seems to me incredible.   (P.)

especially at first, is preferable to written analysis. But
the thing of chief importance is the choice of tests for
analysis.

The monotonous and interminable analyses which impose
on the child the toil of writing more than the toil of reflection, are justly condemned. Their most obvious result is to
disgust the pupil with the study.

"I would have our teachers," says M. Gréard, "without depriving themselves entirely of the resources offered by special collections, become more and more accustomed to look for the tests they
need in their dictations in classical works, and to construct their
examples, or make their pupils construct them, out of the material
furnished by the class instruction. What pages of transparent
language, of exquisite thought, and of every variety, — moral essays, descriptions, narratives, letters, — does our language contain!
The national history is so rich in striking statements, ready-made,
so to speak, to serve as examples in grammar! Let it be at least
on these texts, and on these well-selected examples, that the child
be drilled in analysis. That which has contributed to the disfavor
into which analysis has fallen, is doubtless, first, the abuse which
has been made of it; but it is also the whimsical and tedious character of the texts to which it has generally been applied, and of
the performances to which it has given rise. The use of analysis
is necessary if we wish the child to come to a good understanding
of the relations of the different terms of a proposition or of a sentence. We need oppose only the excess, or the false direction, into
which it has fallen, and for this purpose it suffices to make the
analysis, for the most part, at the board, orally, in sparing terms
on clear and interesting sentences."

355. ORDER TO BE FOLLOWED. — Educators are not
agreed as to the place which should be assigned to grammatical and logical analysis. The official programme of
1882 gives the preference to grammatical analysis; but
many writers, on the contrary, would begin with logical
analysis.

"In order to make the analysis of a sentence," says Madame Pape-Carpantier, "we must first make an analysis of the thought which it expresses; in other terms, a logical analysis, or the study of the ideas and their relations, ought to precede grammatical analysis proper, or the study of words as they are formed into sentences."

"In the progressive development of the reason," says C. Marcel, "the perception of an object always precedes the consideration of its parts; and we reach an understanding of our language by passing from the sentence to the words." [1]

Among Swiss teachers, on the contrary, there is a tendency towards the reverse order, or rather towards sacrificing logical analysis completely.

"In the higher schools," says M. Horner, "*if one has time to squander*, he might afford the luxury of a few excursions into the desert of logical analysis."

We are firm in the belief that logical analysis is useful and necessary, but on the condition that we do not indulge in a terminology too complicated and too technical, and that in the classification and naming of propositions we choose the simplest and clearest method.

356. EXERCISES IN INVENTION AND COMPOSITION. — The child in the primary school ought to be discreetly drilled in composition, or at least in the elements of composition.

"Where is the child that would dare flatter himself that he will never have a letter to write, a memorandum to dictate, or a report to draw up?"

Surely there are such intimate relations between spoken language and written language, that much will already have been done to habituate the child to the work of composition,

---

[1] *L'Étude des langues ramenée à leur véritable principe*, II., p. 26.

if, from his entrance into school, he has been made to converse, and if, in his recitations and in the object-lessons, he
has been steadily required to express himself with correctness. But these oral exercises cannot take the place of
written exercises.

Some teachers seem to put exercises in invention and
exercises in composition upon the same plane.

"Ideas," says M. Gréard, "do not come of themselves into the
child's mind; he must be taught to find them. Still less do they
of themselves take the order and form which they ought to assume; and so he must be taught to compose."

To tell the truth, we do not think that invention ought to
play an important part in school, and the importance which
has been given to it seems to us but a reminiscence of
secondary instruction. At college it may be proper to train
future writers, and in general men who will need to draw
original ideas from their own resources; but at school we
must think only of putting future workmen in a condition to
express correctly and clearly the ideas which spring naturally
and without reflection from the needs and circumstances of
life.

This is why we must not run the risk, with children of the
primary school, when we propose to them a subject for composition, to receive this reply, which often comes to their
lips: "I do not know what to say"! Furnish them with
the ideas they need, by conversations, by lectures, or at
least by the choice of a subject borrowed from their own
experience.

"The first exercises in composition," says Horner, "will consist
in reproducing, partly by writing or in recapitulating, the object-
lessons. . . . There will next be undertaken a written description
of common objects, but this description will always be preceded by

an oral lesson and followed by a methodical recapitulation upon the blackboard.

"The first idea of developing a few sentences, four or five at most, on the start, will be furnished by the teacher. Even the scheme of the development will be prepared, and the pupil will be left to fill it in, by pointing out the causes, effects, and accessory circumstances of time, place, etc. This sort of theme might also sometimes serve as a text for an exercise in orthography. In whatever way the task is accomplished, if the corrections are made in the class, at the blackboard, and if each pupil furnishes the quota of ideas more or less just, more or less happy, which he has found, the teacher will have an opportunity to compare the contributions one with another, and to call into exercise the judgment of all."

And M. Gréard concludes that it is less important to teach children to write than to develop their judgment and their moral sense. We shall not deny this; but it must not be forgotten that the habit of composing easily, correctly, and if need be elegantly, has also its value, and that it is expedient for everybody. "The first quality of language," says M. Bréal, "is propriety of expression, and it may as properly be required of the workman and the peasant as of the man of letters and the philosopher." Now, it is not merely by making him speak, but also by making him write, that the child is taught to form a correct notion of the meaning of words.

357. COMPOSITIONS FROM PICTURES. — There is now such a desire to facilitate the child's work that resort is often made to refinements, to processes which may have their utility, provided they are not abused. Such is the use of *compositions from pictures*, an American importation, and an application of intuitive instruction to exercises in composition. In this case the child has but to see and to tell what he sees in the pictures placed before his eyes. But this

recreative exercise should not be made general, and it will always be much better to describe to children the things themselves, the concrete and living realities.

A refinement of the same sort is the exercise which consists in translating a selection of verse into prose.

"This exercise," says Cadet, "may at least render the service of marking the distinction between poetical language and ordinary language, in the use of words and the construction of sentences."[1]

As for ourselves, we do not believe that there is any great value in practicing this kind of transposition or of *transmutation*, as Belgian teachers say. It is much better to use simplicity, and require the child to describe a walk which he has taken or an event which he has witnessed.

358. EXERCISES IN ELOCUTION. — Elocution is no less important than composition; to know how to speak is even more necessary than to know how to write. Hence the importance accorded by Swiss and Belgian teachers to oral exercises. In France, our official programme requires the oral reproduction of short sentences read or explained, then of narratives recited by the teacher, the résumé of selections read in the class, the report of lectures, of lessons, of walks, of experiments, and recitals of literary and historical selections.

359. LITERARY EXERCISES. — Without presuming too much, we may assert that the primary school itself will tend more and more to initiate the child into the study of literature, and will inspire him with a desire to continue for life, by personal reading, a pursuit full of attractions.

It is mainly in the form of lectures given by the teacher, and of recitations given by the pupil, that this instruction

---

[1] Article *Langue Maternelle,* in the *Dictionnaire de Pédagogie.*

will be given. To these there might be added literary criticisms, which will have the advantage of accustoming the pupil to write, at the same time that they will exercise his taste and bring him into more intimate relation with the beauties of literature. Of course all these exercises should be conducted with discretion. It is especially in the teaching of literature that the instructor ought to recollect this reflection of M. Gréard: "The object of primary instruction is not to embrace, under the different subjects which it touches, all that it is possible to know, but to learn thoroughly in each of them what no one should be ignorant of."

CHAPTER V.

THE TEACHING OF HISTORY.

360. HISTORY IN THE COMMON SCHOOL. — Twenty years ago history had not yet gained an entrance into the common schools of France.

Even in the day of grand projects and at the heroic epoch, I mean under the Revolution, the boldest organizers of the national schools, Talleyrand and Condorcet, had not included history in their programmes. This was because, in the ardor of their struggle against the old régime, and in their enthusiasm, sometimes fanatical, for the new order of things, the early revolutionists had come almost to believe that the history of France dated only from May 5, 1789. Why recall memories of a past forever abolished? Of what use to relate the long history of the French monarchy? That history had disappeared in the night of August 4, with the abuses and the privileges of the time!

But these prejudices have happily disappeared. In 1833 M. Guizot introduced history, and particularly the history of France, into the higher common schools; and in 1867 another historian, M. Duruy, accomplished the same reform for the benefit of the primary schools.

361. PURPOSE OF HISTORICAL INSTRUCTION. — When the history of France is taught to little Frenchmen, the purpose is surely to develop their patriotic emotions and to train them up in civic virtues. In fact, history is an admirable school of patriotism. By means of it one's country ceases

to be a cold abstraction; it becomes a real, living being, whose destiny the pupil follows through the centuries, gladdened, elated by its successes, moved and affected by its reverses. Instructed by the principal events of the national history, familiarized with the names of its illustrious men, the child will believe himself a member of a great family, which he will love the more because he will know it the better. He will feel himself pledged to defend the heritage of his fathers, when he knows at what a costly sacrifice it has been acquired and preserved. He will be ready to imitate the beautiful and noble examples of his ancestors, when a faithful narrative has nourished his imagination with them.

362. INFLUENCE OF HISTORY ON THE DEVELOPMENT OF THE MIND. — But history offers still other advantages. Even reduced to its simplest elements, and brought within the comprehension of children, it contributes to emancipate the reason and to train the judgment. Between the man ignorant and narrow, whose thought does not pass beyond the horizon of present events, and him who, moderately instructed in the history of his country, has some idea of the progress of the ages and of the painful crisis out of which modern France has issued, what a distance, what an abyss! There are studies of which it may be said that they are the liberators of the spirit; history, with the sciences, ranks among the first of these. How many belated souls would be relieved of their prejudices if history, intelligently studied, presented to them the spectacle of the changes that have been accomplished and of the marvelous transformations that have renewed the face of the world! How many adventurers and sectaries would be cured of their folly, if they could be sent to the common school for a few months, and in history made to touch with the finger the necessary

slowness of social progress! History teaches patience to those who lack it, and hope to those who grow discouraged. On the one hand, it gives wings to the imagination; on the other, historical knowledge is as ballast which gives equilibrium to the spirit and moderation to the judgment.

363. CHARACTERISTICS AND LIMITS OF THIS INSTRUCTION. — It cannot be proposed in the common school to undertake the study of universal history. Here the national history ought to be the single object of instruction. The facts of ancient history or of general history should be introduced only by reason of their intimate relations with the nation's history, and in the same proportion as they explain its destinies. It is important, moreover, that the national history be taken up at its beginning in order that it may be continued and carried forward to the end. In American schools the middle age is almost completely ignored. This is well enough for a nation hardly a century old, but it should not be the same with us. Our history is a whole which cannot be divided. In order properly to comprehend the Revolution, we must know the feudal system and the absolute monarchy. We can be indifferent to nothing which our ancestors have done, to nothing which they have suffered. Moreover, the old history of the Middle Age is particularly interesting to the child; here the picturesque predominates and dramatic incidents abound.

It is not merely by fragments and detached narratives, but in a regular and consecutive course, that the history of their country in its vast compass should be presented to children. Doubtless with beginners it is well and perhaps necessary to resort at first to anecdotes and biographies; but as soon as possible we must require the child to follow the march of time and teach him the succession of facts in their chronological order.

"Do not proceed at random," says M. Lavisse. "Weave firmly the woof on which you are to delineate the grand facts and the grand figures of history."

Complete and regular, the teaching of history ought at the same time to be temperate without ceasing to interest and to please. Especially in the common school it is necessary to avoid the dryness of a simple chronological nomenclature and the diffusiveness of an over-rich erudition. In order to escape fatigue and confusion, the attention must be held to the great facts.

"Our better teachers," says M. Gréard, "know that in history it is the solid framework of great events and of generative ideas that they are to engrave in the intelligence of children, without losing themselves in the details of accessory facts and secondary ideas."

Finally, without omitting anything essential, the intelligent teacher will know how to choose the facts which deserve more than others to retain the attention and to be more fully related and explained. In his choice he will be guided by the definition given by Voltaire: "Real history is that of the manners, the laws, the arts, and the progress of the human spirit." He will not lose his way, like the historians of former times, in tedious details and descriptions which have no practical value.

"Supposing even that you had diligently read," says Mr. Spencer, "not only 'The Fifteen Decisive Battles of the World,' but accounts of all other battles that history mentions; how much more judicious would your vote be at the next election?"

364. FUNDAMENTAL NOTIONS OF HISTORY. — English teachers are troubled, and not without reason, with the difficulty the child experiences in entering into the world of history, in comprehending its fundamental notions, or what

Mr. Bain calls *the elements of history.* From an early hour
the child sees about him hills, valleys, watercourses, plains,
villages, and cities ; it will be easy then to inititate him into
geographical studies ; but society, the state, public offices,
even the idea of the past, — these are things which surpass
the mind of the child, reduced as he is to his sensations
and confined within the narrow circle of the family or of the
school.

Thus English teachers are of the opinion that the teacher
of history should first give a short series of lessons, either
oral or, better, borrowed from a good book, by means of
which he should attempt to make intelligible some of the
simple and fundamental ideas of history, as a state, a
nation, a dynasty, a monarch, a parliament, legislation,
justice, taxes, etc.[1] We cannôt too strongly condemn a
method like this, which, at the beginning of the study of
history, would re-establish the abstractions which have
been discarded with such difficulty from the beginning of
other studies. Those so-called historical *elements* are but
general notions, of which the child has no need for the
understanding of particular facts and for acquiring an
interest in a moving narrative. History is pre-eminently a
science of facts, and it is especially with children that it
must preserve this character. Little by little, and with the
child's progress in study, these notions, supported upon
facts, will classify themselves.

365. TWO SYSTEMS FOR THE DISTRIBUTION OF SUBJECT-
MATTER. — It is a difficult question to know which is better :
the ancient programme, which presented the whole of our
national history to the children of the common school three
times, proportioning the breadth of the treatment and

---

[1] Fitch, *op. cit.*, p. 370.

adjusting the nature of the questions to the child's progress in age and in intelligence; or the order followed in secondary instruction, which consists in dividing the history of France into several periods, in making several portions of it, each of them being allotted to a different class.

366. ADVANTAGES AND DISADVANTAGES OF THE ANCIENT SYSTEM. — According to the ancient method, the teacher passed over the same road three times, but each time the subject was enlarged; and it is impossible to deny the advantages of a system which it was wrong to abandon completely. Through the effect of repetition, the facts were better engraved in the memory of the children; and besides, on this plan, from the elementary course the pupil has an idea, however incomplete it may be, of the general course of the national history. Finally, as they bear three times on the same subjects, the lessons may be skillfully graded and adapted to the age of the pupils.

But the disadvantages of a triple repetition are not less evident. First, *ennui* is to be feared; for in the last two courses there is no longer any surprise; there is nothing absolutely new for the pupil.

Besides, it is to be feared that the teacher, obliged to exhibit the whole history of France at one view, may not be able to make a leisurely survey of the most important epochs. Now, with children particularly, history is valuable only through its details. Hence it would seem to be necessary to divide the course into several parts, so as not to oppress the minds of beginners under the weight of a chronology too extended and too complicated.

367. ACTUAL PROGRAMME. — These reflections seem to have inspired the authors of the programme of 1882, who organized the study of history upon a new plan.

Below is the text of the actual programmes. It will be
noticed that they are very short, that they do not enter into
detail, and that they simply fix the distribution of the
topics, rightly leaving to the teacher the liberty of moving
at his ease within the limits that have been traced for him.

ELEMENTARY COURSE: Narratives and familiar conversations
upon the most important characters and the principal facts of the
national history, up to the beginning of the Hundred Years' War.

INTERMEDIATE COURSE: Elementary course in the history of
France, insisting exclusively on the essential facts since the Hundred Years' War.

HIGHER COURSE: Very summary notions of general history;
for antiquity, Egypt, the Jews, Greece, Rome ; for the middle age
and modern times, great events, studied especially in their relations to the history of France.

Systematic review of the history of France ; a more thorough
study of modern history.

Presented at first in the form of narratives and anecdotes, but always in a chronological order, down to the
Hundred Years' War, the history of France does not constitute a regular exposition, consecutive and didactic, except
in the Intermediate Course. It is completed in this form
during the two years of the Intermediate Course ; but in
the Higher Course it is systematically reviewed from beginning to end, and in its most recent periods it is exhaustively
studied.

The actual system is a just medium between the two
methods which we have indicated. On the one hand, in
the first two courses the history is divided into two parts,
from the beginning down to 1328, and from 1328 to the
present day. On the other hand the third course, save the
addition of some notions on general history, is devoted to a
systematic review, and on certain points is exhaustive.

This mixed system escapes the faults and embodies the

advantages of the two exclusive systems. As it seems to us, however, it has one great disadvantage, — that of keeping the youngest children of the school for too long a period on the remotest epochs of our history.

Is it not to be feared that, expatriated to their ninth year in remote centuries where nothing recalls to them the present, the beginners may not bring to the study of history an interest that is vivid enough?

368. THE SO-CALLED REGRESSIVE METHOD. — This disadvantage is so real that certain teachers have had the idea of recommending a strange method which in Germany is called the *regressive* method, and which consists in teaching history backwards, by beginning at the end and ascending the course of the ages.

"In England, in the primary school," says M. Gréard, "the study of history is begun with the contemporary period, for the purpose of giving the intelligence of the child a good grounding in the ideas of the time in which he is called to live."

This system has had but few imitators in France. I very well know that in geography we start from the village school to radiate little by little over the whole world; but in history it is impossible to follow the same course. We must resign ourselves to the necessary conditions of each study, and it would be absurd to attempt to invert the chronological order.

However, let us retain one just and practical idea from this whimsical scheme; in the teaching of history it will be best as often as possible to compare the past with the present, and to illustrate ancient events by comparisons with contemporaneous events. As some one has said, "In primary instruction every lesson in history should begin with the word *formerly*, and continue with the word *to-day*."

369. GENERAL METHOD TO BE FOLLOWED. — The order to be followed is not debatable, — it is the order of time; but the method, what shall it be?

First, let us say that it should not be the same for the different courses. That which is possible and desirable with the most advanced pupils is not always so with the beginners.

Let us add that the teaching of history, more perhaps than any other, admits a great variety, a great liberty in means. We shall not, however, go so far as to say, with Mr. Bain, "that the teaching of history almost appears to defy method."

No, there are general rules to be followed, there are accessory processes to be employed; and the best proof of this is that the men charged with the inspection of schools always find much to censure in what is done in them with respect to the teaching of history.

370. ORDINARY FAULTS IN HISTORICAL TEACHING. — In the *Rapports* of the Inspectors-General of primary instruction we notice a number of observations relative to the most ordinary defects in the teaching of history.

"The history is recited, but not understood. Almost everywhere history is but a simple repetition. The lesson is explained when it is too late. Pupils recite without comprehending; the explanations are generally insufficient. The teacher is lost in the gloom of the first centuries; there is absolute silence as to modern times. Hardly anywhere is history brought down to the period when it begins to become the most interesting. The attention is usually restricted to the study of dynasties and the chronology of battles. The teacher seems afraid to take up the history of the Revolution. Questions are much too rare. The lesson is rarely prepared by the teacher. History is generally the subject that is most neglected. Most frequently history is taught only in the higher divisions." (*Rapports* of 1879, 1880.)

" Too much time is still given to the accounts of battles. Teachers are satisfied with the pure and simple repetition of the text without any development of the subject. History is too much isolated from geography. The course is begun, but is rarely finished. Written review is most often wanting. The study of history, conducted exclusively from the book, remains profitless." (*Rapports* of 1880, 1881.)

In a word, history is still too often an exercise of pure repetition, in which the book plays an exclusive part. The teacher does not participate in it sufficiently by oral expositions, by explanations, and by comments. Besides, he lingers too long on the ancient period, and, either from having a poor knowledge of his own times or as a consequence of certain scruples, he abridges or even omits the history of the Revolution and of the contemporary period. The accounts of battles weigh more with him than the more useful analysis of institutions and manners. Finally, the processes which are wholly indispensable for good instruction, — interrogations and written reviews, — are totally neglected.

371. RECOMMENDATIONS MADE BY TEACHERS. — After the complaints of the Inspectors, let us hear the recommendations made by the teaching body itself. All of them are not faultless, but most of them confirm the criticisms of the Inspectors-General, and prove that at least the best of the teaching profession are in accord with the wishes of their superiors. Let us say, in addition, that the following recommendations relate only to the elementary division or lowest class :

" Teaching through sight by means of engravings. Instruction through the explanation of pictures. Pass rapidly over the early periods. Costumes, employments ; comparison by means of drawings and pictures of the industries of our ancestors with those of to-day. Let history, made as vivid as possible, be taught to children in the form of biographies or narratives. Instruction in history consists in amusing and instructive anecdotes related by the teacher and repeated by the pupils. Instruction given in the form of object-lessons may and should comprehend only the great facts, the great epochs of our history; and yet it ought to be *integral.* Ascend the course of the ages by making history. The teaching of history should be wholly oral. Charts representing the great facts of our national history. A collection of twenty engravings, representing in a very clear and salient manner the principal characters of French history, is a necessity. Instruction in history will be given by means of short narratives, which children will be called upon to reproduce by means of questions prepared in advance. It will serve to develop in children, not only the memory but the judgment, and especially the principal civic virtues."

372. WHAT MAY BE CALLED INTUITION IN HISTORY. — We must have been struck, on reading the preceding extracts, with the importance which competent judges attach to the methods and processes which render the instruction in history interesting and animating. It is not necessary to address the memory alone, although memory is the chief resort in history; but we must also address the reasoning faculties, and cause events to be comprehended and judged. "It is not of so much importance to know where Marcellus died," said Montaigne, "as why it was unworthy of his duty that he died there." Above all, we must speak to the imagination, and, so to speak, resuscitate the past before the eyes of the child. Let the narrative of the book and the lesson of the teacher have enough relief and color, so that the child may see in some sort the things and the men that are spoken of.

"Animate your narratives by lively and familiar tones," said Fénelon. "Make all your characters speak; and children who have a vivid imagination will believe they see them and hear them." And to the same effect Guizot wrote: "Historical characters must seem to children real living beings whom they love or hate, whom they esteem or despise."

To this intuition of the mind, which is the consequence of a well-told narrative, it is not useless to join, when it is possible, a real intuition of the eyes, by showing to the child vignettes and engravings which represent the principal characters and the great scenes of history.

"Eight or ten well-made engravings," says M. Buisson, "with or without color, teach the children more about the ancient civilizations than many pages of descriptions. A view of the pyramids or of the hypogea of Upper Egypt, an exact reproduction of the monuments, vessels, arms, and costumes of Rome or of Greece, gives a singular animation and support to the narratives of the teacher. It is an object-lesson transported into the most remote past."[1]

However, pictures are but an accessory, and it pertains mainly to the art of the teacher or of the writer to animate the instruction in history and to give the child an interest in it.

"During the first years," says Madame Pape-Carpantier, "history ought to be presented to children in the form of anecdotes. The facts related ought not only to be chosen from the moral point of view, but presented in an animated and picturesque manner. Let the teacher put into them a little of that action which is recommended to the orator, to the end that his recital may produce a picture in the imagination of his little pupils. In a narrative children love what is dramatic. We should give movement to our characters, make them speak, act, and, in a word, live. . . . So far as possible, each detached feature should be accompanied by a sketch of the manners contemporary with the facts related; for example, the mysterious life of the Druids in the forests which formerly covered the soil of our country."

---

[1] M. Buisson, *L'Instruction primaire à Vienne*, p. 181.

373. A Lesson upon the Feudal System. — To show how a skillful teacher may succeed in animating a lesson in history, even on a difficult subject; in interesting an entire class in it by striking descriptions and by drawings upon the board, and in rendering the past clear and vivid by an incessant appeal to the experience or to the reason of the child, the best course will be to give an example, which we shall borrow from M. Lavisse.

The following lesson was given at Paris, in the Faubourg Saint Antoine, to a class of children eight years of age:

"I arrived at the moment when a young teacher began a lesson on the Feudal System. He did not understand his business, for he spoke of hereditary services and privileges in a way which left the children whom he addressed absolutely indifferent. At that moment M. Berthereau, the director of the school, enters. He interrupts the lesson and appeals to the whole class: "Who is there here who has ever seen a castle of the Feudal times?" No one replies. The master then speaks to one of these young inhabitants of the Faubourg Saint Antoine: "Have you never been at Vincennes?" "Yes, sir." "Very well; you have seen a castle of Feudal times." A starting-point has now been found in the present. "What sort of a building is this castle?" Several children reply in concert. The master selects one of them, leads him to the board and obtains a rough drawing, which he corrects. He marks indentures in the wall. "What is that?" No one knew. He defined an embrasure. "What was the purpose of this?" Some one finally guessed that this served for defence. "With what did they fight, — with guns?" The greater number, "No, sir." "With what, then?" A young scholar from the foot of the class cries out, "With bows." "What is a bow?" Ten reply, "It is an arbalist, sir." The teacher smiles, and explains the difference. He then tells how difficult it was with bows, and even with the military engines of the time, to take a castle whose walls were high and broad; and continues: "When you are good workmen, and travel on business or for pleasure, you will meet with the ruins of castles." He mentions Montlhéry and other ruins in the vicinity of Paris. "In each of them there was a feudal lord. What did all these lords do?" The whole class replies, "They fought." Then in the presence of these children, no one of whom lost a single word, the master describes a feudal lord, placing the knights in the saddle and covering them with their armor. "But a castle is not taken with cuirasses and lances, and so the war was not finished. And who would suffer most from the war? Those who had no castles, the peasants who in those times worked for the lord. Then the cabins, belonging to the peasants of the neighboring lord, were burned. 'Ah! you burn my cabins,' said the lord who was attacked; 'I will burn yours.' He did so, and burned not only the cabins, but even the harvests. "And what happens when the harvests are burned? There is a famine. Can people live without eating?" The whole class: "No, sir." "Then is war very necessary to find a remedy?" He then speaks of the Truce of God, and adds: "This is truly a singular law. Why, it was said to the brigands, remain quiet from Saturday evening till Wednesday morning, but for the rest of the time do not trouble yourselves, — fight, burn, pillage, kill! Were these people madmen then?" A voice: "Most certainly." "No; they were not madmen. Pray listen to me. Here are indolent people. I do the best I can to have them work the whole week; but I would be half-satisfied to have them work till Wednesday. The church would much prefer not to have them fight at all; but as she could not help it, she attempted to make the lords keep quiet half of the week. Something is always gained in this way. But the church was not successful. There must be force against force, and it is the king who brought all these people to terms." Then the master explains that the lords were not all of equal rank, and that below the master of such a castle there was a more powerful lord, and one of higher rank living in another castle. He gives a fairly correct idea of the gradations in rank, and at the top places the king. "When people are fighting with each other, who stops them?" Reply, "The policeman." "Very well; the king was a policeman. What was done with those who fought and killed somebody?" Reply: "They are brought to trial." "Very well; the king was a judge. Can we do without policemen and judges?" "No, sir." "Very well; the ancient kings were as useful to France as policemen and judges. In the end they did evil, but they began by doing good. What did I say, — as useful? Much more so; for there were more brigands then than now. These lords were ferocious fellows, were they not?" The class: "Yes, sir." "And the people, my children, were they any better?" Unanimous reply, in a tone of conviction: "Yes, sir." "No, no, my children. When they were cowards, the common people were terrible people. They also pillaged, burned, and killed; they killed women and children. Reflect that they did not know what was good or what was bad. They had not been taught to read."[1]

374. THE BOOK. — There is a great distance between this varied and attractive instruction and the method too often in use, which consists in making the pupil read a book, and sometimes making him learn it mechanically by heart.

As soon as possible the teacher ought to intervene, by familiar conversations in the lower classes, and by a consecutive exposition with the older pupils.

However, we do not think of proscribing the book, which, especially in history, is necessary for accuracy in dates and the memory of facts. It would be unwise to abandon the child to the hazards of memory and the possible errors of note-books.

In default of a special book, as in Germany, it is at least necessary that the reading-book, that "encyclopedia of the common school," should contain among other things the historical notions the knowledge of which is thought to be indispensable.

Better still are the elementary historical books, composed with exclusive reference to the common schools, and

---

[1] *Revue des Deux Mondes.*

similar to those which have been published for several years
in France, which avoid dryness, long nomenclatures, gene-
alogies, and superfluous details, which give children general
impressions, clear views, and a taste for history.

375. SUMMARIES AND NARRATIVES. — An elementary
book on history should comprise at least two essential
parts, — summaries and narratives.

The summaries should be as complete and at the same
time as brief as possible.

The pupil will learn these by heart ; for even in history
there is a part for literal recitation to play. The special
purpose of these summaries is to assure precision of ideas.
They will fix in the child's mind the rigorous succession and
order of events. By this means we shall escape the method
of scattered anecdotes or of disconnected biographies, which
is proper only for little children.

There should not be too many narratives in an elementary
book on history. They ought not to be learned by heart,
and should receive only an attentive reading, enlivened
by oral explanations, by the interrogations of the teacher,
and by the responses of the pupil. It is especially by these
narratives that the child will be interested in the study of
history ; he will find in them the portraits of great men,
sketches of manners, beautiful examples, everything which
characterizes the different epochs.

Of course, besides the summaries and narratives, the book
is also composed of a *text*, more or less complete, in which
the events are presented in their order and with the reflections which they suggest. In a less elementary book this
text will of itself constitute the whole work.

376. THE DUTY OF THE TEACHER. — It cannot be too
often repeated that the teacher plays the principal part in
the teaching of history.

"It was long ago that Lhamond said that the best book is the living voice of the teacher. For this purpose we do not demand that he *profess;* for this word suggests the idea of pedantry, and the teacher who listens to his own voice has few chances of making himself heard. Simple and modest explanations, preceded or followed by questions to illustrate them, — this is what Lhomond recommended." [1]

The teacher ought to explain the book, and comment on it ; but he ought also to do without the book and venture himself to sketch the narrative of an event or of an historical period. Especially in the higher course he will substitute the living voice for the dead book, too often not comprehended. If he will prepare himself for this in advance, and know just what he is going to say, and in what order, his oral exposition will be worth much more than the best of books.

377. THE DUTY OF THE PUPIL. — In the study of history, the pupil ought not to be merely a reader or an attentive listener ; he must be made to speak and relate what he has learned from his book or from his teacher. No subject is better adapted to interrogations and to drill in speaking than history. Besides, as Gréard recommends, the pupil should be invited to make a summary of the oral lesson. Short written themes and reproductions might also be required of him on the subject which has been studied in the class, so that his own labor may be added to that of the teacher, and the history may not be for him, as it is too often the case, simply the occasion for easy reading, accomplished with distraction and without real profit.

378. INCIDENTAL AIDS. — The imagination of teachers, and especially that of authors, has multiplied inventions of

---

[1] M. Gréard, *L'Enseignement primaire à Paris.* Notwithstanding M. Gréard, it is necessary that the teacher profess, that he be a professor.

every sort to facilitate the study of history. In general we count but little on these auxiliary aids, such as synoptical and genealogical tables. Nevertheless, competent educators recommend the use of mural charts.

Nor are pictures in all their forms to be despised. "It is to be hoped," says M. Buisson, "that popular art, escaping finally from its trivial uses, may become with us, as it already has in other countries, a means of diffusing useful knowledge, and above all that of the national history."

379. HISTORY AND CIVIC INSTRUCTION. — History is the natural preface to civic instruction, — that is, to notions relating to the actual constitution of the society in which the child is called to live.

"The Americans," says M. Buisson, "teach history in view of political education. Their reading-books contain quite numerous selections relative to the ancient republics. In modern times they dwell particularly on social and political institutions. . . . Themes like the following are assigned to the pupils: A parallel between Pitt and Washington."

"Certain educators," says M. Braun, "think that history and civic instruction ought to be united, and taught one with the other, one by the other."

Without going so far as to blend these two subjects, we ought not to forget the relations between them. Instruction in civics can be but the coronation of historical studies; and while relating with impartiality the history of his country, the teacher will be right in shaping his instruction in view of the political education which is proper to be given to children.

380. HISTORY AND GEOGRAPHY. — History has still more intimate relations with geography, and the recital of historical events should not be separated from a description of the country where the events took place. Geography and

chronology, says an old adage, are the two eyes of history; and in fact, if we do not know the theatre where men have acted, it is difficult to form a just idea of their activity.

381. CONCLUSION. — Thus understood, history is a truly profitable study and a branch of instruction adapted to children. Let us give ear neither to Jacotot, who denies its utility absolutely, nor to Mr. Bain, who asserts that of all the studies of youth there is none so beset with difficulties as history. In order to interest children, it suffices that it is at once "clear and living," according to Guizot's expression, that it appeal at once to their imagination and to their memory. In order that it may be useful to them, it is sufficient that it be regarded above all as a school of morals and of patriotism. Doubtless, it would be assuming too much to demand that the child of the primary school should know, like a philosopher, the causes and connections of events, and that he discern the principles that lie back of facts. It is however necessary, in a certain measure, that for the ordinary child historical instruction should be something besides a simple narration of facts, and that he should be trained to judge of the good and the evil in human actions. "History is not really history," says M. Guizot, "except as we grasp the connection of events which succeed one another, and except it appear in its completeness as the evolution of a people." By reflection, then, let us connect the detached narratives with the great facts, and with the great personages which are as the mountain-tops of history; let us require of the child that the chronological succession of events be clearly fixed in his mind; let us distinguish the important periods, — all this without ceasing to be as simple, as elementary as possible, and while recollecting that in history, as in other things, we must know much in order to be capable of teaching a little.

CHAPTER VI.

THE TEACHING OF GEOGRAPHY.

382. PROGRESS IN GEOGRAPHICAL STUDIES. — Geographical studies are surely making progress in France. We have been so often told that we were the most ignorant people in the world in geography, that our sense of honor has at last been touched, and we have made serious efforts to overtake our neighbors, the Germans. Even in the common school, the teaching of geography is on a quite respectable footing. The reports of the inspectors-general show that there is progress everywhere, that geography is carefully taught, and that this study is perhaps the one that pleases pupils the most.

This progress is due doubtless, above all else, to the moral effect which recent disasters have produced on our minds. Since the day when our soil was invaded and our territory mutilated by foreigners, who by means of their maps seemed to be at home, we have better understood the importance and the value of geographical studies.

But this progress is also due to the happy change which, in late years, has profoundly modified the conditions of geographical teaching. For a dry and barren nomenclature of proper names and the repetition of an unintelligible vocabulary, modern pedagogy has substituted a living study, full of attraction, which addresses itself to the senses and to the intelligence ; which brings before the child by vivid and clear descriptions the nook of earth where he was born, the

362

country for which he ought to feel willing to die if need be, and finally the entire earth, where in default of real travel he is happy to be able to make at least imaginary journeys. And at the same time that the general spirit of geographical teaching has been changed, art has placed at its service and introduced into the school new instruments of study, such as globes, maps in relief, wall maps, maps of all sorts, — in a word, a complete outfit, which facilitates the task of the teacher and enlivens the work of the pupil.

383. NEW METHODS: ROUSSEAU AND PESTALOZZI. — Of all subjects geography is the one which seems best adapted to the processes of the new pedagogy, to the method which ordains that things shall precede words. Rousseau went so far in this direction that he admitted no other means but travel for learning geography. But here, as always, he goes astray through the exaggeration of a just idea. But he at least defines with wisdom the starting-point of all geographical instruction.

"For Émile the two first points in geography shall be the city where he lives and the country residence of his father; then the intermediate places, next the rivers in the vicinity. . . . Let him make a map of all this for himself." [1]

Pestalozzi, like Rousseau, demanded that the teaching of geography should be connected with the first sensations of infancy. At Burgdorf he made the pupils observe the little tract of country where they lived, not upon a map, but upon the very soil.

Through the sight of actual things he gave them an idea of hills, mountains, rivers, and of the various geographical features. Then, when the child, through direct intuition, or at least by analogy, by proceeding from the small to the

---

[1] *Émile*, Book III.

great, from the puddle of water to the sea, from a ditch to a
river, has acquired a knowledge of the terms in physical
geography, Pestalozzi initiated him into political geography
by analogous methods. Taking as a starting-point the
family residence, he thence directed the children's attention
to the village, the church, the school-house, the mayor's
office, the route which led to the city, the city itself, and to
the magistrates who resided there. Finally, proceeding to
mathematical geography, he placed the pupil in presence of
astronomical phenomena and made him observe the rising
and setting of the sun, the Great Bear and the Pole-star;
thus he drilled him in finding the points of the compass, and
determining the position of one place through its relation to
another.

384. DEFINITION OF GEOGRAPHY. — It would not be exact
to say, with an American author, that "Geography is not so
much a science in itself, as it is a collection of matter
belonging to a number of sciences." [1]

On the contrary, the object of geography is perfectly
definite, — it is the description of the surface of the earth;
it studies everything that relates to the form of our globe,
and to the exterior and superficial phenomena of the earth;
though it must be admitted that certain geographers, taking
advantage of the fact that their science has some sort of
relation to everything, extend their domain perhaps beyond
all proper bounds. Geography has such intimate relations
with several other sciences that a natural tendency impels
the geographer to pass the frontier which separates it from
them.

On the pretext that watercourses are fed by the rain,
geography ought not to permit itself to become a course in
physics and in meteorology. Because the description of the

---

[1] Wickersham, *Methods of Instruction*, p. 367.

soil affords an indication of the nature of the rocks, geography must not be confounded with geology. And so with botany, zoölogy, and political economy; we must not take advantage of their relations with geographical studies, to trespass upon their peculiar domain.

This caution has not always been observed. Thus Mr. Bain takes as a starting-point in the study of geography a series of lessons upon tools and instruments, minerals, plants, and animals. In our opinion, geography must not be encumbered with these parasitic notions which have only an indirect relation to its proper object.

But we would not forbid the teacher of geography to make any incursion on the subjects that border on the study of geography itself. It is both profitable and interesting to enrich this subject in every way possible, as by giving an explanation of the facts which it relates, or by giving animation to the instruction by interesting and fruitful comparisons.

385. THE UTILITY OF GEOGRAPHY. — First, geography pursues the same end as history. If, so to speak, the history of France is the soul of the country, the national geography is its body. In its way it teaches patriotism by making known the territory of the country, and the frontiers that have been lost and those that have been saved; and by making the child love the beautiful soil of France, its agreeable and temperate climate, and the natural riches that make it a privileged country.

The Père Girard, in his *Explication du plan de Fribourg*, exhibited, though with some exaggeration, the moral bearings of geography.

"Geography," he said, "is marvelously adapted to this sublime purpose. . . Let the reader judge of this from the following essay. As an harmonious whole, it is an introduction to social life, which speaks to the sense and to the mind, and which surely ought to say something to the heart. It is calculated to inspire love of country and the emotions which are associated with it."

However, let us not overstate the case and say that the principal aim of geographical instruction is to develop the intelligence and the heart, " to stimulate the religious senti- ment." No ; geography is chiefly valuable on the score of its practical utility. It furnishes the future artisan with the necessary knowledge, the positive notions, which he will need in his trade or industry. Besides, it has the merit of intro- ducing the mind to the world of science proper, and of reveal- ing to it some of the laws of nature.[1]

386. DIVISION OF GEOGRAPHY. — Everybody understands the distinction between physical geography and political geography.

Physical geography, says the *Dictionnaire* of Littré, is the description of the earth with respect to the division of its surface into continents, oceans, valleys, mountains, etc.

Political geography is the description of the earth with respect to societies and states.

In other terms, physical geography studies the natural features of the earth, while political geography adds to these the consideration of the work of man, the description of the inhabitants, of their industries, and of their social life.

It is evident that the study of physical geography should precede that of political geography, but it may be profitable, even in an elementary course, to unite the two subjects, were it only to create an interest.

" Ordinarily, physical geography is sharply distinguished from political geography. This separation is a mistake, and hardly

---

[1] For a somewhat different view of the value of geography, see Appendix D.

facilitates the process of learning quickly and well. On the contrary, the practice of teaching proves that physical and political details are mutually complementary and helpful, and that the former aids in retaining the latter, and *vice versa*." [1]

There is still to be distinguished astronomical geography, which is a description of the earth with reference to the heavens, the climates, and the seasons ; and economic geography, which treats of the industrial productions of each country, of agriculture and commerce. But the first may, in a sense, be connected with physical geography, and the second with political geography.

Mr. Bain gives a very high significance to physical geography, which holds an intermediate place, he says, between the ordinary geography and the higher sciences, physics, chemistry, meteorology, botany, zoölogy, and geology. It introduces considerations of cause and effect into geographical facts, by selecting and stating in empirical form the principles methodically taught in the regular and fundamental sciences.

"A course of physical geography is subsequent and supplementary to proper geography," — which Mr. Bain calls descriptive geography, — " while reacting upon it in a way that causation operates upon the knowledge of facts." [2]

M. Buisson has eloquently characterized the scope of an advanced instruction in physical and political geography.

"Through the progress accomplished in their respective domains by the physical and natural sciences, and also by the historical and political sciences, geography neither is nor can be any longer an isolated and restricted science. It does not merely describe, but it explains. The sight of actual phenomena suggests both for the past and for the future the most fruitful inductions: irregularities of surface, which were formerly regarded as so many

---

[1] M. Foncin, *Le Deuxième Année de géographie.*

[2] *Education as a Science*, p. 279.

freaks of nature, have found their laws, their causes, their place, in one universal harmony. The whole surface of the earth becomes a living and moving world, and the monotony or the disorder which ignorance saw in them gives place to lofty general conceptions, as important for their practical applications as for their scientific import. It is no longer required to retain names, but to grasp grand phenomena, both in their aggregate and in their details. It is the physiognomy of a whole orographic relief, of a whole hydrographic system, which must be considered; it is the structure and the configuration of each region which must be grasped in order to connect with them the innumerable phenomena which depend upon them, and no one of which is a thing of chance, from the peculiarities of soil and climate to those of the fauna and the flora which are there developed.

When we come to know in this way the physical theatre where human activity is to be displayed, is there anything richer in the way of instruction than historical, political, and statistical geography? The moment we enter upon this science, the study constantly presents a double movement, that which is exercised on man by the situation, climate, form, and nature of the country where he lives, and in return that which man displays for modifying all these circumstances, for opposing them, or for making use of them for deriving profit from the earth and the soil, the air and the sea, according to the degree of intelligence and energy with which he is endowed. Thus the study of geography is not divorced from that of civilization; it is a sort of universal monument, on which is engraved in all its striking episodes, from the age of caverns and lake-dwellings to the hour in which we now live, the history of the influences of nature on man, and of the conquests of man over nature. It is of this science, thus understood, that Herder was able to say with exultation, ' Charge geography with aridity! We might as well charge the ocean with dryness.' " [1]

387. Why this Study should Begin early. — As Nicole

----

[1] *L'Instruction primaire à Vienne*, p. 185.

had already remarked, "Geography is a study very proper for children;" first, because it depends greatly upon the senses; then, because it is really entertaining; finally, because it requires no reasoning, which is well-nigh lacking at that age.

Let us add that other studies cannot dispense with geography. History and geography should go hand in hand.

On the contrary, it is Mr. Bain's opinion that the study of geography should be delayed, on the ground that geographical notions involve the faculty of pure conception, — that is, of the representative imagination, without any appeal to emotion and sentiment. But, in opposition to Mr. Bain, we think that the faculty of concrete conception is highly developed in the child, and besides, that it is possible to give a living interest to the study of geography.

388. TWO METHODS POSSIBLE. — In history we raised the question whether it was best on the start to give the child a general view of the course of the centuries, or to proceed by partial studies and by periods. Likewise in geography it is a question whether it is better at first to give a general idea of the whole world, or to concentrate the beginner's attention exclusively on the geography of his own country, and not undertake the geography of Europe and the globe till a later period.

The reply cannot be doubtful. The point of departure in geographical instruction is certainly in the study of local geography. Between the ancient system, which first studied the globe, which began where we ought to finish, as Père Gréard said, and the new method, which starts from the village or the city where the pupil lives, and extends from place to place till it finally embraces the entire earth, there can be no hesitation in our choice.

But, on the other hand, the child must not be kept too long

on these preparatory studies. The teaching of geography, — that is, a science whose object is the description of the earth, — would not respond to its definition nor to its purpose, if the child were not placed as soon as possible in the presence of the earth. General geography ought to be united and combined with local geography. All portions of geography are in some sort co-ordinate, while the periods of history, to a certain extent, are independent one of another. Hence a profound difference in the methods to be followed.

"After the preliminary notions drawn from the child's knowledge of the department, and before he enters upon a detailed study of France, I would have the teacher," says M. Levasseur, an authority on this subject, "with globe in hand, give in a few hours a general idea of the form of the earth and of its oceans and continents. It is important that the child should clearly know what place France occupies in Europe, the situation of Europe upon the globe, and what the form of the earth is."[1]

389. NATIONAL GEOGRAPHY. — The centre of geographical instruction in the common school ought to be our own country. In French schools, France is the point of departure and the goal of the geographical excursion which is proposed to the child; but there are rightly added to this general notions of the geography of Europe and of other parts of the world, just as in history the national history is completed by some notions of general history.

And as in history it is necessary for real mental enlightenment to compare the present with the past, so in geography it is well to institute frequent comparisons between one's own country and foreign countries.

"Tell the pupil that France produces seventeen million tons of coal a year, and he yawns and at once forgets the number; but tell him that France produces only one-eighth as much coal

---

[1] As to sequence in the study of geography, see Appendix A.

as England, and he understands you, and, as a Frenchman, is touched to the quick."

390. THE CORRECT METHOD. — Then let us follow the method which consists in starting from the village school, but on the condition that we do not forget to go farther. A teacher may halt so long in giving details on the commune and the canton that at the end of several months he has not gone beyond them. As soon as possible the instruction in geography should open vast horizons to the child, and extend his vision over the entire world.

"Certainly," says M. Élisée Reclus, "we must always take as a starting-point what the child sees; but does he see nothing more than the school and his village? That is the tip of his abode; he also sees the infinite heaven, the sun, stars, and moon. He sees the storms, the clouds, the rain, the distant horizon, the mountains, the hills, the downs or simple undulations, and trees and shrubs. Let him attentively notice all these things, and let them be described to him. This is the real geography, and to learn it the child has not to go beyond the things which surround him, and which are exhibited to him in their infinite variety."

To-day the method of geographical teaching seems to be everywhere established in accordance with this spirit. Mr. Bain says "that geography, after arithmetic, is the study that is most advanced in respect of method." This method may be defined as follows:

"The teacher will speak to the children principally of the things they have seen. After a rain he will show them the ravines which the water has worn in the sand of the yard, the manner in which this water forms lakes, surrounds islands, descends slopes in thin streams which finally unite to form large brooks farther down, and explain to them how they have before their eyes a picture in miniature of rivers and of their affluents.

"He will make them notice thát the sun illumines the school in a different way morning and evening, and will teach them to know the points of the compass and to find their bearings.

"He will trace for them the plan of the school on the board, and accustom them to distinguish what is at the right from what is at the left, what is in front from what is in the rear. He will not fear to insist on this process, to measure if need be, in the presence of the children and with their aid, the length of the walls, the width of the court and the garden, and to record these measurements on the board. He will also trace a plan of the neighborhood of the school, or even of the village, and will have attained his purpose in this respect when his pupils are capable of showing upon this plan, with the pointer, the road which must be followed to go from the church to their homes."

391. The Function of Memory. — Formerly geography was recited; to-day it is at the same time told and shown. It is told, — that is, the teacher gives an exposition of the subject: he gives a lesson in geography as he does in history. It is shown, — that is, an incessant appeal is made, either to the very reality or to a picture of it reproduced by maps.

"With very young children," says M. Levasseur, "the teacher will scarcely indicate the relations of cause and effect, which ordinarily surpass the ability of a nascent intelligence; he will rely on descriptions, and he will cause the different conceptions of geography to be understood, as much as possible by pictures, by sensible forms, and whenever possible by the sight of the objects themselves and by familiar examples."

However, there is a part for memory to play; in all grades of geographical study there are things which the child ought to be capable of reciting. As the multiplication-table is not learned without a mechanical and habitual use of the memory, so we cannot dispense with learning by heart the names of geographical positions.

" The teaching of the geographical nomenclature seems to us to be one of the three principal points in the study of geography, and this nomenclature ought to be learned by heart. We first cause the word to be learned, without which the precision of the idea would be lost; but let us illustrate this nomenclature by such notions as will give to each word a fit idea." [1]

Of course these words, at the same time that they are intrusted to the memory, ought to be localized on the map by the imagination of the child.

392. Maps in General. — Geography has always been learned by the aid of maps; but it is particularly in our time that the process of map-making has been perfected and really adapted to the needs of the child.

" Means of expression in geography," says M. Buisson, "are becoming perfected so rapidly that before long the entire ancient system of cartography will be no more than a dead language." [2]

Without entering into details which would be appropriate in a complete study of the subject, and which will be found in special works, let us indicate at least a few essential points.

We must first distinguish ready-made maps which are shown to the pupil from those which he is required to prepare for himself.

Ready-made maps are either maps in atlas form or wall-maps.

393. Maps in Atlas Form. — These maps are made to be seen near at hand and to give detailed information; but there is danger, however, of placing too much upon them, and of multiplying the signs so as to prevent a clear and

---

[1] Article *Géographie*, in the *Dictionnaire de Pédagogie*.
[2] *L'Instruction primaire à Vienne*, p. 186.

definite view. The best will be the simplest and the clearest. The most scientific and the most beautiful are not always the most useful from an educational point of view.

The custom has now been introduced of no longer separating the map from the text; but separate atlases should not be discarded.

394. WALL-MAPS. — Wall-maps are not less necessary than maps in atlas form. They are made to be seen at a distance, to give contours, broad lines, and general views. They are especially designed to call into play the faculties of the child, his memory and his reason. It is on the smaller maps that he first learns geography; but it is on the wall-map that the pupil is interrogated, and this is why certain geographers think that this study-map ought by preference to be unlettered. It is with the same intent that on German wall-maps the names of rivers and mountains are written in very small characters, so that pupils cannot read them mechanically and are obliged to recognize them by their form and position.

"Wall-maps," says M. Buisson, "are the most important geographical apparatus of the primary school. The Germans have seen sooner than we have all the importance which is to be ascribed to them. The great physical maps of the five divisions of the world, by Von Sydow, have made an epoch in geographical teaching; they have proved that we can place within the range of the schools a graphic representation, at once compendious enough to be very striking and scientific enough to give of each important division an exact, if not complete, idea."[1]

395. RELIEF MAPS. — The services which can be rendered by relief maps are universally recognized. "What is done on ordinary maps may be done at least with as much advan-

---

[1] *L'Instruction primaire à Vienne*, p. 196.

tage on relief maps representing the different geographical features, or merely those of such or such a country."[1]

Of course we must be on our guard against exaggeration in such matters. Ingenuity has taken hold of relief maps, and has often made of them a fancy article, purely conventional, a plaything rather than an instrument of study.[2]

But, with these reservations, it is undeniable that relief maps are the best of all for giving the child an exact idea of the country, for raising him to the conception of the reality of which the map is but a picture.[2]

396. MAPS DRAWN BY THE PUPIL. — The first thing to do, and it is not without difficulty, is to teach pupils to read the map and to find their own place upon it. The official programme recommends that in the elementary course there be simply given an idea of the mode of representation by maps and that the child be drilled in the reading of plans and maps; but for the intermediate and higher courses, it demands exercises in map-drawing on the blackboard and on paper, without tracing, and also exercises in map-drawing from memory.

These exercises need no justification. They train the pupil's hand, they are a preparation for drawing, and are the most direct means of fixing geographical facts in the mind.

"The drawing of maps," says Mr. Bain, "impresses a country, just as copying a passage in a book impresses the author's language and meaning."

But care must be taken not to make a misuse of exercises in map-drawing, the first defect of which, when indiscreetly

---

[1] *Conduite des écoles chrétiennes*, p. 59.

[2] The most valuable helps to geography are models, and if these could be multiplied in schools the conceptions of the general form of countries would be vastly enhanced. (Bain, *op. cit.*, p. 276.)

employed, is to take altogether too much time. Specialists recommend that there be required only map-drawings but slightly complicated and comprised within natural limits ; this last recommendation excludes maps which represent only an isolated department.

397. THE GLOBE. — The inventive art of our contemporaries has devised even globes in relief ; but these attempts "seem destined," says M. Buisson, " to give intuitions that are grossly false," without any advantage to compensate for this greater disadvantage.

It is otherwise with ordinary globes, which render important services to instruction.

"Besides cosmographic notions, the indispensable complement of geography, there is a mass of large comparisons between seas, continents, divisions, and configurations of the earth's surface, which are almost impossible without the frequent use of the sphere." [1]

398. TEXT-BOOKS. — " Formerly," says M. Buisson, " these were the principal means of instruction. Geography was taught from a compendium of a few pages bristling with proper names, and calculated to repel the mind the most thirsty for knowledge." However, the text-book must not be absolutely proscribed ; it is sufficient to reduce the importance which it had in the old methods. It is especially necessary that it be well written, that the text always be illustrated by a map placed on the opposite page, and if need be by illustrations. The Americans have brought into fashion, and the French have copied from them, these elementary books in which the child finds, along with the definition of geographical terms, a gulf, an island, a cape, a mountain, at the same time delineated in a picture and represented on a small map.

[1] Schrader.

399. THE FUNCTION OF THE TEACHER. — In geography, as in other subjects, the voice of the teacher is the great teaching instrument.   It impresses on the intelligence of the pupil the first decisive impetus ; it illustrates the points that are obscure, and gives animation to the instruction. But the oral exposition of geographical notions has special need of being sustained by a collection of school apparatus, by the geographical aids of which we have attempted to give an idea.

400. CRITICAL OBSERVATIONS. — Let us here collect for the teaching of geography, as we have done for the other branches of instruction, some of the critical observations of the inspectors-general.

"Geography is made an exercise of the memory.   Instruction is given from the book, and not from the map.   Geography is regarded as hardly more than a knowledge of names.   Enough geographical sketches are not made on the blackboard.   The study of geography generally begins too late.   Sufficient use is not made of the globes which adorn the teacher's room or remain covered with dust.   Pupils do not know what latitude and longitude are.   Too much stress is put on geographical terms, which, instead of being presented to the child in succession, and to meet the wants of each lesson, are taught in a mass before going to anything else."

Finally, geography ought to become more and more a knowledge of things, and not, as it formerly was, a knowledge of words.   It ought to be a prolific mine of positive knowledge, which gives the child information, not only on the natural features and physical phenomena of his country, but also on its industrial resources and its economic phenomena.   Moreover, it will not limit its instruction to the sentimental frontiers of France.   In a time when the country is making great efforts to develop its colonial power and its territories beyond sea, it is right and it is necessary that geography should make known to the sons of our working-men and peasants the physical and economical resources of distant countries. By this means there will be developed among some of them a taste for travel and colonial enter-prises, and our possessions will not remain colonies without colonists.

CHAPTER VII.

THE TEACHING OF THE SCIENCES.

401. THE TEACHING OF THE SCIENCES IN THE COMMON SCHOOL. — Instruction in the sciences has been noticeably enlarged and developed in the programme of our common schools. At all times arithmetic has been taught in them, and constituted, with reading and writing, the three elements of the old instruction; but to-day the programme comprises, besides arithmetic, geometry, and also the ordinary elements of the physical and natural sciences.

402. IMPORTANCE OF ARITHMETIC. — Belgian teachers count no less than twelve distinct results from the teaching of arithmetic. Without desiring to adopt an enumeration so complicated and so pedantic, we call attention to the fact that arithmetic, of all the subjects taught in the school, is the one that contributes most to the training and development of the faculties of reflection, and particularly the reason. Doubtless grammar, history, and geography, when well taught, may co-operate in this education; but while they call into exercise the reason only occasionally and accidentally, we may affirm that arithmetic gives it constant exercise.

The abstract sciences in general, proceeding by trains of reasoning and rigorous demonstrations, have the farther advantage of compelling the mind not to be satisfied with mere words. They accustom it to demand perfect clearness, absolute precision, logical and concise sequence.

"Mathematics . . . has a marked and peculiar method or char-acter; it is by pre-eminence *deductive* or *demonstrative*, and exhib-its in a nearly perfect form all the machinery belonging to this mode of obtaining truth. Laying down a very small number of first principles, either self-evident or requiring very little effort to prove them, it evolves a vast number of deductive truths and applications, by a procedure in the highest degree mathematical and systematic. Now, although it is chiefly in the one domain of Quantity that this machinery has its fullest scope, yet, as in every subject that the mind has to discuss there is a frequent resort to the deductive, demonstrative, or downward procedure, as con-trasted with the direct appeal to observation, fact, or induction, a mathematical training is a fitting equipment for the exercises of this function. The rigid definition of all leading terms and no-tions; the explicit statement of all the first principles; the onward march by successive deductions, each one reposing on ground already secured; no begging of either premises or conclusions; no surreptitious admissions; no shifting of ground; no vacillation in the meanings of terms; — all this is implied in the perfect type of a deductive science. The pupil should be made to feel that he has accepted nothing without a clear and demonstrative reason, to the entire exclusion of authority, tradition, prejudice, or self-interest." [1]

Of course it is principally an advanced course in mathe-matics which admits of these characteristics and assures these advantages to the general training of the mind ; but even in its elementary stage the study of the mathematics will result on the start in imposing on the pupil a great con-centration of attention ; for in mathematical truths there is complete interdependence and connection, and a single moment of inattention causes the whole fruit of previous toil to be lost. Besides, the rigorous character of mathematical demonstration accustoms the pupil not to take up with words, not to yield except on proof. There is no better

---

[1] Bain, *Education as a Science,* pp. 148, 149.

school for teaching order, precision, and at the same time continuity and rigor in thinking.[1]

403. PRACTICAL UTILITY OF ARITHMETIC. — But without speaking longer of the advantages of arithmetical study considered as a mental discipline, it is evident that this instruction is indispensable by reason of its practical utility. To know how to compute is but little less necessary than to know how to read and write. Even ignorant peasants who can do without reading to no great disadvantage, cannot do without making simple calculations as to their expenses, the wages they ought to receive, the sacks of wheat which they have to sell, and the animals which they tend. Computation is of daily and universal use.

404. THE CHILD'S TASTE FOR NUMBERS. — We might think that on account of their general character of abstraction, exercises in number would not suit the taste of the child, fond above all else of sense perceptions. But this is not so.

"In the large number of classes of very different grades which it has been our privilege either to inspect or to visit, we have often observed that arithmetic was one of the things with reference to which the child manifested the most vividly that joy in learning which comes to him so naturally, when we do not carefully spoil it by throwing around him things that are difficult and incoherent."[2]

---

[1] "Numbers," says M. Frieh, "is a positive science, and there are no two different ways of conceiving its primal elements. In it everything is fixed and invariable, so that the wisest mathematician and the youngest pupil of a primary school find the same result by employing exactly the same process. What is particularly remarkable in the science of numbers is that everything is related and connected with a precision that is perfect; one notion prepares for another, and one principle gives rise to another."

[2] Mademoiselle Chalamet, *op. cit.*, p. 165.

405. THREE COURSES IN ARITHMETIC. — In all the grades
of the common school the programme requires exercises in
mental and written arithmetic ; but it distributes the matter
of instruction progressively, reserving theory mainly for the
higher course.

In the elementary course the four rules may be applied
intuitively to numbers that do not exceed 100. So much for
mental arithmetic. The tables of addition and multiplication are studied. For written work pupils are drilled on the
first three rules by the use of whole numbers. Division is
limited to divisors which contain no more than two figures.
Simple problems, oral or written, complete the instruction.

In the intermediate course, after a review, which is particularly necessary in arithmetic, in a science where sequence
is so important, the division of whole numbers is learned ;
the study of fractions is begun ; the four rules are applied
to decimal numbers ; and the legal system of weights and
measures is studied. It is more and more required that the
problems give rise to rational solutions.

In the higher course, a new review with more marked
attention to theories and to the reasoning process, the metric
system is thoroughly learned. The most difficult parts of the
arithmetic are taken up, such as prime numbers, the divisi-
bility of numbers, prime factors, and the greatest common
divisor. The methods of reduction to unity, applied to
the solution of problems in interest, discount, etc., are also
studied.

406. GENERAL METHOD. — Intuitive in its early stages,
and practical at every step in its development, — such ought
to be the instruction in arithmetic in the common school.
The method of study in this science is henceforth fixed, and
Mr. Bain could say that " the method of teaching arithmetic
is, perhaps, the best understood of any of the methods concerned with elementary studies."

Let us add, that without ceasing to be practical the method in arithmetic should tend to give children a rational knowledge of the science of computation. It is not enough for the child to be mechanically drilled in the operations of arithmetic; it is necessary that he comprehend them, that he render to himself an account of them. By this means he will not only compute better and more surely, but his mind will at the same time be strengthened and refined. "Particularly in arithmetic, to comprehend is to apprehend."

The first requirement is that the child gain an exact idea of number, — an idea which is complete only when it contains the ideas of augmentation and diminution, of addition and subtraction.

407. MATERIAL AIDS. — As a means of making a beginning in numeration, educators recommend the use of small pieces of wood. As a matter of fact, all concrete objects are adapted to this purpose, and the choice is unimportant. The essential thing is, not to plunge the child all at once into the study of abstract numbers, but to resort at first to intuition, to intuitive computation; and for this purpose real objects should be employed, placed in the hands of the child, or points and lines drawn on the blackboard and presented to the pupil's eye.

"Much is involved in the first attempts to work upon number. The distinction between one number and another is shown to the eye by concrete groups of various things, the identity of number appearing under disparity of materials and of grouping. Ideas are thus acquired of unity, of two, three, etc., up to ten in a row. . . . At the outset small tangible objects are used, — balls, pebbles, coins, apples; then larger objects, as chairs and pictures on a wall. Finally dots or short lines, or some other plain marks, are the representative examples to be deposited in the mind as the nearest approach to the abstract idea." [1]

---

[1] Bain, *op. cit.*, p. 288.

408. Transition from the Concrete to the Abstract.— M. Horner very clearly states the process to be followed for gradually withdrawing the mind from the consideration of concrete objects and leading it to the abstract notion. It is first necessary, he says, to show the child material objects, or at least strokes drawn on the board, representing numbers and their combinations. Then, when the child has gained sufficient skill to work with objects, we must conceal these objects from his sight and employ concrete numbers, as 8 nuts, 6 tables, 8 chairs, etc. A new step has now been taken, and after these concrete numbers have been used for some time, the final step in the series must be taken, — we must divest the number of its sensible garment and employ abstract numbers.

409. Numeral Frames. — Instead of employing the first objects at hand, we may resort to apparatus, especially to numeral frames, which are machines designed to facilitate the early steps in numeration.

This device is no doubt serviceable at the beginning of instruction in number ; but we must guard against the abuse of these material means of numerical intuition, lest they go counter to the end we are pursuing.

The numeral frame has been severely criticised.

"This instrument," says M. Eugène Rambert, "corrupts instruction in arithmetic. The principal utility of this instruction is to call into early exercise the child's faculties of abstraction, — to teach him to see with the head, through the eyes of the mind. To place things before the bodily eyes is to go directly counter to the spirit of this instruction. Nature has given children their ten fingers for a numeral frame ; and instead of giving them another, they should be taught to do without the first as soon as possible. It is said that this device makes the teacher's explanations much easier. I have no doubt of this. By means of the numeral frame the child soon makes out that 10 and 10 are 20 ; but the child who counts only in this way loses his time, while the one who has counted in his head has engaged in the most useful of exercises. There is needed a complement and corrective for instruction through the sense of sight, and it is most readily found in computation." [1]

There is some exaggeration in this sentiment, and it would apply more justly to counting-machines. Most teachers recommend the numeral frame for the maternal school, and express the wish that it may be introduced into the common school, at least for the elementary course. It must be intelligently used, however, so as to facilitate the pupil's labor without suppressing it. [2]

410. COUNTING-MACHINES. — The things to be condemned without hesitation are arithmometers, or counting-machines, very complicated pieces of mechanism, real mills, which furnish the result of proposed operations and relieve the pupil of labor.

The use of apparatus, whatever it may be, ought not to make us forget the necessity of mental calculation.

411. MENTAL ARITHMETIC. — Educational opinion is definitely settled as to the value and necessity of mental arithmetic, — that is, of computation made in the mind, without resorting to written numbers.

First, mental arithmetic is an excellent mental gymnastic, because it compels the attention to fall back upon itself, to occupy itself with what is within, without the aid of any material instrument.

Moreover, mental arithmetic responds to the necessities of

[1] Quoted by M. Buisson, *L'Instruction primaire à Vienne*, p. 212.
[2] The numeral frame has been in use since 1812. It is said that it came from Russia, and that Russia herself borrowed it from China.

daily life.　How many times do we need to solve with rapidity little problems of domestic economy which demand but a moment's reflection!　The merchant and the housewife have not the time to resort to written calculation; they have not always at hand pen, paper, and ink.　They need to find an immediate solution.

Finally, mental arithmetic is a preparation for written arithmetic.　At first mental computation will be required, especially of beginners; but during the whole length of the course in arithmetic, mental work will accompany written work.

"Mental computation," says M. Rendu, "is to the mind what gymnastic exercises are to the body. . . . It has its processes, its methodical and progressive procedure, its great variety of exercises, its numerous applications.　Like all other lessons, it demands a thorough preparation."

Certain English teachers are accustomed to use the term economic arithmetic to describe the arithmetic proper for the primary school.

"The purpose of teaching arithmetic in elementary schools, apart from its influence as a discipline, is attained when such a command has been given over numbers as enables a young man or woman to calculate with facility all those questions which arise in the ordinary course of life.　This may be called economic arithmetic." [1]

412. CHOICE OF PROBLEMS. — The subject of the problems ought to be borrowed from the ordinary circumstances of life, from the facts of rural or industrial economy.　The choice ought to vary with the conditions of the child's life; it will be one thing in the city and another in the country.

---

[1] Laurie, *Primary Instruction*, p. 107.

"There is an important principle of economy in education,"
says Mr. Bain, "that applies to arithmetic, but not to it alone;
that is, the utilizing of the questions or exercises, by making them
the medium of useful information. Instead of giving unmeaning
numbers to add, subtract, multiply, and so on, we might, after the
more preliminary instances, make every question contain some
important numerical data relating to the facts of nature or the
conventional usages of life, anticipating, as far as may be, the
future exigencies of the pupils in their station in life. . . . For
example, the leading dates in chronology might be embodied in a
variety of questions." [1]

413. THE FUNCTION OF MEMORY. — Mr. Spencer somewhere says that the multiplication table is now often learned
by the experimental method. We confess that we do not
quite understand the thought of the English educator. Mr.
Bain is very much nearer the truth when he says:

" The memory has to receive with firmness and precision all that
is included in the addition and multiplication tables; and the test
of aptitude for the subject is the readiness to come under this
discipline. It is a kind of memory that in all probability depends
on a certain maturity or advancement of the brain; so that no
amount of concrete illustration will force it on before its time.
. . . . .The multiplication table is a grand effort of the special
memory for symbols and their combinations, and the labor is not
to be extenuated in any way. The associations must be formed
so as to operate automatically, — that is, without thinking, inquir-
ing, or reasoning; and for this we must trust to the unaided
adhesiveness due to mechanical iteration." [2]

414. THE METRIC SYSTEM. — The study of the metric system is connected with that of arithmetic proper. Here again
it is important to show to children the objects themselves,
the metre, the litre, etc. It would amount to nothing to

---

[1] Bain, *op. cit.*, p. 202.
[2] Bain, *op. cit.*, pp. 289, 290.

learn by heart the abstract words whose meaning has not been clearly fixed in the mind by the concrete realities.

"Do you speak of the metre? Cause the pupil to measure the length of the school-room, of the benches, the board, the pupil's desk. The decimetres, the centimetres, the millimetres will naturally present themselves; and if the children carry a stick of the length of a metre, they will ask to have the subdivisions marked upon it."

"Instruction through the sense of sight," says M. Buisson, "is applied naturally and without any difficulty to the metric system."

It has been justly observed that the tables of the metric system will not suffice. Each school should have in addition a collection of real weights and measures, which the child can see and handle.

415. RESULTS OF INSTRUCTION IN ARITHMETIC. — Here are some of the faults reported by the inspectors in the lessons in number:

"A more frequent use of mental calculation should be required. — There are too many theoretical demonstrations. — The pupils who have the best knowledge of the metric system are greatly embarrassed when they handle the metre or the balance. — Most teachers forget that primary instruction ought to be eminently practical.— The work is too abstract and too mechanical. Memory plays the principal part, and the reasoning process is wanting. — The pupil counts tolerably well, but he is usually unable to explain what he has done, for the very simple reason that he has not been accustomed to reason. The intuitive method is mainly followed with the youngest children; but the moment the pupils know how to apply the four fundamental processes, all trace of the method disappears. Theoretical questions are put aside, and books of problems replace the teacher's instruction. Mental calculation is taught without method, and when we interrogate the pupil he seems to employ the same processes as though he had a pen or pencil at his disposal. The study of number is too often reduced to an exercise of memory, and children do not acquire the art of reckoning in the mind, so useful as a mental gymnastic, and so indispensable to those who must do without pen and paper for making their computations. The elements of arithmetic are not made sensible enough. The mechanism of the operations is learned; but pupils do not comprehend clearly enough what they do and why they do it. Too many teachers are still fond of abstractions. They cannot make up their minds to teach number by means of the numeral frame, pebbles, and sticks; but they always begin by having the numbers written before the children have an exact idea of quantity. The metric system is taught, but no one has seen a metre."

The same reports state some instances of progress in the teaching of arithmetic.

"Arithmetic is of all the subjects the one which gives the best results. In most schools the computation is done well enough and quickly enough with the pen or pencil in hand; but pupils are not sufficiently accustomed to mental work. Calculation is taught from the first entrance at school, at first mentally and orally, then with written numbers. Teachers are rarely found who limit themselves to mechanical operations upon abstract numbers. The problems are practical and well chosen. The instruction in arithmetic is rational; the demonstration is always made at the blackboard, and the definitions serve only to sum up and fix the reasoning processes."

416. GEOMETRY IN THE COMMON SCHOOL. — In the programme of 1882 geometry appeared for the first time as a topic of obligatory instruction in the common school. It surely cannot be intended to push very far the study of a science which comprises parts of such superiority and difficulty. It is intended simply to borrow from it some notions which are the natural complement and sometimes the auxiliaries of arithmetic.

Moreover, it is not without protest that the innovation has been sanctioned by our school legislation. Swiss teachers formally declare that "geometry proper should not have a place in the programme of a common school."

But geometry proper is not under discussion; only the elements and applications of this science.

417. PURPOSE OF INSTRUCTION IN GEOMETRY. — In the common school, in the three courses, the purpose of instruction in geometry should be exclusively practical. The aim is to make the following items of knowledge available: 1. A comprehension of the metric system; 2. The measurement of surfaces and volumes required by the needs of life; 3. A knowledge of the simplest operations of surveying and leveling.

418. METHOD TO BE PURSUED. — For geometry, as for the other sciences, there is a necessary initiation, an intuitive preparation. It is especially in the infant school that it is expedient to communicate the primary notions of geometry in a concrete form. The official programme recommends, for the infant class, a selection from Froebel's "occupations," shunning technical terms, definitions, and excess of detail in the analysis of geometrical forms.

What must be avoided above all things, at the beginning, is the abuse of technical terms and abstract definitions, which the child repeats like a parrot, without understanding them. M. Leyssenne advises that with little children we wholly renounce the use of the terms sphere, circle, etc., and that we speak to them only of balls and round bodies. Without going to this extreme, for it seems to us necessary to accustom the child as soon as possible to the special vocabulary of each science, we think that at least the technical term should be used only in the presence of a material object which may furnish the mind with a sensible represen-

tation of it. Do not begin by showing to the child ideal
forms drawn on the blackboard. Show him real things,
figures and solids, whose parts and properties he must be
made to observe.

Says M. Leyssenne: "We should take solids in wood, clay, or
card-board, and place them in the children's hands; then, when
they have thoroughly seen them, touched them, and turned them
in all directions, they should be told that this is a line, this an
angle, this a square, this a circle, etc.; and finally, they must draw
that line, angle, square, and circle, upon the board."

419. ELEMENTARY COURSE. — In the elementary course
hardly more will be done than to continue these exercises
which are the alphabet of geometry, and teach the child to
unravel that science. To these there will be added exercises in the measurement and comparison of magnitudes by
simple judgments of the eye; the child will be taught to
estimate distances approximately; and these will be expressed in terms of the metric system. The difficulty in
making these estimates will be seen when they depend on
the senses alone.

"A stock of geometrical conceptions having been obtained,"
says Mr. Spencer, "a further step may in course of time be taken
by introducing the practice of testing the correctness of all figures
drawn by the eye. . . There can be little doubt that geometry
had its origin in the methods discovered by artisans and others, of
making accurate measurement for the foundations of buildings,
areas of inclosures, and the like. . . Geometrical truths should
be introduced to the pupil under analogous circumstances. In the
cutting out of pieces for his card-houses, in the drawing of ornamental diagrams for coloring, and in those various instructive occupations which an inventive teacher will lead him into, he may
be for a length of time advantageously left, like the primitive
builder, to tentative processes; and he will so gain an abundant

experience of the difficulty of achieving his aims by the unaided senses.[1]

In the intermediate and higher course the instruction in geometry ought to be more exact, more didactic. Intuitive methods should give place to processes purely abstract, in which reasoning should play the important part.

420. INTUITIVE GEOMETRY. — There is now such a craze for intuitive processes that the attempt has been made to apply them, not only to the elements of geometry, when they are in place, but to the whole subject. This is the system known as *tachymetry*, or rapid measurement, a sort of intuitive geometry.

This system may be illustrated as follows : By means of contrivances made of card-board or of wood, there is made an actual decomposition of the different volumes which are to be estimated ; then the parts so decomposed are grouped in different ways, so that the theorem, which would otherwise be demonstrated *in abstracto* by a long train of reasoning, is made intuitive and tangible. This method of physical and concrete demonstration is applied even to the measurement of the circle and the sphere, even to the properties of the square of the hypothenuse and of similar triangles. In a word, *tachymetry* is materialized geometry.

" The aim of *tachymetry*," says one writer, " is eminently practical, — to teach the farmer to compute how many hectolitres of wheat there are in a pile of wheat in his barn ; the road-master how many cubic metres, decimetres, and centimetres in a heap of stones ; the civil engineer how to proceed in forming an estimate of the work he is to perform."[2]

---

[1] Spencer, *op. cit.*, p. 148.

[2] This empirical geometry is all very well for such cases as those mentioned above ; but it should be recollected that no system of mere measurements can ever prove that the sum of the three angles of a triangle is equal to two right angles. (P.)

421. ARE THERE OBJECT-LESSONS IN ARITHMETIC AND GE-
OMETRY? — We do not think that there can be real object-
lessons either in arithmetic or in geometry. We should note
the fact that when we give the child sticks in order to teach
him to count or solids in order to teach him to estimate
dimensions, it is not the things themselves, the sticks or the
solids, that we wish him to study; but we place these
objects before his eyes or in his hands, in order that he may
as soon as possible disengage, from these concrete realities
the abstract idea of numbers, the abstract idea of geometrical forms.

422. THE PHYSICAL AND NATURAL SCIENCES. — In introducing the physical and the natural sciences into the common
school, the purpose has been both to give the child a certain
amount of positive knowledge, of an infinite value for practical life, and to teach him the habit of observation. While
the mathematical sciences are especially valuable for developing inward attention and power of reasoning, the natural
and the physical sciences call the senses into play and teach
the habit of seeing, and of seeing completely. Now, as
some one has said, "the spirit of observation is the best of
professors." The child who is endowed with it learns for
himself a multitude of things which forever escape minds
that are indifferent and incapable of observing.

Every specialist is disposed to exaggerate the importance
of the specialty which he teaches. We are not astonished,
then, that Paul Bert attributes to the physical and natural
sciences a part absolutely preponderant in primary instruction. But we must allow that no study is better adapted
for teaching to see accurately, to take nothing on authority,
and to divest the mind of superstitions and prejudices.

423. PROGRAMMES AND METHODS. — The French official
programme purposely insists on the very elementary char-

acter of the instruction given in the physical and natural sciences in the common school.

It recommends object-lessons for the first course, — lessons, moreover, graduated according to a regular plan, bearing on man, animals, vegetables, minerals. These objects will be shown to children, and the teacher will add to these some simple and familiar explanations.

Physics appears only with the intermediate courses, and provides for only summary notions on the three states of matter, upon air, water, and combustion. Simple experimental demonstration will complete the lesson. On the other hand, in the intermediate course, didactic lessons will be given on man, animals, and vegetables. It is evident that this course ought to be as descriptive as possible.

Chemistry is introduced in the higher course under this description : *The notion of simple bodies, compound bodies, metals, and common salts.*

Physics is studied in its essential laws, — weight, heat, light, electricity, etc. Instruments are described and explained.

Finally, in this same course, mineralogy is in turn added to the two other natural sciences, botany and zoölogy, the study of which is continued. At the same time that human physiology is taught, the principal functions of the human body are explained.

424. NECESSITY OF A BOOK. — The physical and natural sciences cannot be taught without apparatus, instruments, and museums.

Now it must not be forgotten that for the most part the common schools are destitute of scientific instruments and natural history collections. The book is then indispensable, a book that is well written, which requires but inexpensive experiments, — an elementary book, and not merely an abridgment.

"To select in each science," says Paul Bert, "the dominant, fundamental facts; to set them forth with sufficient details to make them clearly apparent to the child's mind and to fix them firmly in his memory; to neglect facts of secondary importance; — such are the general rules that should be followed."

425. PRACTICAL CHARACTER OF THIS INSTRUCTION. — In the teaching of the physical and natural sciences, particular care should be taken to avoid all fine-spun theories, and everything which cannot be made really intelligible to the child. Special attention will also be given to the practical application which may be made of the different parts of these sciences. The official programme enjoins this course upon teachers when it requires them to dwell upon "the transformation of crude material into the manufactured articles of every-day use," and again when it offers practical suggestions on hygiene and upon the effects of tobacco and alcohol.

Doubtless the first result of scientific instruction is mental development. These studies open the intelligence, extend the intellectual horizon, and train men.

"A training in the natural sciences must be raised to the dignity of a regular educational appliance; and for this purpose the quantity must be reduced; but what is learned must be perfectly assimilated, and must be used, not to increase the volume of what is known, but to establish habits of attentive observation, of exact analysis, and of a fruitful and well-regulated curiosity."

But the material results of this instruction are no less valuable. The sciences of nature appear to us particularly useful and commendable, because they are a necessary introduction to professional instruction, and are a preparation for the arts and the trades.

426. SCIENTIFIC EXCURSIONS. — Nothing is more helpful

to the teaching of the physical and natural sciences than scientific excursions, whether they be directed to the fields, woods, and farms, or to some shop or manufactory. But it must not be forgotten that these excursions ought to preserve their character of recreation and diversion. The instruction that is given in them should take place in the presence of pupils in the form of familiar conversations, and the instructor should not carry outside of the class-room the habits and the didactic method of the school.

CHAPTER VIII.

MORALS AND CIVIC INSTRUCTION.

427. MORAL EDUCATION AND THE TEACHING OF MORALS. — In 1881 some of the inspectors-general complained that "at present moral education is not included in the programme of common-school instruction." It will never be included in it; for though it is the principal and the essential purpose of instruction, it is not a part of the programme. Moral education is a general and delicate subject which cannot be imprisoned within the limits of a regular course of technical instruction. It is otherwise with morals itself, which ought to be separately taught as a science, and the highest of all the sciences. Doubtless a course in morals, however well it may be taught, will not suffice to make a good man; but it will aid in doing this, and it is with reason that the legislation of 1882, in imitation of what was done abroad, gave to morals a place in the programme of the common schools.

428. MORALS MAY BE TAUGHT IN EVERY SCHOOL EXERCISE. — Instead of being the definite object of a regular course, taught at certain hours, the teaching of morals ought to be the constant care of the teacher and the natural result of all the exercises of the school.

Says M. Janet: "There is a capital mode of moral instruction which pervades the whole course of teaching, all the studies of the child, and even all the acts of his life. We may teach morals through reading, writing, grammar, history, and even through the

sciences. Children will be taught to read in good books contain-
ing short moral lessons; they will be made to write, as models,
maxims and sentences which will remain in their memory;
dictation exercises may be given them borrowed from the records
of the moralists; and history at each step is a school of morals.
Even arithmetic may be used for this purpose; for from the rule
of interest, for example, this practical inference may be drawn,
that no debts should be contracted, or if they are they must be
paid. There is a lesson in morals in the acts of the child at all
hours of the day, even in his sports and recreations. At each
moment the instructor is obliged to teach neatness, politeness,
obedience, industry, and the spirit of peace and concord. From
this first point of view the school as a whole is in itself a school of
moral instruction."

429. THE SPECIAL TEACHING OF MORALS. — But outside
of this diffused and almost unconscious teaching of morals,
which results from all the exercises of the school, there
ought to be a regular course of instruction in morals, very
simple, of course, and very modest, but distinct from all
the others. Morals is a science which may and should be
taught on its own account, in the common school as everywhere else. It is only by this means that there will be a
cure for what is irregular, indefinite, and insufficient in
moral education, when it is supported merely on indirect
lessons and a disconnected instruction.

On this question there may be differences of opinion
among men of good judgment. M. Buisson, in his *Rapport
sur l'exposition de Philadelphie*, declared that morals differs
from the other topics of the programme in the fact that it
cannot have a fixed time in the scheme of daily exercises.
The official programmes of 1881 have, as it seems to us,
rightly come to a. different conclusion, for they say expressly:

" There shall be each day, in the two lower grades, at least one
lesson which, in the form of a familiar conversation or by means of

appropriate reading lessons, shall be devoted to moral instruction ; in the higher grade this lesson shall be, as far as possible, the methodical development of a systematic course in morals."

430. TOPICS OF MORAL INSTRUCTION. — The object of instruction in morals in the common school is the practical knowledge of duties much more than the theoretical expression of moral principles. It is of less importance to have the child reason as a philosopher on the nature of his actions, than to prepare him to fulfil as an upright man all the obligations of life.

"It should be the duty of all teachers," says M. Janet, "to instruct their pupils during the whole school course in their duties towards their family, their country, their fellows, themselves, and God."

Learned discussions on good and evil, on the character of the moral law, on the principle of moral obligation, ought to be nearly proscribed in elementary instruction in morals. These things are proper in a college course, but it would be useless to require them of children in the common school, whose minds are insufficiently prepared for such studies.

431. SCOPE AND LIMITS OF THIS INSTRUCTION. — The teaching of morals in the common school ought not to be connected with any religious doctrine. Universal and common to all children, to whatever confession they may belong, it speaks but the language of reason and common sense ; it remains human, and does not encroach on the peculiar beliefs of any religious body.

"Lay instruction in morals is distinguished from religious instruction without contradicting it. The instructor substitutes himself neither for the priest nor for the head of the family; he unites his efforts with theirs in order to make of each child an honest man. He ought to insist on the duties which bring men

together, and not on the dogmas which divide them.   Every theological and philosophical discussion is manifestly forbidden him
by the very character of his functions, by the age of his pupils,
and by the confidence of families and of the state ; he concen-
trates all his energies on a problem of another nature, but not
less arduous, for the very reason that it is exclusively practical ;
and this is to make all children serve an actual apprenticeship in
right-living.   •

"Later, when they have become citizens, they will perhaps be
separated by dogmatic opinions, but at least they will be in practical accord in placing the aim of life as high as possible ; in
having the same horror of whatever is low and vile, the same
admiration for whatever is noble and generous, the same delicacy
in the appreciation of duties ; in aspiring after moral perfection,
whatever efforts it may cost ; and in feeling themselves united in
the general homage of the true, the beautiful, and the good, which
is also a form, and none the less pure, of the religious feeling." [1]

432. DIVISION OF THE COURSES. — In the teaching of
morals, more perhaps. than in any other subject, it is necessary to follow a progressive plan, to proceed at first by examples, by familiar talks, to rise little by little to abstract
laws and to general rules.

It is in accordance with these principles that the official
programme has organized the different courses in the common school.

In the infant class the instruction comprises only simple
talks mingled with the various exercises of the school, short
poems learned by heart, and stories told by the teachers.

In the three grades of the common school, the programme
regulates the succession of topics as follows :

ELEMENTARY COURSE.—Familiar conversations; readings with
explanations, narratives, examples, precepts; learning by heart.

INTERMEDIATE COURSE.— Readings with explanations as before

---

[1] Programme of 1882, *Éducation morale.*

(narratives, examples, precepts), but co-ordinated and graduated according to a methodical plan.

HIGHER COURSE.— Short graduated lessons in moral instruction, illustrated by examples in accordance with the programme.

It is then only in the higher course that the instruction will assume a didactic, doctrinal form, and that the teacher will give formal lessons.

433. THE INDUCTIVE AND DEDUCTIVE METHOD. — In whatever way we may teach morals, the method followed is always either inductive or deductive.

We may start from an example, from a fact furnished by history, from a fiction invented by the teacher's imagination, from an experience of the child, from an incident which has occurred in the class, in the school, or in the village, and then lead the pupil to discover the moral truth concealed behind this particular event. This is to proceed inductively.

Or we may lay down a moral rule, the definition of a virtue or a precept of conduct, and after having explained it in itself, we may help the pupil to find practical applications of this general rule. In other terms, we may proceed deductively.

"At one time," says M. Janet, "maxims will be regarded as the consequence of a story or a fable ; and at another they will be presented as principles, and the story or the fable will become the proof or the application of the maxim."

434. PROPER CHARACTERISTICS OF INSTRUCTION IN MORALS. — The clearness, logic, and intellectual qualities which may assure the efficiency of every other topic, will not suffice in the teaching of morals. In this case the teacher is an educator rather than a professor. He does not address himself alone to the mind, — he must touch the heart, penetrate the

conscience, and insinuate himself into the depths of the soul. He has need of gravity, and also of fervor and communicative emotion; he himself ought to feel vividly the moral truths which he communicates to others.

"In order that moral culture may be possible and effective, it is an indispensable condition that this instruction touch the soul to the quick; that it shall be confounded with an ordinary lesson neither in tone, character, nor form. It is not sufficient to give the pupil correct notions and store his memory with wise maxims; but we must succeed in developing within him emotions so true and so strong as to aid him in the day of trial in triumphing over passions and vices. It is required of the teacher, not to adorn the memory of the child, but to touch his heart and to make him feel, by a direct experience, the majesty of the moral law. This is equivalent to saying that the means to be employed cannot be like those which are proper in a lesson in science or grammar. They ought to be not only more versatile and varied, but more intimate, more affecting, more practical, of a character less didactic on the whole, but more serious."

435. Teaching through the Heart. — We have been sharply criticised for having said, in our *Élements d'instruction civique et morale*, that " the practice of morals is based on the sensibilities." But yet this is the simple truth. Feeling, whether it be the feeling of affection for one's family, one's companion, one's fellow-citizen, or even religious sentiment, that noble emotion of the soul for the good, — these are the most fruitful sources of virtue. On this point educators are unanimous.

"With the child," says M. Marion, "the heart anticipates the head, and it is rather through the heart than through the reason that we have our hold on him. It is then to the heart that we must first address ourselves. The sensibilities of the child are already very active at a time when his intelligence is yet scarcely awakened. It would then be a waste of time to teach him general precepts, but to the same degree it would be a useful undertaking to devote our energies to touching his heart, to giving him a love and, so to speak, an agitation for the good, a longing for what is better."

"From the hearthstone of the tender and generous emotions," says Madame de Saussure, "there radiates over the intelligence a kind of animation, that gentle ardor with which it is intimately penetrated. . . . The feelings are not only necessary to the mind as a complement to its knowledge, but they decide its very character, its nature, and the mode of its action." [1]

436. EDUCATION THROUGH REFLECTION. — Convinced as we are of the prerogatives of the heart and the emotions in the matter of moral culture, we have not the least thought of depreciating the influence of the intelligence itself in moral education. Virtue is an affair of judgment as well as of feeling. We must first know where duty lies. To know accurately in what it consists, what reasons constrain us to follow it, what consequences will result from it, is not without use in deciding us to fulfil it.

The teacher will then appeal to the child's judgment and reflection. "In the intermediate course," says M. Janet, "we ought to address ourselves to the reflection, if not more, at least as much, as to the feelings."

"The instructor," says M. Marion, "ought to give the child general modes of thinking, general rules for forming sound judgments, and a larger sense of his own responsibility. If we would have the child accustom himself to do nothing without asking himself what is good or bad in the given case, we must evidently furnish him with general precepts as to good and evil, and give him true *moral instruction*." [2]

437. EDUCATION THROUGH PRACTICE. — When we have assigned the mind and the heart their respective parts in the

---

[1] *L'Education progressive*, I., p. 277.

[2] Marion, *op. cit.*, p. 392.

teaching of morals, we must hasten to recognize the function of habit and will. It is of pre-eminent importance that by his vigilant endeavor the teacher assure to every moment of school life the accomplishment of acts in conformity with the moral law. The intelligent application of school discipline will furnish him the means for doing this. He will allow liberty of thought and action, but will indicate to his pupils their errors or their mistakes. He will teach them a horror for tale-bearing, dissimulation, and hypocrisy. He will place above everything else frankness and uprightness, and for this purpose he will never discourage the frank speech of children, their objections or their questions.

"The teacher ought to give the child habits. . . . At the age of seven the child has not yet all the good habits which he ought to have, and even those which he has are not as strong as they ought to become. We must continue to train him to what is good by inspiring him without his knowledge, so to speak, with correct modes of acting and feeling. General precepts would be useless at that age; they are repulsive and dry because they are abstract and remain without effect. Let us recall the remark of Herbert Spencer, "that it is not only with children, but with all inattentive and slightly cultured minds, that admonitions fail of their purpose."

"We do not teach a child morals in order that he may know, but in order that he may do. In the ordinary sense of the term, it is not a question of teaching but of inculcating, which is an entirely different thing. In introducing morals into the programme of the common schools, it was not intended to introduce a new branch of instruction analogous to the others, new lessons parallel with the other lessons; but it is the education of the heart and of the character that it is proposed to assure and direct in the best manner possible."

438. PRACTICAL EXERCISES. — This necessity of appealing to the moral habits is so evident that the authors of the official programme have taken special pains to recommend

practical exercises which tend to embody moral principles in action, both within the school and outside the school. An attentive supervision is thus imposed on teachers.[1]

These practical exercises ought first to take account of individual characteristics. The teacher ought to know the peculiar disposition of each pupil for the purpose of intervening to correct their faults and to call into play their good qualities. To a far higher degree than intellectual education, moral education requires the particular, personal care which aims at each natural bent of the child.

The teacher must also endeavor to correct the bad habits, the prejudices, and the superstitions which the child brings from the family into the school, upon which he has been nourished from infancy, and which the influences of the environment in which he lives continue to perpetuate in him.

"The child does not reach the age of seven absolutely inexperienced and morally unaffected. A sort of moral perversion has already begun in him through default of proper care, and the teacher who receives him into school ought not only to do what has not been done, but more often to undo what alone has been done."

439. THE EXAMPLE OF A TEACHER. — But it is not alone the child with his habits already formed, with his prejudices contracted from birth, that must be supervised in his acts and trained to think better and to do better; but, above all, the teacher ought to supervise himself.

"In order that the pupil may be penetrated with that respect for the moral law which is a complete education in itself, the first

---

[1] "In some schools the children are polite and respectful to everybody, and they are early inspired with the sentiment of duty; but this is far from being true in most schools. Teachers do not supervise their pupils enough outside of school; they do not apply themselves sufficiently to training the hearts of children, and too often forget that instruction is nothing without education."

thing necessary is that by his character, his conduct, and his language, the teacher himself should be the most persuasive of examples. In this order of instruction, what does not come from the heart does not go to the heart. The teacher who recites precepts and speaks of duty without conviction and emotion, does much worse than lose his effort; he is guilty of a fault."

It is not only when he speaks of morals, it is always and everywhere that the teacher ought to present himself to the child as a living example of uprightness and honesty. A real model acting before the eyes of the child will always be more efficient than the models borrowed from history or fiction.

440. INCIDENTAL MARKS. — It is doubtless necessary in the teaching of morals not so much to preach as to do; but yet exhortations made with gravity are not without their value.

M. Pécaut wisely recommends the managers of schools to call together, at least each week, the pupils of the lower classes for the purpose of conversing with them for half an hour.

"Let them then enter into more direct communication with them; let them pass in review the history of the past week, doing justice to all; and let them point out, along with the faults and shortcomings, the honest efforts and good results. Let them reserve for this conference some interesting article, adapted to raise the children above the ordinary level of their studies, and to inspire them with a taste to read for themselves some good books from the school library. For this purpose let them give their pupils discreet advice as to their ordinary life, their family duties, and books that are to be avoided. Such conversations well prepared, serious without stiffness, in which a skillful manager would never fail to associate his subordinates, might be made the principal *educative* lesson, a cordial, interesting, and undogmatic moral lesson. The child would leave the school better prepared to profit by the good influences of the family, and better armed against the bad examples and the unwholesome excitements of the street."

441. READING. — It is particularly by reading that good moral inspirations are to be insinuated into the head and into the heart of the child. This reading is either done in class, with commentaries which throw into relief the important parts of the text, or is done personally by the pupil.

"School libraries," say the *Rapports* of the inspectors-general, "when they are well maintained, will furnish the teacher powerful aids in education and moral instruction. The influence of good books is very important, and so their influence should be extended everywhere in order to develop, by this means, a high state of moral sentiment."

442. POETRY. — We have noted in another place the relations between the beautiful and the good, between art and morals. In our schools we have not yet learned to draw from literary studies all the advantage which education is entitled to expect from them.

"If the moral and religious sense consists above all in respectful homage and submission rendered to what is better than one's self, to the ideal, to the good, and finally to the perfect Being, what is more proper for awakening it than to make an appeal to the sense of admiration for what is beautiful, — beautiful in thought, sentiment, form, and order; for everything which, by surpassing our low level, solicits us to step out of ourselves and to mount higher? Let us recognize a great want here, which I will only indicate. The official, dogmatic religion has retired from our schools, and nothing has yet come to take its place; moral instruction has no more than appeared on the threshold; and art in its various forms, but particularly in the eminently educative form of poetry, does not fulfill in any degree its office of high culture. Even choral singing, which has always been the chosen instrument of religious, moral, and patriotic education, nowhere exists, so to speak, in our schools."

443. Theoretical Morals. — While the teaching of morals in the common school has mainly a practical aim, the instructor need not neglect to give to his lessons an elevated general character. It does not suffice to teach pupils their individual duties, and put them in a condition to practice them ; but it is necessary that the course in morals be also an occasion to awaken the reflection of the child on the nature of man and on his destination in the world.

"The last course," says M. Janet, " will not be finished without having given the children some notions of what we call theoretical morals, — that is, the explanation of the principles of morals, the distinction between good and evil, duty as distinct from personal interest, conscience and the moral sense, merit and demerit, moral sanction and the future life founded on the justice of God."

In other terms, the teacher has not only to favor the particular dispositions which will prepare the child for the accomplishment of such or such a duty ; but he ought to aim higher and by all possible means, by the strict application of rules, by the judicious use of rewards and punishments, by exhortations and reprimands, and on occasion by theoretical explanations, he will do his best to develop in the soul of his pupil that which is the basis of all morals, the feeling of personal responsibility.

444. Civic Instruction. — Recently introduced into the programmes of primary instruction, civic instruction might in a sense be confounded with morals, of which it is but the complement. It is impossible, in fact, to become a citizen if one does not begin by being a man. The firmest basis of the civic virtues will always be the practice of the individual and social virtues.

It is with reason, however, that a special place has been given to civic instruction, were it only to bring into clearer

view its importance and utility. But it is not proposed to
give merely indirect instruction in civics, such as might
result from history, geography, etc.; but there is opportunity to give direct instruction in all the topics included
in this expression by connecting them with the courses in
history and geography.

445. Necessity of Civic Instruction. — It is not enough
to say that instruction in civics is useful; the truth is that it
is necessary. It is especially so since political liberty, that
conquest of the Republic of 1848, has been added to civil
liberty, that conquest of the Revolution.

In a country which governs itself, where each individual
through his vote participates freely in the direction of public
affairs, why permit the majority of citizens, those who
attend only the common school, to remain in ignorance of
their political and social obligations?

You require them to respect and love the Constitution, and
they do not know the Constitution!

You require them to exercise their rights and perform
their duties, and they are ignorant of the meaning and the
scope of these rights and duties!

Citizens who boast of this glorious name without knowing
what obligation it imposes on them; electors who vote without knowing the importance of their vote; tax-payers who
pay taxes without comprehending the use made of them;
inhabitants of a country who have not been taught to love
her; — such are necessarily the members of a people who
have lacked instruction in civics.

Doubtless the newspapers repair this ignorance in part,
but there is no regularity and system in the teaching of the
press; it is subject to a thousand hazards. Moreover, all
the newspapers are not what they should be; and, finally, the
newspaper often comes too late to heal the political preju-

dices which have been left to take root in the soul of the child and the young man.

A distinguished writer, Vitet, said a few years ago, "Love of country is not taught in France." If this assertion is true, it is important that it cease to be so, and that the children of France learn to love not only their country, but also the institutions of their country.

"Without civic and political education," wrote Pestalozzi, "the sovereign people is a child playing with fire at the risk each moment of burning down the house."

In 1877 M. Gréard demanded the introduction into French schools of what abroad has long been called civic instruction.

"What good sense demands," he said, " is that to the respect for the national traditions which is the basis of enlightened patriotism, there be joined in the minds of children who have reached the age of reason, a knowledge of the general laws in common use in their country. What our pupils know the least, is that which for themselves and for everybody they should have the most interest in knowing. It is surely not without use for them to have an idea of the capitularies of Charlemagne; but how much more important it is that they shall not be left in ignorance of the principles of the social organization in the midst of which they are called to fulfill their duties as citizens! Doubtless the child should not be an absolute stranger to the régime of our ancient provinces; but is it not still more indispensable that he have an exact notion of all that actually constitutes the organic life of a commune, of a department, of the state? How many pupils there are who might explain in a fashion what in their day the Mayors of the Palace were, who would be greatly embarrassed to define the function and the prerogatives of the mayor of their arrondissement or of their village! And if these notions are not taught them at school, as they might be, and as they are in all the countries about us, where and how shall they be learned?" [1]

---

[1] M. Gréard, *L'Enseignement primaire à Paris de* 1867 *à* 1877, p. 281.

446. METHOD TO BE PURSUED. — There is nothing dryer or more monotonous than a course of instruction in civics, if the teacher does nothing more than enumerate to the child the administrative and political notions of which it is composed. But it is easy, if one takes the trouble, to ani-́ mate and vivify this instruction by citing examples, by availing one's self of history, and above all by aiming to excite without cessation national ideas and to enkindle the flame of patriotism.

The purpose of civic instruction, in fact, is not only to introduce into the mind of the child a certain amount of positive knowledge; but it is, above all, to cultivate in his soul at an early hour his natural inclination to love his country and to respect her laws.

The official programme indicates the course to be pursued, which consists, as in geography, in taking the commune as the starting-point, and thence passing progressively to the study of the department and the state. Familiarized at first with the institutions which are, so to speak, within his reach, and which he sees in operation in his village, the child will have no difficulty in rising higher, and will be wholly prepared to conceive the more complicated play of the government itself. But all this on the condition that the teacher knows how to avoid dryness, that he does not multiply useless details, that he excites the child's curiosity, that he appeals to his patriotic feelings, that he always shows him what advantage he will derive in life from the knowledge which he acquires at school, and how much he needs to know all that can be taught him on this point, in order to fulfill later his duties as a citizen and to exercise a citizen's rights.

447. CIVIC INSTRUCTION AND HISTORY. — History, which teaches us the past of our country, is one thing, and civic

instruction, which makes known to us its present state, its actual organization, is quite another. However, we must never separate "to-day" and "formerly"; and civic instruction will not be fruitful unless it is ever stimulating a comparison between contemporary institutions and ancient institutions.

Of course a large spirit of toleration, and even of respect, should animate the instructor in the comparisons which he will have to make between the past and the present. In praising the actual state of affairs, he should have a fear lest he unduly undervalue and misrepresent what now is no more. This has been eloquently said by Jules Ferry:

"I do not like to have it said to children, 'There is nothing but contemporary history.' Ah! it was doubtless a happy thought and a real step in advance to introduce contemporary history into the programmes of our elementary instruction; but let us be on our guard against an opposite extreme. Do not think it wise to say to youth, 'Back of 1789, back of that brilliant and renovating date, there is nothing, nothing but sadness, nothing but misery, nothing but shame.' In the first place this is not true, and then such talk is not wholesome for youth."[1]

448. CIVIC INSTRUCTION AND POLITICS. — By reason of its relations with politics, civic instruction falls upon rocks where it is easy to make shipwreck. The instructor should be on his guard against making of his pupils little journalists and embryo politicians, without forgetting, however, what he owes his country and the respect which is due to the established government.

As some one has said, we ought not to carry politics into the school, "if we mean by politics what occurs day after day in the Chambers, who is the Minister to-day, and who will be the Minister to-morrow."

---

[1] *Discours au Sénat,* du 10 Juin, 1882.

But if we understand by politics a knowledge of the great principles of liberty, of equality, and of fraternal solidarity, which are the foundation of modern societies, and which the sons of the Revolution had to defend against the laggards and against the impatient; if we understand by politics love of country and attachment to the Republic, we say yes, and believe that it is never too soon to inculcate the idea of it, and that this sort of politics is fit for all periods of life.

The law of March 22, 1882, put moral and civic instruction among the obligatory topics of instruction in the primary schools for boys and girls. Hereafter moral and civic instruction will take among the required studies, between grammar and arithmetic, the place which it has the right to claim as a valuable instrument for popular education and as a branch of instruction particularly necessary in a land of universal suffrage, in a great democracy which it would be of no use to emancipate if it were not at the same time enlightened as to its rights and its duties.

449. LAY RIGHTS IN THE MATTER OF MORAL EDUCATION. — The work of the teacher is not done when he has cultivated and adorned the minds of his pupils, and has furnished them with technical knowledge for the combats of life. He derives from his title as teacher, he has received from the confidence of families, a still higher office. By virtue of his office and according to his position, he is the educator of the rising generation.

It would certainly be easier, supposing this were possible, to confine himself strictly to his professional duties, to be simply a teacher of French, history, or mathematics; to go no deeper than the surface of the mind; not to touch the living and inner reality of beliefs, and in a word, as some one has said, " to be nothing but a sort of dancing-master of the intelligence."

But whether he will or not, by the very nature of his duties, by his ceaseless influence on the souls of the children confided to his care, the teacher necessarily assumes a higher responsibility. He intervenes not only through direct moral lessons, but through the spirit which proceeds from all his instruction, and still more through his example, in the moral training of his pupils; and I do not hesitate to say that this is his duty and his right.

Yes, we boldly claim for lay teachers the title of educators and moralists. In order to perform this august part, it is not necessary to wear the robes of a priest. It is sufficient to be a man, an upright man.

By what right, some one will say, do you teach morals? By the right which every good man has, who is at the same time a teacher, to communicate to his pupils that which is his most precious treasure, — moral truth, the most essential and most important of all. Do I need to say that this task, if it is the most noble, is also the most delicate? It is especially on this point that the intentions of the University are misunderstood and its work suspected. We are treated as usurpers and as the enemies of religion; and, in the language of certain political partisans, "the common school became a godless school on the day when the teaching of morals was officially introduced into it."

We would have deserved these reproaches if we had for a single moment forgotten what respect and regard we owe to the religious consciousness and the confessional belief of our pupils; but it must be evident to every candid man that in undertaking to teach human morals, the eternal moral law, we do not purpose in any way to trespass on the rights of parents or of the ministers of religion. Though we are the sincere and ardent defenders of the rights of modern society, we are none the less conscious of the respect which a government worthy of the name owes to the consciences of religious men. What is more worthy of our respect than the conscience of a child, a nascent and as yet undeveloped conscience, an easy prey to all doctrines, which offers itself to our instruction with the ingenuous docility of early years, and which would so easily allow itself to be fashioned in the mold where it might please us to put it? But this conscience, God forbids us to touch it and to take it in hand, not only because this child's conscience is the whole future of the man and has its individual rights, but also because back of it, if we were guilty enough to wish to turn it aside from its natural aspirations, we would perceive the will of the parents, the rights of the family, and the whole inheritance of traditional beliefs.

If there is still any one who imagines that in giving moral and civic instruction to all grades of public education, we have desired to raise altar against altar, to oppose the teacher to the priest or to the pastor, to establish some competition between the manual and the catechism, that we have desired by the side of each temple or each church to establish a school of irreligion and impiety, so that the child on leaving the primary school passes before the doors of the church or the temple with the spirit of indifference or of scoffing, he is mistaken ; and we protest against these imputations with all the power of our conscience as a man, a patriot, and a republican.

Our only thought has been that, at a time when we are concerned with what is of vital interest to a great nation, — I mean the moralization of the people, — it is not expecting too much of the good-will and devotion of all, that moral lessons should not lose all their efficacy for not being clothed with an ecclesiastical character ; but that lay teachers might participate in this instruction. And when we have thus assumed our part of the common task, instead of being cursed as adversaries, perhaps it may be more just to give us thanks as co-laborers.

We shall not lose heart.   We shall continue to invite all
the pupils of our colleges and schools to the neutral ground
of instruction in morals, where we attack no religion, where
we preach justice, charity, and tolerance, which is charity
towards ideas.   We shall continue to build upon these solid
foundations the human city, while leaving to the ministers
of religion the task of building by the side of it what St.
Augustine called the City of God.[1]

---

[1] The public school system of France, taken collectively, and
including all the grades of instruction, is known as the " University of
France," and is under the direction of the Minister of Public Instruction.   The significance of paragraph 449 lies in the fact that the
schools of France have been *secularized*, — that is, taken wholly from
the hands of ecclesiastics and administered by laymen.   The church
is naturally aggrieved at this, claims the teaching of morals as one of
its prerogatives, and pronounces the state schools godless.   (P.)

CHAPTER IX.

DRAWING. — MUSIC. — SINGING.

450. DRAWING IN THE COMMON SCHOOL. — Drawing has long been considered as an accomplishment, as a fancy study reserved to people of leisure or to professional artists. It has resulted from this that drawing has for a long time been omitted from the programme of common school instruction. But it has now gained the day. For several years past the teaching of drawing has been obligatory in most of the schools of Europe. As some one has said, " there is an advent of drawing, as well as of science, in education." It is acknowledged on all sides that drawing is not only an elevated recreation and a preparation for an appreciation of the beautiful, but it is also the prime condition of all progress in the different branches of artistic industry.

" Without drawing, no skillful workmen, no good superintendents of manufactories, no progress and excellence in the highest industries, those which give proof of civilization."[1]

" The advantages which can be derived from drawing, through its happy applications to the mechanic arts, are infinitely valuable. It is the soul of several branches of commerce; it is drawing which gives the preference to the industries of a nation; it increases the value of crude material a hundred-fold. Cloths, jewelry, trinkets, porcelain, carpets, — all the trades relating to the arts cannot be carried on, except through the principles of drawing."[2]

---

[1] See the article DESSIN in the *Dictionnaire de pédagogie.*
[2] Bachelier, *Discours sur l'utilité des écoles élémentaires.*

451. HISTORICAL : ROUSSEAU. — Rousseau was the first in France to recommend the study of drawing, — drawing from nature, moreover, with the intention of making skillful workmen rather than elegant artists.

" We could not learn to judge correctly of the width and height of objects except by learning to know also their shapes, and even to copy them ; for at bottom this copying is absolutely dependent on the laws of perspective ; and we cannot estimate the size from these appearances except we have some perception of these laws. Children, who are great imitators, all try their hand at drawing. I would have my child cultivate this art, not especially for the art itself, but in order to make his eye true and his hand dextrous ; and in general it is of very little consequence that he understand such or such an exercise, provided he acquire the perspicacity of sense and the correct habit of body that are generally acquired through that exercise. I would be very loth, therefore, to give him a drawing-master *who should give him only imitations to imitate, and who should make him draw only after drawings ;* I would have him have no teacher but nature, and no other models but objects. I would have before his eyes the very original, and not the paper which represents it ; and I would have him sketch a house from a house, a tree from a tree, a man from a man, in order that he may accustom himself to observe bodies and their appearances correctly, and not to accept false and conventional imitations for real imitations. I would even discourage him from tracing anything from memory, in the absence of objects, until by frequent observations their exact shapes are firmly impressed on his imagination ; for fear that by substituting odd and fantastic figures for the actual things, he lose all knowledge of proportion and a taste for the beauties of nature.

"I very well know that in this way he will scrawl for a long time without making anything that is recognizable, and that he will be late in acquiring elegance of contour and the light touch of draftsmen, and perhaps never the appreciation of picturesque effects and fine taste in drawing ; but on the other hand he will certainly acquire a truer vision, a steadier hand, a knowledge of the real similarities of size and shape among animals, plants, and natural bodies, and a more ready acquaintance with the shifting of perspective." [1]

Rousseau is wrong in absolutely proscribing the imitation of artificial models. Another error is that he very sharply separates drawing from geometry. "Geometry," he says, " is for our pupils but the art of making a good use of the rule and compass ; and it must not be confounded with drawing, which will employ neither of these instruments."

452. PESTALOZZI AND FROEBEL. — After Rousseau, Pestalozzi and Froebel are the ones who have done the most to popularize elementary instruction in drawing.

For Pestalozzi, geometrical forms constitute the very essence of drawing. The pupil will first draw straight lines, squares, triangles, and arcs of the circle. Later, when the æsthetic element of form is separated from the purely mathematical element, and the pupil has gained a clear consciousness of it, exercises in linear drawing will be followed by lessons in perspective and in artistic drawing.

The drawing of lines is but a preparation for the drawing of objects.

"It is not lines," he says, "that nature gives the child; she gives him only objects ; and we should give him lines only to aid him in seeing objects correctly, and we should guard against removing the objects from him and making him see only lines."

Pestalozzi did hardly more than lay down principles ; Froebel has applied them. Like Pestalozzi, he takes geometrical figures as the starting-point.

" From the start the child has before him a table divided into squares, and then a slate divided into squares. Balls, cubes, thin strips of wood, taken in turn, familiarize him with geometrical

_____

[1] *Émile*, I., II.

forms; yarns and strips of paper drill him in distinguishing
colors. What he has seen he will naturally reproduce. For
guiding his first attempts it suffices to make him begin with
elementary forms. He commences by seeing concrete and tangible lines, so to speak, represented by sticks; at first he has only
to lay down and arrange in different ways the laths or the cubes
in order to obtain regular figures. Very soon, by weaving the
strips of paper, he himself produces mosaics in little squares of
several colors. Finally, when he takes the pencil in hand, it is
easy for him to represent on the slate or on paper the combinations which he has produced with these sticks, cubes, and strips
of paper, and by means of the incitements of analogy and the
help of the squares which guide him without restraining him, and
by means of the growing instinct of harmony and symmetry
which kindergarten training marvelously develops, he cannot
restrict himself to imitating, but he invents almost at once new
combinations of lines whose regular arrangement delights him and
gives his ceaseless encouragement to new efforts."[1]

453. DEFINITION OF TERMS. — Usage has sanctioned certain expressions, according to which drawing would comprise different varieties which are wholly distinct, such as
linear, geometrical, ornamental, artistic, or imitative drawing. Linear drawing is in truth nothing but geometrical
drawing, — that is, drawing which is more specially applied
to the representation of objects geometrically defined. Ornamental drawing is but a development of geometrical drawing. Finally, artistic or imitative drawing is generally
applied to the representation of the human figure.

454. ACTUAL PROGRAMMES. — The teaching of drawing
was not made obligatory in the common schools of France
till 1882. The decree of July 27, 1882, requires that the
teaching of drawing, begun with very short lessons in the
elementary course, " shall occupy in the two other courses
two or three lessons each week."

---

[1] M. Buisson, *Rapport sur l'exposition de Vienne*, p. 247.

The programme indicates, as matter for the elementary course, the tracing of lines and the first principles of ornamental drawing.

For the intermediate course, *free-hand drawing*, ordinary geometrical curves, and curves borrowed from the vegetable world ; copying from casts representing ornaments, and the first notion of geometrical drawing as related to the dimensions, form, and position of the parts of an object ; finally, geometrical drawing with the use of the rule, the compass, the square, and the protractor. In this part of the course the effort will be limited to making pupils understand the use of those instruments which they are to handle in the higher course.

For the higher course, elementary notions on the orders of architecture and the drawing of the human head are added to the free-hand drawing. As to geometrical drawing, the traces hitherto executed on the board will now be made on paper with the aid of instruments. The principles of tinting are given, and decorative drawings are executed in china ink and color.

455. At what Age should Instruction in Drawing Begin? — When the child writes rapidly and well, said Locke, I think that it is proper, not only to continue to exercise his hands by writing, but even to give extension to his skill by teaching him to draw. In fact, there are striking similarities between writing and drawing, and these two exercises may and should lend one another mutual support. So in imitation of Froebel we cannot too much encourage the teaching of drawing even in the infant school.

"Nothing could be better adapted to a little child than drawing, which occupies his eyes and his hand, and compels him, by the very nature of the exercise and without the necessity of inviting him to it, to observe attentively, to compare, and to *combine*.   We intentionally underscore this last word, because it correctly indicates the superiority of drawing over the other exercises in observation, where the child looks without having to reproduce what he sees.   In the most modest attempts at drawing, there is an element of creation, an active personal part which constitutes one of the greatest attractions of this kind of work.   With the pencil in hand, the child invents even more than he copies." [1]

456. CHILDREN'S TASTE FOR DRAWING. — All the observers of human nature, and notably Mr. Spencer, have observed the child's taste for drawing.

"The spreading recognition of drawing as an element of education is one amongst many signs of the more rational views on mental culture now beginning to prevail.   Once more it may be remarked that teachers are at length adopting the course which nature has for ages been pressing upon their notice.   The spontaneous efforts made by children to represent men, houses, trees, and animals around them, — on a slate, if they can get nothing better, or with lead-pencil or paper, if they can beg them, — are familiar to all.   To be shown through a picture-book is one of their highest gratifications; and as usual their strong imitative tendency presently generates in them the ambition to make pictures themselves also.   This attempt to depict the striking things they see is a farther instinctive exercise of the perceptions, — a means whereby still greater accuracy and completeness of observation is induced. And, alike by seeking to interest us in their discoveries of the sensible properties of things, and by their endeavors to draw, they solicit from us just that kind of culture which they most need." [2]

457. TASTE FOR COLORING. — Mr. Spencer has also observed that the process of representation which most charms and attracts the child is coloring.

---

[1] Mlle. Chalamet, *L'École maternelle*, p. 135.

[2] Spencer, *op. cit.*, p. 140.

"Paper and pencil are good, in default of something better; but a box of paints and a brush, — these are the treasures. The drawing of outlines immediately becomes secondary to coloring."

But is it possible to introduce the use of colors into the common school? The programme admits of it in a certain measure, since it is prescribed for the infant classes in the following terms:

"Combination of lines. Representation of these combinations on slate and paper with an ordinary pencil, or by *tracing in color.*"

Also in the higher course of the common school, the programme, as we have seen, recommends exercises in tinting with china ink and in color.

458. TWO DIFFERENT METHODS. — It is none the less true that the most important thing in drawing is the line and its combinations, and not color and its shades.

What method shall be followed to familiarize the child, as surely and as rapidly as possible, with the study of lines? Two systems are before us, — on the one hand, that which would not have geometry made the basis of instruction in drawing, which asserts that the human form, — being that which is most perfect and most harmonious in its proportions, — it is with it that the study of drawing should begin; on the other hand the classical method, which proceeds logically, analytically so to speak, and which, before presenting wholes for the imitation of the child, drills him in reproducing the elements of every figure and of every form, — that is, the lines in their different combinations.

459. MR. SPENCER's OPINION. — Mr. Spencer vigorously condemns the method which consists " in making straight lines and curved lines and compound lines, with which it is the fashion of some teachers to begin." This is, he says, to renew in the teaching of drawing the exercises which

have been abandoned in the teaching of languages; it is again placing the abstract before the concrete.

It is difficult to prove, however, that lines, even though they are but the elements of real forms, constitute anything abstract. This is as though, in the teaching of reading, we should forbid the child to learn the letters which are the elements of words. It seems to us that it is best to place at the beginning of the studies in drawing the tracing of lines, their division into equal parts, and the estimation of the relation of lines to one another. This, according to Mr. Spencer's expression, is a "grammar," or rather an alphabet, of forms, which must necessarily be learned before going farther.

Mr. Spencer's opinion is also that which is advocated in France by M. Ravaisson.

"In its most elementary processes," he says, "to which all others may be reduced, drawing reposes. on a judgment of a special nature, entirely different from that judgment which is employed in mathematics. . . . The best means of drawing any object whatever will then be to study the objects in which are found in the highest degree those qualities which constitute their harmony and beauty, in such a way as to appropriate, at least as much as one is capable of doing and as his time will permit, the spirit which characterizes them. This will be to study the complete types of the highest perfection which nature presents to us. Even for him who will have, in the practice of the trade to which he devotes himself, only to execute the more modest task of imitation, the best method for succeeding as promptly as possible in fulfilling his duties properly will then be the one which all teachers have always prescribed, and which consists in studying for a long time, and as long. as one is able, the types in which is exhibited the unity which impresses on forms their character, and especially the higher unity in which beauty resides." [1]

---

[1] See article *Art* in the *Dict. de pédagogie.*

The method proposed by M. Ravaisson is undoubtedly the most favorable for the development of the æsthetic faculties and of the sentiment of the beautiful. It is the one perhaps which we would recommend if it were proposed in a common school to train artists ; but in the humble sphere in which the destinies of elementary instruction are placed, it seems to us more rational to follow the other method, that which is based on the solid elements borrowed from geometrical representations.

460. CLASSICAL OPINION. — This method has been brilliantly defended by M. E. Guillaume,[1] and it is impossible more strongly to enforce the reasons which justify the preference which we have given it. M. Guillaume observes that it is not so much a question of sentiment as of practical habits, and that drawing ought not to remain in the domain of uncertainties, but that it must have a rational basis.

"From the fact that drawing serves as a mode of expression in the fine arts, it is inferred that art is its principal, if not its unique object, and that in the teaching of drawing it is art that should be principally kept in view. The general and useful phase, the means of precision which it borrows from science and which serve as a necessary support even to the conceptions of the artist, are despised ; and before knowing how to draw a line or recognize its direction, moral expression becomes the theme. In a trice accuracy is sacrificed to sentiment. Taste is exalted as the supreme rule, and the fundamental principles and exercises, without which, farther on, neither inspiration nor actual works can be produced with certainty, are treated with disdain. The ideal is exalted and pupils are enamored of æsthetic theories, before being inured to practice and becoming masters of the laws which control it. Finally, the attention is

---

[1] See article DESSIN in the *Dictionnaire de pédagogie.*

fixed on the artistic vocations which are the exception, while an appeal should be made to the mass, where it is a question of children whose intelligence is developed progressively, and most of whom are destined to be workmen. Is there not a danger in appealing to the initiative and independence of sentiment when the only proper course is to give direction and discipline to minds? However little a child may follow a course in drawing, he should carry away from it definite ideas and practical habits which will be of use to him during his entire life."

M. Guillaume concludes that in practice, as in theory, it is geometry that is the basis of the science of drawing, and that we have to do with industrial drawing or with artistic drawing. If any other course is taken, it is very difficult to arrive at exactness, and the draftsman will run a great risk of always remaining in indecision and vagueness.

But this rigorous and scientific method does not exclude the pursuits of the beautiful and the education of the æsthetic sense; only, instead of being the point of departure, the human figure will be the coronation of the studies in drawing. In the higher course, the copying of figures after the antique will exercise the taste.

"From these admirable specimens of an art which has never been surpassed, the pupil will develop the artistic faculties which may exist within him. Trained from the first to drawing with exactness and precision, he will never remain powerless to translate the delicate or strong works which have been transmitted to us by the most brilliant epochs of art."

461. PARTICULAR ADVICE. — It would require too much time to enter into a detail of the school usages which are best adapted to the teaching of drawing. Let us note merely a few essential points.

I. So far as possible, the first models ought to be rèal objects. The programme of the maternal schools rightly places by the side of the drawings made by the mistress, which the pupil reproduces, " the representation of the most simple objects of daily use." In other terms, the pupil ought not to be exclusively restricted to the study of pure geometrical forms. It is well that he be early exercised in reading and translating the forms of natural objects.

II. At first only figures of two dimensions — that is, planes — must be drawn. Figures in relief ought to be reserved for a later period.

III. Ornamental drawing ought to follow geometrical drawing.

IV. Elementary instruction in drawing, even when we have in view only industrial drawing, ought not to neglect the human form.

V. The principles of industrial drawing ought to be taught *pari passu* with exercises in drawing. " The acquisition of technical skill by the hand is hastened, rather than retarded, by the study of these principles."

462. SINGING IN THE COMMON SCHOOL. — The teaching of the arts proper in the common school is reduced to singing and drawing. But drawing is especially a useful art, the study of which prepares the ordinary child for his future vocation as a laborer or an artisan ; it is only incidentally an element of æsthetic education. It tends rather to develop manual skill than to cultivate the sentiment of the beautiful. On the contrary, music and singing have not the same practical utility. They have been introduced into the common school chiefly as measures of gratifying the feelings, of touching the heart, and of exciting the noblest emotions of the soul. Hence the particular importance of singing, which seems to involve all that can be demanded of æsthetic education in the common school.

463. Singing in the Maternal School. — On· this subject we cannot do better than reproduce the very judicious observations of Mlle. Chalamet.

"Singing has always had a place in our infant schools, and with justice. It may render important service in the education of little children. It brings a valuable contribution to physical development by fortifying the lungs and giving suppleness to all the vocal organs. These organs are less liable to the many and grave maladies which might affect them, especially in early years, if they have been subjected to regular exercise. By this means we provide for the education of the ear; we cultivate and refine a sense which plays along with vision a pre-eminent part in the intellectual existence of the child. Finally, singing exercises over the mental condition of children an influence which makes of it a potent instrument of education, and one of the surest and most salutary means of discipline which can be employed. Who does not know the effect produced by a song introduced at the right moment into a sleepy, languid class, or it may be into one agitated and disturbed? Music has the gift of calming children, and at the same time of urging them to activity by an agreeable excitation. The child loves music. Singing makes him happy, and is for him a natural need, like running and jumping. Can we conceive an assembly of little children where there is no singing? This would be as little normal and as funereal as a garden whose plants never saw the sun." [1]

Since 1882 singing has been one of the obligatory topics of common-school instruction.

"Lessons in singing," says the regulation, "shall occupy from one to two hours a week, independently of the exercises in singing which will take place every day, either in the intervals between classes or at the opening or close of school."

464. Moral Influence of Music. — The ancients as-

---

[1] Mlle. Chalamet, *L'École maternelle*, p. 255.

scribed to music a sovereign influence in moral education. A well-educated Athenian must know how to sing, and the education of Themistocles, who had not this accomplish-ment, was thought to have been neglected. Music was regarded as the best means of habituating citizens to order and social harmony. "A rule of music cannot be touched," said Plato, "without disturbing the foundations of the state." It is to the same effect that Napoleon the First said, "A piece of moral music, executed by the hand of a master, infallibly touches the feelings, and has much more influence than a good book, which convinces the reason without influencing our habits."

"From the intellectual point of view," says a contemporary author, M. Dupaigne, "the result of music is to *elevate* the mind, to give it a taste for the beautiful, of which it is perhaps the most sensible example, and to lead from a taste for the beautiful to a love of study which will give in several other ways satisfaction to this taste. In this respect music is one of the most powerful auxiliaries, which gains time instead of losing it, because it prepares the way for the things of the spirit, for things delicate and exalted. In primary instruction it is music which first represents the æsthetic phase of education, so necessary to be mingled with the commonplaces of the first elements. It is music which, better understood and more easily grasped than literary beauty, more easily permits children to feel the charm and emotion produced by what they have known to be *well said*, and the delicious satisfaction of having had their part in the production of something *beautiful*. The importance of such impressions for the progress of a child's intelligence is not necessary to be demonstrated to earnest teachers; but we know that they require in him who would produce them at least that profound sentiment of art which is called *taste*, and that they necessarily exclude pretence and charlatanism.

"From the moral point of view, the effects of music are not less valuable. It may become for young people the most powerful preservative against the dangers of other pleasures, but on the conditions of a careful choice in selections, and of admitting within the school only the works of a pure and exalted sentiment, and of not fearing to appeal, as much as possible, to the great masters."

465. MUSIC AND DISCIPLINE. — It is useless to dwell on the part that music may play in school discipline. Music not only makes the school attractive, but is an excellent means for regulating the movements of pupils as they enter and leave the school-room, and of introducing order and harmony into it ; it is, moreover, an excellent recreation, which gives repose from serious studies, and which may, during the progress of the classes, reanimate the activity and the spirits of the pupils.

466. CHOICE OF PIECES. — It is a matter of complaint that there is not yet a good selection of pieces for use in the common schools ; and yet this selection is a matter of capital importance. These pieces ought to be simple, entertaining, with words adapted to the age of the child, — old melodies, patriotic songs, hymns to great men.

"Success in the teaching of singing depends, in great part, on the selection of pieces which are given children to sing. Their first exercises in language had been but the expression of their own ideas, of their own impressions. . . . It should be the same with their first exercises in singing. A collection of pieces, simple and well graded, is of extreme importance. . . . . . The words ought also to be as similar as possible to the very language of children, so as to be perfectly clear to them ; but this condition does not exclude real poetry. The subjects chosen will be of various characters; they will vary from serious to gay." [1]

---

[1] Roger de Guimps, *Philosophie de l'Éducation.*

467. METHODS AND PROCESSES. — The first thing to do is to train the ear and the voice. The ear will be trained by hearing and the voice by singing.

In the elementary course, as in the intermediate and higher courses, the songs will be learned by audition.

As at first musical theory will be purposely avoided, it is merely the practical which is of importance.

"Singing, like a speech, is a matter of imitation. . . . The song must be grasped simply by the ear, by singing it to children, as many times as it may be necessary in order that the better endowed among them may retain it in a manner well-nigh correct."

Obvious infirmities in the sense of hearing are due in general merely to the lack of exercise.

"There is no incurable infirmity," says M. Dupaigne. "It is never the ear unless one is deaf, but it is exercise which is lacking."

The beginning will be made, then, by requiring much practice of the children. When they have succeeded in singing in unison, — that is, in exactly reproducing the sounds which they hear, — the half of the work has been done.

An excellent piece of advice given by M. Dupaigne is to select from the children those who have an agreeable and reliable voice, and make them sing alone as an example for the others.

468. INTUITION IN SINGING. — Pestalozzi was right in thinking that as the child learns to speak before knowing how to read, he ought to learn to sing before knowing the conventional signs which serve for writing music. The child speaks because he has heard speaking; so he will sing from having heard singing.

469. MUSICAL THEORY. — In the elementary course, musical theory will be limited to the reading of notes. In the intermediate and higher courses, on the contrary, the study of theory proper should be added to the practical exercises.

But care should be taken not to extend the study of theory too far. Teachers should spare their children theoretical difficulties, but train them to utter sounds distinctly, to control their voice, to notice shades of sound, and to have a clear and correct enunciation.

The important thing is that the child, on leaving the common school, shall have a taste for singing, and that his musical aptitudes shall be so developed that he may be able, when he has become a young man, to become a member of a choral society, which is one of the most commendable and useful forms of popular association. By this means the study of singing will have co-operated in general education; it will have contributed to turn aside souls from gross pleasures and material enjoyments, to direct them towards innocent and elevated pleasures.

CHAPTER X.

THE OTHER EXERCISES OF THE SCHOOL.

470. MANUAL LABOR IN THE COMMON SCHOOL. — All the studies, all the school exercises, which we have so far examined are connected with intellectual and moral education, although some of them may receive an immediate practical application. But physical education, considered either as the development of the powers of the body or as an apprenticeship in the qualities of expertness, agility, manual dexterity, promptness and sureness in the movements which are particularly important to future workmen, — physical education also demands its place in the programme of the common schools.

Hence the importance accorded to gymnastics on the one hand, and to manual labor proper on the other.

"Gymnastics," says the order of July 27, 1882, "will occupy each day, or at least every other day, one recitation hour during the course of the afternoon."

"For the boys, as well as the girls, two or three hours a week will be devoted to manual industries."

What we have said in the first part of this work (Chapter II.) makes it unnecessary for us to dwell on the utility and the nature of a normal course of instruction in gymnastics.

471. IMPORTANCE OF MANUAL LABOR. — "The national school, in a democracy of laborers like ours, ought to be essentially a school of labor."[1] It is a question, not only of

---

[1] Jules Ferry.

developing the intellectual and moral faculties and of giving
a general education which no one in any occupation can
dispense with, but of preparing workmen for the shop and of
training the manual aptitudes. Without losing anything of
its proper character, the common school ought to be in part
a preparation for the professional school.

The time is no more when manual labor was considered a
low occupation. The programme of moral and civic instruction, ordered by the higher council of public instruction,
contains an article with this title: "Nobility of Manual
Labor." For three centuries educators like Locke and
Rousseau have demanded that the apprenticeship to a
manual industry should be introduced even into the instruction of the middle classes, and in general into the education of all men. If we have not yet reached this point,
we have at least placed manual labor in the programme
of the common school; and this is surely a considerable
step in advance.

"Be assured," says Jules Ferry, "that when the plane and
the file shall have taken, by the side of the compass, the map
and the history, the same place, the place of honor, and shall
have been the object of a rational and systematic instruction,
many prejudices will have disappeared, many caste distinctions
will have vanished. Social peace will appear on the benches
of the common school, and concord will illumine with its
radiant day the future of French society."

M. Gréard has pithily expressed the same thought.

"In our opinion it is not without some foundation that our
common school studies are charged with being too classical, in
the sense which tradition attaches to this word. With respect
to history, geography, or language, we are pleased with the
methods which befit an education of leisure. Everything draws
the higher classes of society to the great questions of history

and philosophy which constitute the development of human civilization, and they have the time to devote themselves to them. But such is not the condition of those who live by the labor of their hands, and it seems that we do not sufficiently consider the special conditions of the aid which it is the object of the common school to assure to them, and which ought to be as the intellectual and moral *viaticum* of their whole existence."

Finally, the author of the law of 1881 on primary instruction, Paul Bert, said to the same effect :

"There is no need that any one should misunderstand our real thought. We do not demand that the common school become a professional school; we do not believe that one ought to come from it either a locksmith or a vine-dresser. This is the business of trade-schools or shops, which ought to train artisans, while the school, accomplishing a much more general work, trains men and citizens. But we believe that scientific instruction ought not to rest in the domain of pure theory, but that practical applications to the different industries ought to hold a large place in it. Now it seems to us necessary, in order that this practical instruction may bear all its fruits, that the child should learn to handle the principal tools by the aid of which man is made the master of the materials which are furnished him by nature and the fundamental industries, — wood, the metals, leather, etc. In this innovation we think we see a triple advantage : — a physical advantage, for in learning to use the plane, the saw, the hammer, the child will complete his gymnastic education, and will acquire a manual dexterity which will always be useful to him, whatever he may afterwards do, and will hold him in readiness, now and always, for all apprenticeships; an intellectual advantage, for the thousand little difficulties which he will meet with will accustom him to observation and reflection ; a social advantage, it may be said, for after having appreciated by his own experience the qualities necessary for success in professional duties and for becoming a skillful workman, there is not the least fear that if fortune favors him, to whatever position he may afterwards come, he will despise those of his companions who always work with their hands."

472. MANUAL INDUSTRIES IN SCHOOLS FOR BOYS. — The orders and the programme of 1882 have organized manual labor in the common schools for boys, as follows:

"For the manual labor of boys the exercises are divided into two groups: One comprises the different exercises intended in a general way to limber the fingers and give dexterity, suppleness, rapidity, and accuracy of movement; the other group comprises graduated exercises in moulding, which serve as a complement to the corresponding study of drawing, and particularly of industrial drawing."

ELEMENTARY COURSE. — Manual exercises intended to give manual dexterity. — Cutting of card-board in the forms of geometrical solids. — Basket-work: Union of splints of different colors. — Moulding: Reproduction of geometrical solids and of very simple objects."

INTERMEDIATE COURSE. — Construction of objects of card-board covered with colored drawings and with colored paper. — Trinkets of wire: lattice-work. — Combinations of wire and wood: Cages. — Moulding: Simple architectural ornaments. — Notions on the most common tools.

HIGHER COURSE. — Combined exercises of drawing and moulding; rough drafts of objects to be executed, and construction of these objects according to the sketches, or *vice versa.* — Study of the principal tools employed in wood-work. Practical graduated exercises. Planing and sawing wood, simple unions. Boxes nailed or put together without nails. Wood-turning, the turning of very simple objects. — Study of the principal tools used in iron-work, the use of the file, paring or finishing of rough objects from the forge or foundry."

473. BY WHOM THE LESSONS IN MANUAL INDUSTRY OUGHT TO BE GIVEN. — In the actual state of affairs, the elemen-

tary lessons in manual labor in the common school are
given by the teacher. In the higher common schools resort
is most often made to outside workmen who bring to the
school the co-operation of a thorough experience in the
trade which they have practiced all their life. The ideal
would be, however, that in the higher common school the
manual labor, like the school exercises, should be intrusted
to the teachers themselves; and this is why a recent order
has required that the examination for a higher certificate
should include an obligatory test in manual labor.

474. ORDER TO BE FOLLOWED. — During the first years
of the common school, the child, who is ignorant of everything, has so many things to learn that it is only with discretion that we must impose on him exercises in manual
labor, but in the higher courses we should become more
exacting.

During the period from seven to ten years we must not
require a great display of physical force; the child must
be exercised only in slight tasks which develop his manual
dexterity. Drawing, cutting, making boxes of card-board,
which permit him to obtain objects of various forms and
colors, will call into play at the same time his intelligence,
his attention, and his versatility. To these tasks will be
added the making of little pieces of basket-work and the
construction of metallic lattice-work, making necessary the
use of light tools. At this stage the purpose should be to
make children really produce objects which they can take
home and exhibit as their own work. Some specimens
marked with the name of each child will be left at school
and will form parts of the school museum.

During the period from ten to twelve years the children
should be familiarized with most of the tools used in wood-
work, and trained to use the lathe and initiated to the handling of the file.

During the whole period of school life the practice of moulding will serve to promote the skill and the deftness of the hand.

Of course this professional education ought to be kept within wise limits, so as not to do prejudice to the ordinary studies. The school ought not to become a workshop; it ought merely to prepare for the different manual industries by inspiring the taste and by beginning to train the aptitudes which they require.

475. THE TEACHING OF AGRICULTURE. — The most of our common schools are rural schools. The majority of the children who attend them are to become field-laborers; hence the particular importance of lessons in agriculture.

It is in the garden of the school that these lessons ought at first to be given; later they will be continued in excursions. They will not constitute, at least during the first years, a consecutive and didactic course. They will bear on the nature of the soil, upon fertilizers, upon the ordinary farm tools, and upon the different varieties of field-labor.

In the higher course, the purpose will be to give to these subjects a more methodical character; and an extension will be given to them by calling the attention of children to domestic animals and even to the keeping of farm accounts.

There will be added to these general notions exact information on arboriculture and horticulture; upon the principal processes for the multiplication of vegetables, and on the most important methods of grafting. Outside of the special lessons, it will be easy for an attentive teacher to give to his instruction a rural coloring through the choice of dictation exercises, problems, and reading lessons. The teaching of the physical and the natural sciences is particularly adapted to this purpose, and as often as possible there should be drawn from them practical conclusions which pertain to rural industry.

476. MILITARY DRILL. — A child of our common schools is not only a future workman, but a future soldier. The school would fall short of its mission, which is to prepare for life, for complete living, if it did not devote a few hours to military drill.

"The most of our country conscripts reach the regiment awkward, ungainly, heavy in body and sometimes in mind, without carriage, without ever having had a sword in hand, and too often without ever having fired a gun. For two years they must with great difficulty be taught what they might have learned with so much pleasure while they were children; and it is very fortunate if the drudgery, the punishments, and the dry theory do not give them a hatred for the military vocation." [1]

Through the military exercises of the school the legislator will be permitted to shorten the period of actual service in the regiment without compromising the national strength. From the moment of joining the regiment we shall have, not ungainly conscripts, but young men already broken to military tactics, and capable of handling a gun and of using it. By this means also we shall repair in part the military reputation of the French nation, which precisely, because it loves peace, and wishes to preserve it, ought to prepare itself to be, in the day of danger, a people of citizen-soldiers.

The evolutions of these school battalions, which are becoming more and more customary, are not, then, a vain parade. The children, who take great pleasure in them, are not playing soldier, but are seriously doing a serious thing,

---

[1] Paul Bert, *De l' Éducation civique.*

a useful and patriotic thing. They are preparing to be the defenders of the country and of the Republic.

477. DRILL IN SHOOTING. — The official programme is right in requiring not only drill in marching, counter-marching, alignment, etc., but also in imposing preparatory drill in shooting and a practical study of the mechanism of the gun.

On leaving school, and during the interval between the thirteenth and twenty-first year, the child should become a member of the shooting societies which are established almost everywhere in the country, and which are called to render important services. But this cannot be unless in the school itself he has received an adequate preparation. But the military drill should not encroach on the hours devoted to study; and the order of 1882 wisely directs that the battalion drill shall take place only on Thursday and Sunday, the time to be devoted to the purpose to be determined by the military instructor in concert with the director of the school.

478. OTHER PRACTICAL EXERCISES. — It is not only the natural and physical sciences which lead to practical appli-cations. Geometry also leads the pupils of the common school to the simpler operation of surveying and leveling; and arithmetic conducts them to an apprenticeship in book-keeping.

In general, a practical turn must be given to each branch of study, and it must never be forgotten that instruction is an apprenticeship in real life.

479. MANUAL INDUSTRIES IN SCHOOLS FOR GIRLS. — It is especially in the manual industries that the distinction of the sexes ought to occasion noticeable differences in procedure. On this subject the programme of 1882 speaks as follows:

" The manual labor for girls, besides the work in cutting and sewing, allows a certain number of lessons, conferences, and exercises, by means of which the mistress will attempt, not to give a regular course in domestic economy, but to inspire young women,. through a great number of practical examples, with a love of order; to make them acquire the substantial qualities of the housewife ; and to put them on guard against frivolous and dangerous inclinations."

480. Needle-work. — Even in the maternal school, after having been initiated into the little kindergarten exercises (weaving, folding, plaiting), the little girl will be trained in little tasks of knitting.

The weaving consists in doing with a warp and woof of paper a work analogous to that of a weaver.

The folding consists in giving different forms to a square piece of paper.

481. Domestic Sewing. — Doubtless we must not over-look the exercises in embroidery, tapestry, lace-making, fine sewing, and fancy work, which are carried on in a great number of schools ; but what is even more important, and what should be encouraged above all else, is work of current use, simple, ordinary work, which gives proof of a wholly practical purpose, and which does not aim at passing beyond the requirements of ordinary domestic needs. A single word is sufficient to characterize what the sewing in the common school ought to be : " Domestic Sewing." Official instruc-tions have often been given that no work in sewing shall be done in the school which is not required for household use in particular.

Let us add that it is less important to have the child pro-duce fine pieces of work at once, than to put her in a condition to use her fingers with agility and skill in her future work. M. Gréard thinks that some entertaining reading ought to take place while the pupils are devoting themselves to manual labor. He demands besides that we distinguish the labor of the workshop, which employs children rather than trains them, — the "workshop" deriving advantage from its products, and the products being as much more valuable as the same operations are always intrusted to the same hands which have here acquired a marvelous dexterity, — from the teaching of the school, which requires all its pupils to pass through the progressive series of all the useful exercises.

482. ABUSES OF MANUAL LABOR. — For our part we cannot consent to quote as models to be followed the schools where the teacher has her pupils do work in sewing which she sells at the ordinary price, and then divides the proceeds among the children.[1] This spirit of gain and these commercial habits are not in keeping in a school.

From this point of view, Madame Pape-Carpantier has vigorously denounced the abuse of manual labor in the case of children.

"No; the child cannot fairly become a producer, — that is to say, have something to dispose of, except after having previously acquired all that he needs within himself and for himself. Does the silk-worm spin before having been nourished on the leaves whence she draws her precious web? Must not the child, like the earth, be cultivated before producing? And what can a child produce at an age when everything in him is frail, tender, and still filled with maternal milk? I have been told what he produces: 'A few cents a day.' A few cents! Is such a revenue indispensable? And how is the child made to produce such a wretched pittance? By making him perform the function of a low-priced instrument; by con-

---

[1] See M. Vincent, *Cours de pédagogie*, p. 270.

straining his young turbulence to exercise only certain muscles; to execute only such movements as he will have to repeat every day of his life; by developing to excess in him the force which is needed by his trade, to the detriment of those which he has no occasion for; and finally, by breaking without scruple, in those young organizations, that equilibrium, that balance of forces, which is the very power and the most admirable mani-festation of God in the universe."

483. DOMESTIC ECONOMY. — Sewing is not the only oc-cupation of the household now, consequently the only item in the school apprenticeship of girls, with respect to manual labor. Ideas on domestic economy in general, with the practical exercise connected with them, ought also to form a part of their elementary instruction.

"Why is not the common school which receives the daughter of the laborer practical enough to descend to the teaching, appar-ently so undignified, but so fruitful in hygienic and even in moral results, of the cost of alimentation or of cooking, if we must call it by its proper name ? "

By way of illustration, here is the programme followed in the schools of Belgium, for instruction in domestic economy :

1. Conditions necessary for a healthy home. Ventilation. Cleanliness.
2. Furniture and its care.
3. Warming and lighting.
4. Washing. The use of soap and of liquid chlorides. Re-moval of grease.
5. Care of linen, bed-clothing, and garments.
6. Practical suggestions as to alimentation, quality of foods, and their preservation.
7. General instruction as to culinary preparation.
8. Drinks.

---

[1] F. Cadet.

9. Kitchen closets.
10. Toilet of young people.
11. Family receipts and expenses.

In a programme so extended there are doubtless some unnecessary items; but in a general way, instruction in domestic economy ought to bear on these different subjects.

484. CONCLUSION. — We have now reached the limit of our studies on the different parts of the programme for the common schools. In order to sum up their general spirit we cannot do better than reproduce in this place one or two pages from M. Gréard.

"If such is the aim of common-school instruction, it is evident that its value depends mainly upon its method, and the method which is best adapted to it may be described in a few words.

"Shun all written tasks which give a false direction to instruction on the pretense of raising its character, such as complicated and curious specimens of penmanship, inordinate transcripts of lectures, written tables of analyses and conjugations, definitions that are not understood; be sparing in precepts, but multiply examples; never forget that the best book for the child is the speaking voice of the teacher; use his memory, so supple and sure, only as a point of support, and proceed in such a way that your instruction penetrate to his intelligence, which can alone preserve its fruitful impress; lead the pupil from the simple to the complex, from the easy to the difficult, from the application to the principle; conduct him by well-connected questions to discover what you wish to show him; habituate him to reason, make him discover, make him see; — in a word, keep his reason incessantly in motion, his intelligence on the alert. For this purpose leave nothing obscure which deserves explanation, push demonstrations even

---

[1] M. Gréard, *L'Instruction primaire à Paris de* 1872.

to the material representation of things whenever it is possible; in each subject disengage from the confused facts which encumber the intelligence the characteristic facts and the simple rules which illumine it; in every subject wind up with judicious applications, useful or moral; in reading, for example, draw from the selection read all the instructive explanations, and all the advice bearing on conduct which it permits; in grammar, start from the example in order to reach the rule divested of the subtilties of grammatical scholastics; choose the texts for written dictation exercises from among the simplest and purest selections in classical works; draw the subjects of oral exercises, not from collections constructed at pleasure to complicate the difficulties of language, but from matters of current interest, from an incident in the school, from the lessons of the day, from passages in sacred history, in the history of France, or in a recent lesson in geography; invent examples before the eyes of the pupil to sharpen his attention; let him invent them himself and always record them on the blackboard; reduce all arithmetical operations to practical exercises borrowed from the usages of life; teach geography only from the map by gradually extending the child's horizon from the street to the quarter, from the quarter to the commune, to the canton, to the department, to France, to the world; animate the topographical description of places by picturing the peculiarities of configuration which they present, by explaining the natural and industrial productions which are peculiar to them, and by recalling the events which remind us of them; in history give to the different epochs an attention corresponding with their relative importance, and traverse the first centuries more rapidly in order to dwell on those which are more directly related to us; sacrifice without scruple details of pure erudition in order to throw into relief the broad lines of national development; look for the sequel of this development, less in the succession of wars than in the rational concatenation of institutions, in the progress of social ideas, in the conquests of the mind which are the true conquests of Christian civilization; place before the child's eyes

men and things through paintings which enlarge his imagination and elevate his soul; make of France what Pascal
said of humanity, a grand being who subsists perpetually, and
by this means give the child an idea of his country, of the
duties which she imposes, of the sacrifices which she requires.
Such ought to be the spirit of the lessons of the school."

CHAPTER XI.

REWARDS AND PUNISHMENTS.

485. SCHOOL DISCIPLINE. — Discipline is that part of education which, on the one hand, immediately assures the industry of pupils by maintaining good order in the school and exciting their zeal, and which, on the other hand, working for a more remote and higher purpose, prevents or represses irregularities of conduct and tends to train resolute wills and energetic characters capable of self-control. It has the double purpose of establishing the actual government of the school and of teaching pupils to govern themselves when they shall have left the school and escaped the tutelage of their masters.

486. MEANS OF DISCIPLINE. — The means of discipline are as various as the instincts of human nature. Children may be led by very different mobiles, which are connected with three or four principal groups : 1. The personal feelings, as fear, pleasure, and self-love ; 2. The affectionate sentiments, as the love of parents and affection for the teacher ; 3. Reflective interest, such as the fear of punishment and the hope of reward ; 4. The idea of duty.

To tell the truth, none of these principles ought to be excluded from the internal government of schools. It would be unwise to forego the precious resources which each of these mobiles furnishes the teacher for securing silence, order, and attention, for encouraging ardor in toil, for cor-

447

recting the faults and developing the good qualities of his pupils. Doubtless the ideal would be that the child, conscious of his interest and comprehending his duty, should work and obey through a disinterested act of his own will; but the nature of the child does not yield to this pure régime of a liberty enlightened and truly mistress of itself. Even the mature man is not always capable of self-direction through the idea of right alone; he needs the stimulants of emulation, the solicitation of pleasures, and the salutary fear of the laws. Then do not require of the child an effort which surpasses his powers, but in order to discipline him, appeal in turn to the different inclinations of his soul.

Means of discipline consist precisely in acting on these inclinations; they call into play the springs of activity. The best are those which interest the greatest number of feelings at the same time, and which are supported by the greatest number of ideas. There could be nothing worse than a system of exclusive discipline which tended to develop but a single emotion, as fear, or self-love, or affection itself.

487. EMULATION. — Of all the principles of action which make scholars studious and classes orderly, there is none more powerful than emulation. It is to emulation that is due the efficacy of rewards, and it is emulation above all which animates the school and gives it the spirit of industry. As a disciplinary motive, emulation owes its superiority mainly to its complex character and to the multiplicity of the feelings which it puts in train.

488. DEFINITION OF EMULATION. — Emulation, like all the feelings of the soul, is a thing difficult to define. There enter into it different elements which disturb its simplicity, the analysis of which is difficult. Emulation is above all a personal feeling based on self-love. It might be defined

self-love in act, which is not satisfied with the advantages it already has, but wishes to acquire new ones. By its nature it resembles ambition or the desire for glory; but it is an ambition which has reference to others, which is a rival with concurrent ambitions, which aspires to success, not for the success itself, but for the purpose of surpassing others.

489. THE DIFFERENT ELEMENTS OF EMULATION. — Certain educators are wrong in confounding emulation with the instinct of imitation. Doubtless the emulous man the more often imitates his rivals; but often he also wishes to do differently from them for the purpose of doing better. We do not deny that imitation plays an important part in emulation; but it does not constitute the basis of it, and is but one of the means which emulation employs to reach its ends.

Although composed chiefly of self-love, emulation is still not a desire exclusively personal and selfish. When it is what it ought to be, a noble and spirited sentiment, there is always mingled with it a secret aspiration towards what is good, something of a pure love of perfection. Of course the emulous man wishes above all else to equal or surpass his competitors, but he also pursues an ideal. In every case the duty of the teacher ought to be to develop emulation in this direction, by diverting it from its selfish tendencies, in order to direct it towards the pursuit of the good.

Diderot clearly defined the double nature of emulation, without neglecting to throw into relief the predominance of self-love, when he said:[1]

"Emulation is not exactly the desire to do the best that is possible, — that would be a pure virtue; but it is the desire to do better than others, which approaches vanity. Notwith-

---

[1] See especially the article *Émulation*, in the *Dictionnaire de pédagogie.*

standing this defective side, it is none the less the source of
the most beautiful things in society. Superiority is a general
inclination. The most active pleasure is that of glory; the
thing is to present to it estimable objects; and self-love will
always be the greatest resource in a civilized land."

490. EMULATION IN THE HISTORY OF PEDAGOGY. — In
all times emulation has been known and commended as one
of the essential means of discipline. At Sparta it may be
said that emulation was pushed even to fanaticism; preference was given to him who was the most courageous, the
most temperate, the most insensible to pain. At Athens
how emulous was Themistocles, whose sleep was troubled
by the laurels of Miltiades! Rabelais said of his model
preceptor, that he introduced Gargantua to a company of
learned men, " to emulate whom inspired him with the spirit
and the desire to do valiantly." It is well known that
Bossuet, in order to counteract the indolence of the Dauphin, made him compete with the children of his own
age. "Emulation," says Fénelon, "is a spur to virtue."
According to Locke, all is done, everything is gained,
when we have stirred the pupil's spirit of emulation!
Rousseau, who isolates Émile and allows him no companions, wishes at least that his pupil should find a rival in
himself, and so invents a sort of personal emulation. And
in an article in the *Encyclopædia* he wrote as follows:
" Emulation is a disposition dangerous to the truth, but
education can transform it into a sublime virtue." Rollin
would have us appeal to the reason of children, stimulate
the sense of honor, and make use of praise, rewards,
and caresses.

---

[1] "There is," says M. Feuillet, "in solitary education a species of
emulation, or rather an image of emulation, which is the result of
the comparison which one is led to make of himself with himself;
and hence arises the desire to surpass one's self."

"Children," he says, "are sensible to praise. We must take advantage of this weakness, and try to make a virtue of it. We would run the risk of discouraging them, if we never praised them when they did well. Though praise is to be feared on the score of vanity, we must try to make use of it to animate children without enervating them. For of all the motives adapted to touch a reasonable soul, there are none more powerful than honor and shame; and when children have been made sensible to them, all has been gained."

Madame Campan declared that "emulation constituted the strength of public education." It there reigns over young minds, directs them toward the good, and does no harm to the generous sentiments of the heart and soul.

491. EMULATION IN A DEMOCRACY. — It is useless to prolong this historical review, for it would almost always lead to the same result, a more or less complete approval of the use of emulation in discipline. Let us merely add, that in a democratic society like our own, at a time when it is necessary to summon millions of children to exertion, emulation becomes more and more important. This has, been forcibly expressed by M. Feuillet.

"Emulation was formerly but the worst species of ambition; its purpose was to reach the highest places to which only a small number of subjects could have access. In this way emulation was concentrated instead of being extended. . . . It ought to be otherwise in a republic. . . . It is felt that the main purpose of education can no longer be to obtain a small number of exceptional but superior men, but that its essential purpose is to train that immense majority of good, wise, and useful citizens who, in all the places where circumstances have carried them, unite to form what is called the state. The methods of education then necessarily change with its purpose. Emulation is diffused, so to speak, so as to embrace all ranks and to bring all individuals under its influence."

And Feuillet concludes as follows :

"*Equality*, and by a necessary consequence *reciprocal depend-ence* and *general emulation*, are the conditions to which the happiness of men is invariably attached in all the circum-stances composing the state of society; and consequently these are the conditions which ought to be provided for by the education thât is alone good and true, that which trains citizens."[1]

492. ERROR OF THOSE WHO CONDEMN EMULATION. — The educators who condemn emulation deceive themselves on two points. On the one hand they have too great a dis-trust of human nature ; in their eyes the feeling of self-love is like a poisonous stock which can bear only evil fruit ; they think that to favor emulation is by a necessary con-sequence surely to engender envy, jealous rivalry, and malevolence.

We must reply to them, with La Bruyère, " that, whatever connection there may seem to be between jealousy and emulation, there is between them the same distance that is found between vice and virtue. Emulation is an energetic, courageous sentiment, which renders the soul fruitful, makes it profit by great examples, and often carries it above that which it admires."

On the other hand, by a contrary illusion to forego the aid of emulation is to count too much on the powers of the human soul, and to believe that the child can be excited to exertion by purely disinterested motives, by the simple idea of the duty to be performed, without the need of calling into play his personal instincts. This is to forget what Pascal said :

" The children of Port Royal are falling into indifference through default of ambition."

---

[1] M. Feuillet, *Mémoire sur l'emulation*, crowned by the Institute in **1801.**

493. Rocks to Shun. — The educators who exclude emulation have pointed out the rocks on which we are liable accidentally to fall when we make a bad use of it, but have not been so successful in discovering the irremediable dangers to which all those who employ it are inevitably exposed.

The charges they bring against emulation are the following : " 1. The attention of children is turned aside from the thought of duty and is fixed on the reward. 2. Children are made to honor success rather than merit. 3. The vanity of some is unduly excited, while the others are forever humiliated and discouraged. 4. Hatred and jealousy among companions is provoked. 5. There is contracted for life the detestable habit of seeking for distinction, of striving for the highest place, of seeking honors, and of not being contented with a modest position and an obscure tranquillity."

As a fact, these disadvantages may result from emulation, badly conceived and directed ; but they will be shunned without much difficulty by a skillful teacher, who will take care not to materialize emulation, not to take account merely of the material qualities of his pupils, who will not make a misuse of artificial rewards, who will know how to reassure the conquered and prevent them from feeling too keenly the bitterness of their defeat, at the same time that he will recall the conquerors to a sense of modesty ; who, in a word, will not give too great attention to the spring of emulation, and will not allow it to fall into the dangerous over-excitement of ambition.

494. Rewards. — When we admit emulation as a principle of discipline we at the same time admit rewards. In fact, rewards are the best means of vivifying and animating the feeling of emulation. However desirous we may be that the child shall actually find the best of rewards in the feeling of a duty done or in the consciousness of his progress, it would be folly to deprive ourselves of the aid which might come to discipline from rewards skillfully chosen and discreetly distributed.

495. DIFFERENT SPECIES OF REWARDS. — But there are rewards and rewards. They vary especially according to the nature of the feelings which they aim at and which they affect in the child. For example, they are sometimes addressed only to the affectionate sentiments, as endearments ; or they flatter self-love and the desire of approbation, like praise ; or they respond only to the lower tastes of the sensibility, like dainties ; or, finally, they awaken the selfish instincts, like prizes. Let us add that these different elements may be confounded in the rewards that are given, and that in order to estimate their educative value it is necessary to take a strict account of the character of the different feelings which they excite.

496. SENSIBLE REWARDS. — We must absolutely proscribe purely material rewards, which are not permissible save with very young children, who may be influenced by the allurement of sweetmeats. As soon as possible the child ought to be accustomed to seek the reward of his toil and his efforts in the satisfaction of his higher inclinations.

497. PRAISE AND COMMENDATION. — "The best rewards," says M. Rendu, "are those which, divested of material value, call into play the delicate sentiments without exciting any idea of personal interest." Of this sort are the words of approbation and the commendation of the teacher. They excite the feeling of honor. They are, moreover, as much the more efficacious as the teacher has been able to make himself loved and respected by his pupils. In a school where the teacher's authority is firmly established, and where the pupils

have self-love, the rewards may be reduced to commendations. But care must be taken to employ this means only with caution, for fear of exciting pride and vanity.

" The schoolmaster's means of reward is chiefly confined to approbation or praise, a great and flexible instrument, yet needing delicate manipulation. Some kinds of merit are so palpable as to be described by numerical marks. Equal, in point of distinctness, is the fact that a thing is right or wrong, in part or in whole; it is sufficient approbation to pronounce that a question is correctly answered, a passage properly explained. This is the praise that envy cannot assail. Most unsafe are phrases of commendation ; much care is required to make them both discriminating and just. They need to have a palpable basis in facts. Distinguished merit should not always be attended with pæans; silent recognition is the rule, the exceptions must be such as to extort admiration from the most jealous. The controlling circumstance is the presence of the collective body; the teacher is not speaking for himself alone, but directing the sentiments of a multitude, with which he should never be at variance ; his strictly private judgments should be privately conveyed." [1]

498. OTHER REWARDS. — In general, rewards ought to be but the exterior signs of the teacher's approbation.

Of this description are good marks, place in class according to records of recitations, certificates of approval, inscription on the roll of honor, prizes. Some teachers also recommend medals and decorations.

499. THE DISTRIBUTION OF PRIZES. — We cannot too much encourage the custom, recently introduced into the common schools, of formal distribution of prizes.

" Many common schools," said the ministerial circular of 1864, " have no celebration at the end of the year, where

---

[1] Bain, *Education as a Science*, pp. 113, 114.

good conduct and industry are publicly rewarded. The result is that we find in these schools but little emulation, and that a part of the pupils desert them for a portion of the year. It were well, however, that each village should have its annual celebration for children and their work. The expense involved would be small, and if this could not be met by public tax, individuals, I am sure, would think it an honor to bear it. It will not be difficult for you to persuade the proper officers of each department that the money spent on children is, from every point of view, the money invested at a high rate of interest."

"I am firm in the belief," says another circular, "that this custom would be excellent, on the express condition that the prizes shall be distributed with discretion, so as to be given only to the most deserving pupils."

500. PUNISHMENTS. — Punishments are based on almost the same principles as rewards. Rewards appeal mainly to the feeling of honor or to self-love. Punishments sometimes have the same character,— they tend to humiliate the pupil, to make him ashamed of his faults publicly denounced. But in general their purpose is to wound the sensibilities of the child by depriving him of things which he loves, just as rewards excite him by giving him what pleases him.

501. REPRIMANDS. — Just as praise and words of approbation are the best and the most convenient of rewards, so reprimands, censure, and tokens of disapproval are the promptest and the surest of punishments ; on condition, of course, that the children have previously been made sensitive to shame, and that they love and esteem their teacher.

The very fact of revealing before companions a fault that has been committed, and that the culprit cannot deny, is in itself an effective punishment. There will be added to this, when the nature of the offence requires it, words of censure which will make the pupil blush.

The thing of most importance in the use of reprimands and censure is, first, not to make an over-use of them. Teachers who are always scolding finally cease to be heeded. If the reprimand becomes stale, if it is resorted to too frequently, it loses all its effect. In the second place, it must be exactly proportioned to the fault which it points out and which it proposes to correct. The teacher will no longer be respected if he does not exhibit the strictest spirit of justice in his words. Besides, the tone of the reprimand ought always to be moderate, calm, and dignified. If the teacher loses his temper, his anger, as Mr. Bain remarks, is a real victory for the bad pupils, even when it has inspired them with a momentary fear.

"Never correct a child," says Fénelon, "either in the first flush of his anger or of your own. If in yours, he sees that you are acting from passion or from impulse, and not from reason and affection, and you lose your authority without recall. If in his, he has not enough liberty of thought to acknowledge his fault, to conquer his passion, and to feel the importance of your advice; it is even exposing the child to the risk of losing the respect he owes you. Always show him that you are your own master; and nothing will better make him see this than your patience."

502. THREATS. — Before proceeding to actual punishment it is wise to warn the child of the consequences that will follow a repetition of his fault. He must not be summarily punished, but must first be warned. But threats ought always to be followed by acts. The pupil laughs at a teacher who never goes further than words, who never executes his threat.

503. ACTUAL PUNISHMENTS. — The penal code of the school contains many articles, especially if we study it in the ancient systems of education; but with the progress in manners it has been gradually moderated.

In the maternal schools the only punishments allowed are the following : "Interdiction, for a very short time, of study and play in common; withdrawal of good marks."

In the common schools the teacher ought to make use of the same punishments, — partial loss of recreation, keeping the pupil after school, suspension, or expulsion.

Privation of recreation ought never to be of long duration. On the pretext of punishing the child, he should not be denied the rest and play which are as necessary for his physical health as for his intelligence.

"Detention from play," says Mr. Bain, "or keeping in after hours, is very galling to the young; and it ought to suffice for even serious offences, especially for riotous and unruly tendencies, for which it has all the merits of 'characteristicalness.' The excess of activity and aggressiveness is met by withholding the ordinary legitimate outlets." [1]

The expulsion of the pupil is evidently an extreme remedy and a sort of confession of the weakness of the school discipline ; but the fear of this punishment, if it has overtaken incorrigible pupils in one or two cases, is a very effective example for all the others.

504. Tasks or Impositions. — A great abuse was formerly made of *pensums*, or supplementary tasks ; perhaps it has been a mistake to proscribe them absolutely.

"Tasks or impositions," says Mr. Bain, "are the usual punishment of neglect of lessons, and are also employed for rebelliousness; the pain lies in the intellectual *ennui*, which is severe to those that have no liking for books in any shape. They also possess the irksomeness of confinement and fatigue-drill. They may be superadded to shame, and the combination is a formidable penalty." [2]

---

[1] Bain, *Education as a Science.* pp. 115, 116.
[2] Bain, *Education as a Science,* p. 116.

505. CORPORAL PUNISHMENTS. — In France the regulations, as well as the manners, absolutely condemn the corporal chastisements which for so many centuries were comprised among the *legitima pœnarum genera*. Even Pestalozzi, the good and mild Pestalozzi, used and abused this mode of punishment, and had their use sanctioned by the unanimous consent of his pupils. In England public opinion is still generally favorable to corporal punishment, and it is sanctioned by Mr. Bain.

"Where corporal punishment is kept up, it should be at the far end of the list of penalties; its slightest application should be accounted the worst disgrace, and should be accompanied with stigmatizing forms. It should be regarded as a deep injury to the person that inflicts it, and to those that have to witness it, as the height of shame and infamy. It ought not to be repeated with the same pupil; if two or three applications are not enough, removal is the proper course." [1]

We shall not enter upon this casuistry of corporal chastisements. They must be absolutely forbidden, and in every case, because, as Locke says, they constitute a servile discipline which renders souls servile.

506. GENERAL RULES. — Whatever may be the punishment employed, it will always be necessary to follow some general principles.

First, let the punishment always be accommodated to the fault committed, and also to the sensibility of the culprit. A given pupil may be profoundly affected by a light punishment which will leave less sensitive pupils absolutely unaffected.

Punishment should not be employed lavishly; repetition

---

[1] Bain, *Education as a Science*, pp. 116, 117.

soon destroys its efficacy, and there is nothing good to be expected of a child hardened by punishment. "Carefully avoid punishing all the faults of your girls," said Madame de Maintenon; "the punishments would become common, and would no longer produce an impression."

Penalties should be carefully graduated. "It is a rule in punishment," says Mr. Bain, "to try slight penalties at first. With the better natures the mere idea of punishment is enough; severity is entirely unnecessary."

Special efforts should be made to establish in the child's mind an intimate relation between the penalty and the wrong that has been done. For this purpose the punishment should, so far as possible, be connected with the fault. If a child has told a falsehood he should be humiliated by no longer believing his word; if another is indiscreet, confidence is no longer placed in him; if another is always quarreling, let him be shunned by his companions. In this way the punishment is better understood and is more effective, because it seems to the child the natural consequence of his fault.

507. THE DISCIPLINE OF CONSEQUENCES. — In our day Herbert Spencer has popularized the system which consists in suppressing the whole machinery of artificial punishments, in order to leave a free field for the action of nature. The purpose is to make the child feel the consequences of the acts which he commits. What more striking punishment than these very consequences!

"All the punishments of human invention are powerless. The only chastisements truly salutary are those which nature creates on the spot and applies. No threats, but a silent and rigorous execution. The hot coal burns him who touches it the first time; it burns him the second, a third time; it burns him every time. There is nothing like this immediate, direct, inevitable correction. Observe also that the penalty is always in proportion to the violation of the order of things, the reaction being in correspondence with the action; and that it introduces along with it in the mind of the child the idea of justice, the chastisement being but an effect; and finally, that there is no effect more certain. Universal language testifies to this. Experience dearly bought, bitter experience, is the great lesson, and the only one by which we profit." [1]

508. CRITICISM OF THIS SYSTEM. — However seductive this doctrine of natural reactions may at first appear, it is evident, after reflection, that it could not suffice to constitute with respect to the correction and repression of faults, a system of school discipline. For a certain number of cases to which it may be usefully applied, how many others there are where it would be absolutely inefficient! Let us admit, although it is not true, that every fault, every violation of the order of nature, entails by a natural necessity a painful result. In most cases this will be but a remote consequence on long credit; and the culprit will be able to repeat his faults thousands of times before the punishment flashes upon him. School delinquencies are for the most part of such a nature that the child has not to suffer immediately for being allowed to have his own way. Lack of application and indolence will compromise the entire life of a negligent scholar. Having become a man, he will repent at the age of thirty in an idle existence which he will be unable to employ to any good purpose, for having been an inattentive and an irregular pupil. But when he perceives the consequences of his indolence, it will be too late, — the evil will have been done. The punishment will doubtless be striking, pitiless, justly deserved. The culprit will be obliged

---

[1] We borrow this analysis of Mr. Spencer's opinion from M. Gré ard's *Memoir sur l' Esprit de discipline dans l' éducation*.

to bow before it, as before an inexorable but just fate. But the purpose of punishments is even more to prevent wrong and to correct it in time, than to cause expiation for it in an exemplary way.

509. OTHER CRITICISMS. — It would be easy to show that, from still other points of view, Mr. Spencer's theory is not in accord with the ideal punishment.

"The pain produced by natural consequences," says M. Gréard, "is most often enormous with respect to the fault which has produced them; and man himself claims for his conduct other penalties than those of a hard reality. He would have us judge the intention as well as the fact; he would have us give him credit for his efforts; and would have us punish him, if need be, but without destroying him, and while reaching out a hand to lift him up."

In a word, there is nothing more brutal, more inhuman, than the system which, suppressing all human intervention of the teacher in the correction of the child, leaves to nature alone the task of chastising him. Slow in certain cases, the justice of nature is often violent and murderous. Let us add, finally, that the system of natural consequences suppresses moral ideas, — the idea of obligation and duty. It confronts the child only with the blind and unconscious forces of necessity. And so Mr. Spencer does not hold to his theory to the end, but to the reactions of nature he adds the reactions of the feelings which manifest themselves through the esteem and the affection, or through the censure and the coolness of those who surround the child, and whom he loves. The discipline of nature can be but a preparation for the discipline of sentiments and ideas.

CHAPTER XII.

DISCIPLINE IN GENERAL.

510. PREVENTIVE DISCIPLINE. — Discipline does not depend merely on a system of rewards and punishments *ex post facto*, as so many sanctions to incite to the good or to divert from the evil. True discipline foresees and prevents, even more than it represses and rewards. In a well-organized school which satisfies certain material conditions, and in which the teacher fulfills certain moral conditions which assure his authority, it will hardly ever be necessary to resort to punishment, and rewards will appear rather as a disinterested act of justice than as a means of discipline.

511. MATERIAL CONDITIONS OF DISCIPLINE. — All teachers know how much the regularity and system which they introduce into the exercises of the school facilitate their task and contribute to the good order of their class. Pestalozzi, who had so many moral qualifications, who possessed to such a high degree the art of making himself loved by children, who employed such devotion and zeal in the service of his pupils, was never able to establish an exact discipline, because he was lacking in method and taught in a disorderly manner, without subjecting himself to fixed rules for the length of his lessons and for the order of exercises; in a word, for the distribution of his time.

512. DISTRIBUTION OF TIME. — "The distribution of time," says Rendu, "is the principal means of establishing

463

discipline. . . . The question of discipline is in great part a question of instruction and method."

Through the indications of the programme, which determines at once the topics of instruction and the number of hours which it is advisable to give to each study in the three grades of the common school, the teacher is now guided in the distribution of his time, and no longer runs the risk of falling into mistakes. Let us add, however, that circumstances, such as the requirements of time and place, the number and relative proficiency of pupils, ought, as between one school and another, to justify considerable differences. We are not of those who dream of an absolute uniformity, and wish that at a given moment the millions of children who attend the schools of France should be engaged in the same exercise.

"The ingenuity of an intelligent teacher ought not to be paralyzed by the rigid inflexibility of a schedule. We do not assume to impose a time-table upon teachers, as a vise which binds them; we offer it to them as a rule to guide them. Doubtless, in the domain of common-school instruction more than in any other sphere of teaching, there must be required regularity, exactness, and the spirit of system; but here as everywhere else it is best to leave something to spontaneity, to personal reflection, and to free choice. We dread the absence of method, which leads to school anarchy; but we detest the circumstantial tyranny which, sinking the man in the master, gives to mechanical education the place due to intelligence." [1]

513. GENERAL PRINCIPLES FOR THE DISTRIBUTION OF TIME. — The distribution of time ought not merely to be regulated in advance by the teacher, but it ought to be brought to the knowledge of the pupils by schedules posted in each class-room.

---

[1] E. Rendu, *Manuel*, p. 32.

Without describing in detail the distribution of study hours and of the different topics of instruction, we will state the general principles which result from all that we have said in the preceding chapters.

1. Each section ought to be engaged in several different exercises. With the pupils of the common school, in particular, we must renounce prolonged lessons upon the same subject. Such lessons are not possible, save in the higher classes of the colleges or in the courses of higher instruction.

2. Each session ought to be interrupted, either by the ordinary recess or by marching and singing.

3. In schools taught by one master, the teacher will each day come into direct communication with all his pupils, and consequently with each one of the three grades. Hence the necessity of *collective lessons*, which may bear on certain parts of history, of morals, etc.

4. Each item in the programme ought each day to have its share in the exercises of the school. None of them ought to be sacrificed, even if but a few minutes can be devoted to some of them.

5. The most difficult exercises, those which require the most attention, ought by preference to come in the early part of the day.

6. The length of each lesson and of each exercise should not as a rule exceed twenty or thirty minutes.

7. Every lesson, every lecture, should be accompanied by oral explanations and interrogations.

8. The correction of tasks and the repetition of lessons take place during the periods assigned to these tasks and lessons. According to the rule the tasks are corrected at the blackboard at the same time that the note-books are inspected. The compositions are corrected by the teacher out of school hours.

514. CLASSIFICATION OF PUPILS. — That which hinders the maintenance of discipline as well as the progress of pupils, is that by the very necessity of things there are united in the same class pupils very unequal in age, in degree of instruction, and in intellectual development. Disorder is almost the necessary result of this disproportion and of these inequalities. Nothing is more important, consequently, than the classification of pupils.

"Each year, at the opening of school," says the official order of 1882, "the pupils, according to the degree of their instruction, shall be distributed by the director in the different classes of the three grades under the supervision of the primary inspector."

This rule is applicable not only to large schools having several teachers, but also to schools with one teacher. And even in the latter the classification ought to be even more exact if it be possible, because the one teacher, obliged to distribute his time among the three grades, ought to be able to depend a little more either upon the initiative of pupils or upon the aid of some intelligent monitors.

515. CONSEQUENCES FROM THE DISCIPLINARY POINT OF VIEW. — Who does not see that discipline will gain from a school organization regulated in this spirit? Invited to an instruction which responds exactly to his powers and to his needs, sustained by the variety of the exercises, reanimated by frequent recreations, always subjected to an invariable rule which he knows, never remaining unemployed, instructed in advance with reference to what he ought to do at the different hours of the day, the pupil will find himself in the best conditions for working with order and profit.

516. NECESSITY OF VIGOROUS SUPERVISION. — Formal rules, however, are not sufficient. The pupil is not yet sufficiently master of himself, sufficiently energetic and well-disposed, to follow spontaneously the course that has been traced for him by a carefully arranged programme. There must be taken into account the weaknesses of will and the thoughtlessness of early age, and the dissipation, indolence, and ill-will common to masses of children. The execution of the laws of the school is dependent on the vigilant eye of the master. How much easier the discipline becomes with an active teacher who observes all the movements of his pupils, who watches their dispositions, who stops by a word or a look the beginning of a conversation, who reanimates the attention at the moment when it begins to flag, who, in a word, always present in the four corners of the class-room, is, so to speak, the living soul of the school.

517. The Teacher's Duties out of School. — But the vigilance and solicitude of a good teacher do not cease at the threshold of the school ; they ought to follow the pupil even into the family, and accompany him in a certain measure on the road which leads him from the school to the home. He may discreetly inform himself of what children do when they have reached home, and how they conduct themselves in the streets or on the roads. Through the influence which he will discreetly exert upon the conduct of his pupils outside of the school, he will assure their correct deportment and the silence and order of the school-room itself. Children who are too wild at home, or who have been too disorderly on the streets, have great difficulty when the bell rings to become by an instantaneous transformation attentive and quiet pupils.

By the personal labor which he will impose upon himself, the teacher will also contribute to the maintenance of good discipline in the school. A well-prepared lesson is worth much more than punishments for gaining the attention of the scholars. When the teacher reaches his desk, well knowing what he ought to do and what he ought to say; when wholly pervaded by his subject he can pursue his thought without effort, he will first have that assurance that he will more easily interest his auditors and that he will more surely conduct them to the desired end ; and at the same time, relieved from the anxiety of hunting up his ideas and his words, and of organizing his class on the spur of the moment and by a sort of improvisation, he will the more easily be able to survey his little auditory, to be all things to all, and to let nothing escape that is incorrect or abnormal in the conduct of his pupils.

Let us add that in order to assure the discipline so far as the pupils' diligence and exactness of works are concerned, the industry of the teacher is particularly necessary. The child of the best intentions is discouraged if the written exercises which he has prepared with the greatest care are never corrected. It is not merely because the faults which he has allowed to pass are proofs of his ignorance, that the lack of correction is mischievous, but mainly because the negligence of the teacher emboldens and partly excuses the negligence of the pupil.

518. CO-OPERATION OF TEACHERS WITH PARENTS. — The best of teachers can do nothing in the matter of discipline without the co-operation of parents. "There is no system of education so poor," says Gréard, "as not to improve in quality by the intervention of the family, and none so good that it cannot gain by it." Rollin regarded the participation of parents in all that concerns moral development as one of the essential factors in the internal government of colleges. What is true of secondary instruction is also true of primary instruction. It is necessary, then, that the teacher should be in constant communication with the

families, that he keep them regularly informed as to the work and progress of their children, and that he bring their faults to their notice. Hence the utility of reports to parents. Happy the teachers who can co-operate with parents and induce them to second their efforts and to supervise the lessons which are to be learned and the tasks that are to be written. From this point of view, the lessons assigned for home study, besides compelling the pupil to work more than the thirty hours required in the school, have this advantage, that they oblige parents to interest themselves in the studies of their children. But home lessons ought to be easy, and should not require the formal machinery which cannot be realized in most families.

"Home duties," says M. Gréard, "ought to be adapted, as the others are, not only to the very limited time which pupils have at their disposal after school, but also and above all to the intensity of the effective efforts which the pupil can make. I am not ignorant of the fact that in assigning these lessons our teachers sometimes do no more than respond to the demands of parents who fear the lack of occupation in the evening, and who estimate work by the quantity of paper that is used. But we ought not to yield to unintelligent desires. It is doubtless well that the pupils of the higher grade should be occupied at home in the evening. Let them engage in the reading of history and geography, in reproducing the explanation of words taken from a lesson in grammar, or in solving some problems in arithmetic. This is all well, but on the express condition that these exercises offer no difficulty which repels the child left to himself, and that they be connected with a lesson on which his memory is fresh, and particularly that they be short."

519. MORAL INFLUENCE OF THE FAMILY. — That which the teacher ought particularly to demand of the family is that it should not dissipate his own efforts, that it should

not contravene his instructions, but that it should add its own more secret, more intimate, more personal action to that which he exerts himself.

"We have the right to expect much from the active co-operation of parents, however little they may desire it. We are not ignorant of the difficulties and obstacles which their perspicacity may encounter. We make allowance for illusions and weaknesses. By reason of their very affection, they are in danger of entertaining too high hopes and of despairing too quickly. The cool and disinterested judgment of a teacher is often necessary to re-establish moderation. And who is nearer the heart of the child than father and mother? Who can better take into account his instinctive propensities and his nascent passions; separate his good qualities from his bad; in his departures from duty distinguish the swooning or transient revolt of radical weakness from obstinate resistance? Who better knows his sensibility, and how to excite it when necessary; to subject him, according to circumstances, to the necessities which arise, and to make him triumph over the difficulties which pertain only to himself? Who can better follow the crises which arrest or hasten his development? In a word, who is better fitted to treat him in all his transformations according to his temperament, and give him the moral régime that is best for him?" [1]

520. MORAL CONDITIONS OF DISCIPLINE. — The co-operation of teachers and parents proceeding in concert, hand in hand, to correct the faults of children and to develop their virtues, is in itself one of the moral conditions of discipline.

Another condition is the character of the teacher, his authority, his moral power. What is true of programmes and methods in instruction is also true of rules in discipline, — their value is given to them by those who apply them. It is at this point that we must always start, whether we have

---

[1] M. Gréard, *Memoir sur l'esprit de discipline.*

to do with the internal government of schools or with that of other human institutions. Begin by having men, and all the rest will be given to you to boot.

521. QUALITIES OF A GOOD TEACHER. — Treatises on pedagogy draw up long catalogues of the qualities of a good teacher. We do not propose in this place to present one of these catalogues in which the pedagogic virtues are numbered, and which require the teachers to have ten or a dozen of them, more or less. The moral education of a teacher has nothing to gain from these fastidious nomenclatures. We shall simply say that the best teacher is he who has to the highest degree the disposal of intellectual and moral qualities; he who on the one hand has the most knowledge, method, clearness, and vivacity of exposition, and on the other is the most energetic, the most devoted to his task, the most attached to his duties, and at the same time has most affection for his pupils.

It would be easy to show that each of these qualities or virtues is an element of discipline.

A teacher whose knowledge is not questioned, who is never obscure in his lessons, who speaks with exactness, will always be listened to with respect.

A teacher whose every act is known to be inspired by love for his pupils, has only to speak to be obeyed. He will govern by persuasion.

Especially a firm teacher, who possesses the serenity of conscious power, will inspire his pupils with a salutary respect which will make it impossible for them to fail in their tasks.

In discussing the law of 1833, Guizot stated the principal qualities which he expected of a teacher in the new schools, as follows:

"All our efforts and all our sacrifices will be useless, if

we do not succeed in finding for the reconstructed public school a competent teacher worthy of the noble mission of instructing the people. It cannot be too often repeated that as is the teacher so is the school. And what a happy union of qualities is necessary to make a good school-master! A good school-master is a man who ought to know much more than he teaches, in order to teach with intelligence and zeal; who ought to live in an humble sphere, and who nevertheless ought to have an elevated soul in order to preserve that dignity of feeling and even of manner without which he will never gain the respect and confidence of families; who ought to possess a rare union of mildness and firmness, for he is the inferior of many people in a commune. But he ought to be the degraded servant of no one; not ignorant of his rights, but thinking much more of his duties; giving an example to all, serving all as an adviser; above all, not desiring to withdraw from his occupation, content with his situation because of the good he is doing in it, resolved to live and die in the bosom of the school, in the service of common-school instruction, which is for him the service of God and of men. To train teachers who approach such a model is a difficult task; and yet we must succeed in it, or we have done nothing for common-school instruction. A bad school-master, like a bad curé or a bad mayor, is a scourge to a commune. We are certainly very often compelled to content ourselves with ordinary teachers, but we must try to train better ones, and for this purpose primary normal schools are indispensable."

522. IMPORTANCE OF PHYSICAL QUALIFICATIONS. — The physical qualities of the teacher are not themselves to be despised as an instrument of discipline. Form, physiognomy, and voice play their part in well-conducted schools. It is useless to insist on those qualities which depend wholly on nature; but what an earnest purpose can control are the general bearing of the body, the appearance of the face, and gestures.

"Never assume without an extreme necessity," said Fénelon, "an austere and imperious air, which makes children tremble. Often it is affectation and pedantry in those who govern."

Without requiring, as Fénelon wished, that the teacher should always have a smiling and jovial face, it is especially important that he be generally amiable and affectionate, and that he shun pedantry and despotic ways.

523. MORAL AUTHORITY OF THE TEACHER. — But physical qualities are of little account compared with moral qualities, which are the principal element of authority. By dint of patience, energy, and activity, a teacher, even physically uncomely, may acquire a real ascendancy over his pupils. The teacher is not truly worthy of his name of master, except when he masters his school by the ascendancy of his moral authority. External and in some sort mechanical means of discipline are worth nothing, unless they are seconded by the moral force which only good teachers possess, and in schools where this moral authority is well established they become almost useless.

"To control the wills of children, to root in their minds the conviction that it is not possible not to follow the orders and suggestions of the teacher, to inspire them with an absolute confidence in his judgment, — these are the essential conditions for the good government of the school."[1]

To begin with, the teacher ought to make himself loved. Affection is one of the mainsprings of human activity. What will not one do for those whom he loves? How easily he obeys them! And the best means to make himself loved is himself to love. But the teacher ought also to make himself respected and feared. The true discipline is the mingling of mildness and severity.

---

[1] E. Rendu, *Manuel*, p. 91.

524. Continuity in Discipline. — One of the reasons which the most often weaken the authority of the teacher is the disorder, the looseness, and the contradictions which he introduces into the discipline that he imposes. A government which passes from extreme rigor to extreme weakness, which at one time tolerates an excess of liberty and at another treats the lightest faults with severity, is the worst of governments in education as in politics. A rule once established should never be departed from. I well know that this unvarying tension, this uniformity which never wavers, is a difficult thing; but it is a thing that is necessary. The actual education, said Richter wittily, resembles the harlequin of the Italian comedy, who comes on the stage with a bundle of papers under each arm. "What do you carry under your right arm?" "Orders," he replies. "And under your left arm?" "Counter orders." Thus pulled in different directions, disconcerted by contradictory orders, always thinking to escape a rule which is not imperiously followed, the pupil loses all control of himself and goes adrift.

525. Versatility in the Use of Means. — If it is true, on the one hand, that discipline ought to be inflexible in the rules which it imposes, it is none the less necessary, on the other, that it be supple and variable in the means which it employs. All pupils have not the same character, the same disposition. What is relative mildness with some would be extreme severity with others. Just as the professor studies the diversity of intelligences in order to find access to them, and adapts his instruction to the degree of aptness of each mind, so the educator ought to take account of differences of character, and estimate the degree of power and of weakness in each temperament, so as to adjust aid to need and to distribute equitably as the case requires reward or punishment.

"His object," says M. Gréard again, "is to follow the child across the different phases of his moral life, and in the common life whose rules he follows to assure to him the development of his individual life."

With some the teacher must ever be affectionate and good ; with others he must use severity. At one time he must multiply excitations to arouse a sluggish nature ; at another he must use moderation and constraint.

With one he must always talk reason ; with another he will make a constant appeal to feeling.

526. THE HIGHER PURPOSE OF DISCIPLINE. — Discipline does not tend merely to establish silence and good order in classes, assiduous and exact labor; but it thinks of the future and aims at training men. Its purpose in some sort is to make itself useless. School authority ought to be exercised only with the intention of making the child independent of the yoke of all external authority. Not that an absolute enfranchisement of the human person is to be dreamed of ; at every age and in all conditions man will always have to obey, — his superiors under the flag and in the workshop, the law and its representatives in society. But this necessary subjection does not prevent liberty, which is the discipline that one imposes on himself ; and the object of education of all grades is to make men free.

Hence the characteristics of the discipline truly liberal, which does not attempt to establish obedience by fear and passive habits, but which ever addresses itself to the personal activity and the will, which respects the dignity of the child, which exalts rather than humiliates, which does not stifle the natural powers, but which trains them to govern themselves.

"This reflective enfranchisement, which is the purpose of education," says M. Gréard, "requires in the child two indispensable conditions of inward toil, — reflection and activity; — reflection, which renders account to one's self, and activity, which comes to a decision. No one attains to self-direction except at this price.

"To put to use the moral aptitudes which lie concealed in the consciousness of the child and to make him know their tendencies, the evil as well as the good; to accustom him to look clearly into his mind and heart, to be sincere and true, to make him put in practice in his conduct, little by little, the resolutions he forms; insensibly to substitute for the rules which have been given him those which he gives himself, and for the discipline from without that which is from within; to enfranchise him, not by beat of drum after the ancient manner, but day by day, by striking off at each step of progress one link of the chain which attaches his reason to the reason of another; after having thus aided him in establishing himself as his own master, to teach him to come out of himself and to judge and govern himself as he would judge and govern others; finally, to show him above himself the grand ideas of duty, public and private, which are imposed on him as a human and social being; — such are the principles of the education which can make the pupil pass from the discipline of the school under the discipline of his own reason, and which creates his moral personality by calling it into exercise."

APPENDIX.

A. Page 133.

The Doctrine of Memory.

.In stating the doctrine that the memory should not anticipate the intelligence, M. Compayré is doubtless in accord with most modern writers on education; yet it seems to me that this ground is taken rather as a recoil from an old error than from a due consideration of the relation which the memory bears to the other intellectual faculties. It must be plain that the exercise of the intelligence presupposes the presence of some material on which the mind can react in the way of elaboration, and that this material must be held within the range of the mind's elaborative power. Retention and representation must therefore precede the process of thought. To say that we should memorize only what we understand is very much like saying that we should commit nothing to the, stomach until it has been digested. We eat to the end that we may digest; and we must confide material to the retentive power of the mind in order that the intelligence may have something to work upon. The only question in the case seems to me to be this: Shall this material be held loosely, by what the author calls the "liberal memory of ideas," or exactly, by what he calls the "strict memory of words"?

This last is doubtless what is usually called "memorizing," or "learning by heart." In many cases informal, or loose, memorizing will suffice; but in other cases exact or verbal memorizing is best. But in either case the memory must anticipate the intelligence.

Material that has been transformed by the elaborative power of the mind (the understanding) must then be held for the permanent use or adornment of the spirit by a sort of organic registration; and it is doubtless this final and perfect form of the retentive process which writers have in view when they say that nothing must be memorized which is not understood. If it is recollected that there is also a form of retention which *precedes* the act of thought proper, all the real difficulties of this subject will disappear, and there will be no antagonism between psychological theory and the universal practice of mankind. (P.)

B. PAGE 282.

ANALYSIS AND SYNTHESIS.

THAT writers on education use the terms analysis and synthesis in directly contrary senses, and that great confusion has thereby been introduced into the discussion of method, is a fact which must be admitted and one which is greatly to be deplored; but the important question still remains, Is there a real and an intelligible sense in which these terms are descriptive of mental phenomena? Is there a mode of mental activity in which aggregates are resolved into constituent parts, and another mode in which parts are reconstructed into aggregates? If there is, then the term analysis may be intelligently applied to the first and the term synthesis to the second.

As to the psychological fact there can be no doubt. Perhaps the clearest statement of this law of mental activity has been made by Sir William Hamilton in these terms:

"The first procedure of the mind in the elaboration of its knowledge is always analytical. It descends from the whole to the parts, from the vague to the definite."

"This is the fundamental procedure of philosophy, and is called by a Greek term *Analysis*."

"But though analysis be the fundamental procedure, it is still

ERRATA.

For *analytic*, in Appendix C, line 15, read synthetic; and for *synthetic*, line 17, read analytic.

Material that has been transformed by the elaborative power of the mind (the understanding) must then be held for the permanent use or adornment of the spirit by a sort of organic registration; and it is doubtless this final and perfect form of the retentive process which writers have in view when they say that nothing must be memorized which is not understood. If it is recollected that there is also a form of retention which *precedes* the act of thought proper, all the real difficulties of this subject will disappear, and there will be no antagonism between psychological theory and the universal practice of mankind. (P.)

B. PAGE 282.

ANALYSIS AND SYNTHESIS.

made by Sir William

" The first procedure of the mind in the elaboration of its knowledge is always analytical. It descends from the whole to the parts, from the vague to the definite."

" This is the fundamental procedure of philosophy, and is called by a Greek term *Analysis*."

"But though analysis be the fundamental procedure, it is still only a means towards an end. We analyze only that we may comprehend; and we comprehend only inasmuch as we are able to reconstruct in thought the complex effects which we have analyzed into their elements. This mental reconstruction is, therefore, the final, the consummative procedure of philosophy, and is familiarly known by the Greek term *Synthesis.*"

It thus appears that the terms analysis and synthesis, employed in the very same sense as in chemistry, are necessary in order to formulate a fundamental law of mental activity; and this law is the safest clew we have in the discussion of method, as it evidently underlies the whole art of presentation. **(P.)**

C. Page 298.

The Problem of Primary Reading.

This problem admits of what might be called a psychological solution, and furnishes a typical illustration of the deduction of a method from a general principle. This problem may be stated comprehensively as follows :

To assist the child in making the most direct transition from spoken to written language.

Or, the problem may be stated analytically in these terms :

(1) *To teach the child a small and select vocabulary of printed words; and* (2) *to give him power to name new words for himself.*

1. The principal methods that have been employed for introducing the child to the art of reading are the following : (1.) The *Alphabetic;* (2.) The *Phonic;* (3.) The *Phonetic;* (4.) The *Word;* (5.) The *Sentence.* The first three methods proceed from elements (letters) to aggregates (words), and are therefore analytic; while the last two proceed from aggregates (words or sentences) to elements (syllables and letters), and are therefore synthetic. The question now at issue is this : Which procedure conforms to the organic mode of mental activity, the *analytic* or the *synthetic?* From the psychological law stated under B,

the inference is irresistible that preference must be given to methods which are analytical; so that our choice is now between the WORD and the SENTENCE methods. Both are correct in principle; but as the smaller aggregate seems to me the more convenient and manageable, I give my preferences to the WORD METHOD.

2. In order to name (pronounce) new words for himself, a child must know three things : (1.) The letters of the alphabet; (2.) The elementary sounds of the language; and (3.) The association of letter and sound. It must be plain that in order to pronounce a new word of his own accord, the pupil must be able to infer its *name* from its *form*, and reading aloud might be called translating form into sound; and this power of inference, though never infallible, can be gained from a ready knowledge of these three elements.

The question now presented is this: How can these three things be taught the most expeditiously? Without entering into any explanation or discussion the following summary answer may be given : (1.) The easiest way to teach the elements of words is by requiring the pupil to print or draw them on slate, board, or paper; (2.) The best way to teach the elementary sounds of the language is by phonic analysis or slow pronunciation; (3.) The association of letter and sound is best taught by oral spelling.

According to this analysis the successive steps in teaching a child to read are as follow:

1. Teaching the names of familiar words (say two hundred), at sight upon the authority of the teacher;

2. Teaching the names of the letters by printing words;

3. Teaching the elementary sounds by the analysis of spoken words;

4. Teaching the powers of the letters by oral spelling. (P.)

D.   PAGE 366.

THE VALUE OF SUBJECTS.

THREE ideas should be embodied in a course of study : (1.) The idea of training or discipline; (2.) The idea of practical utility;

(3.) The idea of culture, one chief mark of which is contemplative delight. Under another form this thought may be expressed as follows: Education should form or train the mind, and furnish it with knowledge for two purposes, — practical use and enjoyment. The three values involved in studies may be called the *disciplinary*, the *practical*, and the *culture* values respectively. Every subject doubtless has these three values, though in different degrees, but each subject is characterized by what may be called its *major* value. In other terms, there are three lines of defence for the various studies included in a curriculum, and a subject which is known to have a high value of either sort is entitled to a place in a course of study.

A disciplinary study communicates power; a practical study furnishes knowledge for use; and a culture study communicates organic power and furnishes knowledge for enjoyment. With this distinction, and with major values in view, the studies of the common school course may be grouped as follow:

1. PRACTICAL STUDIES : Reading, writing, spelling, the fundamental processes of arithmetic, language lessons, hygiene, civics.
2. DISCIPLINARY STUDIES : Arithmetic and grammar.
3. CULTURE STUDIES : Geography, history, and literature.

Geography has the same kind of value as travel, and it might be called traveling by proxy. The direct practical value of Geography, that is, its value as estimated by the actual use which each individual makes of it, is very small; while its indirect value, that is, the value which comes to us through the knowledge which other persons have of it, is very large. One may be ignorant of an art or science, and yet may enjoy all the practical benefits flowing from it. In all such cases its value is of the indirect order. In constructing a course of study for a common school, only direct practical values must be taken into account. In Chapter III. of my "Contributions to the Science of Education" I have discussed this subject at some length. (P.)

INDEX.

Industrial Education: *A Pedagogic and Social Necessity.*

Together with a Critique upon Objections Advanced. By ROBERT SEIDEL, Mollis, Switzerland. Translated by MARGARET K. SMITH, State Normal School, Oswego, New York.

A good idea of the value of this book may be gained from the following

TABLE OF CONTENTS.

D. C. HEATH & CO., Publishers,

3 TREMONT PLACE, BOSTON.

NEW BOOKS ON EDUCATION.

Compayré's History of Pedagogy.

Translated by Professor W. H. PAYNE, University of Michigan. Price by mail, $1.75.
The best and most compi hensive history of education in English. — Dr. G. S. HALL.

Gill's Systems of Education.

An account of the systems advocated by eminent educationists. Price by mail, $1.10.
I can say truly that I think it eminently worthy of a place on the Chautauqua Readin
List, because it treats ably of the Lancaster and Bell movement in Education, — a ver
important phase. — Dr. WILLIAM T. HARRIS.

Radestock's Habit in Education.

With an Introduction by Dr. G. STANLEY HALL. Price by mail, 65 cents.
It will prove a rare "find" to teachers who are seeking to ground themselves in th
philosophy of their art. — E. H. RUSSELL, Prin. of Normal School, Worcester, Mass.

Rousseau's Émile.

Price by mail, 85 cents.
There are fifty pages of Émile that should be bound in velvet and gold. — VOLTAIRE.
Perhaps the most influential book ever written on the subject of education. — R. H. QUICK

Pestalozzi's Leonard and Gertrude.

With an Introduction by Dr. G. STANLEY HALL. Price by mail, 85 cents.
If we except Rousseau's "Émile" only, no more important educational book has appeare
for a century and a half than Pestalozzi's "Leonard and Gertrude." — *The Nation.*

Richter's Levana ; The Doctrine of Education.

A book that will tend to build up that department of education which is most neglectec
and yet needs most care — home training. Price by mail, $1.35.
A spirited and scholarly book. — Prof. W. H. PAYNE, University of Michigan.

Rosmini's Method in Education.

Price by mail, $1.75.
The best of the Italian books on education. — Editor *London Journal of Education.*

Hall's Methods of Teaching History.

A symposium of eminent teachers of history. Price by mail, $1.40.
Its excellence and helpfulness ought to secure it many readers. — *The Nation.*

Bibliography of Pedagogical Literature.

Carefully selected and annotated by Dr. G. STANLEY HALL. Price by mail, $1.75.

Lectures to Kindergartners.

By ELIZABETH P. PEABODY. Price by mail, $1.10.

Monographs on Education. (25 cents each.)

D. C. HEATH & CO., Publishers,